THE GREAT TRANSITION

Successful corporations of the future will have little resemblance to traditional corporations. We are in the early stages of a global revolution that is fundamentally changing jobs, business, management, and corporate architectures. Ultimately this great transition will be more devastating than the Industrial Revolution. The forces shaping it include worldwide information highways, investments in cheap-labor countries, worldwide partnerships, downsizing, the concept of value streams, value-stream teams, the quality revolution, powerful microelectronics, cyberspace, virtual operations, agile manufacturing, and the reinvention of management.

To succeed with the changes requires discipline—a family of disciplines that extend from strategic vision to detailed implementation.

Enterprise Engineering is an integrated set of disciplines. Its strength lies in the synthesis of seven different disciplines. Without such disciplines and their synthesis, corporations will not survive the brutal worldwide transition that is evolving.

Enterprise Engineering is a holistic and pragmatic approach to building or changing an enterprise to increase its profitability, competitiveness, or effectiveness in meeting its goals. It is concerned with identifying the most appropriate enterprise architecture and establishing the most effective change methods. It is concerned with integrating these change methods so that the whole is greater than the sum of the parts.

Enterprise Engineering teaches management, in practical terms, how to adapt the change methods to unique situations. All the change methods are concerned with enabling employees to contribute more value. The goal is an enterprise that constantly evolves, adapts to fast-changing demands, and (particularly important) continuously learns at all levels. The enterprise must be based on an intimate partnership between people and technology, anticipating the onrushing, unimaginably pervasive effects of information technology in the twenty-first century.

THE GREAT TRANSITION

Using the Seven Disciplines of
Enterprise Engineering
to Align People,
Technology, and Strategy

JAMES MARTIN

amacom

American Management Association

New York • Atlanta • Boston • Chicago • Kansas City • San Francisco • Washington, D.C.
Brussels • Mexico City • Tokyo • Toronto

**To
Carmac**

Library of Congress Cataloging-in-Publication Data

Martin, James, 1938–
    The great transition : using the seven disciplines of enterprise
engineering to align people, technology, and strategy / James
Martin—1st AMACOM pbk. ed.
        p.   cm.
    Includes bibliographical references and index.
    ISBN 0-8144-0315-8 (pbk.)
    1. Reengineering (Management)   2. Strategic planning.
I. Title.
HD58.87.M368   1995
658.4'063—dc20 95-35180
                                                        CIP

Printing number

10   9   8   7   6   5   4   3   2   1

Table of Contents

Acknowledgments   x
Preface   xi

Part I   Change or Die   1

Chapter

1   Tidal Wave   3
    *Postcapitalist Society • The Cybercorp Revolution • Second-Order
    Transition • Proponents or Victims? • Reengineer or Begin Afresh?*

2   Reinventing Employment   12
    *A Twin Revolution • Constant Corporate Learning • Empowered
    Employees • Maslow's Hierarchy of Human Needs • Taylorism • Personal
    Energy • A Paradox: Continuous Change vs. Excellence • Maximizing
    Everyone's Value • Experimentation: The Learning-Laboratory
    Enterprise • Enterprise Redesign • "Boundarylessness" • Key Themes of the
    Future • The Good News*

3   The Wrong Use of Automation   32
    *Do Not Automate Yesterday's Processes • Automation Without
    Reinvention • Unwieldy White-Collar Processes • Integration vs.
    Fragments • Back to Dickens*

4   The Electronic Organism   42
    *Automation • When Distance Disappears • Corporate
    Transparency • Consolidation • The Multicorporate Organism • The Decline of
    the Intermediary • Electronic Reaction Times • The Strategic Importance of
    Software • Tools for Decision Making • Cybercorp Complexity • The Attacker's
    Advantage • The Age of the Entrepreneur • Sheep and Goats • Profits and
    Propellerheads • Chief Organizational Architect*

5   The Seven Components of Enterprise Engineering   58
    *Integrating the Most Powerful Methods • The Spectrum of Change
    Methods • Infrastructure Change • Continuous-Process
    Improvement • Discontinuous Change • Value-Stream Reinvention • Examples
    of "Breakthrough" Results • Outrageous Goals • Both TQM and Value-Stream
    Reinvention • Scrap and Start Again • Procedure Redesign • When Our
    Intuition Is Wrong • Enterprise Redesign • The Simplification of
    Work • Strategic Visioning • Fused Methods • A New Type of Professional • Off-
    the-Beaten-Track Thinking*

6 Teams and Virtuosos 84
*The Team: A Special Type of Cluster • Teams and Working
Groups • Pseudoteams • Becoming Real • High-Performance Teams • Value-
Stream Teams • Loners Who Are Different • Virtuosos*

Part II Value-Stream Reinvention 101

Chapter

7 Value Streams 103
*End-to-End Redesign • Value Streams • The Basic Idea of VSR • Value Streams,
Not Hierarchies • Dramatic Results • Top-Down Culture Change • IT
Development • Synchronized Change • Summary*

8 Mapping the Value Streams 118
*Primary vs. Support Value Streams • Silos and Stovepipes • The Customer of the
Value Stream • Customer-Delight Factors • The Elapsed-Time–Work-Time
Ratio • Simultaneous Engineering • One-Person Value Stream • Unhealthy
Value Streams • What Should You Redesign First? • When Should You Avoid
Rebuilding Value Streams? • Strategic Value Streams • Fluidity • Evolutionary
Transition • Start-up Corporations*

9 Outrageous Goals 139
*Dramatic Improvement • High-Level Questions • Aladdin's Lamp • What Does
the Customer Really Need? • Speed • Instant Results • Instant
Information • Image Processing • Speech Storage • Intelligent
Documents • When Paradigms Shift • The Value Stream as a Learning
Laboratory • Aspects of Knowledge Acquisition*

10 Customer-Delight Factors 153
*Raving Fans • The Voice of the Customer • Types of Customers • Beyond-the-
Call-of-Duty Awards • Raving-Fan Recipe • The Importance of Customer
Focus • Who Is the Customer? • Ask the Customer • Breakthrough
Ideas • Quality Function Deployment • Zero Defections*

11 Sewer Pipes, Not Stove Pipes 165
*Value-Stream Teams • Targeted Teams • Integration of Work, Not Division of
Labor • Integration of Work • Benchmarking*

12 Sacred Cows and Barnacles 174
*Sacred Cows • Superstitions • Control Procedures • No-Lay-Off
Rule • Compensation • Craftsmanship Cows • Cash
Cows • Barnacles • Organizational Interaction Chart • Removal of Work Which
Does Not Add Value • Self-Reliant Value-Stream Teams • Avoidance of Politics*

13 Reinvention of Work Flow 187
*Reinvention of Work Flow • Simultaneous Activities • Triage • Bypassing the
Middleman • Value-Stream Executive Information Systems • Lean
Manufacturing • Computerized Choreography • Identifying Problems • A Value-
Stream Laboratory*

Part III   Continuous-Process Improvement   **199**

Chapter

14   *Kaizen*   201
     Constant Improvement • P-Criteria and R-Criteria • Quality, Productivity, and
     Kaizen • The PDCA Cycle • The Journey to Zero Defects • Kaizen Is a Vital
     Value-Stream Goal • A Change in Culture • Kaizen-*Capable*
     Computing • Reengineering the System Development Process
15   TQM and the Quality Revolution   216
     The Drive for Quality • Delighting the Customer • Quality Circles • A
     Systematic Suggestion Scheme • Nine Types of Waste • Problems are
     Opportunities • The Five Whys • International Quality Standards • The
     Malcolm Baldrige Quality Award • The Deming Prize
16   Statistics and Problem Solving   232
     Example: The Telephone Problem • Cause-and-Effect Diagrams • Pareto
     Diagrams • Statistical Quality Control • Design of Experiments • Six-Sigma
     Quality
17   Failures in TQM Programs   241
     Reasons for Failing • Bottom-Line Payback • Big Q and Little q • *Commitment of*
     Top Management • Reward Systems • Fads and Wall
     Posters • Bureaucracy • The Quality Czar • Inward-Looking
     TQM • Requirements for Big Q • TQM versus Mozart
18   TQM vs. Revolution   250
     Quantum Leap before TQM • TQM vs. Quantum-Leap
     Redesign • Multicorporate TQM

Part IV   Procedure Redesign   **259**

Chapter

19   Nontraumatic Redesign   261
     The Difference between Procedure Redesign and Value-Stream
     Reinvention • The Difference between Kaizen *and Procedure Redesign • The*
     Risk of Suboptimizing • All Three Are Needed • Evaluation of the Three
     Alternatives
20   Counterintuitive System Behavior   267
     Webs of Activities • Long-Span Activity Webs • Counterintuitive
     Consequences • System Dynamics • Oscillations in a Distribution
     System • Lessons from the Story • Redesigning the System • IT Actions
     Needed • Leverage
21   Dangerous Feedback   281
     Positive Feedback • Negative Feedback • Multiple Interactions • Corporate
     Learning • Actions That Are Needed

Part V Strategic Visioning **291**

Chapter

22 The Strategy Revolution 293
Planning vs. Visioning • Good-bye to Stability • How Do You Build a Tiger? • Strategic Skills • Five Whys for the CEO • Long-Term Investment • Innovation • Strategic Stagnation • Discontinuities in Technology • Top-Management Radar

23 Core Competencies 305
Competencies and Capabilities • Core Competencies • Vertical Inflexibility

24 Strategic Value Streams 311
Unique Capability • Capability Predators • Linking Core Competency to Value Streams • Startling New Successes • Strategic Learning Laboratory • Outsourcing • Management at the CEO Level • Summary

25 Discontinuities 324
Dangerous Shifts • The Life-Cycle Curve • Failure to Manage Discontinuities • The Investment-Life-Cycle Curve • Falling Technology Cost • Draw the S-Curves • Sudden Reversals • Reluctance to Switch • False Sense of Security • Protection of Investment • The Attacker's Advantage • Fast Development • Continuous-Discontinuity Management

26 Scenarios and Mental Models 343
When the Official Future Is Wrong • Mental Models • Scenarios at Shell • Telling Stories • Three or Four Scenarios, Not More • Names That Convey the Story • Pictures and Legos • What Is Predictable? • Warning Signals • The Test of Scenario Effectiveness • The Process of Using Scenarios

27 The Corporate Gospel 358
Vision and Excitement • Criteria for an Effective Vision • Consensus about the Vision • Translation into Action • Value-Stream Visions • Vision and Advertising • Cynicism • Hard Vision • Vivid Expression • A Leader's Use of Language • Flawed Visions • Summary

Part VI Enterprise Redesign **371**

Chapter

28 Old-World vs. New-World Corporations 373
Design for Ongoing Change • Redistribution of Power • Changing the Role of Managers • How Much Do We Need to Change? • Partial vs. Holistic Transition • Reengineering the Entire Enterprise • New Units • The Context of Strategic Visioning • Types of Organizational Change • A Continuum of Change • A Long Journey • Constancy of Vision • Passionate CEO Leadership • Summary

29 What Replaces the Hierarchy? 393
Command and Control • Self-Reinforcing Cultures • Parkinson's Law • Declining Middle Management • Becoming Horizontal • Residual Hierarchy • New Organization Charts • The Corporation and the Brain • Loose and Tight Coupling • Summary

30 The Many Facets of Enterprise Learning 407
Types of Enterprise Learning • Four Types of Learning • Paradox: Empowerment vs. Cohesion • Value-Stream Learning • Joint Learning with Trading Partners • Maximizing Experiential Learning • Barriers to Experiential Learning • Insufficient Innovation • Insufficient Capacity to Act • Insufficient Capacity to Reflect • Inadequate Recording of What Is Learned • Insufficient Capacity to Disseminate • When Learning from Experience Is a Delusion • Single-Loop and Double-Loop Learning • The Measurement of Learning • Summary

31 The Corporation as a Learning Laboratory 430
Chaparral Steel • Research Cemeteries • Four Characteristics • Experiments in Steel Making • Experiments in Software Development • A Multicorporate Learning Laboratory • Risks • Holistic Interplay • Selecting and Keeping Employees • Incentives • Establishing a Learning-Laboratory Corporation

32 The New Employment Deal 445
Vanishing Job Security • The New Deal • Full Explanation • Changing Compensation Schemes • Gain Sharing • Pay-for-Knowledge Schemes • Employee Appraisals • Employee Stock-Option Plans • Different Classes of Employment Package

33 The Changing of Corporate Culture 455
The Protective Barrier • Alien Life Forms • Three Cultural Components • Sudden Shifts • The Level of Cultural Change • Pounding Home the Vision • The Cost of Attempting to Change Culture • Stage-by-Stage Cultural Change • The Cultural Change Process

34 Managing the Risks of Corporate Change 472
High-Management Roadblocks • Ishikawa Risk Charts • Methodology for Reengineering • EE Laboratory • Pilot Operation • Kaizen during Operation • IT Failures • The Need for Speed • Risks Associated with Hand-overs • Dysfunctional Behavior • Pavlov's Dogs • Fear of Reorganization • A Counter-Anxiety • Different Risk Profiles

35 Starting Afresh 490
Green-Field Value Streams • Green-Field Business Units • Reinventing Government? • Global Rebuilding

Glossary 496
Index 498

Acknowledgments

This book is based on the highly pragmatic experience of executives who have succeeded in making radical changes and of consultants who have implemented solutions. The text reflects the experience of consultants who have blazed the trail of Enterprise Engineering: John Wyatt, Kevin Murphy, Mike Beck, Richard Skriletz, Jim Stockmal, and many others at James Martin & Co. (JM & Co.). Throughout the project James Brown has been a constant mentor, original thinker, creative critic, and purveyor of experience. The author is extremely grateful for, and very impressed by, the skills and creativity of these contributors.

The author is grateful to Mark Brunswick and Marlene for creatively molding the manuscript into shape. John Collins of Savant Research Inc. had many valuable suggestions. The book is condensed from a five-volume report published by Savant Research Inc.

The JM & Co. production department created the first manuscript and diagrams. The author would like to thank Supervisor Joellyn Kinzer, Jim Weidenhamer, Mia Chin, Sumalee Cholvijarn, Sallee Winton, and Michael Bryant.

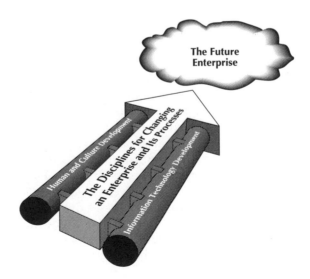

Preface

There is a tide in the affairs of men,
Which, taken at the flood, leads on to fortune.

On such a full sea we are now afloat,
And we must take the current when it serves,

Or lose our ventures.

—Shakespeare

Most managers and workers in today's enterprises are cogs in obsolete machinery. They sometimes have a vague feeling that the machinery needs scrapping and replacing, but they do not know what to do about it. The management structures and work processes of most enterprises were designed decades ago, before modern technology. The processes need radical reinventing and the management structures need replacing. The jobs of most people need to be drastically redesigned so that the value of people increases in an age of software and superhighways.

We are in the early phase of a revolution that will fundamentally transform enterprises around the planet. A survey of twelve hundred corporations indicated that in the U.S.A. alone by 1997 more than $52 billion per year would be spent on "business reengineering," and business reengineering is only one component of Enterprise Engineering.[1] The transformation is a paradigm shift of immense magnitude. Some corporations will take the new opportunities "at the flood" and thrive; others will be swept away. None can ignore this Great Transition.

In April of 1970, *Fortune* magazine released its list of the 500 largest American corporations—the companies that had built such a revenue base, customer base, and reputation that they were for the most part considered stable, even unassailable by some. Their employees were confident that, although social stresses were unknown quantities, at least their employers were stable. Thirteen years later, in scarcely the tenure of an established executive, *one-third of these corporations had ceased to exist.* Today, worldwide competitive stresses dwarf those of the 1970s. We are living in a time of profound change. The corporate death rate is increasing. Competition is becoming global and brutal. The corporations of the 1990s must reinvent themselves or they will sink without a trace. It is clear that the rate of change is too great for many top management teams to cope with. Within a decade or so, fully one-half of today's great corporations may no longer exist.

We constantly hear about competitive threats, but for every threat there is a corresponding opportunity. However, the opportunities are often seized by new, sometimes faraway, corporations. The nations of the world are now competing for global businesses in the same way that companies compete for customers. Although everybody senses these sweeping changes, few executives have any appreciation yet of the magnitude of the vortex into which they are being swept.

Terms such as *business reengineering, business-process redesign*, and *process innovation* have become popular but are often imprecise. They may refer to a single methodology for change, when multiple change methods are required. Enterprise Engineering is a family of change methods. Its intent is to identify the most valuable change methods and integrate them. The integrated family of methods is greater than the sum of its parts. It is only when the different approaches are integrated that the extent of the problem becomes clear: most corporations have the wrong procedures, most computer systems being built today are the wrong systems, most total quality management (TQM) efforts miss their true potential, and most corporations have major learning disabilities.

Enterprise Engineering is concerned with the architecture of future enterprises, and the methods needed to change the enterprise. It is concerned with how we get from here to there and make a profit while doing so. It is *not* a codeword for "downsizing."

> *Many executives realize that radical changes are needed; however, they have to increase today's level of performance while making those changes. The have to drive the car fast at the same time as they reengineer it.*

In the same way that building architects have to know something about construction technology in order to build good skyscrapers, executives have to know something about information technology in order to build the kinds of organizations that can survive into the twenty-first century. Many executives leave this to technical staff members who do not have the business overview. To make the changes described in this book, executives must understand the aspects of IT (information technology) that permits those changes.

The seven components to Enterprise Engineering are described in Chapter 5. To navigate through the Great Transition, professionals are needed who understand all seven components. It is the synthesis of these components that facilitates the most successful navigation.

> *A new type of professional is emerging—the Enterprise Engineer. Enterprise Engineers become skilled in all the change methods that are part of Enterprise Engineering—the complex subject matter of this book.*

The term *enterprise* refers to an *extended* enterprise. The Enterprise Engineer's task does not stop at the boundary of the organization but extends to its customers, suppliers, and other trading partners.

The term *engineering* implies that the subject is a discipline having teachable methodologies whose results can be measured and tested. Enterprise Engineering describes the various change methods in terms of an orderly progression of tasks that can change an enterprise. Executives must be able to measure how the transition is proceeding and correct it when needed. The discipline of Enterprise Engineering is codified but complex. Enterprise Engineers need to be skilled in alternative change methods; they need to understand the techniques for changing organizational culture and the information technology that results in most of the changes.

Some corporations today are achieving order-of-magnitude improvements (not just 10-percent improvements) in end-to-end business processes. This technique requires fundamental reinvention of those processes using a diversity of technologies. It needs new approaches to IT linked to management of major cultural change. The reinventions that are starting today will be the basic teaching of business schools twenty years from now.

A graphic image for Enterprise Engineering—an upward-slanting arrow pointing from today's enterprise to the enterprise designed for the future—is used throughout the book. Later, the arrow divides into more-detailed components. The arrow should continually focus the reader's attention on the following:

- Architects work toward a vision of something that does not yet exist. The vision should be exciting. It should inspire employees to expend vitality on bringing about change.
- Reengineering must be driven by a strategic business vision. Strategic visioning is fundamentally different from the strategic planning practiced in most corporations.
- The organizational architect never has a "clean slate" to work with, only an existing set of assets and problems that always influence the future design. There are immense pressures in most corporations for fast improvements in profit, revenues, and productivity. The CEO has to drive hard for short-term results, at the same time transforming the organization for long-term results.
- The corporations that survive are those that continuously learn. Learning must involve all employees, at all levels, all the time. An organization and its systems must be designed to encourage and optimize the learning processes.
- Most processes in most corporations need radical reinventing. But a nonradical culture of continuous improvement is also needed. Both radical upheaval and nonradical improvement, therefore, are required.
- The value of almost all employees can increase if we redesign their work, empower them, excite them, and challenge them to use their brains. Often

this can be done by building cross-functional teams. Such an approach usually requires major changes in structure and culture.

- Electronics, software, and information highways will make the future corporation startlingly different from the past. It cannot be built effectively unless business change agents and technology professionals work together intimately.

Enterprise Engineering provides management with a toolbox of change methods. It aims to select and integrate the most powerful methods so that management can plan and succeed with complex change while continuing to run the business. The change must be driven by an overall understanding of why the Great Transition is occurring and a top-level vision of how to "take the tide at the flood."

Reference

1. Survey by *Systems Reengineering Economics,* a newsletter published by Computer Economics Inc., Carlsbad, CA, 1994.

Part I
Change or Die

Part I describes how revolutionary changes sweeping through the corporate world, driven by technology linked to rapidly intensifying worldwide competition, are rendering most corporate structures obsolete. Chapter 5 presents an overview of the seven components Enterprise Engineering.

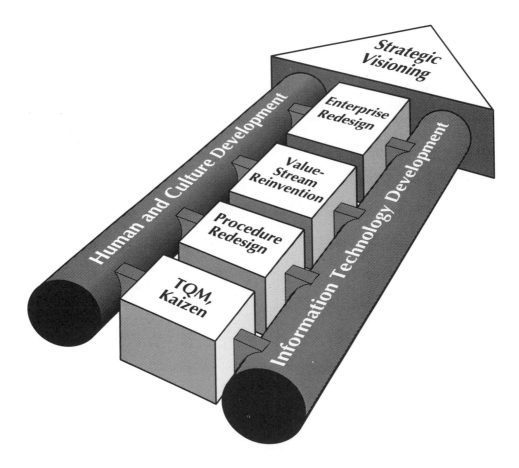

1

Tidal Wave

Today, networks of computers interact worldwide in seconds. A designer in London interacts with a designer in Tokyo as though the two were in the same room. Everything that Shakespeare wrote in a lifetime can be transmitted over an optical fiber in a hundredth of a second (literally!), and fiber optics span the globe. Traders in New Zealand or Stockholm are on-line to computerized futures exchanges. Benetton opened eight thousand shops, in more than a hundred countries, linked to computers in Italy so that its wealth-generating processes could be monitored and adjusted as they happened internationally. This is *today's* reality.

Most of our corporations, however, have structures that are decades old. Their hierarchical management divides work into functional areas designed for an era before the advent of information technology. When communism collapsed after the fall of the Berlin Wall, it signaled the start of an immense change in the enterprises of the communist world. At the same time, a momentous change began in the capitalist world. It dawned on the West that its enterprises needed fundamentally different architectures. The immense power of Information Technology (IT) was being poorly used because enterprises had not changed to take advantage of it.

> *Many U.S. corporations are run like the Soviet economy. In order to survive they plan ahead comprehensively . . . They specify policies and procedures in meticulous detail, spelling out for practically everyone what can and what cannot be done in particular circumstances. They establish hurdle rates, analyze risks and anticipate contingencies. As planning processes have burgeoned in these companies, strategic thinking has gradually withered away.*[1]
>
> —Kenichi Ohmae in *The Mind of the Strategist* (1982)

The Soviet system was not one in which every individual contributed his or her ingenuity to improving its processes.* Most people "tuned out." The surviving corporations of the future will be the opposite. Rather than being "tuned out," every employee should be excited about being able to apply native ingenuity to

---

* From now on we frequently use the inclusive designations *he* and *his* to mean "he or she" and "his or her."

improving the way work is done, challenged to expand his or her skills and use to the fullest extent. Every individual should be challenged to become increasingly valuable.

We are now beginning to design organizations that work in that way: as in bringing water to a boil, we need to energize employees so that ideas constantly bubble into improved processes. The design must take place within a vision and direction set by strategists who constantly strive to improve their insight.

A new approach to organization is evolving that will change jobs, management, and corporate structures everywhere. The average individual ought to have more satisfying and energizing work. To maximize profit, corporations should maximize the value of *all* employees.

Postcapitalist Society

Peter Drucker calls the new era "postcapitalist" society. This does not mean the end of capitalism; it means The basic economic resource, "the means of production," to use the economists' term, is no longer capital, nor natural resources, nor land, nor labor. *It is knowledge.*[2]

Knowledge is made valuable by applying it to work. A corporation needs an infrastructure for maximizing the use of knowledge. The most successful corporations are those that learn in every way possible and put what is learned to the best use. Knowledge, constantly renewed and enhanced, is the primary source of competitive advantage.

> *Francis Bacon said, "Knowledge is power." The modern executive should say, "Knowledge is money."*

Knowledge permits more profitable decisions to be made. It facilitates timely inventory control. It makes automated production possible. As knowledge flows over networks, it enables events to take place more efficiently, saving intermediate steps.

Corporations succeed because they have greater expertise than their competition in such fields as design, management, and marketing. Human expertise is amplified by computers. Software is an encapsulation of knowledge.

The modern corporation must enhance the knowledge of all employees and support them with a knowledge infrastructure that facilitates learning and experimentation at all levels.

An era in which the key economic resource is *knowledge* is startlingly different from an era in which the key resources were capital, raw materials, land, and labor. Most knowledge, unlike traditional economic resources, is endlessly replicable. It can reside in computers, on disks, or in exceedingly complex software. It can be transmitted worldwide in a fraction of a second, customs officials having no idea that the most valuable economic resource has just flitted past them. Customs forms ask, "Are you carrying more than five thousand dollars in cash?"

when worldwide networks are transmitting 2 trillion dollars *per day* between banks. Organized crime transmits more than 3 billion dollars *per day* across national frontiers.[3]

Corporations in the knowledge era must constantly *learn*. Most knowledge can be copied. Only a tiny fraction of knowledge can be protected by copyright or patent laws. Corporations rapidly learn to do what their competition has done. Almost no process improvements can be protected by intellectual property laws. The only way to stay ahead is to learn faster and better than the competition.

> *Unshared knowledge is power.*

Unshared knowledge can make an individual powerful. Knowledge that everyone has does not convey power.

A corporation should employ all the knowledge it can muster. If this knowledge is not shared with other corporations, it provides a unique advantage. It must, however, be fully shared *within* the corporation.

"Intellectual property rights" can protect little corporate knowledge with a few striking exceptions. Most knowledge leaks to other corporations; so learning, which creates new knowledge, provides the primary competitive advantage.

> *The ability to learn faster than your competitors may be the only* **sustainable** *competitive advantage.*
>
> —Arie de Geus, when head of planning for Royal Dutch Shell

The Cybercorp Revolution

Cybernetics is a field of study, originating with a classic book of that title by Norbert Weiner, that compares the nervous system of biological creatures to complex electronic mechanisms.[4] The modern corporation can be thought of as rather like a biological organism except that the corporation consists of people and electronics organized to achieve certain goals. It has an electronic nervous system that links all desks. It is appropriate to call it a cybernetic corporation, *Cybercorp* for short.

Weiner defined *cybernetics* as "the science of control and communication in the animal and the machine." One might extend that definition to include control and communication in the corporation. A corporation, like an animal, is exceedingly complex and cannot be described with simple equations. Its mechanisms for control and communications are changing immensely as we pass into an era of microelectronics, Internet, information superhighways, and complex software.

The prefix *cyber* became popular when hackers started to explore computer networks and discovered the extraordinary worldwide plethora of systems, software, bulletin boards, games, and databases that were accessible. Roaming the world on computer networks was very different from roaming the world physically. The hackers could connect to anywhere almost instantly and explore complex realms of software. They referred to this instant electronic world as *cyberspace*. The traditional sense of geographic space became obsolete and was replaced by that of cyberspace. A computer in Singapore or Paris is as accessible with a keyboard command as the computer in the next room. The modern enterprise exists in cyberspace (whether or not it takes advantage of it).

Employees can access any information anywhere instantly. Computers in a corporation can interact instantly with computers of its suppliers, agents, customers, and trading partners, if the machines are so programmed. Corporations use global networks today, and optical superhighways will greatly increase the speed of interaction. The *cybercorp*—the enterprise of the knowledge era, of Drucker's postcapitalist society—is worldwide. In it distance disappears.

The first "story box" is a case study of a cybernetic corporation, VISA International. Other examples are very diverse in nature. There are innumerable ways to use automation, software, information highways, and the partnership between electronics and people that is the essence of the cybercorp.

A critical aspect of the great success stories is that they begin with a business vision. The story in Exhibit 1.1 was driven by the search for how to grow VISA revenues although card penetration was already high. The reengineering or building of new corporate operations must be driven by a clear *strategic vision* of how to beat global competition in the cybercorp era.

Second-Order Transition

When the knowledge era is mature, successful corporations will operate very differently from those of the 1980s. A fundamental transition will have occurred. The most advanced of today's corporations are living in an intermediate stage, experimenting with new forms. They live on the edge of something we cannot yet know in detail.

Anthropologist Gregory Bateson distinguishes between first- and second-order changes. *First-order* changes are attempts to adjust or improve an existing culture or process incrementally, try to achieve high-level morale or increase productivity, or improve standard operating procedures. First-order changes are *reversible*. We can repeatedly adjust the change effort.

Second-order changes are *irreversible*. They set off forces that are in some way uncontrollable. They trigger a change so dramatic that they cause a break with the previous culture. An avalanche is started. The 1991 transition in Moscow, for example, was a second-order change. A new order was unleashed. Few people liked the conditions that followed; but whatever happened once the avalanche began, there was no way to return to the old Soviet Union. The best one could do was attempt to steer the situation until a new order evolved.

The journey into the cybercorp era is like that. Old mass-production factories are being swept away. Ordered hierarchies of the 1980s are doomed. New organizational structures are taking their place. Organizational knowledge resides in software of ever-growing complexity. The cybercorp architecture relates to its

Exhibit 1.1

In the early 1990s VISA was the world's largest credit-card group, but it wanted to become much larger. It had already signed up more than half the world's eligible cardholders, so much of its growth would have to come from inducing existing cardholders to use their cards more often. How could this be done?

VISA created a strategic vision of how to increase its credit-card business faster than the competition. The vision required a worldwide computer system with unique software and 9 million miles of optical fiber cables around the planet. It estimated that, with the system, the volume of card transactions could grow from $458 billion in 1993 to $1.1 trillion in card transactions in 1998.[5]

A key to the new capabilities of the system is that every transaction from every retailer anywhere in the world has a *unique* identifying number. (This has to be a large number!) The unique identifier stays with the transaction for life. It indicates which card, which customer, which retailer, and which bank are involved. The unique number eliminates the manual handling of "chargebacks" when mistakes have been made. Manual handling is slow and costs about $25 per transaction. More than 12 million transactions per year had errors that needed manual handling of chargebacks, so about $300 million per year can be saved.

In addition, banks handling VISA cards lost about $125 million a year as a result of counterfeiting.[6] The new system is designed to detect tampering instantly because powerful encryption codes are programmed into the card's magnetic strip.

The elimination of most chargebacks and counterfeiting makes the VISA card more appealing to retailers. Retailers who follow the system guidelines can be offered guaranteed payments. Customers need not be antagonized by lengthy disputes over errors.

The unique number for each transaction tells the VISA computer system even more about the card user. Gold cardholders can be spotted immediately when the card is used and can be given a different level of service. Several categories of cardholders can be detected when the card is used.

Computerized categorization of the cardholders permits sophisticated marketing techniques. When the card is used, the system can know what activities allowed the cardholder—such as use of automatic-teller machines, debit transactions, large transactions, telephone charges, frequent-flier services, automatic travel insurance, parking fees, and so on. VISA would like to eliminate the use of cash altogether.

The global system is designed to capture, refine, and activate the wisdom that VISA International collects from credit-card processing. The knowledge is encapsulated in tens of thousands of rules that are in the company's two large computer centers in Basingstoke, England, and McLean, Virginia. Every transaction from many millions of retailers around the world is filtered through these systems, the unique transaction number helping to build the body of knowledge that VISA thinks can make it grow faster than its competition.

The global system cost $50 million to develop. It is estimated that VISA's growth in transactions will be more than $220 billion larger by 1998 than it would have been without the system—an extraordinary return on investment!

knowledge infrastructure, and "reinvented" jobs challenge all employees to improve corporate know-how. New teams with new technology are designed to
please customers. The enterprise at all levels is equipped to learn rapidly and
efficiently and to accumulate its learning in procedures and software. To survive,
the enterprise must continuously expand its pool of knowledge. Transnational
corporations are growing much faster than nations, and transnational crime syn-
dicates are growing even faster. We are irreversibly heading into a global cybercorp vortex.

Two decades from that dramatic time in history when the USSR disinte-
grated, a transition comparable in magnitude to the industrial revolution will
have occurred. The world's political map will have been redrawn. The ex-
communist countries will re-create themselves after the depression of the 1990s.
Japan, reacting to *its* economic turmoil, will aggressively build worldwide corporate empires with "lean" robotic factories and chips in everything. Southeast Asia
will compete furiously. China, perhaps in fragments, will strive with devastating
energy to compete. Corporate reinvention is not an American phenomenon; it is
taking place worldwide. Often the best way to accomplish improvement is not by
"reengineering" but by building new business units based on new principles; this
is happening worldwide. Internet, satellites, cellular systems, and optical superhighways make the mechanisms of the cybercorp global.

Markets will become enormous because of global media and because an international baby boom has occurred that is fifty times the magnitude of the American baby boom. A tidal wave of new consumers is rolling through the world's
demographics. In ten years there will be two billion teenagers. Half of these will
watch global networks such as MTV and CNN, shop in worldwide stores such as
Benetton, listen to the same pop tapes on portable players, go to the same movies;
and most of them will have an intense drive to better their economic situation.
Fewer than 5 percent of them will be in America and Europe.

> *"We are living in a transformation that will rearrange the politics and
> economics of the coming century. There will be no national products
> or technologies, no national corporations, no national industries."*
>
> —Robert B. Reich, *The Work of Nations*

Some businesses are purely local and unaffected by global forces, but some
that thought they had this characteristic were surprised. Flower shops, for example, were organized to sell flowers grown locally so that they were fresh. The
stores thought of their businesses as immune from distant competition. Then suddenly techniques evolved for shipping refrigerated flowers worldwide. Beautiful
or exotic flowers, grown year-round in massive computer-controlled greenhouses,
were shipped globally. Networks evolved enabling us to use a free phone number
to order flowers and have them delivered, beautifully packaged, anywhere in the
world. Computer networks allow us to learn about, and experiment with, flower
arranging and then to ship the flowers for the arrangements.

Global competition will become fierce as industry in China, India, the new
"tigers" of Southeast Asia, and other emerging countries grow. Countries with

high wages and welfare costs will increasingly be in head-to-head competition with cheap-labor countries. Corporations from high-wage countries will build factories in low-wage countries. It will be easier to send abroad not only manufacturing but also key-punching, programming, routine design work, and many white-collar jobs. (Swiss Air does its corporate accounting in India.) Unemployment will continue to plague some high-wage countries.

To maintain higher wages and entitlement programs, the high-wage countries must keep ahead in the race for corporate know-how. The only thing that can sustain high salaries and living standards is the application of high levels of knowledge. There is a global race to improve the knowledge that corporations put to use.

Proponents or Victims?

Some people thrive on complexity; others are victims of it. Some executives have carefully thought out the changes needed and determinedly engineered a new corporate architecture. In other corporations the flattening of the hierarchy and the growth of empowerment have occurred in ad hoc fashion, without deliberate engineering. There was a comment in *Business Week* after an article on "The Horizontal Corporation": "The most critical point is that the phenomenon of the flattening organization is occurring in most corporations *by accident.* Most companies are victims, not proponents, of this trend."[7] This comment applies to every aspect of the cybercorp. Some executives understand what is happening and are ahead of the curve; most are victims, not proponents. The leaders will be those that deliberately learn the new possibilities, create a strategic vision of how to take advantage of them, and reengineer their enterprises to place them in a competitively unassailable position.

However it happens, those organizational structures that inhibit flexible rapid change, worker empowerment, and constant learning will be swept away. The Great Transition will be driven by brutal Darwinian international competition. Only the fittest will survive.

How many of these corporations are familiar to you?

American Cotton Oil Company	Pacific Mail
American Steel Company	People's Gas
American Sugar Refinery	Tennessee Coal and Iron
Continental Tobacco Company	U.S. Leather
Federal Steel	U.S. Rubber
National Lead	

They were 11 of the top 12 U.S. corporations of 1900—long since gone. Most corporations, even great ones, have a lifespan much shorter than that of people.

The new leaders will be corporations designed for an era of intense, global, knowledge-driven competition, with worldwide information highways, massive computing power, and management styles that challenge all employees to contribute more than they do today. The corporation of the future will be designed to learn constantly at all levels, accumulate its learning, and put it to good use.

Reengineer or Begin Afresh?

A vital question for top executives of traditional corporations is Can you convert today's corporation to the new world, or is its embedded culture too difficult to convert? Particularly important: Can you convert fast enough?

The story is told of two executives walking in a jungle who are suddenly confronted with an angry tiger. The Asian executive opens his briefcase and puts on a pair of running shoes. The Western executive says, "You're crazy. You can't outrun that tiger." The Asian says "No, but I can outrun you!"

If reengineering a business takes years and has a high probability of failure, it may be prudent to start new subsidiaries or affiliates that can move fast. They will be the new-world corporations that avoid the slow and inflexible old-world structures. Every CEO must ask Can we reengineer or should we start afresh? Often the best course is to grow new branches, like an apple tree, and prune the old.

Countries with new or reinvented enterprises will pull ahead of those stuck with traditional enterprises. Germany and Japan became powerhouses twenty years after World War II because their old industries were replaced with new-technology factories. The parts of the world that have vigorous new growth, such

Great Transition

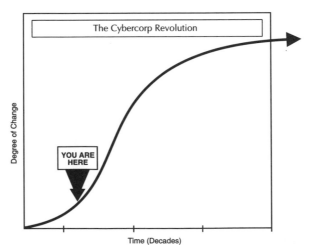

as Southeast Asia, will build new-style corporations capable of competing better than large nonreengineered Western corporations.

The old establishment, dining at country clubs, seems almost totally unaware of the tidal wave heading in its direction. The Great Transition is inevitable and manageable; managing it requires knowledge and professionalism. Within two decades or less today's great enterprises will have been fundamentally reinvented or swept away.

In aggregate, the changes we describe are momentous. They are a revolution in the nature of the enterprise. This revolution is characterized by massive automation, fluid organizational structures, dynamic intercorporate relationships using worldwide computer networks, electronic reaction times, virtual operations, and intense global competition.

The revolution requires fundamental changes in the nature of work that require new patterns of management, new organizational structures, and a new human-technology partnership. When it has run its course in society, this transition will be much larger than the Industrial Revolution.

References

1. Kenichi Ohmae, *The Mind of the Strategist* (McGraw Hill: New York, 1982).
2. Peter Drucker, *Post-Capitalist Society* (Harper Business: New York, 1993).
3. "Global Mafia, A Newsweek Investigation," *Newsweek*, December 13, 1993.
4. Norbert Weiner, *Cybernetics: Control and Communication in the Animal and Machine* (MIT Press: Cambridge, Mass., 1961).
5. "VISA International, Digital Credit," *The Economist*, September 25, 1993.
6. Robert B. Reich, *"The Work of Nations"* (Knopf: New York, 1991).
7. "The Horizontal Corporation," *Business Week*, December 20, 1993.

2

Reinventing Employment

It would be a mistake to think that the Great Transition is all about electronics and networks. It is primarily about the changing role of people in organizations.

A Twin Revolution

The cybercorp revolution is caused partly by powerful technology and partly by a new understanding of how to organize, motivate, train, and energize people. These two types of change feed on each other. Technology permits the change in work, and work must change radically in order to take advantage of technology. The instant flow of information, decision making by software, and the openness of electronic networks fundamentally change the power structure of corporations. An employment revolution is linked to the technology revolution.

Either the technology revolution by itself or the employment revolution by itself could change civilization. The marriage of the two has devastating consequences that require the fundamental reinvention of enterprise structures.

Enterprise Engineering is concerned with the change methods for achieving this human-technology partnership with maximum success.

Constant Corporate Learning

In the days when Cadillacs had fins, the corporate world was fairly stable. America had the luxury of dominating most of the markets it operated in. Corpo-

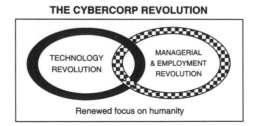

THE CYBERCORP REVOLUTION

TECHNOLOGY REVOLUTION

MANAGERIAL & EMPLOYMENT REVOLUTION

Renewed focus on humanity

rations and mass-production lines were designed to churn out products repetitively at low cost. Today, constant change and international competition are the norm. The corporate world has gone from the predictability of floating on calm blue water to a state of rafting down turbulent white water. The tumult of the white water will last until the Great Transition nears completion.

Once-loyal customers are shopping around and have new expectations. New competition is springing up everywhere. Exhibit 2.1 lists reasons for intensifying competition.

As competition intensifies, the central problem for the enterprise is to stimulate learning and experimentation, capture what is learned, and spread the results of learning throughout the enterprise. Learning produces knowledge, and knowledge produces profits.

> *Unutilized corporate knowledge of how to improve operations is as undesirable as unused inventory. Corporations design systems to solve*

Exhibit 2.1 Reasons why competitive pressures are becoming more intense

- More competitors are emerging in many industries, at home and abroad. Customers have more choice.
- Increased competition has often brought oversupply and lower margins.
- Corporations with radically reinvented processes give more customer satisfaction.
- Corporations with new structures are faster on their feet.
- The spread of the quality movement encourages customers to demand quality.
- Rapid growth of new technology leads to new business opportunities and renders many existing operations obsolete.
- New technology enables new entrants to attack established markets.
- Reengineered factories having lean or agile manufacturing challenge traditional factories.
- Products designed for automated fabrication drive down prices.
- Previously regulated (and protected) industries are being deregulated (for example, finance, banks, airlines, telecommunications, utilities).
- Reinvented business alliances (reinvented using electronics) strengthen competition.
- Alliances among nations, as in the European Union, change the rules of international competition.
- International networks and computers facilitate aggressive worldwide competition.
- Aggressive high-tech countries (for example, Japan and Korea) grow in capability.
- Cheap-labor countries (for example, India and China) grow rapidly in population and compete vigorously in certain markets.
- New product design-to-launch cycles are shortening.
- Everything is speeding up because of computers, networks, and just-in-time techniques. There is less time to respond to new threats.

the problem of unused inventory. They must also solve the problem of unused knowledge.

As an enterprise learns and enhances its knowledge, this knowledge may be recorded in manuals, electronic documents, databases, and expert systems. Complex holistic knowledge resides in the mental models of executives and planners. Managers can act as coaches, showing employees how to use existing knowledge and how to build on that knowledge.

Empowered Employees

Until recently, most employees other than managers and professionals had tedious, repetitive jobs and had no say about how work processes were accomplished. They might as well have hung up their brains with their overcoats when they entered the workplace. Work was drudgery. Employees were only too glad to go home and forget about their jobs. Today this is changing. The new enterprise challenges and empowers employees to be creative, use their brains, take initiative, and make improvements in work processes.

Empowerment is at the heart of the change in attitude. Empowered employees are challenged to make their own decisions about how to work instead of following step-by-step procedures designed by somebody else. When managers empower employees, as either individuals or teams, they must ensure that those employees have the necessary training and skills to do the work well.

Empowerment needs *leadership,* not merely management. Leaders must spend time *coaching* employees in how to work as effectively as possible. To claim that somebody is empowered without the necessary skill building and coaching is nonsensical (but it often happens). People feel empowered when they feel confident that they can do their work excellently. They feel in control; they can learn how to improve their work methods.

Empowerment *means delegating responsibility for results, not tasks. A person or team must be free to work out how best to achieve results. People must be trained and coached to do this with confidence.*

It has been discovered that most employees can improve their work processes when challenged. Many small improvements add up to major changes in quality, productivity, and customer satisfaction. Small, self-directed teams with challenging goals can be enthusiastic and effective in improving work processes. As a result, employees have increased energy and are more productive.

Hewlett-Packard (HP) gave its engineers the task of finding out how the defect rate in soldered connections could be cut. The engineers succeeded in cutting the defect rate from 4 to 2 in every 1000 connections.

> Later HP charged its workers with solving the same problem. The company made many changes in the process and eventually cut the defect rate *a thousandfold,* to under two defects in a million.[1]
>
> Wealth generation increases in a modern society not because people work harder but because they work smarter. A modern enterprise with its computers and networks should be so engineered as to encourage all employees to use their brains to the fullest.

As computerized tools, robot machinery, and automated-process control become more powerful, people tend to move into jobs requiring higher skills. People no longer need to act like robots on a relentlessly moving production line; book-keepers no longer add up columns of figures. Staff of many types, working with computers, spreadsheets, and decision-support tools, are expected to make better and larger-scale decisions. Designers have powerful tools that enable them to be more creative. Computers can often do the drudgery work; human beings should do work that is uniquely human.

The annual revenue generated per person is several times higher in corporations that have automated in the right way than in corporations having little automation. The best automated corporations demand greater skill for greater pay.

We must grow human potential as fast as we grow technological potential.

Some employees become so adept with technology that their managers do not understand what they are doing. Virtuosos with computers can build up a level of skill that enormously exceeds anything their managers can envision. This is true of investment analysts, factory-schedule planners, market analysts, chip designers, and users of many advanced software tools.

Virtuosos do not need Ph.D.s; often they are college dropouts or low-level employees hooked by the fascination of computers.

A characteristic of the cybercorp is that virtuoso *employees* have *to be empowered because their managers cannot understand what they are doing.*

Maslow's Hierarchy of Human Needs

The psychologist Abraham Maslow categorized human needs in a hierarchy (Exhibit 2.2).[2]

When industry first evolved, it did little more than satisfy the needs for food and shelter. Later, corporations became concerned with safety. Many corporations in recent decades satisfied the need for belonging, creating a familylike environment. The movement toward empowering employees seeks to satisfy the higher needs: self-respect and self-actualization. An enormous reservoir of untapped

Exhibit 2.2   Maslow's hierarchy of human needs.[3]

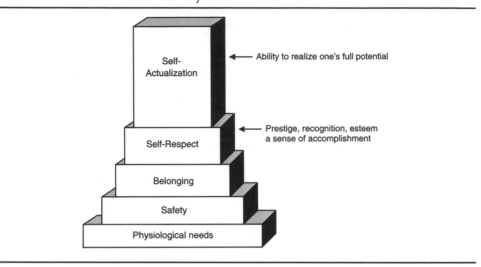

potential in most people can be channeled more productively. Individuals need to be proud of what they are doing and feel fulfilled because they have made special contributions.

For many years the concept of self-actualization was only applied to managerial and professional groups. Organizational psychologist Edgar Schein stated in 1980: "There is clear evidence that the drive toward self-actualization is an important—perhaps crucial—aspect of managerial and professional behavior. It is not clear, however, how relevant this motive is to the lower level employee."[4]

Today's view is that self-actualization is vitally important for *all* employees. The Japanese have demonstrated that when all employees can make valuable improvements in the processes used, these contributions add up to major improvements in quality, productivity, and profit. There is more scope for self-actualization and creative contribution from lower-level employees than ever before because automation has changed the nature of work. Routine jobs can be done by machines; people do work that cannot be automated. This offers workers more scope for improving their work processes. As we empower employees, we enrich jobs.

While this change has been occurring, there has been simultaneous growth in the understanding of how to maximize human contributions with techniques such as total quality management (TQM—discussed in Part III). The use of techniques for enabling workers to contribute to quality improvements and customer satisfaction has become highly refined in some corporations.

Many professional and managerial people find their primary means for self-actualization in their work. They take work home, socialize with colleagues, and "talk shop" at dinner. In corporations in which employee empowerment has become ingrained, a high proportion of nonprofessional employees find as much self-actualization in work as professionals do. They socialize with team members. They constantly try to improve their work processes. They dream about their work at night just as managers and professionals do.

Taylorism

In earlier times, management's goal was to make work as simple as possible. It was then easy to teach and replicate the tasks. By breaking work into simple repeatable steps, the lowest-cost workers could be employed.

The year the United States of America was born, Adam Smith wrote *The Wealth of Nations*. He described how to achieve what, in those days, seemed extraordinary productivity by making each worker repeat a single, simple task. For example, in a pin factory: "One man draws out the wire, another straightens it, a third cuts it, a fourth points it, a fifth grinds the top for receiving the head."[5] By breaking work into simple, repetitive tasks, he claimed, thousands of times as many pins could be made per day as when each worker made an entire pin.

Early in the twentieth century, the most influential authority on work processes was Frederick Winslow Taylor, who preached a doctrine of "industrial efficiency." Taylor stated, "It is not the job of the worker to determine how work is done." Efficiency experts were to do "time and motion study" to determine the precise actions that workers should repeat when operating machine tools and other devices. Taylor, in what was called "scientific management," sought to make work more specialized, precisely defined and optimized, and interchangeable. Taylorites observed workers with stopwatches. It was thought that there was one best way to perform a task. Efficiency experts designed work, and management compared the performance of workers to predetermined standards. Taylorism averred that the role of the worker was to follow directions quickly, precisely, and without argument.

The mechanistic nature of work was increased with the spread of production lines such as those of Henry Ford. Charlie Chaplin's film *Modern Times* satirized the unspeakable drudgery of the worker. Henry Ford kept workers under control. He reportedly kept a pool of five thousand toughs, many of them ex-convicts, on hand at his company to be used as strike-breakers.[6]

Taylorism and similar systems were concerned with reducing work to simple, repeatable activities. Corporations had *thinkers* and *workers*; workers were not allowed to think. Today, we feel that all employees should be challenged to think and devise improvements in work routines. They become excited about doing so; they enjoy seeing their improvements in operation and constantly try to refine them. Matsushita had six million written suggestions for improvement from employees in 1985. This stands in stark contrast to Taylorism. Taylor lamented, late in his career, "I have found that any improvement is not only opposed but aggressively and bitterly opposed by the majority of men."[7]

More recently automation spread through factories, with numerically controlled machine tools and intricate mechanisms for doing repetitive work. Most blue-collar workers were no longer regarded as automatons. Robots, not people, should do the work of robots. It was found that most employees like to think about their work process and can be highly ingenious in finding ways to improve it.

> Motorola gave tests to its workforce in some factories and found (to is amazement) that 40 percent could not answer questions such as "10 is what percent of 100?" Motorola's vice-president of training commented, "About half of our 25,000 manufacturing and support people in the United States failed to meet the seventh-grade (age 12) yardstick in English and math."[8] Nevertheless, Motorola found that those same employees created extraordinary improvements in productivity in their plant. Workers everywhere can be very creative about improving their own work.

The modern corporation challenges its employees to redesign their work processes and to seek out any possible improvement. The Japanese in the 1970s and 1980s achieved massive improvements in productivity and quality by developing a work culture that encouraged constant improvement and suggestions for redesigning work from the workforce. Ko Nishimura, president of Selectron, exemplified this approach: "People are much more capable than you think they are, and they are willing to do much more than you think they will."[9]

Although many workers in old-style corporations have jobs that require no thought, employees are often remarkably ingenious outside. I grew up in a coal-mining district in England. The miners had one of the most awful jobs imaginable. In the pubs in the evening they would discuss their study of horse-racing forms whose complexity bewildered outsiders, or they would restore old cars and constantly tune and redesign parts of them to obtain better performance. They were clever at their hobbies, highly skilled at gardening or home construction. Such people would have enjoyed helping to improve their work processes and products but were not allowed to.

An enormous reservoir of untapped potential can be channeled more productively. Most people can work out how to do things better, but they have been deterred from doing so in our enterprise structures.

In Britain in 1993 there was a furor about closing unprofitable government-run coal mines. The papers reported that the government would spend £500 million ($800 million) per year to keep unprofitable mines in operation so as to save 15 thousand jobs.[10] This is $53,333 per year per job. Imagine what could be done if this money were spent on retraining the mine workers to participate in modern industry. They and their union officials proclaimed with great emotion on television that if the pits were closed the workers would be "thrown on the scrap heap." Nobody in British politics discussed the lost opportunities of condemning people to work down in coal mines when they could have been trained and coached to do far more valuable jobs that are enjoyable.

The work revolution associated with Henry Ford, mass-production lines, Frederick Taylor, time-and-motion study, and so forth, created jobs that were utterly boring and dehumanizing. Today's work revolution—associated with self-directing teams, workers searching for better methods, value-stream reinvention, a knowledge infrastructure, and the learning enterprise—is creating jobs that are challenging and exciting.

In the late 1980s absenteeism at General Motors plants averaged an appalling 10–14 percent. However, at GM's totally reinvented Saturn plant it is just 2.5 percent. At Saturn work, at Maslow's fifth level, is more enjoyable. Workers are respected members of teams that they do not want to let down. The low-priced Saturn became the highest-rated American car for quality. In a 1992 survey only Lexus and Infiniti beat it for customer satisfaction.

Personal Energy

To maximize their contributions, people need to apply energy and enthusiasm to their jobs. Human energy arises from meaning and excitement. When people believe that what they are doing is meaningful, they put energy into it. When it excites them, they can work very hard.

Energy increases with the perception of the value of one's ideas and activities. The energy of an enterprise is the sum of the energies of its employees. Therefore, all employees should have the freedom to create and introduce meaningful ideas. They should be able to align their own meaning with the purposes of the enterprise.

Unemployment is a serious concern in many countries today. Worry has been expressed that reengineered corporations can employ only the brightest and best educated. In reality everyone can contribute native intelligence and ingenuity. Shure Brothers, a manufacturer of hi-fi components, demonstrated this at its plant in Juarez, Mexico.

The goal was to improve the manufacturing process of Shure's top-selling microphone products. Shure established cross-functional teams called "paradigm busters." Some team members could not read and had little education. The teams were empowered to reinvent the process and were challenged to show the Shure head office in Evanston, Illinois, that they could work wonders. TQM was applied at every stage of the reinvented process. The teams cut manufacturing steps from 349 to 96 and production time from 32 days to 2. The teams also recommended significant product-design improvements. Manufacturing changes instituted by the teams cut the workforce on one product from 56 to 29. All this happened because there was a no-layoff guarantee. The challenge of team empowerment won the loyalty of Mexican employees. The turnover rate fell from a high of 8 percent per month to 2 percent or less.[11]

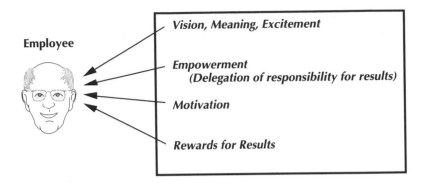

To make jobs meaningful, management must create a corporate *vision* that excites people and fires the imagination of everyone in the organization. People must believe in the vision, and it must give meaning to their work. Management should empower people to achieve results related to the vision and should offer rewards and motivation.

An overall corporate vision may guide the creation of a narrower vision relating to a particular work process. When the vision for the work process is clear, individuals or teams should have freedom to improve how they work so as to achieve results that meet the vision. Energy arises from the challenge to be creative in achieving results that have meaning in the context of a vision.

A Paradox: Continuous Change vs. Excellence

For survival, enterprises need two characteristics that at first glance appear contradictory.

Most authorities stress the extreme fluidity of today's environment. Success comes from responding to market demands with more agility than one's competitors. Enterprises must be dynamic; we need breakthrough thinking and a stream of new products and new ideas. People must be encouraged to try new things. However, constant change without control cannot produce skills and excellence. We call a person "flakey" if he pursues a new idea every day but never makes anything work well. Corporations can become flakey by doing what they think the management magazines are advocating.

To succeed, an organization must (1) *become good at something*. It must improve continuously until it outshines most of its competition. There must be constant changes; most failures of well-established corporations occur because of failure to change. In addition, the adaptive, fluid, flexible changes must (2) *be directed at a specific goal or mission*. They must be the fast changes of a missile pursuing an evasive target rather than those of a bluebottle buzzing in a jar.

The enterprise, then, needs a vision and strategic alignment—the commitment of everyone in an enterprise to a common, energizing purpose. Enterprises that have such a vision are able to succeed in a dynamic environment because their diverse talents and capabilities are more aligned than their competitors'.

In 1992 Britain's flamboyant Richard Branson was the world's second-youngest self-made billionaire (after Bill Gates). Branson compared dealing with employees to raising children. He quoted his father as saying that the ideal way to bring up children was to lavish them with praise and, unless safety was endangered, to encourage them to experiment. "The same thing applies to staff." [12] People who are lavished with praise try harder. They know when they have made a mistake and do not have to be told.

In 1992 Branson sold Virgin Music to Thorn EMI for almost a billion dollars and undertook to operate an unconventional airline, Virgin Atlantic. Much of Branson's success resulted from constantly challenging employees to be creative and letting them make decisions. Branson told his airline crews to choose their own uniform and to be sure that it was attractive. He conducted impromptu brainstorming sessions with employees to encourage their imaginations to run wild with new ideas. One group suggested a hot tub on the roof of the London airport lounge; another suggested an old Russian submarine periscope for waiting passengers to use in scanning around the airport.

Virgin was the first airline to have seat-back videos. It introduced "upper class," giving first-class service at business-class prices. It tried in-flight entertainers, a music library, and performing magicians in the aisles. It gave passengers kits for minimizing jet lag.

Hong Kong has Saville Row-style tailors at a third of Saville Row prices. On Branson's flights to Hong Kong, a crew member was trained to measure passengers for tailoring; the measurements were faxed ahead to Hong Kong so that a tailor could meet the plane and fit the clothes.

Particularly important, Branson regarded the plane as the perfect environment for market research; the customers were trapped there for seven hours or so. He had his crews talk to the customers in depth about the airline, write down what they said, and act on it. He discovered that upper-class passengers especially liked the free limousine service to the airport in Britain and to anywhere within fifty miles of the airport in the United States.

Branson's cash investment in Virgin Atlantic Airways was $2 million in 1984. Its revenue six years later was $700 million, in spite of British Airways' alleged "dirty tricks" campaign to undermine the upstart's revenue.

The task of management is to build an organization that is *both* highly responsive to its environment in the present and has a vision and architecture designed to maximize long-term growth and effectiveness. The corporation must be supremely reactive to the fast-changing environment and strategically skilled at planning and designing a structure that can survive a profoundly uncertain future. The process of building an organization that can respond more quickly than its competitors requires long-term planning and investment—in flexible processes, systems, core competencies, and (most importantly) people.

An organization must continuously learn. We only become great at something if we know what we want to achieve and move steadily toward that vision, learning. All employees should share the vision and press toward it, learning at every step. The learning must pervade the enterprise from top to bottom.

When people in the enterprise learn how to make improvements, the results should be codified and made available to other employees. Information technology should be designed both to help in the learning process and to preserve and improve the results of the learning. *Automation* should be introduced in such a way that it produces *information* that helps employees optimize and improve the automated process.

Human energy arises from freedom, not coerced alignment. This freedom and energy is needed for continuing responsiveness to rapid change. Individual diversity must be respected and made use of for unplanned (and basically unpredictable) changes. However, the freedom and diversity need a shared purpose and vision.

Maximizing Everyone's Value

The capability of any corporation is the sum capability of its people. If we maximize what every employee contributes, we maximize the value of the corporation.

Individuals are employed in order to contribute to the processes they engage in. In an efficient organization individuals contribute a great deal; in an inefficient organization their abilities are not tapped. In some corporations revenue per employee is $25 thousand; in some it is $800 thousand. It is interesting to ask why revenue per employee at Microsoft is four times that per employee at IBM. A goal of a healthy corporation (and, indeed, of an economically healthy society) should be that all individuals contribute to the maximum extent they can.

In today's society it is desirable to look at every individual and ask, How could this person's work be changed to make him or him more valuable? We all should get into the habit of doing this. When we are in shops, in meetings, in government offices, at work, and going about everyday activities, we should ask about the people we interact with: How could these people contribute more? Could we redesign their work so as to increase their value? Most people could contribute *much* more than they do. Many are going through the motions of an ill-designed job. Sometimes they are surly or unhelpful to customers or other departments. When their work is redesigned and they are challenged to make improvements or become members of highly motivated teams, there is a new thrill to their jobs. The boredom is lifted. They are challenged in exciting ways. They are empowered to make a difference and achieve self-respect and self-actualization. What is good for people is usually good for business.

We should ask of everybody, What is the maximum contribution that this person could make? What redesign of work could help achieve this?

One of the great discoveries a man makes, one of his great surprises, is to find he can do what he was afraid he couldn't do.

—Henry Ford

There is a major gap between the actual and potential performance of most people. There is no one whose value to the enterprise cannot increase; a primary management challenge is to find out how to help each person do that. Individuals can contribute more if they have more skill or expertise, more powerful tools, and access to knowledge. Their work can be redesigned to enable them to add more value. Often they contribute more as members of self-directing teams with clearly focused goals. They should be trained to use tools and methods that streamline tasks.

There are numerous ways to empower people: to enable them to do more interesting, satisfying, responsible, valuable jobs. They may be helped with computerized tools, expert systems, access to databases, and information superhighways. Technology, as always, should be a means to an end; it should be a means to improving human decision making, application of skills, and "value-added" communication. Business redesign and effective uses of information technology should have a goal of increasing the value of employees.

Experimentation: The Learning-Laboratory Enterprise

People learn from training courses, seminars, coaching, benchmarking, other people, and (particularly important) doing things—but to learn something fundamentally new, we need to experiment. Traditionally, experimentation has gone on in the corporate laboratory, often in a beautiful countryside environment far away from the turmoil of business. The unwritten law is that the laboratory is where scientists alone do experiments and research.

In a world of dynamic change, with intense competition and copycat products, corporations need to be improving their products and processes continuously. Many employees should be conducting experiments to find better techniques. Experimentation should take place not only in the laboratory but in the factory and in teams trying to find better ways to please customers. (Chapter 31 describes situations in which the whole corporation operates as a learning laboratory.)

Workers on the factory floor, teams with tough problems, and employees trying to please customers should conduct experiments in order to find fundamentally better ways to do things. They should brainstorm for new ideas and decide which ones to try out. A photographer experiments with innovative ways to shoot, a metal worker with ways to make precision castings better, a chef with new combinations of tastes. The more we experiment the more we are likely to improve. Experiments cause people to search for new ideas, to ask questions in new places, to read and research, to make unconventional associations. It is fun. Ordinary employees often produce better ideas than Ph.D.'s.

Most employees and teams thrive on experimentation. They need to be taught how to design experiments that will produce verifiable results. Management must make sure that the search for better methods and mechanisms is coordinated so that employees do not reinvent the wheel but benefit from one another's contributions.

Some activities need more experimentation than others. The strategic-visioning process discussed in Part V addresses core competencies and strategic capabilities that can put a corporation ahead of its competition.

These special capabilities should be focused on. Employees in these areas, not just in the laboratory, should engage in research and development. Inexpensive experimentation should go on continuously in many areas, but sometimes expensive experiments are worth the investment too. A learning-laboratory enterprise needs to identify clearly the line items of budgets for experimentation.

The learning-laboratory corporation could not be more different from the traditional man-in-the gray-flannel-suit corporation. It encourages and rewards innovative thinking whenever this achieves results. A mix of analytical, rational thinking and "off-the-wall" creativity pervades all of its activities. Much of what has been learned about running the R and D function applies to the entire enterprise.

Enterprise Redesign

Exhibit 2.3 summarizes changes in approaches to work. As employment was successfully reinvented with empowered employees, self-directing teams, fundamental reengineering of the work process, experimentation throughout the enterprise, and new relationships with business partners, it became clear that the old hierarchical management structure was being replaced with new structures. Power structures had grown up with fiefdoms at multiple levels in the hierarchy. Vice-presidents protected their empires. The fiefdoms guarded data because un-shared data gives power. The hierarchy's controls and measurements were imposed by a growing bureaucracy.

Most of the controls and measurements are irrelevant to the empowered teams, which span the functions of the hierarchy. The bureaucracy seriously impedes the empowerment of employees and the capabilities for employee experimentation. New management structures are needed. The trend toward new structures is accelerating because a better understanding of how to get the most value from employees coincides with a massive spread of technology that can both minimize the drudgery of work and deliver empowering information to every

Exhibit 2.3   The reinvention of employment: a summary of the changes in work

The Old Way	*The New Way*
Division of labor	Empowerment of employees
Division and simplification of work	Enriched work; employees engaged in multiple tasks and expanding their knowledge
Lowest-cost workers	Highest-value workers
Taylorism	*Kaizen* (Chapter 14)
Workers thought not to have an important effect on quality	Quality considered everyone's job
Workers not knowledgable about the work process	Employees participating in designing of work routines
Management giving orders; workers obeying without argument	Participative management, self-managed teams
One "best way" to do work defined by management	All employees learning continually and contributing to enterprise learning
Experimentation done by scientists	Experimentation done by many teams of employees
Cost of labor minimized through standard work steps	Training and initiative of every employee to ensure their greatest possible contribution
Most tasks simple	Sophisticated use of creative tools and computers
Work dehumanizing	Work that gives self-respect and self-actualization
Most workers not expected (or permitted) to think	All workers expected to use their ingenuity
Hierarchical management	Flat organizations, cross-functional teams
Formal channels for information	Free access to information
Functional fiefdoms	The "boundaryless" organization

worker in an enterprise. This managerial revolution coincides with, and is driven by, the technology revolution.

Traditional organizations are compartmentalized and rely excessively on chains of command. In the new organization information can flow freely to where it is useful. Boundaries and bureaucracies slow down business processes and decisions when speed is critical for success. They insulate people from reality when facing reality with brutal honesty is vital. They garble communications when information passes from one group to another, each with its own "spin doctors." The most successful organizations increasingly are lean and agile, with a fluid structure able to respond rapidly to market changes. Corporations need open minds and systems that reach across functions and hierarchies with candor, challenging all workers to think more. The world is moving at such a pace that boundaries and bureaucracy are serious liabilities.

Many corporations still have the fiefdoms and compartmentalization of the past. The corporate barons enjoy their power and try to preserve it. In some corporations management has become its own worse enemy.

"Boundarylessness"

In General Electric the need for free communication across the enterprise culminated in the coining of the word *boundarylessness* to express an all-encompassing characteristic of the new corporation. Boundarylessness suggests the removal of artificial boundaries to communication and full cooperation across the artificial barriers that have separated people in the past.

Jack Welch, the legendary CEO who transformed General Electric, explains boundarylessness with the image of a house that presents barriers in three dimensions.[13]

- *Horizontal Barriers*—Walls divide a house horizontally. In a corporation they are the barriers between separate functions, departments, product lines, or geographical locations. Marketing should work together with production, production with design, Paris with Manila.
- *Vertical Barriers*—Ceilings and floors divide a house vertically. In a corporation differences in rank can obstruct open communication. Information should pass freely from bottom to top and across layers. The number of layers has been drastically reduced in many enterprises.
- *External Barriers*—In a house external walls and space separate it from neighbors. In a corporation there needs to be close communication, aided by electronics, with customers, suppliers, agents, retail chains, venture partners, and others.

Cooperation across boundaries is increasingly a requirement for competitive success. It is made more practical by technology, but technology can also build barriers, deliberately or otherwise. One group builds databases that others cannot interrogate; system incompatibilities prevent interoperation. Boundarylessness requires a different state of mind. It thrives in a culture of openness and cooperation. Playing politics is a cardinal sin in the cooperative enterprise. If the corporate goals are clear, intricate informal networks among people achieve much more than rigid, traditional organizations. (Part VI of this book describes the redesign of the enterprise.)

ConAgra grew out of the Nebraska Consolidated Mills Company, a milling company that by 1971 had branched out into various food products. In the early 1970s ConAgra fell on hard times. It lost money in 1974, and its market value sank to $10 million. To turn this disaster around, the new president brought in a CEO from Pillsbury, Mike Harper.

Harper immediately engaged senior managers in defining a longer-term vision for ConAgra. He personally drafted a paper that became a small booklet, *ConAgra's Philosophy.*

ConAgra's Philosophy

- Most people want to be involved meaningfully in their work.
- Most people want to feel connected to, and part of, a larger world (to have a sense of belonging).
- Most people want to set goals and use their energies to attain them.
- Most people would like to be themselves, to feel a sense of responsibility as well as a sense of personal uniqueness, and to have the freedom to express themselves as they are.

Harper and his top management team made the philosophy work. After many changes ConAgra achieved a market value in 1988 a thousand times that of the dark days of 1974.

Key Themes of the Future

The following six key themes are critical to all corporate redesign (Exhibit 2.4).

Fundamental Uncertainty

The world is accelerating toward becoming one interconnected system. Financial markets, consumer tastes, political aspirations—nothing is a solely "local" phenomenon any longer. Because of the dawn of global telecommunications and media, "local" markets, tastes, aspirations, and so forth, are increasingly volatile. One hears the phrase "new paradigm" continually, a symptom of the sense that our abilities to predict and to control the future are illusory and must be left behind. Our growing interest in chaos theory and the emerging science of complexity exemplify this theme of the unresolvable uncertainty that we must deal with in designing future organizations.

Radical Changes in How People Work

The purpose of an organization is to coordinate capital, energy, and knowledge to achieve some purpose. Leverage is needed to produce work more effectively than one's competitors, but suddenly the nature of work has changed in much of the industrial world. The essence of this change is the reemergence of the importance of human skill and knowledge in production. This theme is central to the emerging partnership between people and machines in the performance of work. It is already difficult to distinguish whether a human being or a computer is doing much of the routine work in our society—who makes the airline reservation, the agent or the computer? So, the design of organizations must create a framework in order for this human-technological partnership to flourish.

Explosive Changes in Technology

Technology is a crucial element in future organizational design. We are talking about a "sea change" in technology—discontinuous change, not just an extrapolation from the past. This may not be apparent to us because we are experiencing continual, incremental changes in technology each month, but if we look ahead twenty years or so, we can begin to appreciate the impending discontinuity better. By then civilization will have completed its first step toward a pervasive cyberspace "mind" that spans the planet. The ability to learn, communicate, and compute globally is here today, but it is evolving at great speed with worldwide fiber-optic and satellite networks that each of us depend on daily for continual learning, work, and entertainment. Organizations must redesign themselves to participate in this "global mind" more effectively than their competitors.

Renewed Focus on Humanity

At the deepest level, our ideas about who we human beings are, the mystery of our humanity and wisdom, are changing. We are often dissatisfied by our inventions and constructs. Inside organizations this new desire for more than work and rewards results in employee empowerment, increased creativity, and emphasis on the "softer" aspects of organizations, such as relationships and holism. People yearn to reach beyond themselves for something more meaningful. The corporate architect's response to this yearning is an important part of organizational design.

Extreme Rate of Change

Such themes are causing an accelerating rate of change. With computers and international networks we build mechanisms that react at great speed. The windows of opportunities shrink. Many procedures are speeded up. The slow-moving stability of the top-down command structure is replaced with the agile ingenuity of employees challenged to use their brains. Empowered teams can use their skills in unpredictable ways. All around the planet diverse approaches cause rapid, unpredictable changes, like mercury splashing on glass, and these are felt worldwide because of global electronics.

Constant Learning

The permanent white water, the constant uncertainty, the racing changes in technology, demand that enterprises continue to learn and experiment. The term *learning enterprise* is used everywhere, but most writers have a one-dimensional view of what it means. There are many diverse ways an enterprise must learn. Factory workers learn differently from marketing professionals; product designers learn differently from corporate planners. The architecture of the new enterprise must permit it to maximize all types of learning and to capture and disseminate the resulting know-how.

The Good News

In the past what was good for the corporation was often bad for the individual. We created soul-destroying jobs.

With today's reinvention of work, what is good for the corporation is good for the employee who learns the new skills. Most boring jobs can be abolished (but not quite all). The dehumanizing methods of Taylorism are gone. The intense competition and emphasis on quality means that we can buy more interesting goods and services. Unlike Adam Smith's revolution, the wealth of nations is maximized by increasing the value of everybody.

The various change methods of Enterprise Engineering aim toward the highest of Maslow's hierarchy of human needs—the striving to achieve full potential. This possibility energizes and excites people.

The learning-laboratory corporation is the culmination of the twentieth-century journey from treating employees as dumb slaves who must obey orders

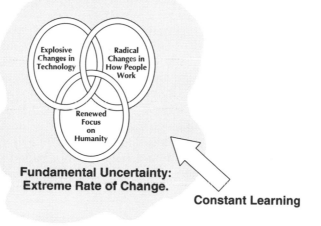

to encouraging employees to use their intelligence to increase their value. The century started with Kafka-like bureaucracy and contempt for employees, with Frederick Taylor timing every motion of workers with a stopwatch. It ends with the challenge of regarding the entire corporation as a learning laboratory, and challenging everybody to achieve full potential.

Turn Your Boilermen into Knowledge Workers!

The progress of civilization can be assessed in terms of the increasing contributions of ordinary people.

In primitive societies most people were idle most of the time or did menial tasks. By the seventeenth century a small, privileged class had most of society's wealth. Its members built beautiful homes and employed people to improve their quality of life while most of society was poor and contributed little. By the eighteenth century, industrialization was underway. There was a small class of "haves" and a vast number of "have-nots," as in India today. By the nineteenth century the have-not class was still large; the lot of the poor was grim. By the twentieth century jobs that required more from many were increasing the wealth of the public and creating the consumer society. By 1950 most people in developed countries were employed, but many were production-line workers or clerks having jobs of mind-destroying tedium.

By the twenty-first century most employees will be trained to do work that is interesting and of substantial value. It will be a complex, competitive, and highly creative society with most drudgery jobs automated. By the twentieth century the aristocracy and courts of kings had lost their power. By the twenty-first century the power structures of corporations will have been radically changed so as to challenge and empower the rank and file to contribute more. Compensation will relate to the contribution of an employee, not to rank or status.

The challenge is to achieve massive reengineering and automation without creating a major underclass that does not participate in the high-value work. In America today such an underclass is growing; the result is violence in the cities.

As we unlock the riches of automation, we must design a society in which all people participate and learn the multiplicity of ways of contributing to it. All people in all parts of society can do some type of work that improves the quality of life. Most do not need to be "symbolic analysts." As automation becomes ever more sophisticated, the value of jobs will continue to increase and will require life-long education and training. It will require leaders who inspire vision, motivation, and excitement.

References

1. "The Quality Imperative," *Business Week Guide* (McGraw Hill: New York, 1994).
2. Abraham Maslow, *Motivation and Personality* (Harper & Row: London, 1964).
3. Ibid.
4. Edgar Schein, *Organizational Psychology* (Prentice-Hall: Englewood Cliffs, N.J., 1980).
5. Adam Smith, *The Wealth of Nations* (Adam & Charles Black: Edinburgh, 1850).
6. Arthur A. Sloane, *Hoffa* (MIT Press: Cambridge, Mass., 1991).
7. John Dos Passos, *The Big Money* (Modern Library: New York, 1937).
8. William Wiggenhorn, "Motorola U: When Training Becomes an Education," *Harvard Business Review*, July-August 1990.
9. Guang Bao and Elizabeth B. Baatz, "How Selectron Finally Got in Touch with Its Workers," *Electronic Business*, October 7, 1991.
10. *London Sunday Times* (Front-page story), January 24, 1993.
11. Martha H. Peak, "Maquilodoras: Where Quality Is a Way of Life," *Management Review*, March 1993.
12. Jeffrey Ferry, *The British Renaissance* (Heinemann: London, 1993).
13. Noel M. Tichy and Stratford Sherman, *Control Your Own Destiny or Someone Else Will* (Doubleday Currency: New York, 1993).

3

The Wrong Use of Automation

By the start of the 1990s a shocking realization had begun to spread among a number of computer professionals and top executives. A vast amount of money had been spent on advanced technology, but most of the time we had built the wrong systems. Worse, most of the systems being built today are the wrong systems.

The service industries of the United States spent a mind-blowing $800 billion on automation during the 1980s, but during that period white-collar productivity went *down* by 3 percent.[1] Employment increased faster than production.

Many corporations installed large mainframe systems—at great expense for computer staff, analysts, programmers, and software—that in some cases produced a net negative return on investment. Personal computers appeared on desks everywhere. The estimated cost per personal computer was well over $10 thousand when support costs were calculated.[2] This did not include the time staff spent tinkering with the devices instead of doing other work. Executives worried that the benefits seemed to be less than the costs. Japanese companies with far fewer computers produced higher profits.

By the 1990s the reasons for the problem had become clear: corporations should have drastically redesigned their processes to take advantage of information technology, but most of the time they had not. Executives should have been thinking in terms of cybercorp opportunities and architecture, but most of the time they had thought about computer applications for existing departments. Using today's technology to automate twenty-year-old processes is like Marconi inventing radio and using it only as a point-to-point wireless telegraph. He did not initially recognize its potential for broadcasting. When broadcasting was first proposed, a man who was later to become one of the most distinguished leaders of the industry declared that it was difficult to see uses for public broadcasting. About the only regular use he could think of was the broadcasting of Sunday sermons because that was the only occasion when one man regularly addressed the mass public!

Thomas Edison once said that the primary value of his newly invented phonograph was to allow "dying gentlemen to record their last wishes."

Do Not Automate Yesterday's Processes

Most people fail to understand the potentials of technology because they think of it in terms of solving problems they have today. They ask, How can we automate what already exists? The great potential of technology is to *replace* what exists with something different and fundamentally better. Tibetans invented the turbine mechanism but used it only for the rotation of prayer wheels.

Many enterprises went through an early phase of office automation that was discredited because the costs exceeded the benefits. Many users did not want to give up "hard copy" when mail or documents became electronic. An IBM systems journal advocated following the desires of the customer: "The customer was anxious to avoid disruption of their established organization by introduction of office communications. As a matter of philosophy, *the system must fit the users and not the reverse.*" [3] This is the wrong philosophy: the users must change their ways in order to maximize profits from automation.

Enterprises sometimes seem unable to take seriously the change needed in their organization until they have spent significant money on computers first. Despite the advice to think before automating, many executives seem to have to automate first in order to understand it and then rethink the process. They spend in order to focus, then think, and then redo. This is expensive and slow. The Enterprise Engineer ought to introduce an appropriate change in process as early as possible. If you must "spend, think, and then redo," be sure that the first unreasoned steps are easily reversible.

From 1975 to 1982 there was a massive drive to automate accounting in the United States, but during this period the number of accountants *increased* by 40 percent. General Electric, known for its superb financial management, had top executives drowning in data they could not possibly use. One GE business produced seven daily reports for top management containing product-by-product sales details on hundreds of thousands of items. Each report made a stack of paper twelve feet high. *Fortune* commented that such practices

> . . . emasculated top executives by overwhelming them with useless information, and enslaved middle managers with the need to gather it. . . . Briefing books had grown to such dense impenetrability that top managers simply stopped reading them. Instead, they relied on staffers to feed them "gotchas" with which to intimidate subordinates at meetings. [4]

Later GE and other corporations learned how to use management information systems to highlight situations that called for executive action.

Automation Without Reinvention

A dramatic example of the effects of technology exists in the world's car factories. Extensive automation was introduced there in the 1980s. On television we repeatedly saw images of robots welding or spray painting cars. One would expect there to be a correlation between automation and productivity, perhaps something like that in Exhibit 3.1.

Unfortunately, such is not the case. MIT carried out a detailed study of the world's car factories—their IMVP (International Motor Vehicle Program) survey.[5] Exhibit 3.2 plots productivity and automation for European and American car

Exhibit 3.1   One might expect higher levels of automation to bring higher levels of productivity as here. Exhibits 3.2 and 3.3 indicate that this is not the case unless the processes are reinvented.

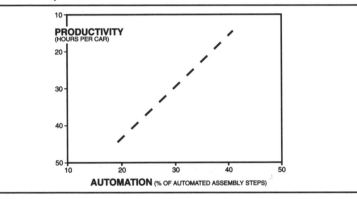

Exhibit 3.2   A comprehensive study of the world's car factories done by MIT[5] reveals almost no correlation between automation and productivity in America and Europe. This is in sharp contrast with Japan as shown in Exhibit 3.3.

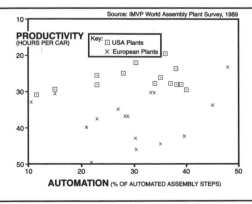

assembly plants. There is almost no correlation between automation and productivity!

Exhibit 3.3 shows the same information for Japanese car factories.[6] With one exception the Japanese factories in 1989 achieved higher productivity than car factories in the rest of the world. Japanese car factories, starting with Toyota, invented "lean" manufacturing and changed every aspect of how a car should be designed and assembled. When automation is applied to the fundamentally reinvented car factories, in Japan and now elsewhere in the world, startling productivity improvements are achieved. A car with ten thousand parts is built in less than 20 hours—and in the best case, 12 hours.

One might expect quality to suffer if cars are built fast. Exhibit 3.4 shows the opposite.[7] The Japanese plants exhibit higher quality (in terms of assembly defects) as well as higher speed of manufacturing. If automation is used in the right way, both speed and quality can be greatly improved. Automation can prevent many of the defects that people make. To do so, both the product and the manufacturing process need to be redesigned jointly to take advantage of automation.

> *The lesson here is Do not apply automation without totally redesigning the end-to-end process.*

Social commentators and unions worry about employees being laid off because of computers. In reality employees are being laid off because foreign corporations are more efficient. Many large American car factories with expensive computers and mass-production lines with robots that look spectacular on television have been closed in the last ten years because they could not compete with Japan

Exhibit 3.3 In Japan the car factory was totally reinvented, using "lean" manufacturing and then applying automation. With one exception higher productivity was achieved than in the West. Lean manufacturing is now spreading to some Western car plants.[5] The factory of the future needs thorough reinvention of its processes to take advantage of new technology.

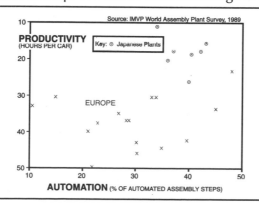

Exhibit 3.4   Increased productivity must not be at the expense of increased defects. Reinvention of processes must seek out those techniques that *both* increase productivity and reduce defects. The Japanese reinvention of car factories did this successfully.[5]

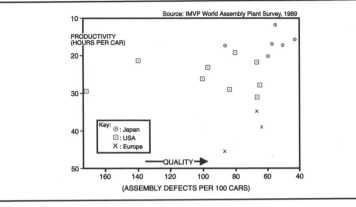

and South Korea. The Japanese had created "lean" manufacturing and were building cars of high quality at lower cost.

It was often assumed in the West that the Japanese competed better because of cheap labor or because they moved like armies of insects (the French prime minister called them "ants"). Neither contention was true. The Japanese are intelligent business people who reinvented their business processes. They changed every aspect of how car manufacturers should design cars, relate to their suppliers, assemble cars, and interact with customers.

Unwieldy White-Collar Processes

The lessons learned in lean manufacturing apply even more to administrative processes. The end-to-end processes in most corporations are clumsy and slow. They date back to the age before computers and networks. We need to scrap most processes and replace them with something fundamentally different that capitalizes on what modern technology makes possible. We have applied expensive computer systems to outrageously old-fashioned processes. The awkward nature of the process itself prevents the computers from making much difference. We can make a big difference if we scrap the entire end-to-end process, fundamentally rethink its goals, and invent something that meets those goals as directly and simply as possible, using modern technology and new teams of motivated people.

Dealing with a customer who reports an error in a credit-card bill may involve multiple letters and perhaps forty process steps. It sometimes takes weeks to resolve the problem. With image processing the procedure can be revised so that the customer need only dial an 800 number to correct the problem, usually in one telephone call. Many administrative procedures have been reinvented to achieve dramatic reductions in the time and work required, and major improvements in the ability to please the customer. Exhibit 5.6 (in Chapter 5) shows examples of breakthrough results in the reinvention of business processes.

Computer professionals acquired sophisticated knowledge about how to make their machinery work and how to create programs for it. The computer industry captivates its professionals with a mind-gripping fascination unlike that in any other occupation. Few computer professionals think about how the *business* should be reinvented, however. They may think about how to automate a procedure that already exists, but that negates the value of the technology. Its true value lies in fundamentally reinventing how the enterprise functions. The more complex the software and electronics become, the more IT (information technology) professionals tend to focus on the technology rather than focusing on the big opportunities it presents. The big challenge is reinventing the business. Because of the intense focus on making the electronics and software work, *most computer professionals are building the wrong applications.*

The financial implications of this are staggering. In most corporations the computing budget is the largest capital budget, but the true cost of computing goes well beyond the computing budget. It includes the time business people spend in IT-related meetings and tinkering with personal computers. The cost across society as a whole is enormous. The financial impact of lost opportunities is much greater than the cost of computing.

> *Most computer systems being built today are the wrong systems.*

Most administrative processes are even more in need of reinvention than manufacturing processes. What has happened in the car industry will happen in other industries. Immense reinvention is needed in service industries. Enterprise reinvention is in the air everywhere, and corporations that fail to do it will go the way of the dinosaur car factories.

In corporations competitive survival will force reinvention; in government some other force is needed. Some processes in government are unbelievably inefficient. A study of Washington's low-interest rehabilitation-loan program found that each civil servant processed an average of only one loan application every three months. Each $20 thousand loan had $11 thousand of administrative expenses.[8]

Integration vs. Fragments

An enterprise can be thought of as an exceedingly complex system—like a piece of machinery with many parts that have to work together.

If each part of a system, considered separately, is made to operate as efficiently as possible, the system as a whole will not operate as effectively as possible.

—Russell Ackoff

Russell Ackoff comments that if many types of car were examined by engineers, with engineers identifying the best designed components and then assembling a car from those best components, that car would not work. The performance of a system depends more on how its parts interact than on how well they work independently of one another.

In a corporation that consists of many departments, each department could try to work as efficiently as possible, using the most advanced computer systems for that department. This would not make the corporation as a whole efficient, however. Optimizing the parts independently is highly inefficient compared with optimizing the whole. This is especially true in an era of reinvention. When a corporation needs reinventing, many of the old parts should be scrapped.

As we build the cybercorp, our primary concern must be integration of the organism. Only when we have done that well should we consider optimizing the components. The departments of the traditional corporation must often be replaced as we build the new-world corporation.

In most corporations employees are trapped in an organization structure. Within that structure they think about what is visible to them. They may think about their own department and what it does or, at a higher level, about production scheduling or the procurements division. Building an efficient corporation needs a broader viewpoint. The end-to-end processes that desperately need reinventing span multiple departments, divisions, and sometimes corporations. The necessary reinvention is not the purview of a department head and sometimes not in that of the vice-president of a division. Most people trapped in an obsolete organization structure cannot change the organization. They build systems for their own department or their own division. *Again, these are the wrong systems.* They tend to cast in concrete the obsolete procedures that ought to be reengineered.

If total quality management (TQM) is applied within an obsolete organization structure, it has the effect of optimizing and polishing procedures that ought to be scrapped and replaced with something quite different. TQM should be applied to the reengineered process, not the obsolete process.

The spread of personal computers, workstations, and local area networks has led to an era of downsizing in IT. Each department started to build its own systems. Control passed from the IT organization to line management. There are clear advantages to business units building and perfecting their own systems if those systems fit into an integrated and optimized enterprise. However, most of the systems were built with no cybercorp viewpoint. They were the wrong systems, expensive because of hidden costs and often difficult to change. Ironically, the CIO lost control in many corporations at just the time when his integrated corporatewide viewpoint was needed. You cannot build a cybercorp out of independent fragments.

It is appalling how many authorities on "business process reengineering" advocate modeling and modifying an existing business process when the right thing to do is *scrap* the process and take an integrated approach to building cybercorp value streams as described in this book.

Enterprise Engineering needs a high-enough-level viewpoint to identify the sets of activities that span multiple divisions of the enterprise and that need reengineering. It is this enterprisewide view that has the large payoff. It raises vital questions about the enterprise's overall architecture, culture, and information technology. Answering these questions effectively should result in the planning of a corporate journey with a pragmatic timetable for needed changes.

Back to Dickens

In a world of lightning-fast electronics, it is amusing to let one's imagination drift back to the days of Dickens. In those days transactions were handled by a clerk with a quill pen, perched on a high stool and perhaps wearing a top hat. Before him lay a stack of thick, well-bound ledgers. If an order was made for a certain quantity of goods, the clerk would deal with the entire transaction. He would look up stock sheets to see whether the order could be fulfilled from stock or some of it had to be manufactured. He would update the order book, and if any goods were sent he would modify the stock sheets, make out a bill for the customer, and make an entry in the customer ledger. If the customer had a query, the clerk could turn to the appropriate pages of his ledgers and produce an answer. He could balance his books at the end of the day. He had detailed knowledge at his finger tips about all the transactions he handled.

The world changed. Business grew until the work needed many clerks with many ledgers. Division of labor made the job easier. One clerk could maintain stock sheets while another did billing, and so on. Mechanization was introduced, and the work was split up into batches. One accounting function would be carried out by one clerk with a machine and the next by another clerk with another machine. When punched cards came along, large batches became economical.

As the volumes grew, different work steps came to be carried out by different departments. The invoicing department knew nothing about product defects. The shipping dock that received the goods created paperwork that went to the quality-control department, the quality-control department sent reports to purchasing, and so on. Paper passed from one "in" tray to another. It was no longer possible to deal with customer problems quickly or to give quick answers to queries about the status of an account or the credit worthiness of a customer.

Early computers had no disks; they needed tapes. It was economic for them to process large batches of work one function at a time. The larger the batch size, the more efficient the computer run. Tapes were shipped to the computer location. One item could not be changed without running the entire batch; so it waited, sometimes weeks, until that batch was processed. Large hierarchical organizations prospered with many departments, each doing a specialized set of tasks. The divisions of the hierarchy became separate power-groups, each defending its own turf.

Today, we can reinstate the Dickensian clerk. He can have all the information he needs at his finger tips, on computer screens. Transactions can be processed immediately. Customer concerns can be dealt with quickly. A customer can always deal with the same person, one who knows all about the customer's problems and wishes. The service representative can retrieve any information about the customer from the computer. Even if the customer is thousands of miles away, the information travels in a second or less. Most paperwork can be eliminated. There is no need for invoices. There is often no need for purchase orders because suppliers' computers trigger the replenishment of stock when it is needed. There need be little keyed input. Electronic documents enter a computer directly. Much data is collected directly from bar scanners or cash registers, so most clerical errors are eliminated. Work can be dramatically simplified.

In this environment, where almost any information is available electronically and distance has no effect on information, we need to concentrate on how to please the customers. How can we understand their needs better? How can we eliminate defects? How do we cut costs? How can we improve quality? How can we make exciting products? Can we climb learning curves more rapidly in an increasingly complex environment?

These issues become too complex for a lone Dickensian clerk, so we may put together small teams of specialists who work closely together. The team has all the skills to do the work it needs to without having to hand it over to people outside the team. They can avail themselves of all the information and computer power they need. Their task is to finish the job whatever it may be and please their customer, whether that customer is inside or outside the corporation.

Unfortunately that is not the way most corporations are organized. The hierarchies have taken on a life of their own. Divisions and departments carry out specialized functions as though they were still in the age of punched cards. Each department plays its own part in the process, with little awareness of what other departments do, and jealously guards its own data. Many departments want their own computer systems. Their latest idea is a *client-server system* in which personal computers are connected to a departmental server. Many enterprises are furiously building departmental client-server systems, which automate the type of work structure that made sense thirty years ago.

To say it again: *Most computer systems being built today are the wrong systems.*

References

1. Stephen Roach, chief economist of Morgan Stanley, *CIO Forum: The Re-Engineering Challenge*, videotape (CCI: Syosset, N.Y., 1993).
2. Ibid.

3. A. H. Engel, J. Groppuso, R. A. Lowenstein, and W. G. Taub, "An Office Communications System," *IBM Systems Journal*, vol. 18, no. 3, Armonk, N.Y., 1979.

4. Noel M. Tichy and Stratford Sherman, *Control Your Destiny or Someone Else Will*, chapter 3 (Currency Doubleday, N.Y., 1993).

5. The IMVP (International Motor Vehicle Program) at MIT publishes a list of its working papers (MIT: Cambridge, Mass.).

6. James P. Womack, Daniel T. Jones, and Daniel Roos, *The Machine That Changed the World: The Story of Lean Manufacturing* (Harper Perenniel: New York, 1991).

7. Ibid.

8. J. D. Davidson and Lord Rees-Mogg, *The Great Reckoning* (Simon and Schuster, N.Y., 1993).

9. Russell L. Ackoff, *Creating the Corporate Future* (John Wiley & Sons: New York, 1981).

4

The Electronic Organism

We commented that an enterprise could be thought of as an organism of people and electronics. Large enterprises are becoming as complex as biological organisms. Like a biological organism, the enterprise needs a nervous system, nerve endings, the right conditioned reflexes, and the capability to learn constantly from its experiences. Many corporations decline or go out of business because of repeated failure to get the right information to management. Other corporations, such as Federal Express, would not have existed without reinvention of operations with technology. Hewlett-Packard moved up suddenly to second place in the computer industry because it reinvented both its machines and its manufacturing processes to achieve high quality at low cost.

As in a biological organism, the corporate nervous system must link all locations. Employees should have access to databases across the enterprise. Some operations are done by computers or automated machinery; some need the unique abilities of people. For most operations people have to work in cooperation with computers. The software becomes ever more complex. A steadily increasing proportion of a corporation's expertise and procedures are represented in software.

The cybernetic corporation has quite different processes from enterprises with traditional structures and isolated computers.

Automation

Computers in Tokyo can decide to make a financial trade in Chicago and transfer the money in a fraction of a second. Bad weather can close certain airports, and computers reschedule the operations of flights, crews, and maintenance worldwide to minimize disruption in service and maximize airline profits. Television sets can be mass-produced on a robot production line at lower cost than would be possible with the cheapest labor in Africa. The competitiveness and survival of advanced corporations depend on how effectively they use automation.

As technology evolves, machines become more impressive, dwarfing human beings in their capabilities but ultimately needing people. A giant excavator is formidable compared to the frail biological creature that drives it. The excavator is highly automated, but it needs its driver. Bond traders have international networks of computers that can detect and take advantage of fleeting investment opportunities. A jumbo jet pilot's responsibilities decrease as more and more functions are performed more reliably by computers than by the pilot, but jumbo jets do not fly without the human pilot.

By contrast the flight attendant's job has little automation. The more the basic mechanisms become automated, the greater the need for people to concentrate on uniquely human roles such as inventing new ways to please customers.

The future corporation has much in common with the bond-trader network and jumbo jet. Its operation is highly automated. Many functions are performed better by machines than by people. Information flashes between locations automatically to keep the jet safe in the sky, but both the human pilot and the human traffic controllers are vital. As automation improves, greater skills are demanded of people. Human services need caring human beings.

Artificial intelligence is a misleading term because it suggests to the unwary that computers can reason in the way human beings do. This is far from reality. The human brain is exceedingly complex and, in the foreseeable future, we will not come close to emulating its capabilities. However, it is slow, and it lacks precision and the computer's capability to handle highly complex calculations and logic. Exhibit 4.1 contrasts the capabilities of the human brain and the computer. Most processes in corporations need both the human being and the computer. Some processes can be completely automated. Few processes can be completed optimally by a human being alone.

One of the few things certain about the future is that electronics (and optoelectronics) will grow in capability at a very rapid rate. Information superhighways will lace the corporate world long before they reach into our homes. Pocket computers will be radio-linked to the Internet.

These trends will shape, profoundly, the design not only of an organization's knowledge infrastructure but of its entire strategy for interacting with customers, employees, and other stakeholders. As the cost of computing drops, low-cost intelligence devices—combination computers/television sets/video games/cellular communications—will become widespread, interconnecting practically everyone with a pervasive, image-oriented, intelligence network. Children a few years from now will say to their parents: "You mean you actually hung up your connection to the network? How did you stay in touch with everything that's going on?"

When Distance Disappears

Telecommunications technology is advancing at a furious rate because of the immense capacity of fiber-optical networks, the growing power of computers, satellites, and the use of increasingly intelligent software.

These advances cause drops in the cost of long-distance circuits and provide circuits that can handle vast amounts of data and images. When I wrote my first book on data transmission, data circuits normally operated at 150 bits per second.

Exhibit 4.1 Comparison of human intelligence and artificial intelligence

Machine enthusiasts have always wanted to believe that we will build machines like human beings. When Babbage created mechanical calculators at the end of the nineteenth century, a firm trying to sell this technology advertised "brains of steel." Computers and networks of computers have immensely powerful capabilities that people and networks of people do not. Human intelligence remains unique, however. Most corporate processes need both human and mechanical capability.

	HUMAN	COMPUTER
Common sense	*yes*	*no*
Ability to set goals and to think about meaning and purpose	*yes*	*no*
Ability to recognize patterns meaningful to human beings	*yes*	*limited*
Ability to draw analogies and associated diverse ideas	*yes*	*no*
Ability to recognize complex abstract patterns	*no*	*yes* (*with neuro-computers*)
High-speed logic	*no*	*yes*
Accurate storage of a vast amount of data and rules	*no*	*yes*
Ability to apply a vast number of rules with precision	*no*	*yes*
Ability to do complex calculations	*limited*	*yes*
Absolute accuracy	*no*	*yes*
Precise replication in many locations	*no*	*yes*
Immediate communication with many locations	*no*	*yes*
Originality	*yes*	*no*
Ability to inspire or lead others	*yes*	*no*
Wisdom	*sometimes*	*no*

Today the fastest optical circuits in public use transmit 6.8 billion bits per second over each hair of glass. And we are still only at the beginning of fiber-optical networking development.

Advanced telecommunications make many of the effects of distance disappear. They facilitate global trading; they cause us to rethink where we should locate facilities; they enable knowledge-based industry to serve locations worldwide from a single place. Most of industry's processes were designed around the movement of paper documents. Electronic information can be at any place at any instant. It enables us to reinvent procedures to make them fast, flexible, and focused on the needs of the customer Exhibit 4.2).

Corporate Transparency

Good corporate networks connect all locations and provide a distributed computing environment. Employees need a common interface (such as Microsoft's Win-

Exhibit 4.2

Information on paper is tied to a physical location. Somebody has to file it, search for it, fetch it, mail it, and so on. The same information handled electronically can be at any place at any instant. It can flash worldwide in a second. Information is freed from constraints of time and distance. Processes and management structures built for an obsolete world of paper shuffling are extremely harmful in an era of electronic information.

The flow of electronic images is completely different from the flow of paper documents. It demands complete redesign of workflow.

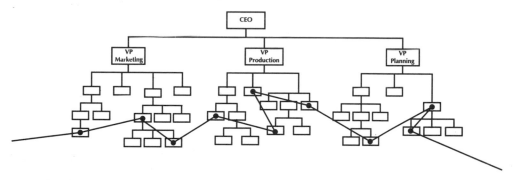

To achieve the promise of image-based multimedia technologies, the reengineering focus must transcend process redesign. Simple process improvement cannot result in the productivity and revenue benefits of a top-down reengineering of an organization's end-to-end operations.

dows) for accessing computing resources across the enterprise. Texas Instruments, in the 1980s, for example, built an international network for its own operations that called it a "single image" network, meaning that it projected to employees everywhere the same image of the corporatewide computing resources.

Because the network connects all locations, events anywhere can be made visible to the computers or "knowledge workers" at the head office or at any other location. This visibility of events is referred to as *corporate transparency*. Most large corporations operate worldwide and should have worldwide transparency. If customers in Sydney go into Benetton shops and ask for clothes of a particular color, the computers near Rome know about it. Any change, anywhere in the world, can be immediately known and acted upon if necessary. Computers are programmed to monitor all events that need attention.

When knowledge workers have powerful computing linked to a corporatewide nervous system, the corporation becomes a human-electronic creature—constantly alert, with worldwide sensors detecting anything that requires action, sometimes acting automatically, and sometimes alerting workers or executives.

There is a mismatch between this human-electronic creature and the way most big enterprises are organized today. A vital question for executives everywhere is How do you organize the human-electronic creature so as to produce the best results possible for your customers? Answering this question requires massive reinvention of the corporate processes and structure, linked to enterprisewide design of the knowledge infrastructure.

With global competition, corporations must increase both agility and stability, empower the individual and at the same time emphasize the enterprise goals. The conflicts among these demands can only be resolved by a fluid organization based on a powerful knowledge infrastructure.

Consolidation

Good telecommunications make it possible to consolidate service centers of many types. When you can be immediately reached with an 800 number or Internet, it does not matter where you are so long as you provide good service.

> In 1987 GE Lighting had a new CEO. He closed down twenty-six customer service centers and replaced them with one center using modern computing and equipment. The same company had thirty-four regional warehouses, costing $35 million. The new CEO closed all of them and invested $25 million in nine state-of-the-art facilities.

In 1988 Texas Instruments had twenty-five computer centers worldwide. The decision was made to consolidate them into two centers serving the world. A high-capacity data network made it possible to funnel all of the traffic into two centers. Users could not tell where the computers were. The two centers, which backed each other up in case of a fire or catastrophe, eventually had more computing power than the original twenty-five but at a much lower cost. Money was saved in hardware, software copies, operating staff, and real estate. With such consolidation, it makes sense to move centers out of those cities or countries in which costs are exceptionally high.

The Multicorporate Organism

One aspect of the cybercorp is quite different from a biological organism: it has electronic links to other corporations.

Corporations have direct computer-to-computer links with their trading partners—their suppliers, customers, retail outlets, agents, banks, distributors, transportation companies, and strategic affiliates. The era of corporate networks has evolved to an era of intercorporate networks that relay information automatically among corporations. A knowledge worker in one corporation can interrogate databases set up for this purpose in another corporation. Transactions such as orders, invoices, payments, and receipts flash electronically between computers in separate corporations.

Intercorporate computing has a major impact on business efficiency. It enables smaller inventories to be maintained with just-in-time techniques. It facilitates closer relationships between manufacturers and suppliers or between chain stores and distribution companies. It permits automatic reordering. Particularly important, it provides ways to improve customer service. It helps organizations react more quickly to changing requirements.

Some interactions between computers in separate corporations become elaborate. For example, a computer in a firm providing steel girders drilled and cut to shape interacts with a building company whose construction schedules change unpredictably. A designer of custom-made parts uses computer-aided design on a machine that interacts directly with the customer computers. Specifications for software are created with a computer in one company that interacts directly with tools in a contracting company that builds the software (perhaps in a cheap-labor country). These, in turn, interact with computers in the purchasing company where the software is tested and requests for modification made.

The world is becoming laced with a vast mesh of intercorporate networks, with the computers in one corporation interacting directly with the computers in other corporations. These networks work well over today's Internet, ISDN, satellites, and leased circuits, but electronic superhighways built with fiber optics will speed the interaction and increase its capacity. The world is very small from the viewpoint of the computer. Global cybercorps interact constantly with other cybercorps.

The Decline of the Intermediary

Computer-to-computer connections between organizations sometimes make it possible to avoid paying fees to agents or middlemen. Airlines, for example, created software that enables corporations to make bookings directly and find the minimum-cost fare without going through a travel agent. Stock-market systems enable customers to analyze and buy stocks at a discount fee if they do not use a stock broker. People can make airline bookings, plan vacations, arrange money transfers, pay bills, analyze investments, make stock purchases, and so on directly from their office or home computer. Corporations set up networks so that such actions can be worldwide where appropriate.

Boundaries between industries blur as computers enable corporations to reach out for new business. Banks are in the information business. Chain stores sell banking services. Software companies sell books in electronic form. Benetton is selling financial services. Auditors sell software. IBM is in the consulting business.

Electronic Reaction Times

One of the key characteristics of the cybercorp is that in it *things happen fast*. When separate organizational locations are linked by computer networks, an event in one location is immediately felt in another. Cybercorps can trigger action in the other cybercorps at electronic speed.

The windows of opportunity in business are of shorter duration when corporations are linked electronically. Price advantages have to be exploited immediately. Computers in many corporations scan the prices of potential vendors electronically and order on-line from their computers. To minimize inventory-holding costs with just-in-time inventory control, suppliers have to deliver exactly when computers tell them to. Computers generate sales proposals while the salesman is with his customer. Networks connecting manufacturers with suppliers are used to facilitate quality control on the supplier's premises and just-in-time delivery. We have just-in-time manufacturing, just-in-time education—just-in-time everything. CCI, an education company, offers its customers just-in-time training with video tapes customized to their needs. Customers wanting a mortgage, insurance, credit, financial quotations, or other such information once had to wait for weeks; now it can be provided in minutes. Young people watch MTV with edit cuts every second. We have rapid food delivery, eyeglasses made while we wait, one-minute managers, microwave ovens, news whenever we switch on television, facsimile mail, instant travel bookings, instant cameras, instant gratification.

Networks connecting retailers to manufacturers enable manufacturers to know immediately when public buying habits shift, and manufacturers react quickly. International events affect computerized stock markets immediately. The stock, bond, or futures trading that used to take place in rooms packed with traders yelling and signaling should now be largely automated, and the traders are all over the world rather than in one room. An event anywhere causes reactions to ripple instantly through the international computer networks.

Because of computers, corporations can design new products and bring them to market quickly with automated production lines. The time between a customer's ordering a product and the product's delivery is reduced to the minimum, sometimes within hours.

The rate of change in technology is likely to go on increasing because technology feeds on itself. Research results facilitate better research. Technologies of many types are creating new products and markets, and scientists in many fields say that the market has barely scratched the potential of technology.

While competitive threats are intensifying, in many corporations the biggest

In most competitive situations *speed* is the deciding factor in the following:

- getting products to market
- implementing new services
- responding to fashion trends or consumer demands
- resolving problems
- eliminating waste
- making effective organizational changes
- controlling inventories and distribution
- making product improvement
- making changes in the organization and its systems

problems relate to their own structure and processes. Corporations have often spent a fortune on computer systems designed to reinforce an obsolete corporate structure and work routines. Worse, the computer systems are difficult to change so tend to lock the corporation into its obsolete structure.

New companies do not have old companies' sluggishness, high overheads, and inability to respond. They can be designed from scratch with the techniques described in this book. They can be nimble on their feet. Whole new industrial sectors such as those in fast-growing Southeast Asia, can build with new and more-efficient processes. One aspect of the Great Transition is in the speed of events. The rate of change is increasing like that of a car with the accelerator hard down and will continue to increase until a steady fast speed of change is accepted and corporations are reengineered to cope with that speed. The illustration on p. 10 makes this point clear. A new generation will grow up comfortable with, and insisting upon, the speed that technology makes possible.

The Strategic Importance of Software

Much of a corporation's expertise and procedures are represented in its software. Corporate software is rapidly growing in complexity. Packages, templates, software objects, and automated development tools will allow increasing complexity as times goes by, encapsulating an ever-growing body of human know-how. Some corporate software has become a valuable strategic resource that could not be replicated quickly by competing organizations.

When American Airlines was highly profitable, its CEO, Robert Crandell, was asked whether he would sell the airline. He replied that given the choice of selling the airline or selling its software, SABRE (which links the airline to booking agencies worldwide), he would rather sell the airline; the software was more valuable.

European airlines struggled to combat the effects of SABRE's moving into

Europe. Two airline consortia built competing systems of great complexity for their time, AMADEUS and GALILEO. The airline business, like other businesses, became a battlefield of competing software. Many enterprises have been badly hurt by failures to acquire and implement effectively the software they needed. The London Stock Exchange was so badly damaged by its failure to build a system for electronic share registration, TAURUS, that the London Sunday Times described the fiasco as "the beginning of the end for the London Stock Exchange."[1]

Software for bread-and-butter operations can be purchased but software that makes a competitive difference usually cannot be bought off the shelf. Unique software must be built, either in-house or by a contractor, and it must be built quickly. If your competition can build a competitive system in three months that takes you three years, you will be in trouble. Fast change is essential for survival. As software becomes more complex and strategic, corporations cannot design and maintain the integration of systems that is needed unless computers themselves perform that task. As systems became more complex, they cannot sensibly be built without rigorous engineering, and rigorous engineering of software cannot be achieved without automated tools. The *automation of automation* is essential.

Many corporations have old mainframe systems and old-fashioned software development methods. Their systems are designed for narrow functions; they are often called "stovepipe systems" because of their narrow vertical set of functions. They do not support the reinvented processes that are needed for competitiveness.

Tools for Decision Making

Many office workers have learned how to use spreadsheet tools which are evolving into more-elaborate systems. We need large multidimensional spreadsheets automatically filled in by the computers that handle operations; spreadsheets linked to tools for trend analysis, forecasting, operations research tools, market analysis, and so forth; spreadsheets with built-in expert systems. Spreadsheets can employ *rule-based processing* so that, when a cell is changed, others change on the basis of rules. We need *intelligent spreadsheets*. Spreadsheet tools are linked to elaborate graphics capabilities that enable decision makers to examine visually the effects of alternative decisions. Some airlines link tables to a route map with colors and symbols showing the effects of decisions on different routes, allowing the user to point to routes or airports or display charts showing details.

New tools for decision making are being developed. Neurocomputers are fundamentally different from conventional computers. They cannot do most conventional computing; they cannot be programmed to execute a sequence of instructions. Instead, they are trained, as a child can be, to recognize certain inputs and behave in certain ways. They can be trained to search for and recognize patterns, the way a person looks for and recognizes patterns in information. But neurocomputers can find patterns that a human being cannot. They can be trained to recognize complex patterns in data that lead to a particular result—for example, reacting to multiple instrument readings to optimize the operation of a continuous process. Neurocomputers have been used to detect patterns of information that indicate fraudulent use of a credit card. They can scan vast quantities of archival data, searching for patterns that provide business insight (such as optimizing the effectiveness of mailing lists, for example).

Computers store ever more vast amounts of data. Impressive decision-making capability becomes available when knowledge workers can access the data and use rule-base automated reasoning, powerful software, neurocomputing, and other tools. The cybercorp interlinks such capabilities across the enterprise and its trading partners.

Cybercorp Complexity

Computer software and the collections of rules embedded in it can become ever more sophisticated. This was evident on Wall Street in the early 1990s when explosive growth occurred in derivatives.

Derivatives are computer-generated financial instruments that play complex professional betting games with assets such as stocks, bonds, and commodities. They give one party a claim on the value of an underlying asset at some point in the future and bind a counter-party to meet a corresponding liability. Many derivatives combine bets on multiple assets. They can be used to hedge against changes in interest rates, commodity prices, currency fluctuations, and prices in general. Derivative designers, often using immense computing power, create derivatives with complex combinations of assets. They often have exotic names such as caps, collars, swaps, swaptions, YEELDS (yield-enhanced equity-linked securities), CHIPS (common-linked higher-income participation securities), LYONS, TIGRS, and so forth. They are computer-generated cocktails of investments that can provide billion-dollar betting opportunities for gamblers who find Las Vegas too small.

Amazingly, by 1993 the United States had $14 trillion involved in derivatives—more than twice America's gross domestic product. Regulators worried that this volume of derivatives threatened the stability of the whole financial system.

Time described this as a "cyberwonderland." Derivatives are designed by genius hackers, sometimes called "quarks," using ever more sophisticated computing techniques. *Time* quoted some quarks as saying that their managers in big investment houses do not, and cannot, understand what the quarks are doing: "Many times what your boss is saying is just hilarious. It's wrong; mathematically it makes no sense. You can't even say 'Look, you don't know what you're talking about!'"[2] Even if they could not understand the quarks, in 1993 the ten senior partners in Goldman Sachs got $25 million each in profit sharing mostly from de-rivatives.[3]

Top Wall Street executives are saying: "Now, quantitative research is the whole deal. If you don't have it, you can't produce the new financial instruments."

Time comments that Wall Street's new products are so complicated and inter-dependent that only the advanced number crunching of the quarks can untangle the risks involved; without it the market crushes you. In 1995 Britain's oldest and proudest bank was wiped out by out-of-control derivatives trading.

In many other fields complexity increases as computer-stored rules prolifer-ate and computer power becomes formidable. Many areas of the cybercorp have virtuosos, perhaps not quite so exotic as Wall Street's quarks.

As computer use grows, reaction times shrink, complexity increases, and decisions become less intuitive.

The Attacker's Advantage

When technology changes, it creates new business opportunities. An old estab-lished operation may be attacked by a new operation using new technology. The attack may come from a new corporation or from a new thrust in an existing corporation. A corporation making money from an old operation needs to defend its source of profit from attackers. However, the attacker may have certain advan-tages over the defender.

The defender has much capital invested in the operation and wants to protect its investment. It does not want to invest in new technology that will lower the large return from its existing investment. The defender tends to be skeptical about the new technology. It is unproven; it is expensive; and today it is not producing results so good as or so profitable as the old technology. The attacker, on the other hand, has no old investment to protect. He spends all his investment on the new technology, expecting that it will eventually work well, drop in cost, and become profitable as its market share increases. New technology often goes through a period of struggle and nonacceptance but eventually succeeds and takes off ex-plosively. This explosive growth may surprise the defender and drastically cut profits.

The evolution of industry is full of examples of the defender supporting an old technology too long and then losing out as a new technology sweeps through the industry. Sometimes the decline of the old technology, when it comes, is pre-cipitous and unexpected. A comprehensive study of competing technologies of the past led McKinsey & Co. to conclude that *when technology changes at a rapid rate, the attacker often has the advantage over the defender.*[4]

Because technology is changing at an ever-increasing rate, the attacker in-creasingly has the advantage. This is one of the factors causing increasingly in-tense competitive pressures.

The Age of the Entrepreneur

In an age teeming with invention, many new corporations spring up and succeed with new technology, software, biochemicals, education resources, and so on. There is a great diversity of creative niche players. This is very much the age of the entrepreneur. The growth and failure rates of the most successful start-ups are higher than ever before in history. The fastest growing, such as Sun, Compaq, and McCaw Communications, sprint past the milestone of billion-dollar annual revenue after five or six years in business. New fortunes are made quickly, and entrepreneurs everywhere dream up schemes that they become excited about.

Many new corporations understand the *attacker's advantage* and attack old corporations where they are vulnerable and where they appear to be locked into an older technology or traditional mode of operation. New niche players are growing at a furious rate. It is clear that much of the successful invention is taking place in start-up corporations. The cost per patent in the entrepreneurial world is a minute fraction of the cost per patent in Bell Laboratories.

Complexity in industry is growing by leaps and bounds, so few corporations can create *by themselves* the product lines they need. Large corporations scan the horizon for small corporations with new ideas that they would like to own. Sometimes a large corporation buys a small one, but this often suffocates the original's inventiveness. Sometimes a large corporation licenses the technology of a small one. Often the large one invests in the small corporation and helps it in return for having access to its technology or the right to market its products.

There are many strategic alliances, with one corporation owning shares in another. It is becoming difficult to know which owns which. Often a major part of the profits of a corporation comes from strategic partnerships. Increasingly the alliances are transnational.

Sheep and Goats

As the rate of change increases, the power of many technologies climbs an exponential, not a linear, curve (Exhibit 4.3.). There is a big difference between corporations that adapt well and those that adapt poorly. The best corporations have a culture and infrastructure that facilitates constant learning, whereas the average corporation learns slowly and so is left behind. The faster the rate of change, the greater the gap between corporations that *learn* efficiently and rapidly and those that do not.

As automation swept the corporate world, a large difference began to emerge between corporations that used it well and those that did not. The best organizations built a human technology partnership to which all employees could contribute; the worst created dehumanizing jobs. The best ones built systems that were fast, fluid, and flexible; the worst built unchangeable dinosaurs. The best used automated tools for designing and building systems; the worst used pencils and plastic templates and hand wrote spaghettilike code that only the original pro-grammer could understand. The best redesigned products for robotic assembly, drove down manufacturing costs, created a culture of quality improvement, inte-grated production with marketing, forged intricate links to trading partners, and redesigned their work processes so that they could please their customers.

The best lean factories with a high level of automation are very impressive. A vast amount of human and technical skill was needed to create them. As the most efficient corporations automated and reinvented their processes, the least efficient ones had difficulty staying in business. Some were bought out, some-times at astonishing low prices (such as Western Union, which was bought by its major competitor for a mere $180 million).

The sales representative of factory automation avoids the backward factories having vine-covered walls. The sales rep of advanced software avoids information technology (IT) departments that are still in the "dark ages." The best organiza-tions reinvent themselves with the most modern tools; the worst are left to founder in their disorganization.

The difference between the sheep and the goats is increasing.

Profits and Propellerheads

To talk about reengineering business without talking about information technol-ogy (as many business publications do) is like talking about politics without tele-vision. Electronic technology changes everything. The cybercorp revolution aims at creating an effective human-technological partnership. Business people who attempt to discuss business redesign without adverting to sophisticated new tech-nology are limited in what they achieve. Computer professionals who talk about business reinvention usually miss major opportunities. The new business para-digms need the *joint* creativity of business people and computer people.

In many corporations the business executives regard the IT organization as an alien culture. The IT professionals tend to live in their own world, preoccupied with technology issues and largely uninterested in the business matters. Business executives refer to IT people using world such as "propellerheads."

In one Canadian corporation business management referred to the IT people as "Martians":

> "They talk a strange language; they live in a world of their own. They describe us as 'end users' and talk as though we were aliens. They ask questions with an astonishing lack of knowledge about our business; they might as well ask, 'Does this end user have three fingers or seven?'"

Exhibit 4.3

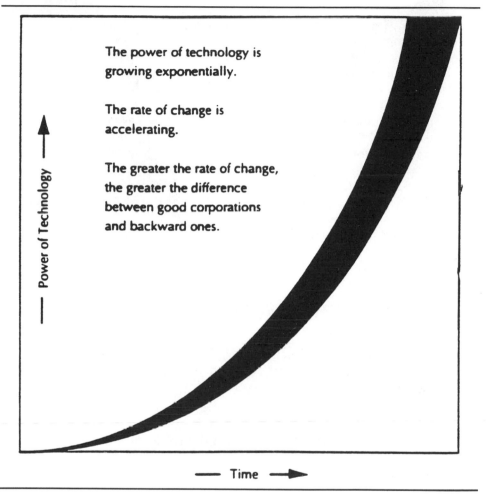

The power of technology is growing exponentially.

The rate of change is accelerating.

The greater the rate of change, the greater the difference between good corporations and backward ones.

Power of Technology

— Time ➤

There is often a massive gulf between business management and the IT organization. IT is far from delighting its customers, the business people who need it. IT is barely on speaking terms with top management which has the task of building a computerized corporation. IT does not build systems that are fluid and flexible and does not build them fast. It uses slow, ponderous processes to build systems that are rigid and difficult to change, and that inhibit the implementation of reinvented business processes.

The cybercorp needs the highest level of trust and communication between top IT professionals and the business leaders.

An amazing number of management books—and many executives—avoid the issues of technology. This makes as much sense as a skyscraper architect not

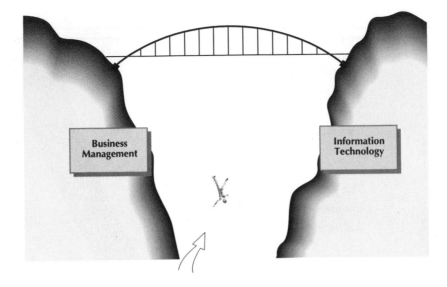

CIO stands for "career is over" unless fusion is achieved between IT and business.

knowing about materials and engineering. Technology, to a large extent, is the driver of corporate change and a major reason for corporate reconstruction. Enterprise Engineering seeks complete fusion of IT to the other areas of corporate change.

Chief Organizational Architect

The *architecture* of an enterprise is the basic overall organization within which work takes place. Most enterprises, however, rely on obsolete architecture. Their organization reflects a slow-moving era before information highways, notebook computers, bar scanners, databases, and today's emphasis on teams, empowered employees, and constant learning. A vital part of Enterprise Engineering is the movement toward architecture appropriate for the cybercorp.

The cybercorp needs a corporatewide ecosystem for focused learning and experimentation. It needs technology that gets the right information to the right people at the right time. It needs new forms of human organization targeted toward achieving a clear vision.

The ultimate responsibility for the enterprise architecture must lie with the chief executive officer. The task of creating the most appropriate corporate architecture is complex, however; many technical, human, and organizational issues are involved. There should therefore be a chief organizational architect—the czar of organizational change.

The chief organization architect needs to ask a crucial question: Can the needed architecture be achieved by "reengineering" the existing organization, or should the corporation develop by creating new organizations or subsidiaries designed for the cybercorp age?

References

1. "Taurus: Bank Takes Bull by the Horns," *The Sunday Times*, Business Section, London, March 14, 1993.
2. John Snow, "Attack of the Data Miners," *Time*, April 11, 1994.
3. John Greenwald, "The Secret Money Machine," *Time*, April 11, 1994.
4. Richard N. Foster, *Innovation, The Attacker's Advantage* (Summit Books: New York, 1986).

5

The Seven Components of Enterprise Engineering

Hundreds of management books have been written in the last ten years. Some are fad-of-the-month books; some describe powerful ways to bring about change.

Integrating the Most Powerful Methods

The goal of Enterprise Engineering is to identify and integrate the most valuable and successful ways to change an enterprise, and to take them into a professional discipline with a teachable methodology and measures of effectiveness.

> *Enterprise Engineering is an integrated set of disciplines for building or changing an enterprise, its processes, and systems. It integrates the most powerful change methods and makes them succeed. The goal is a human-technological partnership of maximum efficiency in which learning takes place at every level.*

There is no cookbook for organizational change. Building successful enterprises is largely an art that depends on the unique skills of the leader and his associates. We can bring more order and methodology to organizational change, however, and much education about what works well and what does not. Most enterprise architectures are obsolete. Most end-to-end processes are clumsy, slow, expensive, and even harmful; they need to be replaced with routines that are fast and focus on the needs of the customer. Many archetypal changes, often made possible by new technology, are repeated from one enterprise to another. Some of these archetypal mechanisms produce major improvements. Change agents should be fully aware of them.

Enterprise Engineers need training to understand the best mechanisms for corporate processes and the family of methods for changing an enterprise. A person steeped in this training and experience can look at an enterprise and its processes and quickly see ways to bring improvements.

Sometimes gentle, continuous change is the right approach; sometimes discontinuous change is needed. Often it is necessary to scrap a process that loosely involves many departments or to replace it with one designed to achieve results simply and directly. Many end-to-end processes designed for an era before modern technology need to be replaced with something much faster and more flexible. A combination of change methods is usually most effective.

There are two aspects to the job of the Enterprise Engineer.

First, the *new mechanisms, new ways of organizing work, and new corporate architectures* must be understood. Although this knowledge is constantly changing because we are in an era of rapid invention, most patterns repeat themselves. What worked in ATT can be applied in British Gas. Toyota's lean factories contained lessons for Hewlett-Packard. There are similarities between Benetton's reinventing itself and United Stationers'. New archetypal processes now evolving will be taught in business schools twenty years from now.

Second, Enterprise Engineers must understand the *methods* that can change an enterprise. The multiple change methods are discussed in detail in the rest of the book. There is a vast difference between Deming's TQM (total quality management) approach[1] and Hammer's business reengineering approach.[2] Both have succeeded spectacularly and failed disastrously in different corporations.

The Spectrum of Change Methods

The Enterprise Engineer needs to understand the whole spectrum of change methods and what is needed to make them succeed, select the most appropriate methods for the circumstances, and create a plan designed to maximize the chances of success. Each of the change methods has its own tools and techniques. Each ought to relate to information technology (IT), which pervades the modern enterprise but which is repeatedly misused.

Some "gurus" who have become popular have an almost religious attachment to one methodology. TQM experts say that everything can be done with TQM. Some procedure-redesign experts contend that everything should be modeled with IDEF (a technique for modeling work flow). Business reengineering experts regard TQM and IDEF as irrelevant because processes should be scrapped, not modeled or tuned. The mature Enterprise Engineer ought to understand the alternative methods, their advantages, and disadvantages, and should be able to apply the combination of techniques that is best for the circumstances.

Two Key Aspects of Enterprise Engineering

What should the enterprise be?	How do we get there from here?
Establish the strategic vision.	Establish the appropriate change methods.
Plan the architecture.	Plan the road map to the future.
Design the future enterprise.	Direct and manage the change projects.

Exhibit 5.1

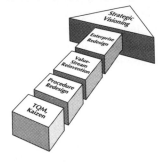

- **TQM, *Kaizen****—*Continuous* change applied across an enterprise, focusing on individual tasks and improvements made by departments or teams
- **Procedure Redesign**—*Discontinuous* reinvention of existing processes, geared toward quick-strike problem solving such as process cost cutting
- **Value-Stream Reinvention**—*Discontinuous* reinvention of end-to-end streams of activities that deliver value to customers, focusing on significant ("breakthrough") jumps in effectiveness
- **Enterprise Redesign**—Discontinuous reinvention of the fundamental structure of an entire enterprise, focusing on new organizational entities and cultures
- **Strategic Visioning**—An ongoing cycle whereby senior management establishes an overall vision and context for change for the entire enterprise

The arrow in Exhibit 5.1 contains five categories of change methods. The following pages summarize each of these five categories of method. The methods are interrelated. They can be applied either singularly or in coordination. Although the change methods are quite different, they use common techniques where possible so that a change agent is comfortable with the whole family of approaches. To succeed, an integrated set of change processes must operate at all levels. The closer to the head of the arrow, the greater the change contemplated, usually. All five levels of method have an important place. A change agent needs to select the methods most appropriate to each situation.

All of these change processes must involve continuous learning as well as making current processes more cost-effective and customer-pleasing. The goal is steadily to make a multidimensional transition to an enterprise in which learning takes place at all levels.

Infrastructure Change

The methods for changing an enterprise must be concerned with culture and the organization of human resources. They must also be concerned with IT and how

Exhibit 5.2 Two infrastructure change processes

- **Information Technology Development**—Processes that build and maintain the knowledge infrastructure needed to support the other five change processes (done before, during, and as a result of these processes)
- **Human and Culture Development**—Processes that build and maintain the structure and culture needed to support the other five change processes (done before, during, and as a result of these processes)

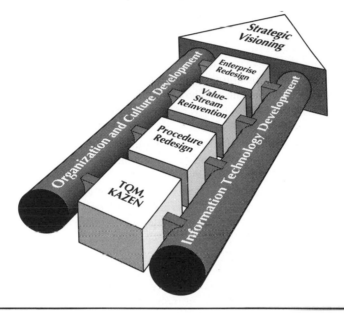

appropriate systems can be built fast enough. These two infrastructure change processes, linked to the arrow of change methods, constitute the basic diagram of Enterprise Engineering (Exhibit 5.2).—*the seven disciplines of Enterprise Engineering.*

As indicated in Exhibit 5.2, the most common reasons why schemes for business redesign fail are that culture and politics block the change and that the IT resources are not put into place adequately.

If the methods for changing the enterprise have limited knowledge of information technology (as they often do), the largest potential benefits will be lost. If reengineered processes are implemented without an understanding of how to change the organization and its culture, the effort will fail.

If the redesign is done in partnership with information technology and organization-and-culture development, remarkable results can be achieved. All of the redesigned processes need to energize employees and draw the best contributions from them. Care and skill are needed in changing the culture and organization. All of the change methods must be designed to take advantage of IT. The development methods need to support Enterprise Engineering as a primary goal. Fast, fluid, flexible development is required of computerized systems.

Continuous-Process Improvement

The lowest level of the arrow of change methods is concerned with creating a culture of continuous improvement. The Japanese masters of this method call it *kaizen*. The term translates as "everybody improves everything all the time." All employees identify problems and make suggestions for correcting them. Work teams are empowered and motivated to make continual improvements in the work processes. Pleasing the customer is an overriding concern whether the customer is the ultimate customer or an internal customer. To help achieve customer satisfaction, attention focuses on constantly improving quality, both of the processes and the products (Part III).

Kaizen is a pervasive corporate culture in Japan. If you continuously make a large number of small improvements, you eventually become very good at what you do. *Kaizen* has been translated in the West into total quality management, (TQM), with ISO (International Standards Organization) Standard 9000, Malcolm Baldrige awards, and the quality movement in general (Chapter 15).

Kaizen and TQM employ a family of techniques that includes quality circles, suggestions schemes, statistical quality control, and diagrams for analyzing problems. There are many TQM training courses. Some Western corporations have built a highly successful and valuable TQM culture. Others, interestingly, have failed in attempts to introduce TQM (for reasons discussed later).

Continuous Improvement in Xerox

In 1982 Xerox was near death. Its market share had fallen from 90 percent to 15 and was still declining. Japanese copying machines were better than Xerox's and sold for less than Xerox's manufacturing cost.

David Kearns, the CEO, reversed the situation with a corporatewide quality campaign that changed everyone's job. Xerox set out to train the hundred thousand Xerox employees in quality techniques. No one was to be exempt. Managers would learn a new technique and then use it, teach it, and verify that it was being used by others. Training started at the top and cascaded to the bottom. Each employee engaged in two sessions (totaling 96 hours of training) on quality. In 1982 Xerox did not have a single machine rated best in class. By 1990 Xerox models were leaders in all seven copier categories, and Xerox offered a total-satisfaction guarantee. Xerox took seven years to complete the culture change to total quality. Kearns comments that corporations today must do it in half the time.[3]

Discontinous Change

Many business processes need fundamental reeningeering of a type that cannot be achieved with continuous-process improvement. Incremental improvements, for example, could not have built a SABRE system for the airline industry or changed a corporation's response time for credit requests from eight weeks to eight minutes. Reengineering often spans areas of the business that have not communicated with one another directly.

The term *"clean sheet" redesign* conveys the need for a fundamentally new design rather than an adjustment to present processes. This approach is particularly important today because of the power of modern technology. Information can be moved from one place to another in seconds, bypassing traditional channels and management. In principle, any employee can access any information with a computer. As mentioned earlier, vast sums have been spent on information technology, often with little improvement in productivity, because enterprises have not been redesigned to take advantage of the technology. Today no major computer application should be created without examining whether business processes should be reengineered.

Discontinuous Change in Xerox

David Kearns, after achieving Xerox's spectacular reversal of fortune with total quality management, realized that quality was not enough:

> "There's no denying that you need quality to play the game in today's world. It's the ticket of admission. But it's not the way to win, anymore than defense alone is the way to win the football game. Xerox can't beat Canon on quality alone. Quality is a big step. In many industries, it may be required to survive, but ultimately it is not sufficient to succeed.
>
> Remember, one thing quality doesn't do is to change the inherent nature and structure of the work in a corporation. In the long term, we believe that some big payoffs for corporations will come from rethinking how they organize work, information, and people— in other words, from entirely new architectures."
>
> —David Kearns, Prophets in the Dark[4]

Value-Stream Reinvention

Like *kaizen* or TQM, value stream reinvention is concerned with improving the work processes so as to please the customer. However, whereas *kaizen* employs an ongoing stream of incremental improvements, value stream reinvention scraps an existing work process and replaces it with a *radically* different process, which often requires major corporate restructuring.

Reinvention takes a clean slate and says, "Forget what we have today. What would be the most effective way to do this work?"

A particularly important concept in Enterprise Engineering is that of the *value stream*. A *value stream* is an end-to-end collection of activities that creates a

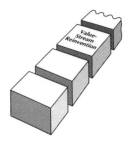

result for a customer. The "customer" (as with TQM) may be the ultimate customer or may be an internal "end user" of the value stream. The value stream has a clear goal: to satisfy (or, better, to delight) the customer. (Exhibit 5.3)

> *A value stream is often referred to as a "process." Unfortunately the word* **process** *is used in many different ways by different professionals. Systems analysts would call accounts receivable a process, for example. Accounts receivable is not a value stream; it is not an end-to-end stream of activities designed to satisfy a customer. We will use the term* **value stream**, *rather than process, to define the end-to-end stream of activities. Sometimes the term* **cross-functional process** *is used, sometimes* **core process.** *Value stream is a precisely defined concept for the end-to-end set of activities that delivers particular results for a given customer (external or internal). Examples of values streams appear in Chapter 7. The term* **process** *is so vague that it should not be used.*

The value streams in most enterprises straggle across multiple functional areas, as shown in Exhibit 5.4. The work is handed from one department to another. Each department has a line-up of jobs waiting to be done, so the overall cycle time is longer than it need be. The sequence of work handovers in Exhibit 5.4 causes many problems.

Value-stream reinvention is concerned with replacing a set of activities such as those in Exhibit 5.4 with a new work flow that is fast, simple, automated where possible, and performed by a small team (or person) sharply focused on pleasing the customer. The value-stream team is *empowered* to find the best way to please the customer with the most appropriate technology and support structure. Fundamental rethinking is applied to the end-to-end work process. (Exhibit 5.5).

As will become clear further on, corporations have achieved dramatic breakthroughs in performance by reinventing value streams. Every corporation (other than very small ones) organized with traditional hierarchical management can achieve major improvements with value-stream reinvention (Part II).

Kaizen or TQM is concerned with an ongoing succession of incremental improvements to existing processes; value-stream reinvention strives for *ten times,* not *ten percent,* improvement. TQM concerns fine tuning; value-stream reinvention concerns replacing the current work process with one that is dramatically better.

Exhibit 5.3   Value Streams

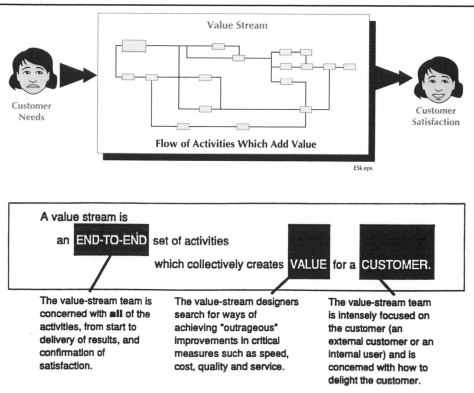

A value stream is an END-TO-END set of activities which collectively creates VALUE for a CUSTOMER.

The value-stream team is concerned with **all** of the activities, from start to delivery of results, and confirmation of satisfaction.

The value-stream designers search for ways of achieving "outrageous" improvements in critical measures such as speed, cost, quality and service.

The value-stream team is intensely focused on the customer (an external customer or an internal user) and is concerned with how to delight the customer.

- An enterprise is a collection of value streams.
- In most enterprises all of them need reinventing.
- Value-stream reinvention usually means total redesign.
- *Kaizen* (TQM) techniques are used to produce continuous improvement of new value streams.

Exhibit 5.4   A value stream that needs to be reinvented

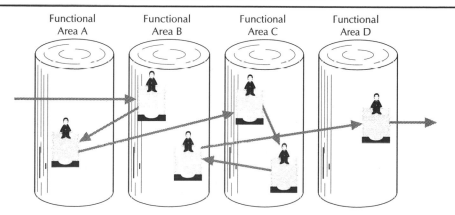

Exhibit 5.5

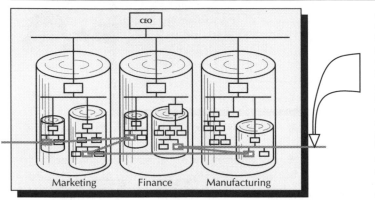

A value stream often crosses multiple functional areas, each with its own goals and measure. The handovers between functional areas are slow, error prone and filled with miscommunications and hidden agendas. There are multiple rules and controls that do not relate to delighting the customer. Backtracking when "things fall through the cracks" is difficult.

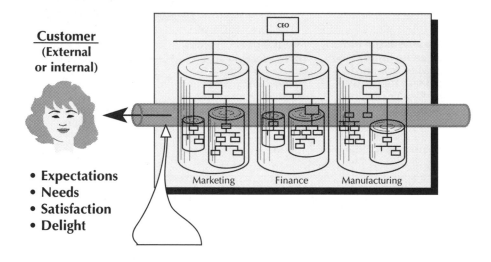

Customer
(External
or internal)

- **Expectations**
- **Needs**
- **Satisfaction**
- **Delight**

The reinvented value stream focuses on customer needs and delight-factors and meets them as directly as possible with small highly focused, highly motivated teams using the most appropriate technology, designed to simplify the process.

Michael Hammer's "business reengineering" is one form of value-stream reinvention,[2] one goal of which is to make the value-stream teams as self-sufficient as possible. This approach strives to avoid handing work over to other departments and to avoid the delays and miscommunication that occur in such handovers. A technology (which has been neglected) that enables value-stream team members to be self-sufficient is the use of expert systems. Expert systems capture know-how and guide employees in using it. They allow the computer-recorded know-how to be steadily improved as learning takes place.

Well-designed expert systems can enable small teams to handle far more complex processes. This is especially true when the expert systems are linked to other forms of automation. Expert systems can be particularly valuable for the reinvention of value streams, whose goal is to focus a small team as directly as possible on delivering results to the value-stream customer. There are diverse ways in which expert systems can help achieve this.

Banc One used to take 17 days to process mortgage requests (much faster than the industry average). It cut this to 2 days—less for many requests. At about the same time it grew from handling 33 thousand to 300 thousand loans[3] and reduced the error rate.

Before reengineering, setting up a loan required action by eight specialized departments in addition to the branch that originated the loan. The request passed from desk to desk and waited at each stage. This process was replaced with value-stream teams, "work cells" that could perform the whole operation quickly. The loan originators in the field were provided with notebook computers, which enabled the field staff to make inquiries and check interest rates. The notebook computer forced the originator to do it right the first time and collect all the needed information. Notebook computers and value-stream teams eliminated most of the paperwork blizzard.

Examples of "Breakthrough" Results

Work flow such as that in Exhibit 5.4 is crying out for replacement with a simple tightly designed value stream. Where this has been done, dramatic results have often been achieved. Value-stream reinvention is achievable in most corporations.

In addition to results that are measurably dramatic, such as those in Exhibit 5.6, improvements in customer service can be achieved that are subtle, often not measurable, but very important to the customer. The new value stream can be designed to allow the customer always to speak to the same company representative, who has information about the customer's desires and needs. The customer representative can seem to know all about the customer's concerns. The customer need not be aware that this information appears on the customer's personal computer screen.

Outrageous Goals

Because value-stream reinvention is powerful and achieves results such as those in Exhibit 5.6, it is desirable to set breakthrough goals. Sometimes the expression "outrageous goals" is used. The team doing the reinvention brainstorms for possible types of breakthrough. Breakthroughs are possible partly because of technology, partly because of scrapping the multiple waiting lines, handovers, miscommunication, politics, and delays inherent in a work-flow routine such as that

Exhibit 5.6   Examples of "breakthrough" improvements for reinvention of work (Similar results are possible in almost all corporations.)

Goodyear built a network connecting suppliers worldwide so that the quality of materials could be checked on the supplier premises. This avoided shipment of bad-quality materials and enabled production rescheduling to make use of low-quality materials.

GE cut the time from customer order to delivery of circuit-breaker boxes from 3 weeks to 3 days.

Canon built a system that enabled lens design to take place 14 times faster; it was then able to explore far more alternative designs.

Bell Atlantic reduced the time it takes to install a high-speed digital link for customers from 30 days to 3—in some cases to several hours.

IBM's Credit Corporation reduced the time it took to arrange financing for a customer purchase from 7 days to 4 hours and enabled the same number of people to handle 100 times the number of financing applications.

Citicorp Mortgage reduced the time for processing a loan commitment (or mortgage approval) from the industry average of 30–60 days down to 15 days or less—and then down to 15 minutes in some cases.

Wal-Mart reduced restocking time from an industry average of six weeks to 36 hours.

Remington reduced the time to convert a block of steel into a finished shotgun receiver from 6 days to 4 hours.[6]

Harley-Davidson reduced the time for manufacturing motorcycle frames from 72 days to 2 while increasing final product quality from 50 to 99 percent.[7]

Hewlett-Packard cut the time to assemble server computers to four minutes by redesigning the machine for automatic assembly.

Citibank changed its process for dealing with credit-card problems, resolving most by consulting an electronic image of the credit slip while the customer is on the phone. Previously the process had taken days and required up to 40 separate steps.

Con Edison in New York redesigned its procurement procedures, reducing its administrative costs by 80 percent.

(*continued*)

Examples of "Breakthrough" Improvements (*continued*)

Motorola reduced the time to respond to a customer request for a pager from 3 weeks to 2 hours.

Ford reduced the number of people involved in vendor payment from 500 to 125.

Federal Mogul, a large auto parts manufacturer, reduced the time to develop a new part prototype from 20 weeks to 20 days, tripling the likelihood of customer acceptance.

Many IT organizations changed to a RAD (rapid application development) process for application building to cut total development time from 2 years to 4 months.[8]

Hewlett-Packard cut the time to design a printer and get it into production from 4 years to 22 months.

Marks & Spencer cut its supply cycle for food in its stores from 10 days to 2, improving the choice of fresh food to shoppers.

Digital Equipment, at its Albuquerque work-station line, reduced inventory from 16 weeks to 3 while reducing defect rate from 17 to 3 percent.[9]

VF Corporation shortened the time for restocking retailers with Wranglers, Vanity Fair, Lee, Jantzen, etcetera from 70 days to 7.

Iomega Corporation reduced the time to make disk drives from 28 to 1.5 days. This dramatically reduced its inventory-holding costs and defect rate (because the cause of a defect was found at the end of a 28-day cycle was difficult to isolate).[10]

DuPont cut its production cycle for Kalrez, a rubbery plastic, from 70 days to 16 and cut its order-filling lead times from 40 days to 16. It also boosted on-time deliveries to 100 percent.

United Electric Controls Co. cut delivery times of industrial sensors and control products from 12 weeks to 3 days.

---

in Exhibit 5.4 and replacing it with direct concentration on the customer. Chapter 9 presents examples of goals that seemed outrageous when first proposed but that were achieved.

The hierarchies and bureaucracies of today's enterprises are inherently inefficient. There is immense scope for fundamentally new thinking. The achievements of many corporations make clear that a revolution in the nature of work is going to sweep through our enterprises.

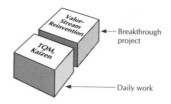

Value-stream reinvention causes many new problems. The new value-stream team should employ TQM to deal with the problems and constantly to search for ways to improve the new value stream.

Both TQM and Value-Stream Reinvention

TQM (total quality management) and value-stream reinvention are not mutually exclusive. The high priests of TQM claim that it is the only correct way, and the high priests of value-stream reinvention (sometimes called business reengineering) claim that that is the only true religion. In reality it is highly desirable to use both. One should not use a hammer for every problem.

In a corporation that does not yet have a TQM culture, when a value stream is reinvented, part of the reinvention should be to have small teams thoroughly applying TQM to the new value stream.

Scrap and Start Again

Value-stream reinvention, in its most extreme form, aims to scrap an end-to-end business process and start again. Designers determine what the results of the value stream ought to be in the future and then work backwards as if unconstrained by the present processes or management. They say, "If this were a start-up company, how would we operate the end-to-end process?"

Fortune quoted an insurance executive as saying "It isn't fair. I've got mainframes to run and agents to pay, and I'm competing with little guys who just have PC's and telephones." [11] This encapsulates why it is necessary to scrap a process and start again.

Scrapping and starting over is shock treatment in many enterprises. Not surprisingly it meets with much resistance. The reengineering czar needs to be the CEO, the COO, or a person with top-level clout. Mike Hammer comments, "A lot of people have to be clouted." He writes that 70 percent of business reengineering efforts fail." [12] Such a failure rate should not occur with determined top management that knows exactly what it is doing and is skilled at changing corporate culture. Failures occur when a sledge-hammer approach is taken to changing corporate culture. (Chapters 32 and 33 discuss corporate culture.)

Scrapping a process and replacing it may sound heavy-handed but it is often the only way to achieve the degree of change needed.

Sir John Harvey-Jones, ex-chairman of the giant chemical company ICI, reflects on a lifetime of beating organizations into shape: "A major change is often easier than chipping away at a succession of minor ones."[13] He comments that bureaucracy does not easily wither away. "Although everyone complains of over-management and obsolete controls, it is extraordinarily difficult to fight free. Over time a sort of cat's cradle is devised so that as one frees oneself from one entanglement, it is only to find oneself in another."

Done right, starting over with new value-stream teams can generate a new level of energy and excitement. Creating excitement about a new way of working can be much more successful than endlessly patching the old way of working.

Procedure Redesign

The reinvention of a value stream requires major surgery. Sometimes, however, redesign of an existing procedure can be done within the existing management structure. The redesign may involve streamlining of work flow, automation of activities, or introducing computer networks for getting better information to managers. Procedure redesign is discontinuous change, different from the continuous improvement of *kaizen* or TQM, but it is not the fundamental replacement of the work activities and management structure implied by value-stream reinvention. On the arrow of change-methods, it falls between *kaizen* or TQM and value-stream reinvention.

Government personnel regulations contain voluminous instructions on how to fill in forms. The *U.S. Federal Personnel Manual* totals 10,000 pages. There are 900 pages alone on how to fill in Standard Form 50 ("Notification of Personnel Action").

By contrast Federal Express automated most of its personnel functions so as largely to eliminate paperwork. Employees and managers enter information about themselves on computer screens. The system enables employees to find what job opportunities are open in Federal Express and is concerned with training, upgrading, and motivating employees. The automated procedures not only save a vast amount of money but increase employee upward mobility and morale.

If major surgery is required, as it often is, procedure redesign is no substitute. Management or Enterprise Engineers should make sure that it is not an excuse for avoiding necessary surgery.

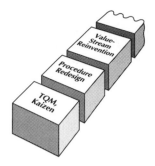

A Canadian firm invented snowmobiles and sea scooters. It organized its factory to make snowmobiles in the summer for winter sale and sea scooters in the winter for summer sale. It did not have good information about worldwide customer demand, however. Sometimes its inventory of sea scooters would run out early in the season. When the Japanese copied the product and moved aggressively to fill the gaps left by a defective distribution system, the Canadian firm found its market share eroding with alarming rapidity.

What the firm needed was a system in which details of customer orders could be transmitted from dealers worldwide to the factory as orders occurred. The factory needed to respond quickly to changes in sales, switching from making snowmobiles to sea scooters and vice versa, to help ensure that orders would not be lost.

This is an example of procedure redesign. It did not need the high-risk changes in management that characterize business reengineering. Urgent non-traumatic change could address the rate of market loss. The necessary worldwide system could be built quickly by outsourcing it to system builders skilled in fast development.

When Our Intuition Is Wrong

The effects of policies and procedures in an enterprise sometimes are the opposite of those intended when a cause-and-effect relationship is not understood by the procedure designers. Organizations have complex webs of interrelated activities that have behavior patterns of their own. Often these patterns are contrary to the intuition of managers who make decisions and create policies. It is only too common to observe government policies that have quite different effects from those that were intended. The same is true of corporate policies. The system seems to have an agenda of its own.

An activity in one place affects other activities elsewhere in a complex web of activities. Webs of activities might be easy to understand if they were linear, but they are not; they are filled with *feedback loops*. Positive feedback loops refer to a trend, good or bad, that is self-reinforcing and so causes continuous acceleration. Negative feedback loops refer to a trend which regulates itself like steering a bicycle, but in doing so might have a balancing effect and often cause oscillations. Feedback loops are familiar to electronics engineers. In electronic circuits, just as in corporations, events trigger other events. The difference is that the behavior happens rapidly in electronic circuits; in enterprises it happens so slowly that we may not be aware of its effect.

Where a web of activities takes place fairly quickly, managers observe it, learn about it, and try to improve it. Where it has long time delays or causes effects in remote places, managers cannot directly observe the results so often do not learn about them. Such long-term webs of activities are becoming far more common because of the trends towards globalism, intercorporate operations, tighter relationships with trading partners, and corporate complexity. It is becoming increasingly common for an action and its results to be far apart.

Learning based on the observable results of our actions is limited in what it can teach us. Managers, policy makers, and system designers need to understand long-term webs of activities, the types of behavior they cause, and the techniques for lessening problems with them.

If managers learn thoroughly from observable experience, they may have superficial intelligence but with a learning disability. Their insight and intuition have not been trained in long-term effects. Their organization exhibits *counter-intuitive* behavior often resulting in severe corporate decline. Management wrestles with a situation that refuses to behave as expected (Chapter 20).

As we reengineer enterprises, we need to analyze long-term causality webs and their counter-intuitive effects that we can deal with in different ways. For example, we can make long-term effects *visible* to decision makers by creating appropriate information systems. We can design processes that avoid the problems caused by long-term effects. We can often do this by designing network systems that span distance, affect separate organizations, and eliminate delays. By building systems that get the right information to the right people at the right time, we can overcome many problems caused by long-term webs of activities. Often we can do this within the existing management structure so that it falls into the domain of procedure redesign rather than the more-traumatic domain of value-stream reinvention.

A procedure (or a value stream) redesigned without an understanding of long-span causality webs will cause harmful side-effects. Enterprises often build information-technology systems to automate existing procedures without understanding the problems inherent in these procedures—another example of building the wrong system. (Chapter 21 lists ways to deal with the problem of counter-intuitive procedures.)

Enterprise Redesign

Most large enterprises are in need of complete redesign. They are steadily downsizing, cutting out layers of management, and moving from hierarchical to more-

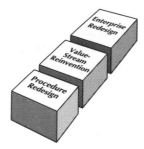

horizontal structures, but this is not enough. Part VI describes characteristics of "new-world" corporations and contrasts them with existing "old-world" corporations. The new-world corporation—cybercorp—should employ cross-functional value-stream teams highly focused on delivering results to the customer or end user of the value stream, backed up by electronics, automation, and a knowledge infrastructure.

New- and old-world corporations differ in just about every aspect of employment—teams, measurements, management, compensation, education, appraisal, rewards, motivation, unions. Electronic links to trading partners raise important questions about what work should be outsourced, which employees should be off the payroll, what business units should be wholly owned, and so on. A cybernetic corporation can link together scattered resources with computerized choreography where many of the resources are not owned or wholly owned. These resources can work together closely with just-in-time interaction.

Corporation change agents are confronted with the question Should reengineering relate to an existing procedure (procedure redesign), clean-slate replacement of a value stream (value-stream reinvention), or holistic redesign of the enterprise (enterprise redesign)?

Redesign of the enterprise, if needed, can be done by reengineering existing organizations, or by building *new* business units, factories, subsidiaries, or affiliates. A corporation so entangled in an obsolete, convoluted culture may choose to make the transition to the new world by creating new business units.

Some enterprises reengineer themselves one value stream at a time. Value-stream reinvention is risky. Unless it is carefully managed, it may fail. To tackle one value stream at a time limits the risk but stretches out the time for enterprise change. It is often desirable to move faster. Some organizations plan an enterprisewide change in management style, encouraging all managers to set up high performance work teams and TQM.

Enterprise redesign often has to take place for other reasons. Two corporations may merge. A set of activities may be spun off to form a separate corporation. Some corporations that have made acquisitions to achieve vertical integration later discovered that this caused harmful inflexibility, so they redesigned to bring back flexibility. Sometimes the basic nature of the business needs to be changed. It may be desirable to split it into separate businesses with different types of operations.

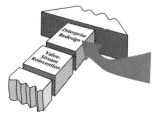

Value-stream reinvention may have a large payoff only after the basic structure of the business has been changed.

Enterprise redesign refers to holistic change to a new-world architecture, sometimes accomplished by building new business units or subsidiaries.

Often the basic structure of a business needs to be changed before reengineering begins.

Agway, a large farm-supply company in the Northeast, experienced losses at the end of the 1980s and decided that reengineering was needed. First, however, top management had to rethink the nature of the business. In the 1980s many small farms had disappeared; the survivors were large, sophisticated farms. Agway's 600 stores sold everything from garden trowels in truckloads of material for large commercial farms. It made sense for large farms to ship goods directly from warehouse or mills rather than have farmers place bulk orders at the stores. On the other hand, the stores were losing general-merchandise sales to discount retailers such as Wal-Mart and Kmart.

Top management reviewed the overall corporate strategy and decided that retailing and commercial farm supply were different types of operation. It split the company into these two businesses, each of which could then use value-stream reinvention differently and create new organizations directly geared to its customer needs.

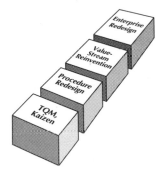

These are all processes for changing processes. They are concerned with simplifying work, as well as improving results.

The Simplification of Work

Enterprise Engineering is concerned with simplification. It changes work to achieve higher quality, better results for customers, and lower costs. In most cases where work is drastically simplified, work methods can be made fast, fluid, and flexible. Reasons for simplifying work:

- *Automation*—Computers can do tasks that were previously done by people.
- *Elimination of Bureaucracy*—Bureaucracy grows like barnacles, reducing an organization's hull speed.
- *Simplification of work flow*—The interactions among departments can often be dramatically streamlined.
- *Refinement of the information infrastructure*—Systems that get the right information to the right people at the right time facilitate simpler and better processes.
- *Working smarter*—Empowered teams with clear goals and smart machines can tackle work in a simple, direct manner.
- *Reduction of middlemen*—Intermediaries, internal and external, can be bypassed with today's networks.
- *Elimination of unnecessary work*—Many historical control procedures can be eliminated as work is redesigned.

Exhibit 5.7 shows how value-stream reinvention eliminated about 80 percent of the work of procurement in a major utility (discussed in Chapter 12).

Strategic Visioning

The head of the EE arrow strategic visioning is vitally important. Many top executives are skilled at tackling operational problems when the real problem is strategy. If the strategic vision is wrong, excellent implementation does little good.

> *A horrifying amount of "business reengineering" is done with the wrong strategic vision. A horrifying amount of IT development is done with the wrong business design.*

As Part V explores, the volatile forces of competition are changing corporate strategic thinking in a revolutionary way. A corporation has to ask how it can continue to excel when so much is changing so fast. It is not enough to be nimble on its feet. Constant change can result in failure to develop excellence. To succeed long-term, a corporation must be exceptionally *good at something*. It must have a

Exhibit 5.7

Before Reinvention

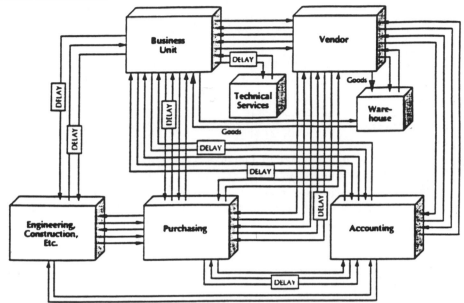

After Reinvention

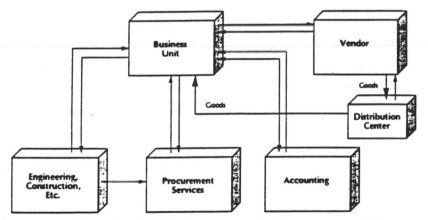

Value-stream reinvention should eliminate much of the paperwork flow, handovers, and delays, and should drastically simplify the process.

core capability that puts it ahead of competition even though products and the marketplace change in a fickle and unpredictable way.

Often the core capability that is the key to growth and survival is a strategic value stream. A top priority in Enterprise Engineering is to identify the core capability that could permit the organization consistently to beat its competition despite product and market change, and to reengineer that capability to make it excellent. If the core capability is unique, the corporation can become a "capability predator" that takes business from its competition or takes over other corporations, improving their performance (Chapter 24).

Making a core value stream unique may demand unique development of technology. Wal-Mart, for example, grew from a small corporation in the American South to the world's largest retailer mainly because it developed a core capability of distribution and logistics to a level beyond that of others. It could get the right goods to the right stores, in the right quantity, at the right time, at the lowest prices. To achieve this, it reinvented its distribution value stream with bar scanners, an elaborate computer network that it extended to its suppliers, unique software, warehouse technology, and a wholly owned transport fleet. The low prices enabled it to attract customers in other ways, such as by having customer "greeters."

Great corporations such as Sony, Hewlett-Packard, the BBC, Toyota, or Banc One have one or more core capabilities (Exhibit 5.8).

A great corporate strategy is generally formulated by an individual or team with exceptional insight. Some corporations have been harmed because the instinctive strategist has been pushed to the sidelines in favor of rational, by-the-numbers planners who use computers. Strategic visioning is a holistic right-brained activity that demands insight. Analysis and spreadsheets are vital, but without insight they produce no strategy.

Insight relates to a mental model that an executive conceives or an executive team uses. Decisions about running the company are based on this model. Important techniques can improve that model, so it is vital to challenge the model constantly in an attempt to improve it. This process is the highest level of enterprise learning.

The mental model of most executives is based on their experience. The past has taught them how to manage. When paradigm shifts occur, however, some of the lessons from the past are no longer valid. In some cases executives have wrecked companies by clinging to "well-proven" assumptions when those assumptions have ceased to be valid (Exhibit 5.9).

The top managers of an enterprise need radar that shows, when possible, the waters into which they are sailing. It is not possible to predict the future. What is possible is the creation of scenarios about the future that challenge the assumptions and mental models of top management. Planning with scenarios has been extremely valuable in enabling some corporations to fare well in an uncertain future. Conversely, planning with one "official" view of the future or with an incorrect mental model has often been disastrous. Often the official future becomes gospel and managers feel constrained not to talk about any alternative.

Scenarios do not predict the future; they improve the insight of executives

Exhibit 5.8

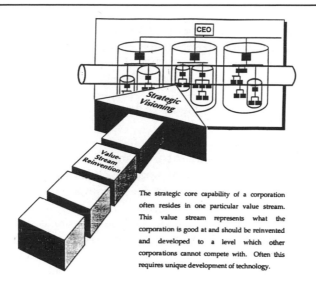

The strategic core capability of a corporation often resides in one particular value stream. This value stream represents what the corporation is good at and should be reinvented and developed to a level which other corporations cannot compete with. Often this requires unique development of technology.

The strategic core capability of a corporation often resides in one particular value stream. This value stream represents what the corporation is good at, should be reinvented, and should be developed to a level that other corporations cannot compete with. Often producing this core capability requires unique development of technology.

Exhibit 5.9

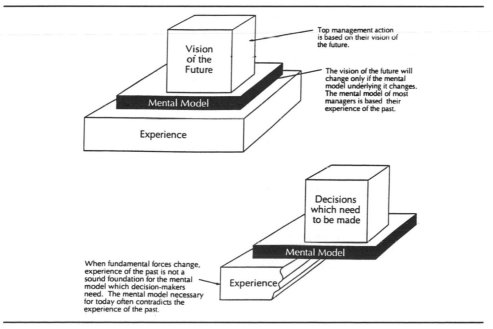

Top management action is based on their vision of the future.

The vision of the future will change only if the mental model underlying it changes. The mental model of most managers is based their experience of the past.

When fundamental forces change, experience of the past is not a sound foundation for the mental model which decision-makers need. The mental model necessary for today often contradicts the experience of the past.

who make strategic decisions. Scenario planning usually needs disinterested review. Outsiders are better able to detect and challenge the deeply held and often-subconscious assumptions of top executives (Chapter 26).

Fused Methods

IT (information technology) has evolved methodologies for establishing the computer systems an enterprise needs. At the same time, enterprises have evolved change methods for transforming their processes. It is essential that these become integrated. IT methodologies must become a component of Enterprise Engineering. Exhibit 5.10 shows this convergence.

There needs to be complete fusion between business and IT because IT makes the modern enterprise and its reinvention possible. It does not make sense to have an IT strategy independent from the business strategy or a business strategy that ignores IT. The IT strategy should be a component and an enabler of the business strategy.

A New Type of Professional

A new type of professional is evolving—the Enterprise Engineer.

Enterprise Engineering represents a substantial body of knowledge that is teachable. The professional Enterprise Engineer needs to understand the subject

Exhibit 5.10   The fusion of business methods and IT methods

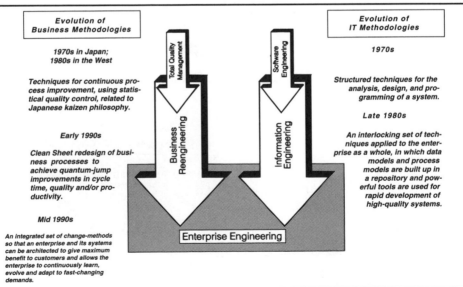

Evolution of Business Methodologies		Evolution of IT Methodologies
1970s in Japan; 1980s in the West	Total Quality Management / Software Engineering	**1970s**
Techniques for continuous process improvement, using statistical quality control, related to Japanese kaizen philosophy.		Structured techniques for the analysis, design, and programming of a system.
Early 1990s	Business Reengineering / Information Engineering	**Late 1980s**
Clean Sheet redesign of business processes to achieve quantum-jump improvements in cycle time, quality and/or productivity.		An interlocking set of techniques applied to the enterprise as a whole, in which data models and process models are built up in a repository and powerful tools are used for rapid development of high-quality systems.
Mid 1990s	**Enterprise Engineering**	
An integrated set of change-methods so that an enterprise and its systems can be architected to give maximum benefit to customers and allows the enterprise to continuously learn, evolve and adapt to fast-changing demands.		

matter in this book and also needs knowledge of information technology, its implementation techniques, and its potential effect on enterprise processes. An Enterprise Engineer needs to be familiar with all of the change methods of enterprise engineering, not just single categories of change method such as TQM or business reengineering. A core of this knowledge stays constant, and the practitioner acquires deeper understanding of it with experience, but technology and its effect on enterprise processes never stops changing. New ideas appear rapidly. Exhibit 5.11 lists the capabilities needed by an Enterprise Engineer.

The Enterprise Engineer should be familiar with the emerging technologies that can change business and the emerging archetypes of new value-streams. He must be familiar with the tools for modeling, simulating, and streamlining business processes, and for linking the models to rapid system implementation. He should understand the techniques that enhance the capability of empowered teams, such as expert systems, and the infrastructure needed to support a learning enterprise.

Exhibit 5.11   Capabilities needed by an Enterprise Engineer

Personal Skills

- A personality and know-how respected by the top management people
- Missionary skills
- Skills in teaching, coaching, communication
- A mental habit of breakthrough thinking

Strategic-Level Skills

- Knowledge of the strategic options and directions of the enterprise (Part V)
- Ability to participate in top-management strategic visioning and exploration of scenarios and discontinuities (Chapters 25 and 26)
- Understanding core competencies and "predator" value streams (Chapters 23 and 24)
- Understanding of new forms of enterprise architecture (Part VI)

Knowledge of Change Methods

- Knowledge of the archetypal ways in which business processes are being changed
- Understanding of TQM, *kaizen,* and the techniques used in continuous-process improvement (Part III)
- Understanding of value streams, cross-functional teams, and the techniques used in discontinuous-process replacement (Part II)
- Understanding of systemic behavior of processes and how it can cause counterintuitive effects (Chapters 20 and 21)
- Ability to model and redesign workflow
- Ability to reinvent value streams and participate in workshops for process reinvention

(*continued*)

Exhibit 5.11   (*continued*)

- Understanding of the techniques used in lean manufacturing or services
- Understanding of the new relationships with suppliers, agents, retailers, customers, and others

Knowledge of Technology

- Understanding of new technologies and their potential for changing corporate processes
- Understanding of IT methods for rapid implementation of systems for new business processes
- Skill with cross-functional enterprise modeling
- Knowledge of how to create a corporate knowledge infrastructure

Cultural Skills

- Understanding of changed corporate values and how to instill them
- Understanding of new forms of human organization, teams, empowerment, participatory leadership, and the "boundaryless" organization
- Understanding of the ways to generate emotional energy at all levels
- Understanding of corporate cultural issues, when culture can be changed, and how to change it (Chapter 33)
- Ability to excite people with the vision of change
- Ability to facilitate workshops for changing processes

Off-the-Beaten-Track Thinking

A major reason for having "professional" Enterprise Engineers, and particularly ones from outside the company, is that managers and employees within the company tend to be trapped in the thought patterns and culture of their own organization. The new processes, new value-stream teams, and changes in management that are needed are likely to be quite different from conventional wisdom in the company. To invent such changes needs an outside viewpoint or the viewpoint of a professional Enterprise Engineer. To make the changes happen needs management with a different focus from that of the current hierarchy. Insiders tend to preserve the inside way of life. Steam engineers did not invent electric power. Monks do not dissolve monasteries.

Breakthrough thinking is needed to change corporations. Real breakthroughs come from people asking questions different from conventional ones. They do not ask How do we streamline paper flow? but What happens if IT eliminates paper? They do not ask How can we make better camera film? but How could electronics change photography? They do not ask How can technology improve what we are doing? but What completely different opportunities exist?

Breakthrough thinking is a habit of mind. Some people never do it; some become good at it. The professional Enterprise Engineer must make it a habit of mind.

References

1. W. Edwards Deming, *Out of the Crisis*, MIT Center for Advanced Engineering Study, Cambridge, MA, 1982.
2. J. Champy and M. Hammer, *Reengineering the Business* (Harper Business: New York, 1993).
3. David T. Kearns and David A. Nadler, *Prophets in the Dark* (Harper Business: New York, 1992).
4. Ibid.
5. "Files with Faces," *Computerworld*, December 14, 1992.
6. Jim Carmichael, "New Guns the Way They Used to Be," *Outdoor Life*, May, 1988, p. 72.
7. O'Neal and K. Bertran, *Developing a Winning JIT Marketing Strategy* (Prentice-Hall, Inc.: Englewood Cliffs, N.J., 1991).
8. James Martin, *Rapid Application Development* (Macmillan: New York, 1991).
9. O'Neal and Bertran.
10. *The Quality Imperative*, A Business Week Guide (McGraw Hill: New York, 1994).
11. "Reengineering: The Hot New Management Tool," *Fortune*, August 23, 1993.
12. Bruce Caldwell, "Missteps, Miscues," *Information Week*, June 20, 1994. M. Hammer's estimate in this article is repeatedly quoted.
13. John Harvey-Jones, *Managing to Survive* (Reed Consumer Books: New York, 1993).

6

Teams and Virtuosos

Corporations are steadily learning that using empowered teams of people is an effective way to achieve excellent results. Instead of obeying detailed orders, these teams create their own way of working. *Empowerment*, as was stated earlier, means "delegating the responsibility for results, not tasks." The team works out how members can best achieve results and constantly learns how to do this better.

Groups of employees can be organized in different ways. Sometimes they are tightly knit teams; sometimes they are loose clusters. Sometimes they are self-managed; sometimes they are managed from outside. Sometimes a group is semi-permanent; sometimes its members gather together to do one task and then disperse. Sometimes a group has members with similar skills; sometimes it consists of people from different disciplines so that it can combine diverse capabilities.

D. Quinn Mills describes the "re-born" enterprise as consisting of "clusters" of employees. The clusters have the following properties.[1]

- They handle their own administrative functions, divorcing themselves from the managerial hierarchy to a great extent.
- They develop their own expertise.
- They express a strong customer orientation.
- They are action-oriented.
- They share information broadly.
- They accept accountability for business results.

The Enterprise Engineer needs to ask, What are the most effective clusters of employees? How should they be organized? What should be the structure of the cluster? How should it fit into the overall corporate structure? or, in general, What is the most effective way for the enterprise to get results?

The answers to these questions have changed because of changes in technology, which demands new skills from people and in return enables people to achieve more powerful results. Technology changes the flow of information. A group can have access to whatever information is available and is needed for a task. A group may be scattered geographically but share a database and computing resources. Technology can automate routine tasks and leave to people those requiring skill and human care.

The Team: A Special Type of Cluster

A particularly important type of cluster is a team. A team is different from a work group, a committee, a mob, or a casually assembled cluster of people.

The word *team* is often misused in business to mean any grouping of people—even an entire corporation. In its true meaning the word *team* refers to a small, tightly knit group of people intensely focused on meeting a specified objective that all members of the team are committed to accomplishing together. Team members subordinate individual goals to those of the team. The individual cannot succeed or fail independently of the team; the individual's success is the team's success. After a basketball game it makes no sense to say "Joe won and Bill lost." All team members win or lose together.

The team's members trust one another. They complement one another's strengths and compensate for one another's limitations. If a teammate has difficulty understanding something, the others explain it. If a team member has problems doing something, the others help solve the problems. Each team member is committed to making the others successful. The team is responsible for each of its members.

The smallest type of team is a two-person partnership. The members of a partnership have a joint set of goals, and succeed or fail together. Great partnerships combine different talents, like those of Gilbert and Sullivan, so that the result is greater than the sum of the parts. Each member of the partnership is committed to making the other successful. A team is like a partnership but with more than two participants.

Good teams become preoccupied with being the best. They learn to employ the most powerful tools and techniques. They find ways to maximize their accomplishments and the quality of their work. They devise pragmatic solutions to problems and search for constant improvements. They have a high level of pride and obtain great enjoyment from their collective efforts to be the best.

A team is a tightly knit group that works in concert to achieve team goals, not individual goals. A sales team is usually not a true team but a collection of independent salesmen, each with different customers and each trying to maximize his own commission. A sales team working with one customer to obtain a multimillion-dollar order is a true team whose goal is well-defined and whose members support one another to achieve it.

A team is usually self-managed. A sales team working on one large order is self-managed; members may report to an industry manager, but the team decides what it does and is collectively accountable for its decisions. A team for developing software applications may be self-managed. Members know what is wanted and work together to produce it, checking out what they are building with the users and making sure that it is right. On the other hand, a team such as of chorus girls in a Busby Berkeley musical is not self-managed. Dancers obey instructions from an external director and must obey them with precision. A sports team too may be tightly directed by an external coach. Every individual must be sure not to let down the team. The legendary British SAS teams for antiterrorist operations or special military operations are self-managed. They determine their own methods and tactics. Here the life of every team member may depend on every other team member. Each member must help the others improve weaknesses.

A self-managed team may or may not have a manager within the team. In many teams all members are equal. This is sometimes the case in teams of three or four people building computer applications. In a rowing eight a cox is part of the team, and oarsmen obey him. Some teams have a leader. An SAS antiterrorist team has one member in charge. Teams are often *coached* by managers outside the team who monitor the team's performance and help it to improve.

With today's technology a team of knowledge workers can be geographically dispersed. Members stay in constant touch with all other members by means of networks and work-group software. Telecommunications of higher band width permit closer communication among dispersed team members. Video conferencing can enable a team to incorporate important specialized talents that do not exist locally.

Teams have always been used and honed to the highest levels of effectiveness in sports and in the theater. Only recently have they come into common use in factories and corporations. It can be very enjoyable to be a member of a great team that functions together in an extraordinary way. Many people remember a time in life when they were part of such a team and regard it as one of their very satisfying experiences. It may have been in sports, in a task force that studied something intensely and clarified its ideas, in a sales team that battled to close a massive order. It may have been in a theater performance that aspired to excellence, or in the army, where shared dangers intensified human cooperation and camaraderie. Some say that they have spent much of their life looking for that experience again.

There are now legendary examples of teams achieving greater success than conventional working groups in corporations. Motorola used teams to bring produce defects to a very low level and to design cellular phones having a few hundred parts instead of a thousand. Hewlett-Packard used teams to halve the time to design new products and get them to market. The 3M Company used teams to achieve as its goal having half its revenues come from new product innovations created in the prior five years. General Motors based its fundamentally reinvented car factory—the Saturn plant—on teams, and demonstrated that it *could* make small cars that were popular, reliable, and profitable.

The most powerful way to manage the introduction of fundamental change is with well-trusted teams, so teams are particularly important to the changes brought by Enterprise Engineering. Radical redesign allows teams more opportunity to accomplish their task and constantly search for improvements that make the design practical. Teams are particularly good at dealing with difficult problems. The greater the challenge, the greater the need for the shared intelligence of a team. Extreme changes are less alarming to teams than to individuals because teams grapple collectively with them. Indeed, good teams welcome and enjoy the challenges that come when such changes occur. True teams, with the characteristics described in this chapter, almost always outperform conventionally managed groups when confronted with tough challenges.

> *The use of true teams is greatly underexploited in most of today's enterprises.*

Teams and Working Groups

It is important to distinguish between a team and a working group. A team and a working group may be the same size and may have the same work to accomplish, but they operate altogether differently. In a work group one individual is in charge, and each member behaves as an individual. There is *individual accountability*. In a team no one individual gives orders to the members; the members work out collectively what to do. The team has *collective accountability*.

When the Berlin wall fell, most factories in East Germany were crude and inflexible; they made goods of atrocious quality. In 1990 GM's Opel bought the assets of a state-run car maker that assembled Wartburgs, an East German car, about as attractive as a warthog, and built a clean-field factory using the principles of lean manufacturing, *kaizen*, and production teams that aimed for zero-defect quality.

Opel used an intensive interviewing process to select East German workers who could work well in teams. It gave them twelve weeks' intensive training and used Lego blocks to demonstrate the new lean-manufacturing process.

The new factory assembles 150 thousand cars per year of extremely high quality in less than 20 hours per car (about half the time of the average European car plant). The purchasing chief at the old Wartburg plant used to keep 90 days' worth of metal parts on hand. The new plant keeps 4-to-6 hours' worth of parts. Two thousand employees are organized into 5-to-8-member teams in which each member can perform each of the team's tasks. The teams are motivated to learn continuously and to invent ways to do the work better. The teams audit their own performance so that costly inspection and correction at the end of the line is avoided. The plant works three shifts a day (whereas Toyota plants work only two shifts so as to leave time for maintenance).[2]

Opel found it much easier to train East German workers in a brand-new reinvented factory than to convert existing West German plants to lean manufacturing of similar productivity.

When a person joins a team, individualism is subordinated to the group. His personal life is based on commitment to the team; the team member must not let the team down. Such solidarity is what is implied by the word *team*. The individual gives up certain rights. When a championship sports team is in training, its members must not drink, keep late nights, engage in sexual relations, or do other things that detract from the intense drive for success.

It is very difficult to convert a "group" into a "team." The group is individual-based; the team is commitment-based. It is easier to form a team from scratch, inviting selected people to join. It is made clear to them that if they join they give up certain rights; the rules associated with being a team member are spelled out. The individual being invited to join should be free to say no without any penalties attaching to that. When a person agrees to join, it is like saying "I do," at the altar. As with marriage, the team member gives up certain freedoms and agrees to obey the rules of the team.

A team is not a permanent structure. It lasts only as long as it is focused on particular achievements and is constantly learning to maximize its success. A car locked up in a garage will be a car in six months' time; a team left idle for six months will not be a team anymore. A car has the property of persistence; a team does not. To remain a team, it needs to be focused and striving. Some teams are put together for one shortlived task. Others are long-lasting resources that tackle a never-ending stream of work. Exhibit 6.1 summarizes the difference between a working group and a team.

Teams have been extensively studied by Jon Katzenbach and Douglas Smith,[3] who illustrate that the best teams achieve far better results than working groups. Katzenbach and Smith identify six basic characteristics of true teams, which are summarized in Exhibit 6.2.

Exhibit 6.1   The difference between working groups and teams

Working Group	*Team*
One individual in charge	Shared leadership
Individual accountability	Joint accountability, mutual support and trust
Separation of thinkers and workers	Team members who think *and* work
Managerial control	Purpose and *modus operandi* decided on and fine-tuned by the team
Excellence through division of work so that each person concentrates on doing a narrow set of tasks with ever-better performance	Some tasks done interchangeably by team members, who teach one another better skills
Measurement of individual performance	Tough goals that make the team battle together jointly with collective excitement about achieving the goals
Employee appraisal by the employee's manager	Employee appraisal by peer team members

Exhibit 6.2   Team basics

There are six basic characteristics of real teams (first described by Jon Katzenbach and Douglas Smith who have studied teams for many years).[3] A deficiency in any one of these characteristics prevents true team effectiveness, but many potential teams ignore one or more of them.

Small Size—Teams are not large in size; otherwise team members have difficulty knowing what is in one anothers' minds. Powerful teams are usually made up of fewer than ten people; occasionally, for some purposes, teams are larger. Teams that need the close interaction among all team members are small, sometimes four people or so.

Mutual Accountability—Rather than one leader the team as a whole is accountable for results. A team does not have a boss who gives orders; instead, team members work out jointly how to do the work. Rather than seeking personal praise, each team member helps the other members to make the team succeed jointly. This mutual help and accountability is the key differentiator between real teams and other employees groups.

By promising to be dedicated to team goals rather than personal goals, each team member earns the right to express personal views about all aspects of the team's work and to be listened to constructively. Mutual accountability needs mutual trust; this grows as the team members get to know one another and is reinforced as they succeed in achieving team results. People cannot be *made* to trust one another. Mutual trust, which is essential to real teams, strengthens as the team confronts tough challenges together. The tougher the challenges, the more mutual dependency tends to grow. Employee appraisal, instead of being done by the employee's boss, is done by fellow team members.

The Right Mix of Skills—Teams must have the set of skills necessary to complete the work. Different team members often have complementary skills. They need, in addition to technical or professional skills, the ability to analyze and solve problems, make good decisions, and intercommunicate well. It is important to assemble the right skill mix when creating a team, but Katzenbach and Smith comment that no team they met had all skills needed at the outset. Emphasis on team performance helps to identify skill gaps quickly. Personal learning and development is essential if teams and team members are to help one another learn what is needed.

Common Meaningful Purpose—Team members must have a common purpose that is meaningful to them. Usually the overall purpose comes from management outside the team, and the team adjusts and clarifies its own purpose. Management may define the boundaries and scope of the team's authority but allow the team the flexibility to shape its purpose within those boundaries. Katzenbach and Smith comment that the best teams invest a large amount of time together exploring and shaping a purpose that then belongs to them collectively and that they are excited about. The purpose needs adjusting as experience grows and conditions change; it is "like an offspring in need of constant nurturing and care," the mutual agreement about purpose that allows mutual accountability and trust to grow.

(continued)

Exhibit 6.2   Team basics (*continued*)

Specific Performance Goals—A team purpose should relate to specific performance goals. More than anything it is the common pursuit of tough goals that makes the team "jell."

Performance measures should have targets—such as getting a product out in 10 months instead of 18, reducing defects from 1 in 200 to 1 in 1000; reducing software development costs to $300 per function point (function points are a measure of software complexity), responding to customers within two hours. Clear targets cause a team to focus on what must be done to achieve those targets. Without clear targets, there is vagueness about whether the team has done well. The target should be progressively raised so as to provide the morale-booster of the team's hitting the target before it is moved higher.

Targets may be adjusted in conformance to changing goals. For example, when a defect rate has been reduced, a new target may emphasize bringing the cost down or speeding up the production cycle.

A Common Approach—A team needs a common approach to how its members work together. Team members need to agree about who does what, how work is coordinated, how schedules are set, what training is needed, what methodology is used, and in general the team modus operandi. Members should share equally amounts of real work (as opposed to planning, reviewing, decision making, etcetera). The team should spend as much joint effort in determining how it works together as in determining its purpose. The roles and methods evolve over time as the team gains experience and circumstances change. Teams develop their own unique processes for working together effectively. Each individual brings unique knowledge, skills, prejudices, and personality. Mutual discovery of one another and progressive skill building are needed for a team to become as effective as possible. The team candidly explores who is best suited for each task and how the individual roles come together. The tougher the performance measures, the greater the forces pulling the team together with mutual trust and dependency.

Most organizations manage on the basis of individual accountability rather than group accountability. Job descriptions, career paths, performance evaluations, and compensation focus on individuals. Our culture focuses on individual accomplishments. The change to focusing on teams and team accountability is sometimes a difficult transition for management to make, so groups called "teams" are often set up without being true teams with the characteristics of Exhibit 6.2. We talk about "the top management team," for example, when usually it is not a true team but a group of strong individuals with individual goals and accountability.

Pseudoteams

Many efforts to create teams have failed, resulting in pseudoteams. A *pseudoteam* is a group that calls itself a team but whose members behave as individuals rather than as team members. It does not focus on collective performance and is not trying to shape a common purpose. A pseudoteam performs less effectively than a working group because it lacks the single-person leadership, accountability, and drive of a real team. The pseudoteam members' interactions detract from each person's individual performance without providing the benefits of a real team. Being on a pseudoteam is a demoralizing experience.

Katzenbach and Smith observe that pseudoteams plague all organizations and that management should take action to change them.[4] They should not call themselves teams or continue to fool themselves but either be converted into working groups with individual accountability or recreated as real teams if possible.

Katzenbach and Smith categorize team efforts as those of pseudoteams, potential teams, real teams, and high-performance teams, as shown in Exhibit 6.3.

A potential team is a group that could become a real team were it to develop all of the team basics listed in Exhibit 6.2. It needs to be given a tough goal with performance measurements and strong motivation to strive for them. The group might need some coaching to become a real team. Katzenbach and Smith comment that a steep performance gain occurs when a potential team becomes a real team. But many never do.

Becoming Real

A real team must have the team basics listed in Exhibit 6.2. Real teams are not created by training people to become a team. They develop when a group is given a difficult set of goals to achieve. Real teams tend to form naturally in organizations that set exceptionally tough performance goals.

The team basics in Exhibit 6.2 should be regarded as a discipline that must be followed to create the conditions in which real teams grow. First, a common purpose must be agreed upon. Then performance measures must be established and tough targets set. People with the right mix of skills should be assembled and the goal established of developing the skills to a high level. The potential team then must set out to refine the common purpose and establish details of how members will work together. A modus operandi is established in which the team members hold themselves mutually accountable for results. As the team goes to work it constantly tries to refine its purpose and modus operandi, helps members to build skills, and works out how to raise the performance targets.

The most important factor in making potential team members work together as a real team is the performance challenge. The team must have targets to hit or obstacles to overcome that can only be achieved if the team works better than the sum of its parts. Corporate leaders should build teams by emphasizing a strong performance ethic rather than by promoting team behavior or having team-building exercises. Many companies reorganize around teams without the drive for exceptional performance in each team, and this results in pseudoteams or potential teams, not real teams. Teams thrive on performance challenges, and without such challenges they flounder. The more urgent and meaningful the goals of the team, the more likely a real team is to emerge—with its members helping one another to focus on the goals rather than continuing to perform as individuals.

Usually the more difficult the challenge, the more fun the team has deciding how to respond to it. Many teams reflecting on their growth tell stories about problems or events that caused exceptional difficulties and made the whole team come together to forge a joint attack. A team leader can initiate such challenges. Many great teams have grown in capability by setting "mission impossible" challenges. There can be great excitement in creating a goal or vision beyond anything that exists today and then driving hard to make it happen. A determined team can sweep away obstacles with a "damn the torpedoes" attitude. "Impossible" goals forge team behavior. They can unleash exceptional energy, creativity, and determination, and cause people to have fun.

High-Performance Teams

A high-performance team has all the properties of a real team, described above, together with extraordinarily challenging goals that require the commitment of every team member to helping every other member to achieve. *Every team member is concerned that every other team member improve the skills and ability that will maximize the chance of exceptional performance.* This applies to both interchangeable and complementary skills. Team members become confident in their dependence on one another.

NASA's mission, in December 1993, to make many repairs to the Hubble space telescope was a stunning example of a high-performance team at work. Every astronaut in the lengthy training for the mission devised every idea he could for helping every other astronaut to prepare better for the five days of extra-vehicular activity in space that was needed to repair both the telescope and NASA's reputation.

Leadership is shared on high-performance teams, although there may be a named leader whose role is largely ceremonial and who may be the spokesman to the outside but, like the leader of the Hubble space-telescope mission, has as much real work to do as the other team members. All team members are empowered and determined to take initiatives but check with the other team members before acting.

High-performance teams—and they are rare—have an abnormal degree of commitment to one another's performance and growth. Such teams tend to develop when goals are tough and exciting. The personal bonds and commitment that characterize high-performance teams are difficult to establish. They do not

Exhibit 6.3   Team performance (based on Katzenbach and Smith)[3]

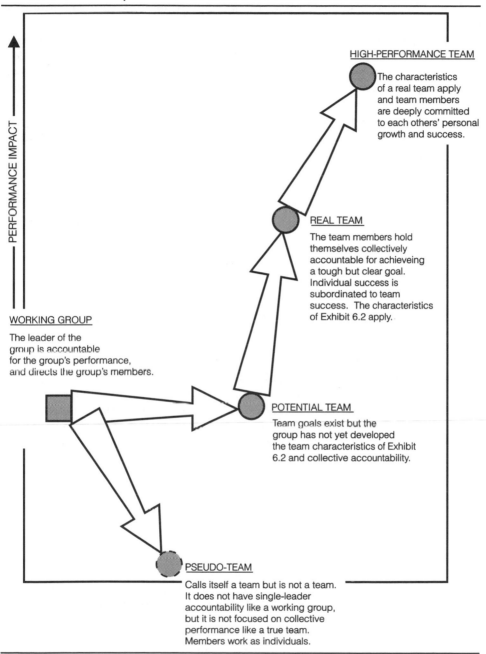

arise from team-building exercises or training but when the right group of people finds itself with a challenge, knowing that members must bond together to confront it.

High-performance teams often achieve results that transcend reasonable expectations. The commitment to building on another's capability adds to the collective feeling of having fun. Katzenbach and Smith comment that a finely developed sense of humor is a characteristic of high-performance teams: "There may be some humorless high-performance teams out there. But we doubt it."[5] Members of such teams describe their experience as participating in something bigger and better than oneself. The team usually improves the performance ethic of surrounding people who are not members of the team.

We few. We happy few. We band of brothers; For he who sheds his blood for me shall be my brother.

—Henry V

The U.S. railroad freight industry changed remarkably little in the twentieth century until 1981, when deregulation gave railroads the opportunity to build a new business combining different modes of transportation. The railroad was then allowed to operate trucks that would go to customer locations, fill up with goods, "piggyback" the truck body or containers on trains across the country, and then deliver the goods by truck to the destination.

A Burlington Northern Railroad team of seven people was established to build a new business unit that combined train and truck transport so as to serve customers better. The team met astonishing obstacles: There was extreme hostility from most of Burlington Northern's established power structure. The railroad did not like truckers. It viewed them as the enemy, unregulated "fly-by-night" upstarts who were trying to take away the railroad's traditional business. Railroaders were hostile to the idea that truckers and railroaders should cooperate and that the railroad should market truckers' business.[6]

Bill Greenwood, the leader of the team, understanding the size of the business opportunity, was enthusiastic about starting intermodal operation. He realized that even his own boss was opposed to it, however: "My own boss was out to get us and was virtually drumming up support from the rest of the marketing organization to bury us."[6]

Severe obstacles often have the effect of making a dedicated team grit its teeth with determination to overcome them. The threat tends to bind team members together. They have to cooperate to survive. Battling tough challenges together can turn an ordinary team in a "high-performance team." This happened at Burlington Northern. The team went to war.

It decided that the right approach to intermodal traffic was to build a cross-functional organization that removed the barriers separating marketing, operations, accounting, information technology, etcetera. Many powerful executives of Burlington Northern felt threatened by such a view. The team wanted to divert dollars and people away from existing boxcar operations to new flatcars for piggyback services. Worse, the team wanted to hire truckers to run operations in the heart of the railroad. This was like making Madonna a Catholic priest.

The obstacles stacked up. One executive rigged an equipment bid to prevent the intermodal group from working with a preferred vendor of a critical flatcar. The railroad set out to make intermodal business units a dumping ground for low performers. They made it difficult to obtain resources, people, and marketing information. Permissions were withheld. The team decided that "it was easier to ask forgiveness than permission." It could not get the IT support it needed so violated company policy to buy its own personal computers. It circumvented the communications department and bought Voicemail.

The team worked night and day to develop a detailed proposal for the chairman and president. It required that 160 railroad ramps be closed down, as they were not convenient for customers, and that new hubs for piggyback operation be opened. The proposal called for capital and many changes to start the combined truck-and-train marketing and its operation. One of the two top executives totally opposed the proposal.

After intense argument the proposal was cut back to only two hubs that could act as pilots for the concept. As though to stack the odds against them, the two worst locations were chosen for these hubs. "It was a test," Greenwood commented, "designed to make us fail."

The problems became worse. One of the two hubs was stalled by cold weather in an exceptionally bad winter, and the nation slipped into recession. Nevertheless, the team battled to make the pilot hubs succeed. Nobody on the team had any marketing experience; they had to learn that. They advertised in a way the railroad had not done; and to appeal to truckers they excluded trains from their ads, further enraging the old railroaders.

The pilot program succeeded, and then nothing stopped the team. Within eighteen months, Burlington Northern had become number one, among U.S. railroads, in intermodal operations. It broke record after record, exceeding even the team's most optimistic expectations. The team had built a billion-dollar business in the face of intense opposition.

Value-Stream Teams

One of the most effective types of team is that which results from value-stream reinvention. The awkward traditional value stream that requires passing work from one group or department to another is replaced so that a team does the whole job, focusing on how it can please the value-stream customer (internal or external).

A corporation is composed of its value streams. As the value streams are reinvented, using technology to the fullest extent, the corporation is increasingly operated with value-stream teams. These teams need careful design. Teams of a variety of different structures are used.

A well-designed value-stream gives a team clear goals and establishes tough performance measures—the primary criteria for the team's success. The value-steam team can be largely in charge of its own destiny and can have challenging targets. It may have difficult obstacles to overcome.

Some teams are established on a temporary basis to achieve a given result; value-stream teams, however, are designed to remain in operation, constantly improving the value-stream capability.

Certain value streams, as we discuss in Chapter 24, are of extreme strategic importance. They represent the core capability of the corporation that enables it to keep ahead of its competition. Unbeatable core capabilities often need unique technology and dedicated teams. The term "capability predator" used in Chapter 30 describes a corporation that develops a core capability to a level that enables it to take over other corporations and increase their value or to play havoc with competing corporations. The high-performance corporation of the future is likely to be composed of value-stream teams, each being challenged to learn as rapidly as possible how to improve the value-stream processes. One or two value streams may be identified as strategic core capabilities, and these will have the most intense focus on building high-performance teams linked to exceptional technology.

Major unpredictable change confronts all corporations today. The stability of earlier decades has gone. Processes that involve passing work from department to department in a hierarchical organization are difficult to change rapidly. Value-stream teams, on the other hand, can quickly adjust their purpose and performance goals. What is needed are value-stream teams with powerful information technology which enables the team to attack new targets quickly and vigorously. The emphasis on tough performance goals makes value-stream teams a potent asset in coping with major organizational change. Change is not so threatening to a team as it is to an individual or to the manager of a working group because, instead of having to fend for himself, the team member shares the collective commitment. A real team thrives on new challenges.

Change demands new learning. Teams tend to integrate learning and performance challenges. They have to learn in order to achieve new goals. Each team member shows the others what to learn so that they can behave collectively. Teams translate longer-term purposes into short-term objectives and develop the skills to meet those objectives.

Loners Who Are Different

While today's management literature is full of advocacy for teams, it tends to say little about the brilliant loner. It is probably the case that brilliant loners change the world more than teams. Thomas Edison, Gloria Steinem, Edward Teller, Alfred Hitchcock, Henry the Eighth, Albert Einstein, Abraham Lincoln, Elvis Presley, Saddam Hussein, John le Carré, Robert Oppenheimer—loners do things that are interesting.

There are many loners in corporations, and sometimes they become exceptionally good at a particular activity; they can apply themselves with a fierce intensity. The loner may be impossible as a team member. He does his own thing. Often a support structure grows around the loner to help put his ideas into practice.

Thomas J. Watson, Sr., and then his two sons built IBM, one of history's greatest corporations. They were totally autocratic; their temper was terrifying. They would smash furniture in meetings if they did not get their own way. Tom Watson, Jr., suddenly fired his entire crew when he was cruising and sailed the boat alone.

A young woman with no degree worked for a company near Chicago that made training products in the early 1980s. She sat up night after night with Lotus 1-2-3. She collected and analyzed data, eventually showing that more than half of the company's products had a net-negative return on investment—something had eluded the company's planners, accountants, and senior management.

Woody Allen played his clarinet in Michael's Pub in New York every Monday without fail. He refused to attend the Academy Awards ceremony even when he was nominated. He was a law unto himself. Maybe that is why he made films that were really different. Many Europeans know the name of only one American film director—Woody Allen.

Sometimes loners are entrepreneurs; sometimes they create startlingly different product designs; sometimes they create excellence in unique ways; sometimes they are devastating perfectionists; sometimes they use computers to do the most complex analysis, modeling, or synthesis. In a world of intensifying global competition and copycat products, a key resource is the capability to innovate. People who think differently are valuable; a challenge is to harness and use such originality. Corporations need the unique capabilities of loners as well as the collective, but often conventional, capability of teams.

> *Reasonable men adapt themselves to their environment; unreasonable men try to adapt their environment to themselves. Thus all progress is the result of the efforts of unreasonable men.*
>
> —George Bernard Shaw

Virtuosos

David Ogilvy, the legendary advertising executive, commented that great copywriters are ten times as effective as the average copywriter. Genius programmers write ten times as much bug-free code as the average programmer.

Today's tools can amplify the capability of bright people. The planner has modeling tools; the architect has computerized design tools with libraries of preexisting designs; the programmer has code generators and repositories of objects. The best professionals make themselves highly skilled with the most powerful tools.

Dedicated computer hackers using networks to break into remote computer systems build up a degree of skill that is truly astonishing. Some business people with computerized analysis tools have become equally dedicated and skilled at handling a certain type of task. Like dedicated hackers, they push computers to the limits of capability, but they are not interested in hacking—they are interested in their particular decision domain, and they become total authorities in this domain. Mike Milken, the junk-bond king, was an example (not a good example because he broke the law). He learned everything he possibly could about junk bonds, using his computer to do calculations nobody had done before. KKR & Co., the firm that drove the leveraged buyout mania in the 1980s, obtained fees of hundreds of millions of dollars with a staff of only twenty. Less publicized are numerous dedicated planners who sit in front of their spreadsheet screens until midnight, the graphics designers, computer-application builders, or market researchers who explore databases and build market models.

Computers hold an uncanny fascination for some people. They work at the screen with an intensity that excludes all else. Bill Gates's parents tried to ban his use of computers for eighteen months because they interfered with his studies.

Hackerlike decision makers exist in many fields. A large bank may have a senior person who deals with the worldwide needs of major Japanese customers. A large airport may use the services of a person using a computer to assign flights to gates. A factory may rely on a person who uses a computer to optimize production schedules. Such a person may be "line," not "staff," in that he makes events happen. He executes the results of his deeply calculated decisions. But this is not conventional "line" management because nobody works for this person. Like the archetypal hacker, he may be entirely lacking in people-management skills.

We will refer to "intellect workers" who are exceptionally brilliant and dedicated as virtuosos. A *virtuoso* is narrowly focused and develops special skill to the highest level possible. Virtuosos exist in many specializations—financial analysis, marketing, customer service, production scheduling, quality control, systems architecture, decision making with computerized models. As computerized tools become more and more powerful and complex, virtuosos became increasingly important. They can often access data from many databases to support their specialized knowledge. They sometimes employ worldwide networks.

As we reengineer corporations, we should develop and encourage virtuosos, and design processes that enable us to obtain the maximum benefits from them. They are sometimes "prima donnas," who have to be managed delicately. Their decisions often have pervasive financial impact. Sometimes they are entirely lacking in people skills. They became virtuosos because they are more comfortable communicating with computers or violins than people.

The traditional Western corporation has rarely respected its virtuosos and has often failed to put them to work. The world of the "organization man" and the "man in the gray flannel suit" tended to want interchangeable conformists rather than brilliant hackers and creative thinkers. Even IBM failed to put most of its brilliant people to good use. It put up notices requiring them to wear white shirts and ties in the cafeteria, to keep the wild ducks flying in formation. Instead of encouraging its virtuosos, it tried to mold them into cogs in the machine. The brightest ones often left.

The more the economy evolves into a knowledge society, the more it needs intellect workers and virtuosos. Corporations need to know how to develop them, motivate them, and redesign work to take advantage of them.

The decline of hierarchical management and the growth of self-directed teams coincides with the growing recognition and use of virtuosos. This is part of the evolution toward intellectual work replacing physical work. Intellectual work introduces great complexities and opportunities for business and computer hackers.

Some virtuosos can work in teams. Others are rugged individualists incapable of team interaction; they cannot be members of real teams without taking responsibility for their peers, and they find such responsibility a distraction from their virtuoso activity. Teams may be designed to pass work to virtuosos or to provide support for them. A brilliant architect may be a loner but needs teams of people to implement what he sketches.

Although some virtuosos work completely alone, most need a support structure. They are most useful as members of clusters. The value of the virtuoso and the value of the team can be combined by designing the team as a support structure for the virtuoso. The virtuoso does the unique, creative, intensive, or brilliant work, and the team does the more routine work. The virtuoso may pass work to the team, or the team may pass the interesting cases to the virtuoso. Much creative work needs a small amount of inspiration and a large amount of perspiration. The virtuoso may provide the former, and the rest of the team provides the latter.

Different types of team design involve virtuosos. It is important to adopt the right team structure. Inappropriately designed teams fail to deliver the needed results. Teams are not antithetical to virtuoso performance. On the contrary, high-performance teams may demand it. The team finds ways to make use of each individual's strengths.

Teams are not the answer to every situation. Sometimes working groups with strong management and individual accountability are more appropriate. A capable craftsman working alone can achieve great results. The corporation of the future needs teams, working groups, and individual virtuosos. The designers of reinvented value streams need to consider all options.

In 1986 one of America's large banks decided to enter the asset-sales business, which involves selling corporate loans and packages of investments to regional banks, subsidiaries of foreign banks, and large institutional investors such as insurance and brokerage companies. Top management aimed to capture this market with an all-out assault described as "like the Allied invasion of Normandy."

This activity needed complex computer application. Medium-term (one-to-five-year) asset sales require computing different from that of short-term asset sales. They include leveraged buyout financing and recapitalizations, loan syndications, and restructurings. Legal requirements are complicated and are constantly changing. Each deal is unique and requires dedicated computer-application writing to support it, often with as little as ten days' advance notice.

The operations vice-president employed a brilliant loner, Mike Joblin, to build the applications, and it was critical that they be built quickly.[7] Joblin had to find a software tool with which he could design and generate code quickly for this type of application. Joblin built his own family of reusable designs. Amazingly he created more than 900 thousand lines of code in slightly more than two years. With the traditional software development life cycle this would have taken hundreds of person-years. Joblin's code for medium-term asset sales had more than 500 menu choices and 250 reports and dealt with a wide array of regulatory requirements. He also built billing and sales-lead tracking systems.

Joblin's systems helped the bank's salespeople get more business. The sales and front-office staff can make any deal they want because they knew that the requisite computer application can be built quickly. Joblin's work was strategically vital for the business. Without it the bank could not have moved with such spectacular success into the new business area.

By 1988 the bank was ahead of the former front-runner, Bankers Trust. It sold $400 billion worth of corporate loan assets in 1988, earning $100 million for the bank, with a staff of about 50—a remarkable profit per person.

Success in business can be short-lived. Competition can quickly replicate a new thrust, and the thrust may relate to only one aspect of the business. The glowing successes that these case studies describe can easily relate to a corporation that becomes known for lack of success in other areas. The bank in this story was Security Pacific.

References

1. D. Quinn Mills, *The Rebirth of the Corporation* (John Wiley & Sons: New York, 1991).
2. "GM's German Lessons," *Business Week,* December 20, 1991.
3. Jon R. Katzenback and Douglas K. Smith, *The Wisdom of Teams* (Harvard Business School Press: Boston, Mass., 1993).
4. Ibid—Epilogue.
5. Ibid—Chapter 4.
6. Ibid—Chapter 2.
7. Quoted from a press release about Security Pacific's Asset Sales Group, from Cortex Inc., Waltham, Mass., August 23, 1989.

Part II
Value-Stream Reinvention

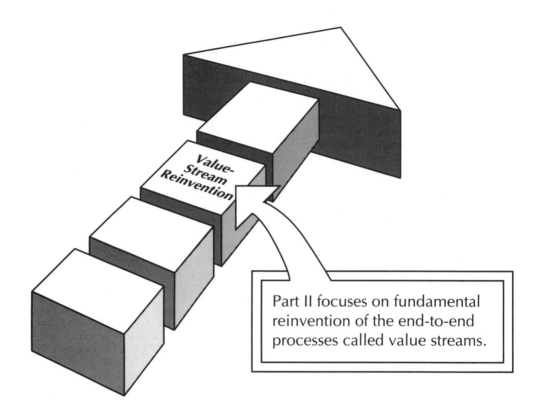

Value-Stream Reinvention

Part II focuses on fundamental reinvention of the end-to-end processes called value streams.

7

Value Streams

End-to-End Redesign

A detailed study at Ernst and Young's Center for Information Technology found that "in many companies the key processes were last 'designed' (to the degree that they were designed at all) well before the rise of information technology."[1] The processes and structures in most corporations were put together before today's market demands for fast, fluid, flexible change. They were designed for an era of hierarchical management, division of labor, inflexible mass production, and rigid procedures manuals—before networks that could instantly transmit any information to any employee.

> *Computers have been used to automate ancient processes and fit into ancient corporate structures.*

It is now becoming clear how these processes and structures should be redesigned. Many of them need total replacement. When we reinvent something designed for an earlier era, we can achieve dramatic improvements in cost, quality, service, and speed.

Exhibit 5.6 presented examples of breakthrough improvements in corporate processes. These are examples of order-of-magnitude improvements—10-times, not 10-percent, improvements. For example, many telephone companies have reduced the time it takes to respond to customer requests for circuits from almost 2 months to about 2 days. Some banks have shrunk the time they take to tell customers whether they will give them a house mortgage from a few weeks to a few hours. Electronic manufacturers have dramatically shrunk the time it takes to design a new product and get it to market. Iomega reduced the time it took to make disk drives from 28 to 1.5 days. Corporations have cut the administrative costs involved in purchasing to one-fifth.

More important, some corporations have rebuilt a core capability so that they do it far better than their competition. They have become a "capability predator" (discussed in Chapter 24), so that they can take business away from their competition or vigorously expand into new markets. Wal-Mart, for example, reinvented its distribution and logistics capability so that it could get goods to the shelves of its supermarkets at the right time at a lower cost than its competition. It grew from a largely unknown retailer in 1980 to the world's biggest retailer by 1993.

These dramatic gains are made possible by the reinvention of end-to-end processes that we will refer to as value streams. All organizations with a traditional structure need to reorganize themselves with fundamental reinvention of their value streams. New corporations should organize themselves from the beginning around value streams.

A common management practice is to implement new management alignments without affecting the manner in which task-level work is performed. In the long run this does not accomplish much. What is needed instead is fundamental reinvention of processes so that results can be achieved for customers in the most simple, direct, narrowly focused fashion.

IT departments often build computer systems to implement the procedures of the old organization. The systems can be expensive and difficult to change. Such systems inhibit the reinvention that is needed. *Many computer systems being built today will make it more difficult to change the enterprise as it should be changed.*

> *The term* **reengineering** *may be inappropriate applied to business processes because the processes were never "engineered" in the first place. They grew like ivy on a tree with a succession of changes motivated by internal economies of scale, empire building, corporate politics, computer software, tradition, geographical distance, use of unskilled people, and rarely a focus on how to please the customer.*

Value Streams

A *value stream* is an end-to-end collection of activities that creates a result for a "customer," who may be the ultimate customer or an internal "end user" of the value stream. The value stream has a clear goal: to satisfy (or, better, to delight) the customer.

The term *value stream* refers to an end-to-end set of activities (Exhibit 7.1). Order fulfillment, for example, is a value stream: the input is the order, and the results are the delivery of ordered goods. Order entry is one activity in the collection of activities that constitute the order fulfillment value stream.

A value stream is a collection of activities that function together. The value-stream customer has certain desires, and the value stream consists of work activities dedicated to serving that customer. Value streams and their customers cannot be separated—the focus on customer gives the value stream its purpose.

The customer is sometimes the ultimate customer of the enterprise; sometimes the "customer" exists within the enterprise. For example, the materials acquisition value stream supplies materials to a company's manufacturing operations—here the customer is the manufacturing function. The value stream customer may be a sales prospect, not yet a customer who has placed an order.

Exhibit 7.1

A value stream is an end-to-end set of activities that is collectively valuable to a customer. The customer may be the ultimate, external customer or an internal user of the value stream.

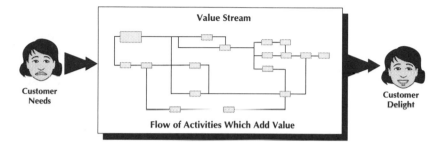

- An enterprise is a collection of value streams.
- In most enterprises all of them need reinventing.
- Value-stream reinvention usually involves total redesign of a system.
- When the reinvented value stream is in use, kaizen (TQM) techniques are used to result in continuous improvement, as described in Part III.

Sometimes the term *end user* is employed to describe an internal customer of a value stream, but *Customer* encourages value-stream workers to try to please the recipient as they would an external customer.

From the point of view of the customer of the value stream, the value stream might as well be a black box; it does not matter how the value stream operates internally. Certain objectives must be satisfied. A customer who has marketplace choices will choose the enterprise that offers the greatest satisfaction.

Process vs. Value Stream

As was mentioned earlier, the term *process* causes misunderstandings. Business people talk about the accounts payable process or order entry process. IT professionals draw data-flow diagrams and other diagrams labeling as processes such areas as "prepare invoice" or "compute order quantity." None of these is what is meant by *value stream.*

Because of the amorphous meaning of the word *process,* the terms *business process redesign* and *business process reengineering* are imprecise. Different users of these terms mean different things, just as different professionals have different meanings for the term *process.* Enterprise Engineering avoids these terms and uses those more precise in their meaning, such as *kaizen, value stream,* and *value-stream-reinvention.*

Value Stream vs. Value Chain

The concept of a value stream differs from that of a value chain, described by Michael Porter in his book *Competitive Advantage:* "The value chain desegregates a firm into its strategically relevant activities in order to understand the behavior of costs and the existing and potential sources of (competitive) differentiation."[1] This analysis focuses on activity costs and margins as a strategic-analysis activity.

A value stream is much simpler than Porter's value chain. Porter's value chain relates to the enterprise as a whole, whereas value streams relate to a set of activities that satisfy a particular type of customer (internal or external). The value-chain perspective is driven by a functional business view evaluating costs and margins as a basis for competitive comparisons. The value-stream perspective is based on streams of work activities in every enterprise that deliver a particular result for a particular type of customer or user. These streams of work are clumsy and slow because they pass through multiple departments and functional areas. In most corporations dramatic improvements can be achieved by scrapping and replacing the awkward value streams with well-organized teams using powerful information systems.

Redesigning the value streams can be a relatively straightforward way to improve competitiveness (although implementing the redesign is a major management challenge).

An enterprise consists of a collection of value streams. Most large companies can be broken down into a dozen or more value streams. IBM identified 18 major values streams, Ameritech 15; Dow Chemical 9, and Xerox 14 in its document-processing business.[2] A major insurance company envisions itself as 14 value streams. Exhibit 7.2 lists a typical collection of value streams in a corporation.

Representing an enterprise as a collection of value streams is a useful way of understanding an enterprise. Reinventing each values stream to make it serve its customer in the most direct, focused way will give a corporation a major competitive advantage.

The list of value streams differs somewhat from one enterprise to another. An insurance company may have a separate value stream for claims processing. A telecommunications company needs a value stream for managing its network. An airline needs a value stream for maintenance of aircraft internationally.

In the top three value streams in Exhibit 7.2, the corporate customer is the value-stream customer. In the other value streams the customer is internal. Each value stream has clear customers, however, and its goal should be to satisfy those customers in the simplest, most direct way.

Although a value stream has many work steps, these should be tightly coordinated and compressed into the minimum time needed to maximize response to the customer. Work steps should be done simultaneously, where this is practical, to increase speed. Unnecessary work should be eliminated. Handovers from one group to another, which tend to cause errors or things "slipping through the cracks," should be avoided where possible.

Exhibit 7.2 A typical collection of value streams in a corporation

- *Customer Engagement*—acquiring customers, determining their needs, selling, ensuring that they are pleased
- *Order Fulfillment*—receiving orders, fulfilling orders, collecting payment
- *Customer Services*—providing customers with services such as help in using the product, planning, consulting
- *Manufacturing*—production of goods, maintenance of inventory, interaction with suppliers
- *Procurement Services*—assistance in supplier selection, contracting, and management
- *Product-Design Engineering*—designing products and facilities for manufacturing them
- *Research*—exploration of potentially valuable science and technology
- *Marketing*—determining what customers need, what products to build, what features are needed; advertising
- *Market-Information Capture*—acquisition of information about sales, locating intelligence about competition
- *Product Maintenance*—repair of products and preventive maintenance on customer sites
- *Legal Department*—solving legal problems, writing contracts
- *IT-Application Development*—developing and modifying systems and software
- *IT Infrastructure*—building the corporatewide network, database, and facilities for distributed computing
- *Human Resources*—assistance in recruiting, training, compensation, career planning
- *Leased and Capital-Asset Management*—management of buildings and capital resources
- *Financial Management*—accounting, negotiation with banks, cash management
- *Enterprise Engineering*—designing, implementing, and improving value streams; engineering the enterprise learning processes

In identifying value streams that are candidates for reinvention, it is important to identify clearly where they start and where they end. This clarifies what the value stream is. Exhibit 7.3 shows the start and end of typical value streams.

Sometimes the start and finish of the value stream is clear and unambiguous. In other cases reinvention of the value stream can change the beginning or end. For example, the table shows procurement as starting with a purchase order. However, the procurement process might be so reinvented that purchase orders are eliminated much of the time. The vendor is given on-line access to an inventory database and signs a contract to maintain the inventory.

Exhibit 7.3   Value-stream start and finish

To clarify what the value stream is, its start and finish activities can be named.

Value Stream	Start	Finish
Order acquisition	Prospect, lead	Order
Order fulfillment	Customer order	Delivery
Procurement	Requirements determination	Payment
Mortgage request	Inquiry	Resolution
Manufacturing	Procurement	Shipment
Product design	Concept	Prototype
Software application	Concept	Cutover
Strategy development	Market requirements	Business strategy
Customer communications	Customer inquiries	Customer interest in products
Claims processing	Accident report	Claim payment

The Basic Idea of VSR

The basic idea of value-stream reinvention is simple. Businesses consist of value streams whose purpose is to achieve specific results for a customer (internal or external). The customer's need can be clearly identified, and the business ought to make the customer as happy as possible. The value stream for doing this may involve multiple work activities. Often these activities occur in different functional areas, as shown in Exhibit 7.4

Historically the corporation has been organized into functional areas and departments within those functional areas. The process for satisfying the customer, in Exhibit 7.4, spans four functional areas. The work is handed from one department to another. Each department has a queue of jobs waiting to be done. Some departments have automated their work. Their computer systems execute rigid procedures.

Most value streams extend beyond departments or functional areas. Order taking at dealer locations may be linked on-line to production scheduling; production scheduling may be linked to electronic placement of orders for precisely timed deliveries; deliveries themselves may trigger electronic payments; deliveries trigger production-planning actions; production planning triggers scheduling of shipments, automatic reordering, notices to dealers; and so on.

There are several things wrong with the work flow in Exhibit 7.4. First, all of the queues increase the time required to complete the work. By reinventing the process we can get rid of most or all of the hold-ups. Second, there are subtle miscommunications between the separate departments; the work delivered has flaws in it. Some items "slip through the cracks." Third, the costs are high. Not every job needs to pass through every step in the procedure. Fourth, when computers are used, some jobs may need special treatment, subtly different from what is programmed. Fifth, the process in Exhibit 7.4 may work smoothly (albeit

Exhibit 7.4

Most end-to-end processes are slow and error prone because they wander across multiple functional areas.

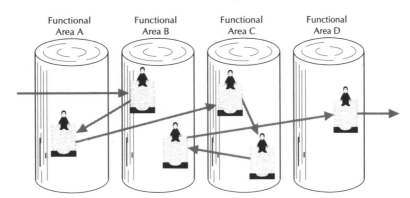

A process such as this must be scrapped and replaced with an empowered team that gets the work done as simply and directly as possible, focusing intensely on the needs of the customer (internal or external).

---

slowly) for most jobs, but sometimes exceptions occur, and it is necessary to go back to the department that did an earlier task and make changes. This backtracking causes problems. The department may not be able to find the transaction, or changing it may upset its routine. Sixth, each function and department in Exhibit 7.4 has its own motivation, code of behavior, and rules for giving employees good marks. Often these motivations and rules have nothing to do with satisfying the customer or succeeding in the marketplace.

Value-stream reinvention asks several basic questions:

- What are the value streams of an enterprise?
- Who are the customers of each value stream?
- What are the customers' needs and desires? What would delight the customer?
- How can the value stream be reinvented to meet customer desires as simply and directly as possible, using the most appropriate technology and information systems, and minimizing the costs of doing so?

Certainly the best way to serve the customer is not to ricochet through the bureaucratic procedures of Exhibit 7.4. How could one person or one tightly knit team deal with a customer's needs? How can facilities and methods permit a team to tackle the entire process without the queues and hand-offs in Exhibit 7.4, responding to the customer's needs directly and flexibly, and focusing full attention on delighting the customer?

Value-stream reinvention goes right to the heart of the matter: How can work be reinvented so that it focuses intensely on pleasing the customer?

Value-stream reinvention is concerned with identifying the end-to-end processes that meet a customer's needs and with reinventing them to serve that customer as effectively as possible (Exhibit 7.5). Modern technology offers spectacular scope for this reinvention.

> Value streams are often more complex than that in Exhibit 7.4. At Hallmark Cards, for example, the process of designing a card was studied. It was found that there were 25 steps between assigning a concept to the creative staff and releasing the card to the printing department. Ninety percent of the time the work sat in one of the 25 "in" baskets. The president of Hallmark's Personal Communication Group had the process redesigned. He commented: "We grouped people together who had been separated by disciplines, departments, floors, and even buildings, to cut down query time, spur creativity, and end the throw-it-over-the-wall-its-their-problem cycle."[3] These new integrated teams brought out cards eight months ahead of schedule.

In a Greek legend, nobody could untie a knot tied by King Gordius of Phrygia. The knot bound the yoke of a chariot to a pole. An oracle of Zeus declared that whoever undid the knot and freed the chariot would reign over all Asia. Many people tried to untie the knot; nobody succeeded.

Value-stream reinvention does not untangle the knots that have evolved tortuously in corporations. It finds unanticipated radical solutions, cuts through the entanglements, and starts afresh, often with new technology.

The person who became Alexander the Great, and later came to reign over all Asia, found a radical, direct solution. He did not try to untie the Gordian Knot; he cut it with a stroke of his sword.

Exhibit 7.5

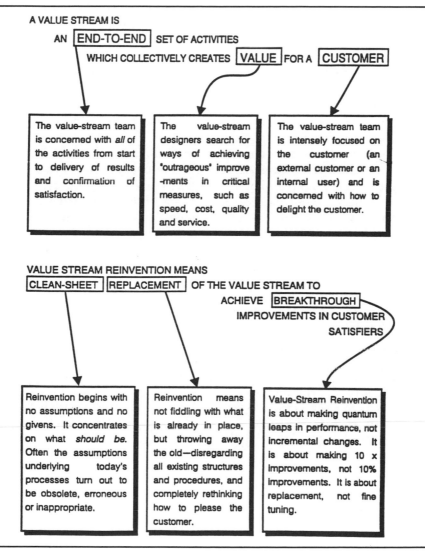

Value Streams, Not Hierarchies

Traditional enterprises have hierarchical management. Data are passed up the management chain and commands are passed down it. Hierarchies were necessary in the days before information technology, but they cause many problems. Corporations around the world have been lowering their number of hierarchical layers, introducing clusters and teams, and generally searching for more efficient forms of organization.

An enterprise consists of its value streams, but most enterprises do not charge executives with managing the end-to-end value streams. Instead, executives manage functions—the vertical cylinders of Exhibit 7.4. Each cylinder has its own hierarchy and politics. Enterprises ought to be redesigned so as to make someone responsible for each end-to-end value stream.

Hammer and Champy popularized the term *business reengineering* for their style of value-stream reinvention. They comment: "Business Reengineering should be brought in only when a need exists for heavy blasting. Marginal improvement means fine-tuning; dramatic improvement means blowing up the old and replacing it with something new."[4]

In many cases parts of a value stream have already been improved, but the customer sees little effect because of poor coordination with other functions. Manufacturing, for example, may have spent years improving cycle time and quality, but orders are not passed to the factory until a credit check has been done, order discrepancies take a long time to resolve, the goods sit in a warehouse before shipment, the goods take time to insure, and the shipper batches the deliveries. A chain is as weak as its weakest link.

Sometimes value streams are complex, employing multiple computer systems, and rebuilding them causes a major upheaval. Sometimes they are relatively simple and easy to redesign. In one clinic, performing a blood test took 18 hours, involving 59 steps and 10 people. The reinvented value stream used advanced equipment and 2 trained paramedics to do the entire job in five minutes. The customer received the results, so corrective action could be taken if necessary, before the patient left the clinic.

As corporations becomes more competitive, more automated, more knowledge intensive, it is increasingly true that *time is money*. The waiting lines of Exhibit 9.4 represent a loss of time; they also represent a loss of money. In Hallmark's card-production process, the time waiting in line for 25 processes instead of getting new ideas to market was a direct financial loss.

Dramatic Results

A value stream that straggles across the hierarchy like the one in Exhibit 7.4 needs to be reinvented from scratch. The designers need to take a clean sheet of paper—forgetting today's rules, regulations, and personalities—and reinvent the work so that is it done by one team (or person), narrowly focused on meeting the customer's desires directly. Where this has been done dramatic results have been achieved.

Because the waiting lines are removed, the cycle time is much shorter. Because a single team concentrates on the whole process without passing the task from one to another, quality and service are greatly improved. The new team can use its creativity and ingenuity to invent major enhancements. Computer systems are designed specifically for the team. Many work steps are eliminated, and fewer people are involved. This and the shorter cycle time both save money. It is usually possible to achieve savings in time and cost, and to improve quality and service, with the same value-stream reinvention. The following is an appropriate symbol for value stream reinvention:

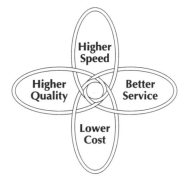

It is important to understand that higher speed does not mean lower quality. We are not advocating "quick and dirty" solutions. Value-stream reinvention should search for techniques that give both higher speed and higher quality. Much of the lack of quality arises from the multiple throw-it-over-the-wall-its-their-problem approach in Exhibit 7.4. Making a team responsible for the end-to-end, customer-focused cycle results in meeting customer needs better, emphasizing service and quality where they are important.

IBM reengineered a factory making visual display terminals, redesigning the product so that it had far fewer parts and so that these parts could be assembled by automatic machines and robots. The number of people on the production line was cut from 130 to 5 at the same time that production capacity was almost tripled. The inventory was cut from about 2 months' supply to 4 days'. With the same redesign, the product's mean time between failures was improved eightfold. These dramatic results could not have been achieved with continuous process improvements or TQM; they required fundamental reinvention.

Bell Atlantic reduced the time it took to install a high-speed digital circuit for customers from 30 days to 3—in some cases to several hours.[5]

Ford reduced the number of people involved in vendor payment from 500 to 125.[6] Hewlett-Packard cut the time it took to design a printer and get it to market from 4 1/2 years to 22 months.[7]

These are not isolated unique exceptions. They all employed methods to achieve results that can be emulated in all corporations. In addition to results that are measurably dramatic, such as those listed in Exhibit 6.6, improvements of customer service can be achieved that are subtle, often not measurable, but very important to the customer. Some companies have designed their telephone system to enable a customer always to get switched to the same representative, one who knows all about the customer's concerns because this information appears on the representative's personal computer screen.

Top-Down Culture Change

Value-stream reinvention cannot be accomplished from the bottom up. The total change in management that it requires can only come from a level of management higher than those affected. Cross-functional change has to come from the CEO.

One of the biggest obstacles is dealing with human concerns and cultural resistance. A plan that seems "obviously" right often fails when management changes and cultural issues are not handled correctly. To make value-stream reinvention work, the CEO has to be passionate about it and determined.

The term *business reengineering* is often threatening to middle managers, and others who are capable of erecting roadblocks to change, because it implies that the whole business and its managers will be *reengineered*. The term *value-stream reinvention*, being more sharply focused and relating for the time being to only a specific value stream, is less generally threatening.

IT Development

The new value stream needs to be as automated as possible—with technology that provides the best information for value-stream workers. Often value-stream reinvention is needed because technology permits a new way of working. IT systems are quite different from the old systems built for functional silos.

The new systems need to be implemented quickly. Sometimes a value stream has been redesigned, staff trained, and employees motivated so that they are excited about their new jobs, but the IT systems are not changed.

The IT organization needs the capability to build new systems rapidly, and to build them so that they can be changed quickly, because the new work involves a period of rapid learning and change. To accommodate the requirements for fast change, flexibility, ease of use, and excellent human factoring with a graphical user interface, client-server technology is often used for new value-stream systems. Excellent tools and methodologies for fast development of client-server systems are available, but many corporations are not using them.

Value-stream reinvention needs careful attention to IT systems building and management of the change in organization and culture.

Synchronized Change

As enterprise is an organism, with its many processes linked by a central nervous system. Both people and computers are part of the processing and communication activity. In redesigning this organism remember that it is essential to align the corporation's business objectives, its human organization, and its electronic infrastructure. These should be designed and implemented together. To implement reinvented value streams, the human changes and the technological changes

must be jointly managed and implemented to avoid problems. Because much of the most valuable value-stream redesign is cross-functional, the human changes in different functional areas must be coordinated, not developed in isolation by the different functional areas. The functional areas must participate in joint workshops for the planning and design of the systems required.

When organizational changes and systems changes are managed separately, there is usually a deadly embrace. New computer systems founder because of cultural resistance and reluctance to change old methods. New business procedures work badly because of inadequate computer systems. It is easy to build an exciting new computer system only to find that its users stubbornly continue their old, inefficient practices or do not "buy in" to the new approach. Conversely, many reengineered business operations fail because IT did not support them adequately.

The new systems can effectively be sabotaged by end users who do not understand the reasons for them or who have parochial reasons for not wanting the change. On the other hand, users excited by the new business vision become frustrated because old IT systems are not changed when needed. Either situation leads to cynicism and a reversal of the initial enthusiasm. The organizational, human, and IT aspects of change need to be integrated.

Fragmented changes to systems or business procedures are unfortunately more common than managed integration. Fragmented initiatives usually go awry. The change in the organization, its management and culture, the training and skill-building of the value-stream workers, and the building of the new IT systems, need to be done in tandem and managed jointly. The three activities need to be synchronized in order to implement the new way of working efficiently.

As technology continues its rapid growth in power, increasingly capable of changing the enterprise, it becomes vital to fuse the organization's technology with its business objectives.

The organizational change, human skills change, and development of new IT systems need to be managed jointly, implemented in tandem

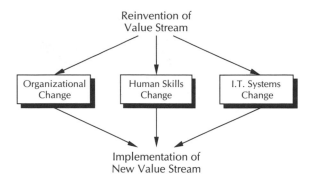

and synchronized, otherwise successful implementation of the new
value stream will not occur.

Summary

Every corporation should be thought of in terms of its value streams, which deliver results if they are designed to do so as simply and directly as possible.
Value streams like that in Exhibit 7.4 do not make sense in an age of computers,
information highways, and high-performance teams. When the concepts of value-
stream organizations have been digested by management everywhere, new corporations will consist of well-managed value streams rather than today's functional organization. Old-style corporations with functional management will have
difficulty competing with the new value-stream corporations, especially when
they are designed to constantly learn, experiment, and improve.

Building a new corporation organized around value-stream teams is likely
to be easier than building a new corporation with a functional hierarchy. Converting an existing enterprise from a functional structure to a value-stream structure, however, can be extremely difficult. Conversion involves a traumatic transformation of the power structure and dramatic cultural change. Many attempts
at "reengineering" have failed.

> *Bruce Rupport, senior vice-president and champion of reengineering at*
> *Agway, comments: "You can survive the old way. You can survive the*
> *new way. It's the goddamn transition that'll kill you."*[8]

References

1. Michael E. Porter, *Competitive Advantage* (The Free Press: New York 1985).
2. T. H. Davenport, *Process Innovation* (Harvard Business School Press: Boston, 1993).

3. Story by Robert L. Stark of Hallmark Cards, Inc., told in chapter 10 of M. Hammer and J. Champy, *Reengineering the Corporation* (Harper Business: New York, 1993).
4. Ibid.
5. T. H. Davenport.
6. M. Hammer and J. Champy.
7. "How Managers Can Succeed Through Speed," *Fortune*, February 13, 1989, p. 6.
8. "Reengineering: The Hot New Managing Tool," *Fortune*, August 23, 1993.

8

Mapping the Value Streams

A value stream has a job to be done with a clear goal: that of pleasing a customer (internal or external). A value-stream team can get excited about achieving that goal, but it needs good tools and good information systems, no unnecessary steps or controls, no politics, no second guessing. The team members just want to do the best job possible. Most work ought to be like this—and most can be reinvented so as to have these characteristics.

A value stream consists of activities that could be mapped with a work-flow diagram. Exhibits 8.1 and 8.2 show illustrations of value streams. Clearly, the value streams in most enterprises are badly in need of reinvention, and dramatic improvements are being achieved in redesigning them. Implementing the redesign requires major upheavals in the organization, management, enterprise structures, and jobs.

At the start of Enterprise Engineering, it is necessary to identify the enterprise's value streams, name them, and identify their start and finish, as in Exhibit 7.3. As a first step the activities in each value stream should be listed. Each activity should be represented as a brief sentence starting with a verb as in Exhibits 8.3, 8.4 and 8.5.

The value streams in a company correspond to natural business behavior. Businesses exist in order to serve their customers; the value stream is the string of activities that provides that service. The value streams have often been unnamed and largely unmanaged because corporations have been structured around vertical functions. These functions evolve their own power structures. Value-stream reinvention identifies the values streams, makes them visible, names them, reinvents them, optimizes them to satisfy their customers as fully as possible, and establishes a value-stream team that does the work, focusing directly on how to please the customer. The team constantly strives to improve its performance in achieving this goal.

Primary vs. Support Value Streams

Some value streams are particularly important and determine what makes a corporation unique or competitive. We will refer to those as *primary value systems*.

Exhibit 8.1 An order-fulfillment value stream

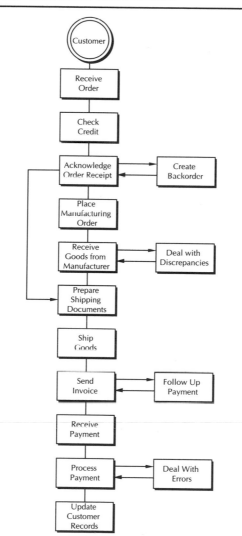

Other value streams are needed for basic support of the business, to enable the business to operate. We will refer to those as *support value streams.*

Primary value streams include such areas as product design, customer engagement, distribution logistics, manufacturing, and marketing. Support value streams include purchasing, operational finance, human resources, facilities management, and IT services.

Exhibits 8.3, 8.4, and 8.5 list the value streams in three corporations, and divide them into primary and support value streams. The support value streams

Exhibit 8.2   A purchase value stream

This value stream has *internal* customers, who require parts.

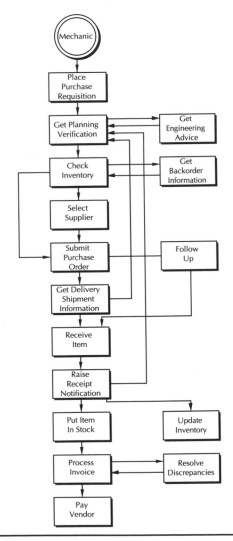

have "customers" inside the enterprise; some, but not necessarily all, of the primary value streams have "customers" external to the enterprise.

One, or maybe more than one, of the primary value streams may be regarded as a *strategic* capability, which top management wants to perform with world-beating excellence. Part of the managers' strategic vision is to make the corporation so excellent with one particular value stream that in that area they can beat the competition. Building a strategic value stream may need advanced use of technology. (Chapter 24 discusses *strategic* value streams.)

Exhibit 8.3 Value streams in a well-known insurance company

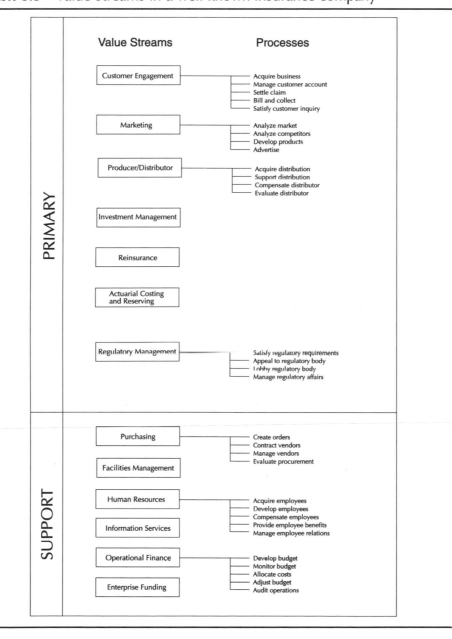

Exhibit 8.4   Value streams of a manufacturer

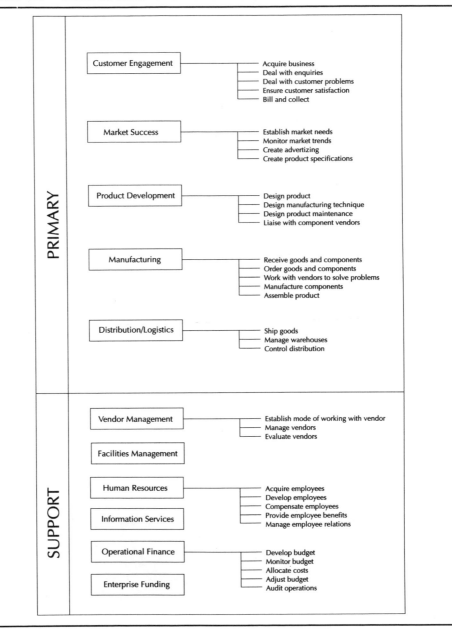

Exhibit 8.5 Value streams in a public utility

Value Streams	Processes
PRIMARY	
Customer Engagement	Acquire business / Manage client account / Bill and collect / Satisfy customer enquiry
Market Success	Analyze market / Analyze competitors / Establish pricing / Adjust offerings
Production	Operate equipment / Maintain equipment / Plan additional capacity / Plan replacements
Distribution	Maintain links to customers / Repair equipment / Preventive maintenance / Plan additional capacity / Plan replacements
Community Relations	
Regulatory Management	Satisfy regulatory requirements / Appeal to regulatory body / Lobby regulatory body / Manage regulatory affairs
SUPPORT	
Purchasing	Create orders / Contract vendors / Manage vendors / Evaluate procurement
Facilities Management	
Human Resources	Acquire employees / Develop employees / Compensate employees / Provide employee benefits / Manage employee relations
Information Services	
Operational Finance	Develop budget / Monitor budget / Allocate costs / Adjust budget / Audit operations
Enterprise Funding	

Exhibit 8.6   Primary value streams in a university

Value Stream	Value-Stream Customer
Student services	Students and parents (Few universities do much to please the parents.)
Academic mission	Faculty and academic bodies
Grants management	Foundations, companies, individual donors
Fund raising and alumni relations	Alumni
Trustee relations	Trustees
Endowment management	University as a whole

A few universities have been reengineering themselves. Most universities need to—badly. The critical value streams in a university differ in nature from those in most corporations. They are illustrated in Exhibit 8.6

Silos and Stovepipes

Every corporation can be represented as a set of value streams. A value stream can be divided into a collection of activities as in Exhibits 8.3, 8.4, and 8.5.

Traditional enterprises are organized by function. An executive having a title like vice-president of marketing or vice-president of finance heads each functional area. Often the functional areas are largely autonomous, and there is limited communication among functions. An employee in manufacturing does not normally pick up the phone and make joint decisions with an employee in marketing. Sometimes it is commented that an enterprise is organized into functional "silos" (Exhibit 8.7).

> Antony Jay described his work as the head of a BBC television production department:
>
> > If I wanted to take on a new production assistant or pay an incumbent one more penny, I had to apply to the establishment department; if I wanted to promote him to producer I had to apply to the appointments department; if I wanted a film editor to work on Saturday, I had to ask the film department; if I wanted to change a set designer, I had to ask the design department; if I wanted new carpets or an extra office, I had to ask the administration department; if I wanted to change studio rehearsal times, I had to apply to engineering allocations; if I wanted to tell the press about a program, I had to do it through the publicity officer. There was no question of doing without an extra office so as to pay a producer more—

Exhibit 8.7 Functional silos

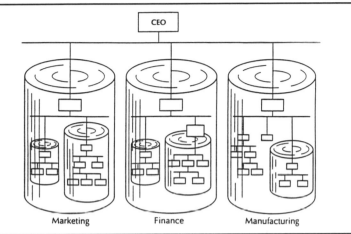

all these budgets were unconnected, and none controlled by me. And none of the heads of these departments worked under the head of my own group, and many did not meet a common boss until three or four levels up in the hierarchy.[1]

Such an activity should be redesigned so as to put the production manager in charge of his own production value stream. He would then use his own discretion about spending his own budget. He would be able to take on or lay off freelance designers, film crews, and so on. He would concentrate on pleasing his customer—the audience.

The computer applications within each function have often been built independently by separate noncommunicating development teams. These so-called stovepipe systems (Exhibit 8.8) often use incompatible data, which prevents or makes difficult communication between the systems (even "open" systems).

Many value streams cross multiple functions in an enterprise (Exhibit 8.9). Work must pass through many hands as it progresses from one functional area to another. This causes delays and errors. It is difficult to trace what may have "fallen through the cracks." Exceptions are time consuming. There is no manager in charge of the value stream as a whole.

In some nonphysical values streams—such as approving a mortgage, processing an insurance claim, obtaining finance, or obtaining a price estimate—the total work done adds up to only an hour or two. The time the customer has to wait is weeks or months, however because the work sits in many "in" baskets and is handed over many times. Redesigning the value stream can reduce the total time to hours.

Exhibit 8.8

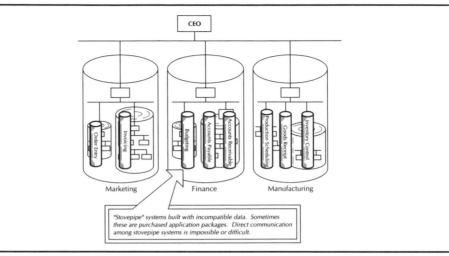

"Stovepipe" systems built with incompatible data. Sometimes these are purchased application packages. Direct communication among stovepipe systems is impossible or difficult.

Exhibit 8.9

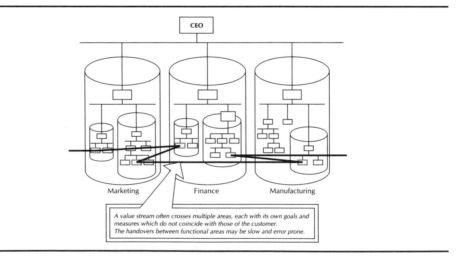

A value stream often crosses multiple areas, each with its own goals and measures which do not coincide with those of the customer. The handovers between functional areas may be slow and error prone.

A major goal of reengineering is to identify the end-to-end work and to have efficient teams do it in the cleanest and simplest way possible, with no "hand-overs," no boundaries, no politics, and the most powerful use of technology.

Exhibit 8.10 shows how value streams often consist of work done in more than one functional area of an enterprise.

Exhibit 8.10 A typical value stream involving activities in multiple traditional departments

This matrix shows the value streams in a large utility and how they relate to the departments that existed before reengineering.

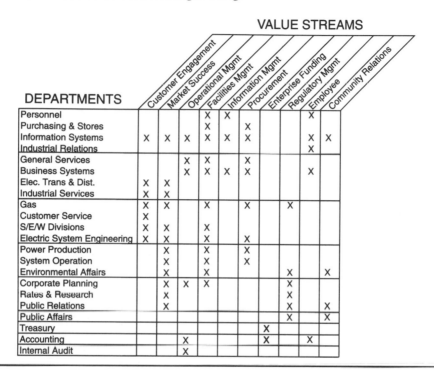

The Customer of the Value Stream

It is important to identify clearly the customer of the value stream because the customer's desires drive the reinvention.

The value stream often encompasses all enterprise work activities with which the customer can interact. This may mean, for example, that service and maintenance are not seen as distinct from selling. Rather, they are part of a single customer-engagement value stream. This approach provides the greatest opportunity to satisfy the customer by having the value-stream manager, or team, focus on *all* the customer needs. The value stream reconciles all the views a customer may have of the enterprise and creates the view of a single, serving enterprise dedicated to the customer. The idea of dedicated service to the customer is the cornerstone of value-stream reinvention.

A common error is to group together customers who are fundamentally different. For example, the person who buys a car and the dealer who sells it are "customers" of two distinct value streams for the car manufacturer. In order to satisfy both the end customer and the dealer, each value stream may be treated separately. This helps to maximize the benefits to the enterprise of each value stream.

Examples of *internal* customers are a manufacturing group that needs parts or products purchasing, a marketing group that needs product development, or a management team that needs a new computer application. As with external customers the internal customers' wishes are analyzed and the values stream reinvented to satisfy these wishes.

Customer-Delight Factors

The team that reinvents the value stream needs to ask the question, What would delight the customer? If the customer could have some order-of-magnitude change in the behavior of the value stream, what would it be (Chapter 10)?

The value stream is redesigned to satisfy the customer's wishes as fully as possible, rather than focus on internal procedures that make accounting or management tracking easier. It is not that accounting and management tracking are unimportant; it is that over time a variety of internal procedures have grown and multiplied, taking on an importance of their own. Managers look inward to internal procedures when they make business changes instead of asking, What changes must we make to serve the customer better?

Executives in charge of functional areas often grow more and more out of touch with what the customer wants or how work is done. People close to the products or customers know a great deal about the products or customers but have to refer decisions to people with no such knowledge. Enterprising ideas never get approved. Action that should be taken immediately is delayed until it is of no value. Ross Perot in his days with General Motors commented, "In a lot of these big companies, what it takes to be successful has nothing to do with making better products, or serving the customer, or the rules of the marketplace. It has to do with following procedures."[2]

The advice given by a functional manager is often dominated by the desire for internal convenience or the personal prestige of seeing his own plan adopted. The functional professional may be passionate about his own narrow area of expertise, so his parochial viewpoint dominates rather than the desire to please the customer, about whom little thought is given.

The team actually doing the work has a much better idea of what procedures are good than a remote executive in charge of a specialized function. If Nelson had had a fax machine, he would never have won the Battle of Trafalgar.

In a training company there was a concern for producing video tapes of high quality. A Ph.D. in "instructional design" was hired who insisted that all tapes meet his standards, which were based on academic theory which was irrelevant to communicating with the customers. Those people who worked with the customers knew what style of tapes they liked and what did not work for them.

Their real-customer knowledge was ignored because the Ph.D. insisted on his own theory.

The team that redesigns the value stream focuses its creativity on finding ways to delight the customer. There are probably opportunities for pleasing the customer not yet perceived by the customer. The operational team that eventually *works* with the customer, performing the value-stream operations, gets to know the customer in new ways and should be able to refine the operations and improve its ability to please this customer. Analyzing the means for satisfying customers requires understanding and interactions of the customer with the value stream. Each of these interactions or events must serve to improve the customer's view of the enterprise. Each interaction provides the opportunity to *exceed* the customer's expectations, binding the customer more strongly to the enterprise.

The Elapsed-Time–Work-Time Ratio

There are many activities for which speed of response is an important customer requirement. A salesman needs fast action in order to close a competitive sale. A manufacturer needs to get a new product out ahead of competition. A bank patron needs to find out quickly whether financing is available.

Many processes in enterprises are slow because they were not designed for speed. Work sits in piles or "in" trays. There are delays when work is passed from one department to another. Each department is concerned with its own tasks. Nobody is responsible for focusing on the customer requirement.

An interesting ratio is *the total time to complete a process divided by the total labor hours needed to accomplish the work.* This should be estimated when speed is a customer requirement. In many insurance companies processing and underwriting an insurance policy takes more than 20 days, but the actual work is done in two or three hours.[3] (Exhibit 8.11).

One study of elapsed-time–work-time ratio revealed that, for the average process, actual working time comprises 0.05- to -0.5 percent of total elapsed time.[4]

IBM provides credit to some of its customers when they make large purchases. It used to take from 6 days to 2 weeks to process credit requests (that is, to find out whether IBM would provide financing and on what terms). When reinventing that process, managers discovered that the actual work took 90 minutes.[5] The rest of the time the request was being handed from one person to another and sitting in piles on people's desks. The elapsed-time–work-time ratio was about 37. When the value stream had been re-created, the average time for processing a request came down to 4 hours. The ratio fell to about 3.

Some corporations (including GE) have done better than IBM in shrinking the time to respond to financing requests. Most financing requests can be handled by computer, whereas some need careful human attention. For those financing requests that a computer can process, the customer can be given a response in minutes.

Exhibit 8.11   Elapsed Time / Work Time

A large ratio of total elapsed time to do a job to the actual work time involved occurs when there are many hand-overs and waiting lines, as in Exhibit 9.4 A large ratio indicates that reengineering is needed.

	Elapsed Time	Work Time	Ratio
Completing a customer's order	3 weeks	6 hours	27
Acceptance of a credit request	8 days	2 hours	32
Processing an insurance policy	20 days	3 hours	53
Processing a mortgage application	3 weeks	1 hour	120
Contract negotiation between lawyers	6 months	6 hours	173
Responding to a customer query	3 days	5 minutes	288

Many processes that are basically information processing take weeks. These can be shrunk to minutes if computers can process the straightforward cases and get the right information to the right people for quick decision making about the more-difficult cases.

Lawyers are notorious for creating delays. A massive consulting firm, which advocated that its clients reengineer their processes to minimize cycle time, took six months to agree on one simple contract. The contract was boilerplate with minor modifications, each of which had to be examined by a lawyer on the other side. The actual work for the whole contract totaled a few hours, but the eventual elapsed time was six months. Each modification sat in an "in" basket until the lawyer on the other side could "get around to it." Nobody dared suggest that the two lawyers should each have a computer connected by a phone line, and should interact in real time.

When I worked for IBM, IBM "censored" the textbooks I wrote to look for violations of IBM policy. It always took longer to censor a textbook than to write it.

Simultaneous Engineering

The elapsed-time–work-time ratio *can be less than 1.* To achieve this low ratio, work activities have to take place simultaneously. A complex time-critical process should be designed so that work activities go on in tandem. When a company redesigns a product, the design work may partially overlap with prototyping activities. Planning of the production facilities may coincide with the design. Creating a marketing campaign may overlap with the detailed design and manufacturing planning. This is referred to as "simultaneous engineering."

One-Person Value Stream

A useful way to think about most value streams is to ask, If a single person operated the entire value stream, with the goal of fully satisfying the value-stream customer, what would that person do? The one person might need help from specialists, work groups, or new computer systems. Sometimes it is more sensible to think about a small tightly knit team rather than one person. With complex operations such as constructing a skyscraper or designing a jet fighter, the one-person question may not be helpful. But for processing an insurance claim, responding to a customer order, purchasing materials, obtaining a mortgage approval, and conducting most of the ordinary processes of business, the question makes good sense. It should be assumed that the one person or team has the necessary information systems (often not yet in place) and that the work is automated where possible.

Sometimes value streams are redesigned so as to give one person the task of meeting each customer's needs or of being in charge of that work. This person is sometimes called a *case worker* or *case manager*. The customer then interacts with one person who pays attention creatively to keeping the customer happy. A large insurance company, for example, may have many case workers for arranging insurance and many for the different value stream of claims settlement.

A one-person value stream differs from a value stream that bounces around multiple functional areas. One person eliminates error-prone handovers. No work sits for days in "in" baskets. Nothing slips between the cracks. Work is designed to meet the goals of the customer rather than those of function managers who do not think about the customer. Because the case worker spends his entire time thinking about his customers, he can grow to understand their needs very well and can invent ways of pleasing his customers. He can think about how to eliminate work and meet the customer needs as fast as possible. Many customer needs that might have taken days to respond to in the past can be handled immediately if a call can be routed to the right individual with the right computer system.

When credit-card users find errors in the processing of their transactions, for example, the credit company may have to perform between ten and forty work steps, mostly done by different people. Sometimes the customer writes a letter and the bank writes back. In some cases, after working months to resolve a problem, a bank tells the customers, "We can't find the record." Citibank reinvented this process, using image processing. Now, when the customer calls, the call is switched to a person at a personal computer that can display an image of the credit slip in question. Usually the error can be corrected while the customer is on the telephone, and the customer's next bill is adjusted accordingly. The ten to forty work steps are replaced by one, and only exceptional cases need more than one.

USAA, the United Services Automobile Association, reengineered its systems so that it can deal with customer car-insurance concerns while the customer is on the telephone. The insurance company aims to give the best customer service.

A customer's file can be accessed electronically and problems can be dealt with over the phone. About 15 hundred agents in locations across America can immediately retrieve documents from a central database. The document, which is sharp and clear on the computer screen, can show details of customers, policies, car crashes, police reports, pictures of the wreckage, maps of what happened. The avoidance of paper processing enables USAA to give better service to customers, do better selling, and settle claims more quickly.

USAA receives more than 10 thousand pieces of mail per day. It scans these into an electronic folder system. An agent can retrieve any letter immediately if a customer calls. The property and casualty unit loses only 2 percent of its customers per year, versus an industry average of 10 percent.

In addition to providing better service, the system saved USAA about $4 million per year.

Unhealthy Value Streams

Some value streams are more in need of reinvention than others. Some, very inefficient (in terms of customer satisfiers), can achieve major improvements. A value stream with a large elapsed-time–work-time ratio, for example, can be redesigned to give much faster responses to its customers, where that is important. If there are multiple steps with waiting lines of work at each stage, there is broad scope for shrinking the elapsed time. Exhibit 8.12 lists symptoms that usually indicate unhealthy value streams, in which much can be gained by reinvention.

What Should You Redesign First?

Corporations cannot rebuild all their value streams at once. When they map out their value streams they need to decide which to rebuild first.

A variety of criteria affect the decision. Certain value streams may be clearly cumbersome or broken and in urgent need of repair. One or more may be exceptionally important. There may be one for which the customers are demanding better service, faster response, or better quality. Competition may be meeting customer needs better. One or more value streams may need to be reengineered to produce results at substantially lower cost.

Often the value streams that are re-created first are the ones for which it is easiest to achieve impressive results. The low-hanging fruit is picked first. Some value streams are relatively easy to rebuild, others require traumatic upheaval. It makes sense to start with the easy ones.

Some may have an exceptionally large pay-off such as cutting cycle time from weeks to days or from days to an immediate response. It may appear possible to eliminate a major group of work activities or a major set of costs.

Exhibit 8.12 Symptoms of unhealthy value streams

- The value stream crosses many functions and involves many narrowly defined jobs.
- There are multiple hand-overs from one department to another.
- There is a high elapsed-time–work-time ratio.
- The value stream has no clear manager or owner.
- Primary employee motivators are unrelated to the value-stream customer.
- Corporate politics abounds.
- Inspection finds many flaws so that products must be sent back for rework.
- Unusual situations cause excessive delay.
- Managers try to increase the number of people working for them.
- There is a major gap between what the customer would consider ideal and what actually occurs.

Sometimes an experienced consulting organization recommends a value-stream reinvention and seems confident that it can be done. Some accept payment on the basis of a measurable improvement. Sound help from the outside may give management confidence to go ahead. A corporation may have decided to initiate a new set of activities, create a subsidiary, or move into a new business area. This new initiative should be designed *from the start* as a set of value streams optimally designed and managed so as to please customers. It is often easier to build value-stream management into a new organization than to change an old organization.

When Should You Avoid Rebuilding Value Streams?

Just as it makes sense to pick the low-hanging fruit first, so it also makes sense to avoid the fruit that is too difficult or risky to pick. A value stream snarled in heavy politics may be a situation to avoid. Management should perform risk analysis (discussed later) and avoid invention where the risks of failure appear higher than benefits warrant. The new ideas may need new computer systems that are beyond the organization's ability to create with assurance.

The payoff from reinventing some of the value streams may be low. It is not worth the trauma. If the risk is high and the payoff is not, find something else to do.

The reinvention effort needs a business sponsor who believes in it and who is absolutely determined to make it succeed. Without a clear sponsor who has management clout, it should not be done. If the commitment is lukewarm, there is a high probability of failure. Value-stream reinvention should not go ahead unless the CEO is *absolutely determined to make it succeed* and to overcome the inevitable obstacles. Management must say, "Damn the torpedoes, we're going to get there."

Exhibit 8.13

Reasons for Choosing a Value Stream to Reinvent	*Reasons for Avoiding Reinvention of a Value Stream*
<ul><li>It is broken.</li><li>Results would be dramatic.</li><li>It is of strategic importance.</li><li>It has core capability and if excellent would achieve a major competitive advantage.</li><li>The customer is demanding better results.</li><li>Competition is close.</li><li>It would not be difficult to achieve.</li><li>Easy gains are possible.</li><li>It is possible to cut costs substantially.</li><li>An experienced consulting firm is confident of success.</li><li>A new subsidiary or operation is being established.</li></ul>	<ul><li>There would be no dramatic results.</li><li>The politics are problematical.</li><li>The process is excessively complicated.</li><li>There is no business sponsor.</li><li>Management determination to succeed is lukewarm.</li><li>The risks of failure are high.</li><li>New IT systems that appear difficult to build would be needed.</li><li>Inadequate skills are available.</li><li>Other changes on the horizon might interfere.</li></ul>

Simultaneous rebuilding of multiple value streams is usually not a good idea, but sometimes the values streams interact in complex ways. Changes in one value stream must be coordinated with those in other processes. An attempt to shorten the time to bring products to market, for example, may need to involve the production value stream, customer interaction, product design, customer service, logistics, and finance. The more complex the entanglements, the more difficult it is to succeed. The situations chosen for reengineering may be deliberately simplified to minimize their interfaces to other value streams, at least initially (Exhibit 8.13).

Strategic Value Streams

To achieve long-term success when markets and products are changing rapidly, a corporation needs certain core capabilities at which it does extremely well. These capabilities are often value streams of special importance. The strategic-visioning process of Enterprise Engineering (described in Part V) should identify what a corporation wants to excel at and should determine how this strategic capability can be built to a world-class level. Some corporations have developed a strategic value stream to a level that the competition cannot emulate. They have become "capability predators," having a capability that enables them to expand vigorously into a new areas, capture business repeatedly from the competition, or take over competing corporations and make them more profitable (Chapter 24).

Sony steadily developed a capability to design miniaturized electronics and introduce variations on its products at an astonishing rate. Benetton invented a worldwide system for responding to the fickle fashion demands of teen-agers much faster than its competition. Hewlett-Packard dramatically shrank the time to design and manufacture new products. Banc A built a capability that enabled its bankers to learn much more about their customers and sink deeper roots into their community than competitors. Banc A became so good at its reengineered capability that it set out on a takeover binge, acquiring other banks and increasing their value.

Identifying what value stream or streams are strategic is important. These are the top-priority candidates for value-stream reengineering. To build a value stream that provides a *unique* competitive advantage requires impressive new invention or the building of unique and complex technology or software. The reengineering of a core capability may need extremely complex computer and network systems. Sometimes a corporation decides to focus intensely on the "predator" capability while allowing everything else to be "business as usual."

Fluidity

Some forms of business process redesign have created processes that are tightly tuned for one activity but are difficult to adapt. When changes occur, as they do today with startling speed, the tightly tuned process may be harmful because it cannot be adapted. A vital characteristic of value-stream reinvention is the creation of value-stream teams that can adapt when they need to.

Done correctly, value-stream reinvention increases, not decreases, flexibility and adaptability.

Evolutionary Transition

Making the transition from a traditional hierarchy of functions and processes to a value-stream organization is difficult, time-consuming, and fraught with both human and system problems. There is a large graveyard of failed attempts at business reengineering. A corporation can be mapped and possibly organized in terms of value streams before any major attempt is made to implement reinvented value streams. This is illustrated in Exhibits 8.14 and 8.15. The processes shown in Exhibits 8.14 and 8.15 are the same. In principle the same departments can be retained while executives oversee value streams instead of functions. This does not by itself improve the efficiency of the enterprise, but it sets the enterprise up for improvement. Each value-stream executive can go to work to streamline his value stream. The executive can be motivated and measured in terms of success with value-stream reinvention.

A major change in computer systems is needed when an enterprise is

Exhibit 8.14 Traditional division of an organization into functions and processes

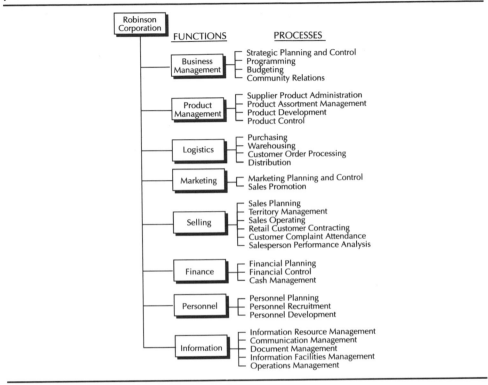

changed to a value-stream structure. The IT organization can map out the enterprise as in Exhibit 8.15 rather than 8.14, and then steadily make plans for the systems, data models, object models, networks, and so on. It can plan evolutionary reengineering of the systems and make sure that new systems support the new organization.

Often the best option for an existing corporation is to establish new units organized in the new way. It is easier to start afresh than to reengineer an organization with deeply entrenched culture, politics, and complex mainframe computers. The choice between reengineering old units and building new units is a vital part of Enterprise Engineering.

Start-up Corporations

Start-up corporations can adopt efficient business practices from the start. Many new corporations are now being designed with a value-stream architecture rather than purely hierarchical architecture. Executives manage values streams, not the

Exhibit 8.15

This chart shows the same corporation as Exhibit 8.14 organized as value streams and processes instead of according to functions and processes. The processes in this exhibit and Exhibit 8.14 are the same.

A corporation can be reorganized in terms of value streams while temporarily retaining most of the departments of the previous organization. Each value-stream executive is then challenged to reinvent his value stream to make it as efficient as possible.

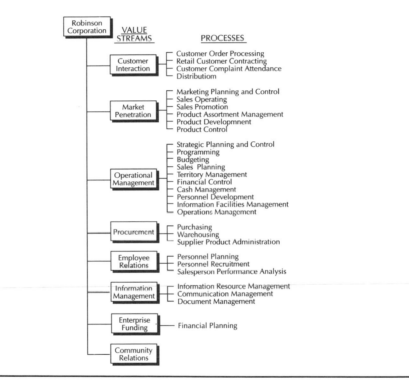

functional silos of Exhibit 7.4, and in this way please their customers better than many large corporations. If large corporations do not reconstruct themselves, their business will rapidly be eroded by new corporations giving better customer satisfaction.

Benetton reinvented the clothing business. Wal-Mart reinvented retailing. Sun Microsystems changed the computer business. Dell became a billion-dollar company at a rate unheard of before the 1980s without creating an original-looking machine; it reinvented how personal computers should be sold—by mail order.

The assets of large corporations become liabilities when they cannot be adapted to customers' needs as well as corporations with new value streams targeted at delighting their customers.

Many new corporations are growing in developing countries. The new growth in the eastern Pacific rim (other than Japan) is phenomenal. These new corporations do not have baggage from the past or "legacy" computer systems. They are building new, from scratch, with new ideas, hoping that the older corporations take a long time to reinvent themselves.

References

1. Antony Jay, *Management and Machiavelli* (Holt, Rinehart & Winston: New York, 1967).
2. "The Man Who Speaks His Mind on GM," *Detroit Free Press*, November 25, 1986, Business Section, p. 1.
3. T. H. Davenport, *Process Innovation, Reengineer Work Through Information Technology* (Harvard Business School Press: Boston, 1993).
4. G. Stalk Jr., and T. H. Hout, *Competing Against Time* (The Free Press: New York, 1990).
5. Davenport.

9

Outrageous Goals

Dramatic Improvement

Value-stream reinvention is concerned not with *improving* existing processes but with *scrapping* and *replacing* them. When we replace processes, the challenge is to do something dramatically better—something that would not be possible with incremental improvement. Technology brings changes that would have seemed like a miracle to earlier generations, and today new technology is arriving at a furious rate. When we replace a value stream, we must brainstorm about how new technology, and new use of teams and virtuosos, can enable us to achieve results that would not have been possible a few years ago.

Working windmills changed the landscape of Europe three hundred years before it was realized that *ships* could be operated with wind. James Watt patented a perfected version of his steam engine in 1769, and the machine was used for a variety of purposes. Thirty-six years later Napoleon's fleet was defeated at the Battle of Trafalgar. After Trafalgar, Napoleon still wanted to invade England, but the British sailing ships were too vigilant. If a value-stream consultant had worked with Napoleon, he would have asked how technology could be used to help meet the customer's desire: to invade England. The first boat propelled by steam was the tug *Charlotte Dundas* three years before the Battle of Trafalgar. With steam tugs Napoleon could have crossed the English Channel unimpeded on a windless day.

In the electronics industry when the microchip replaced the transistor, massive improvements became possible. The old designs were scrapped and replaced. In a similar way empowered value-stream teams with information technology are replacing the multiple queues and handovers of traditional business functions. Most processes in today's corporations were designed for an era long since gone, so massive improvements are achievable.

When a value stream is reinvented, it is desirable to set goals. (The term *outrageous goals* is used.) We should be looking not for minimal improvements but for radical changes, like CitiCorp's cutting its time to respond to requests for mortgages from 30 to 60 days and then to 15 minutes for most cases. Exhibit 9.1 shows examples of goals that were considered outrageous when proposed.

The risks and upheaval caused by scrapping and replacing value streams are worthwhile only if the benefits are great.

High-Level Questions

When setting goals, it is important to ask high-level questions, not low-level ones. Instead of Can we improve the efficiency of the branch offices? ask Why do we need branch offices if salesmen have notebook computers and network links to corporate systems? Instead of Can we get lower-cost airfares? ask Can we avoid the need to fly by using video conferencing, workstation networks, or locally empowered teams? Instead How can we reduce the cost of invoice processing? ask How can we eliminate invoices?

The value-stream focus helps to address high-level questions. How do we deliver results to the customer in the most simple, direct way? As we focus on customer needs, what work can be eliminated? How can we minimize value-stream cycle time?

Value-stream designers must ask new questions:

- Who are the value-stream customers?
- How can we delight the customers?
- How can we do this in the simplest, most-direct way?
- What current problems need to be solved?
- How can we minimize value-stream costs?
- How can we make the new value stream fluid and flexible?
- How can we design the new value stream so that it constantly improves?
- What outrageous goals may be achievable?

Exhibit 9.1   Examples of goals that seemed outrageous when proposed

- Respond to customer requests in a day, not 20 days.
- Have complete information about a customer, including personal information, available when a customer telephones.
- Deal with errors in credit cards while the customer is on the phone by electronically displaying the credit slip.
- Eliminate invoices.
- Eliminate purchase orders by having the supplier continuously replenish the stock.
- Respond to requests for credit within an hour.
- Cut defect rate to 3.4 in a million (six-sigma quality).
- Cut software error rate to 3.4 bugs per million lines of code (an IBM goal).
- Cut supermarket shelf restocking time from 6 weeks to a day.
- Cut time to design and produce new products from 4 years to one.
- Cut application software development time from 2 years to 4 months.
- Cut the television studio staff from 40 to 6.
- Eliminate branch sales office.
- Enable salesmen to generate a proposal while at the customer site, and modify it as needed.
- Tailor insurance contracts to individual customer needs.
- Build top-quality luxury cars in the same cycle time as mass-market cars.

Aladdin's Lamp

Technology makes things possible that were not possible before. When new technologies come into existence, however, we do not grasp their possibilities quickly.

One way to help put technology to use is to focus on the customer. If the customer had Aladdin's lamp, what might he wish for? Could that wish possibly be achieved with technology? If not, could a modified version of the wish be made practical?

You go into a music store, for example. What might you, as the customer, wish for? Many hundreds of thousands of recordings have been made, but the store has only a few thousand. Much of what you would like to buy is not in the store but "out of print." You like comedy in music and would like to know what Alan Sherman recorded, perhaps exploring this in a computerized catalog. There were many Alan Sherman recordings, but the store says it has never heard of him and certainly does not stock any Alan Sherman disks. Aladdin's Lamp: The customer might wish to buy *anything* that has been recorded and buy it now! Is this possible?

CD music is digital. A central library of recordings could keep one digital copy of everything. Any copy could be transmitted to the music store on request. With a T3 circuit, an hour of digital music takes about 40 seconds to transmit in CD format or 8 seconds in the compressed format of the Sony minidisk. It could be recorded on a writable optical disk (such as the Sony minidisk). A high-speed recording device might be used so as not to keep the customer waiting. A color label or booklet could also be transmitted and printed. The customer could have any recording he wished.

IBM signed a contract with the Blockbuster music stores to do this.

The customer might wish to receive the music at home and not go into the music store. With an ISDN circuit to the home, an hour of music might be transmitted in an hour and recorded on a Sony minidisk; over a phone circuit it would take longer. A music-on-demand service could be designed to allow *any* music ever recorded to be transmitted to the home. New technology opens up many new business opportunities.

Many customers and executives are afraid to rub the Aladdin's lamp. Their imagination is constrained by what current procedures achieve. It might seem ridiculous to think of responding to a mortgage request in 15 minutes, rather than 30 days, or to resolve credit-card errors while the customer is on the phone, or to eliminate invoices, or to cut inventory-holding costs to zero (by making the supplier maintain the inventory and paying only when the goods are used), or for an insurance company to pay insured drivers at the scene of the accident. All of these are being done.

What would delight the customers of a real-estate firm selling houses? Today they are being driven around by salespeople and may see three houses in a day—often houses that do not meet clearly specified needs. Many good-candidate houses are not seen at all. The customer would like a much faster process. Imagine a computer showing a map of the area with dots representing all the houses for sale. The buyer can operate sliders on the screen to indicate the price range, number of bedrooms, distance from where he works, size of garage, yard, and so on. A smaller number of dots appears and disappears as the sliders move, showing houses that fit the buyer's preferences. The buyer can then explore electronically the houses, looking at multiple pictures or video clips and doing some price negotiation before visiting a house. The buyer may even want to do this electronic exploration not from the area of the house but from his present location, perhaps on a computer of the corporation that is relocating him.

What Does the Customer *Really* Need?

Value-stream designers should repeatedly brainstorm about the question What does the customer *really* need? This fundamental question can lead to goals' being set that would have seemed outrageous before today's technology.

Otis customers want *no* elevator failures. This requires an endless drive for solutions to all causes of failure. A breakthrough came when Otis built electronics into their elevators that send radio messages to maintenance engineers. The electronics can then be designed for *preventive* maintenance. A weak item is detected that has not failed yet, or a redundant item has failed, so a message is sent to the maintenance person. Many types of machines can be designed to send messages by radio or data link to maintenance staff. A pill box can send a radio signal to a medical computer each time it is opened; a doctor can then know if this patient is failing to take pills that are needed.

When the question is asked What does the customer *really* need? The answer may change the business. Ben and Jerry's may ask an insurance company to cover the contingency of a refrigeration failure in their ice-cream warehouses. What do they really want? They want *no* refrigeration failure. The insurance company may decide to offer them no-failure refrigeration, deciding that it can manage the risk better if *it* manages the refrigeration function, negotiating with the various equipment vendors to create no-failure refrigeration.

Future clinics in the age of human-gene analysis may offer patients long-term programs of *preventive* medicine on the grounds that they can determine from the individual's genes what medical dangers an individual is susceptible to. It may make sense for such a clinic also to offer medical insurance to customers whose genes it has analyzed.

Speed

A particularly important goal in many competitive situations is speed. Value-stream reinvention often permits much-faster operations. Exhibit 5.6 contains various examples of those.

There are two main reasons why a major decrease in time is possible. First, the many waiting piles and hand-overs illustrated in Exhibit 9.3 are avoided. Second, operations can be done concurrently that were previously done sequentially.

If a goal is speed, a value-stream team can be designed that can move fast. It should relentlessly attack every bottleneck until none remain.

Reducing cycle time is a clear, straightforward goal that has many benefits. Inventory and work in progress can be reduced. Errors and failures can be found and corrected quickly. A corporation can be made more responsive to its customers. By filling orders fast a company can reduce its customers' inventory-carrying costs and hence have a competitive edge.

Iomega Corporation took 28 days to manufacture a disk drive. After reengineering the time was cut to 1.5 days. This saved $6 million a year in inventory-carrying costs, on sales of about $100 million. It saved many more millions by making it easier to find the cause of defects. When defects were found at the end of 28-day production cycle, it was very difficult to pinpoint their cause and correct it. This became much easier with the 1.5-day cycle.

Wassan Paper Mills Company had large, wealthy competitors. It could not spend half a billion dollars on new high-volume equipment as they did.

Instead the company decided that it could have a competitive edge if it filled orders faster than its big competitors. If it could fill orders in one day instead of many days, it could eliminate its customers' need to carry expensive inventory. Wassan reengineered its order-to-delivery value stream so that it succeeded in filling 95 percent of its orders in less than 24 hours.

From 1988 to the end of 1992, John Young, the CEO of Hewlett-Packard (HP) made a dramatic turnaround in that company by reengineering everything for speed. The time from concept to first delivery of new printers was cut from 4.5 years to 22 months; Young then set out to drive it down to 10 months. On many products he *halved* the time from concept of a new product to profitability of that product.

Products were redesigned so that they could be manufactured in the most automated way, cutting out as many manual steps as possible and cutting out the possibilities for manufacturing defects. HP spent more money up front on good design in order to lessen the number of changes that would be made later that cause a chain reaction of delays. Profits could be increased by spending an extra 50 percent on development of a product in order to deliver it six months earlier. The faster a product came out, the sooner it could be refined and improved.

Achieving speed in new-product creation required coordinating actions that spanned research, development, manufacturing, marketing, interaction with suppliers, and interaction with out-sourced manufacturers. This tight coordination called for horizontal teams that spanned the traditional functions. John Young carved up HP's bureaucracy, cut out two layers of management, axed many committees, and created value-stream teams that could integrate the cross-functional activities.

Instant Results

Where a process involves obtaining information for a customer and perhaps making a decision using that information, the process may be reengineered to save time. Something that took days or weeks may be done while the customer is on the telephone.

The "outrageous goal" in some processes should be "instant" response. This can often be achieved by having an empowered person equipped with a computer system designed to provide "instant" information.

Instant Information

One of the most important characteristics of information technology is that it frees information from the constraints of geography and time. Any information can be made available at any place at any time. Information on paper is tied to a physical location. Someone has to search a filing cabinet for it or deliver a report. If copied, stacks of paper accumulate in disorganized piles. Paper information is mailed and sorted. Secretaries have to file it. A nurse in a typical hospital walks about 8 miles per day. If the hospital computer systems make information available where she is (for example in or near the patient's room), she need walk only 2 miles per day so that she can spend her time doing what she wants to do—nursing.

Information in electronic form can be retrieved anywhere at any time. Electrons travel in a flash. If the right networks and software are installed, a person with a portable computer can access information from databases across the enterprise. The information can be well organized and up to date.

Information about purchase orders can be available at every location where goods arrive so that the shipment can be immediately correlated with the purchase order. There need be no invoices and no problems trying to reconcile shipping notices, dock-receipt forms, invoices, and purchase orders. When the shipment is received and validated, the purchaser's and vendor's electronic files are updated, and payment is automatically triggered. Processes like these become much simpler, faster, and much less work.

Information about retailer sales can go immediately to wholesalers and to the factory. The factory can plan production with up-to-the-minute knowledge of sales. When latex is shipped from Malaysia, Goodyear's factory in the United States knows its quality before shipment and can plan production accordingly.

Information relating to all aspects of a value stream can be available to the value-stream team even though the team is in different locations.

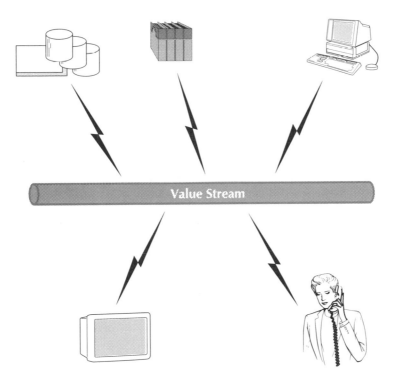

The value-stream team should have electronic access to any information the members need to do their work and satisfy their customers (internal or external). IT systems should be designed for value-stream effectiveness, not stovepipe functions.

Image Processing

In spite of information technology, much information is still on paper. People still search filing cabinets. Image processing takes us a step further toward paperless information. With image processing, systems documents are fed into a machine, which digitizes them. Pictures, signatures, and corporate logos are all stored in digital form along with the text—no keypunching. Credit-card slips, accident reports, pictures of real estate, signed documents, and so on can now be transmitted, stored in databases, and made accessible at work-station screens. With this technology almost no information cannot be made accessible electronically at the time and place it is needed in the value-stream processes. When a customer telephones, his file can be accessed electronically from any location, and problems can be dealt with while he is on the telephone. The avoidance of paper processing saves USAA considerable money; but, more important, it enables the corporation to give better service to customers, do better selling, and settle claims more quickly.

Oticon, a Danish hearing-aids company, had a CEO who aggressively changed the organization and cut the product-development cycle time from 2½ years to 11 months.

The CEO banned all paper, decreeing that it must be shredded after its contents have been scanned into computer systems. Every employee (with a handful of exceptions) had the same standard work station. Employees were not tied to one office but could do the same work from any work station. The employees moved, not the equipment. This provided great flexibility in changing work processes.

The paperless, boundaryless environment came as a shock to some employees. Employees who could not cope were coached, but some left; the best employees stayed and rapidly climbed a learning curve with the new methods.

The CEO, like Attilla the Hun, was an absolute driving force behind the changes.

Speech Storage

Like paper documents, speech can be stored electronically. Comments from various people can be linked to documents. An executive reading a report need not dictate his reactions to a secretary; he can point to locations in the text and speak his comments. The document is then stored and transmitted with his spoken words.

If you have an emergency and dial 911 (999 in the United Kingdom) someone types details of what you say into a computer. The person receiving the message may get part of it wrong, especially if you are upset and agitated. It would be better to store the sound of you voice in the computer. The police or ambulance can then hear your directions firsthand as they drive to the scene of the emergency. No errors.

Television can also be digitized and stored in a computer. The U.S. Federal Aviation Administration has an executive information system with which executives can see summaries of information that might be important to them. This system has been built to display video windows on a computer screen where appropriate. It may be important to see video clips of a plane crash or news commentary that might affect the actions they take.

Today anything can be electronic—text, speech, diagrams, photographs, video, handwriting, fingerprints, voice prints, signatures. Any information can be stored anywhere, replicated endlessly, and transmitted around the world over optical fibers at the speed of light. However, our enterprises were designed before the instantaneous movement of information. Expensive computers were installed without redesigning the flow of work—without reinventing employment. Enterprises are still designed as though information had to be filed in one place.

Electronic documents should not be imitations of paper documents. They bring new benefits. The first cars were called "horseless carriages" and looked as though they were designed to be pulled by a horse. It took years to realize that a good shape for a car is different. Radio was originally called "wireless telegraphy"; it took years to realize that the great application of radio was broadcasting, which has no resemblance to telegraphy. Similarly the "paperless office" should have little resemblance to offices designed for paper. In fact one should question whether there should be an office at all. We must ask What can we do with electronic information that we cannot do with paper?

The world's airlines were completely reinvented with links from travel-agent computers to airline computers, worldwide. Fare structures changed, with airlines allocating multiple prices and deals to the seats, trying to maximize load factors and revenue electronically. Electronics made frequent-flier programs possible.

Intelligent Documents

Electronic documents can be "intelligent." The document becomes an object that has its own behavior with programmed "methods." An "intelligent purchase order," for example, can monitor a customer's inventory. It springs into action when the inventory falls below a certain level and transmits itself to the screen of a person who can authorize it, sets off alarms if it does not receive authorization on time, triggers the shipment of goods, watches for acknowledgment, monitors the correct receipt of goods, monitors whether payment is received, and takes action if payment is late.

When documents are electronic and intelligent, work flow needs complete reinvention, which should revolve around the teams designed to use technology to please value-stream customers.

When Paradigms Shift

One "outrageous" goal should be to change procedures overnight when that is a desirable response to changes in competition, customer demand, or new ideas. A value-stream team can be ready to change quickly, but it may need an infrastructure that supports rapid change. A factory may be designed so that its layout can be changed rapidly; workers can change dies or create a new set-up quickly. In the past, computer systems put procedures in a straight-jacket. Now computer systems should be designed that allow for rapid change and software regenerated rapidly with modern tools.

When changes come at a rapid rate, the large hierarchical firm is likely to be the last to change. The silo executives continue to run their silos with the same rules. In contrast, a value-stream team is very aware that changes are happening. It is listening to its customers and adapting its behavior so as to constantly please them. It is perhaps because we have entered an era of fast change and paradigm shifts that value-stream teams have become recognized as so valuable. They are fast, fluid, flexible, and focused on their customers' changing needs. When radical change comes, they recognize it.

An executive put in charge of restoring a "broken" company commented to us, "It is because it was so successful for so long that its procedures became so ingrained. It assumed all the answers had been found. It became withdrawn into itself." This could describe many once-great companies. Rigid functionally oriented procedures must be replaced with value-stream teams constantly alert to changes, new competition, and new customer needs. In an era of change, the most dangerous form of management is self-perpetuating functional managers with shared assumptions and rigid rules.

> *A small company can shift its behavior fast when it needs to. Value-stream teams can give a large company the flexibility of a small company, while retaining economies of scale of a large company, such as having a large-sales force.*

The Value Stream as a Learning Laboratory

A value-stream team can make major improvements without doing anything particularly original if it replaces the long waits, stovepipes, and hand-overs of the traditional hierarchical organization. It is better if the value-stream teams go further, however, and constantly search for ways to improve the value stream, some of which may require major innovation. The value-stream team has clear goals; it should be highly innovative in the pursuit of those goals. The aim of the team should be to innovate faster than the competition. It often makes sense for a value-stream team to do research and experiments. In effect the value-stream team can operate somewhat as a research-and-development (R and D) organization, focused on improving the value stream and climbing a learning curve as rapidly as possible.

In many corporations experiments are done only in the R and D laboratory, which is isolated from where day-to-day business is done. The laboratory may produce breakthrough ideas, but they are unrelated to today's processes. Research and experimentation is often needed to improve today's processes. The best people to do that are sometimes the teams established to operate a reinvented value stream. The value-stream organization may be run like a learning laboratory. Much of what has been learned about making R and D effective applies to the value-stream teams.

The teams may be trained in the skills needed to perform and evaluate experiments. These skills include the design of experiments, statistical methods, and graphical techniques that permit comparison of a large number of alternatives, techniques for diagramming complex work flows that foster changes in work-flow design, brainstorming, and creativity techniques.

In Chapter 31 that idea is applied to how some corporations, (for example,

Chaparral Steel) have dramatically improved their competitive position by running entire corporations as learning laboratories.

Often a starting point for research in how to improve the value stream is to find examples of value streams in other corporations from which ideas can be taken. Similar values streams may be found in different types of corporation. A manufacturer may learn about improving mail-order fulfillment from a mail order house. It may learn about just-in-time logistics from a retail chain such as Wal-Mart. Often the most powerful insights come from looking outside one's own environment to gain a new perspective. Companies in a different business from one's own can be fertile sources of ideas.

Ongoing investigation can ensure that the best industry practices are uncovered, picked apart, modified as appropriate, and put to use. The search for such practices can be a disciplined process: systematic identification of candidates to study, analysis of what is exceptional in their processes, brainstorming about how the best ideas can be adapted, and measurement of the benefits gained in implementing them.

Value-stream R and D activities may involve setting up experiments and pilot programs, changing computer systems being prototyped, and so on. The knowledge infrastructure should make the fruits of the research and learning available to everyone. This R and D can be done by value-stream teams or by a group that supports the teams. The best new ideas often come from the teams themselves when they are encouraged to brainstorm and experiment.

Best-practice research is a state of mind. It needs everybody involved with the value stream to constantly search for new ideas and debate how they may be adapted. Instead of "not invented here," the attitude should be "steal ideas shamelessly" (SIS), a phrase used by the Milliken Corporation.

Often there are multiple value-stream teams working on one type of value stream. One of these teams may establish a demonstration project to explore a new way of working. Much may be learned on the demonstration project before it is transferred to other teams. Demonstration projects are usually more integrated and complex than ongoing experiments. They may represent a clean-slate break with the past. They use new processes that the corporation hopes to spread to all value-stream teams of that type but that need to climb a substantial learning curve first. Rapid on-the-job learning results from applying the new approach. Once its learning curve approaches a plateau, the demonstration project may be transferred to other teams, perhaps with transfer of team members now experienced in the new approach.

Sometimes a dramatic change to the value stream can be achieved if a major IT system is built. The right team with the right computing can be unbeatable. We need the best combination of IT linked to human care, skill, and attention to customers. Wal-Mart built a logistics system, for example, for getting the right goods in the right quantities at the right time to the shelves of its shops. The reengineering of the distribution value stream gave Wal-Mart a strategic capability beyond that of its competitors. VISA's member banks lost $125 million in 1992 from the counterfeiting of cards, but encryption codes of information VISA put

Exhibit 9.2   Creation and capture of knowledge in a learning laboratory enterprise[2]

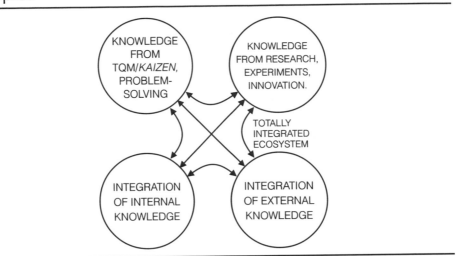

on the magnetic strip of credit cards cut the losses to $20 million or so in 1993.[1] An even larger saving resulted from automating "chargebacks," as described in Exhibit 1.1. The solution involved assigning to every transaction a unique identification number that identified the retailer and the issuing bank. This number always stayed with the transaction, making it easy to track the source of error and eliminate the manual work in chargebacks. Having a unique number for every transaction may necessitate very large numbers, but this is no problem for computers. Such a scheme can apply to many types of transactions. Enciphering transactions to avoid fraud can apply in many industries. Computer systems that get the right information to the right people at the right time are needed everywhere. Value-stream teams should be challenged to develop potential uses of IT, although they may need outside help to implement what they invent.

Aspects of Knowledge Acquisition

Exhibit 9.2 indicates four aspects of the accumulation of knowledge in an enterprise.

> *First*—Knowledge is acquired by the constant improvement that comes with *kaizen*/TQM activities. This is often best achieved with value-stream teams focused on doing their best for their customers or end users.
> *Second*—A knowledge infrastructure is needed to gather knowledge, store it, improve it, disseminate it, and put it to use. Components of the knowledge

Exhibit 9.3 A table contrasting R and D in a traditional enterprise with that in a learning-laboratory value stream

Traditional Enterprise	*Learning-Laboratory Value Stream*
R and D is done in an isolated laboratory.	Value-stream teams do constant R and D, searching for new ideas to integrate into the value-stream processes and products.
Experimentation is rarely done in functional departments or on the factory floor.	The value-stream organization constantly experiments to test better ways of operating.
Invention is the exclusive province of scientists or engineers.	The value-stream teams are challenged to invent.
"It it works, don't fix it."	"If it hasn't been improved recently, it's obsolete."
The R and D organization is isolated in its own area.	The value-stream organization does R and D jointly with suppliers and customers to climb a joint learning curve. It selects suppliers who are willing to help it extend its capability.
Only engineers build prototypes.	Prototypes of new processes and systems are set up to test them and solicit suggestions for improvement.
Functional managers are averse to risks and avoid actions with uncertain consequences.	Risk is accepted as an essential part of experiments to improve the value stream.
Failure is penalized.	Failure is not penalized otherwise experimentation is discouraged. The attitude is "If that didn't work, try something else."
Functional managers preserve the status quo.	Outrageous goals, which cannot be met without substantial innovation, are set.
Laboratory researchers explore the frontiers in a general way.	Value-stream researchers are highly targeted towards the goals of the value stream.
Employees are selected who fit in with today's procedures and do not "rock the boat."	Value-stream team members are selected who are likely to try new things, have innovative ideas, and communicate the results.

(continues)

Exhibit 9.3   Continued

Traditional Enterprise	*Learning-Laboratory Value Stream*
A not-invented-here attitude limits the adoption of ideas from elsewhere.	The value-stream organization constantly examines how other enterprises work, adapts their ideas, and applies benchmarks. The value-stream organization searches for ideas at conferences, at seminars, and in publications.

    infrastructure may include databases, computer-based training, expert systems, and information highways.

Third—Knowledge comes from research, experimentation, and innovation. Instead of being isolated in a remote laboratory, R & D should pervade the entire enterprise. There should be constant research and experimentation with processes.

Fourth—Much of the knowledge an enterprise needs exists outside the enterprise. Constant external learning, research, visits, benchmarking, joint ventures, and cooperation with affiliates can put external knowledge to use.

    The four aspects of knowledge accumulation summarized in Exhibit 9.2 need to be integrated. With value-stream teams constantly pushing the limits and a knowledge infrastructure, knowledge can accumulate from both internal and external sources.

References

1. "Digital Credit," *The Economist,* Sept. 25, 1993, page 119.
2. Dorothy Leonard-Barton, "The Factory as a Learning Laboratory," *Sloan Management Review,* Fall, 1992.

10

Customer-Delight Factors

Raving Fans

The goal of a corporate activity is often described as "satisfying the customers." A new value stream should aspire to do much more than this. It should set out to *delight* the customer. Most customers have low expectations; if these low expectations are met, they are "satisfied." In a world of intensifying global competition, this is not enough.

Ken Blanchard, famous for his One-Minute Manager books, uses the term *raving fans*.[1] He says: "Satisfied customers don't count these days. If you want a booming business you have to create Raving Fans."

Nissan set out to do that with its Infiniti car. It trains its dealers and employees to think of their potential buyers as "honored guests." They follow up each sale by looking for ways to create raving fans; for example, they might pick up the customer's car at the airport for routine service. If the ersatz-wood trim cracks but is not covered by the warranty, they replace it anyway. The expense generates an equivalent amount of good will. The raving fan will tell his friends.

The value-stream designers should ask, "What would delight the customer (external or internal)?" The designers should identify customer-delight goals, even if they do not yet know how to achieve them. We would avoid the commonly used term *customer satisfier*, because the goal is to not merely to satisfying but to create raving fans.

The Voice of the Customer

Much of an organization's learning ought to center on the customer. The designers of products and processes must listen acutely to the "voice of the customer." Future enterprise success ought to be defined in terms of responding to this voice. Amazingly, many organizations still listen to their own internal voice far more than the voice of the customer. They believe that they already know what the customer wants. They imagine the customer is saying what they want to hear. The corporation needs to take steps to capture the *actual* voice of the customer. What does this entail?

Exhibit 10.1

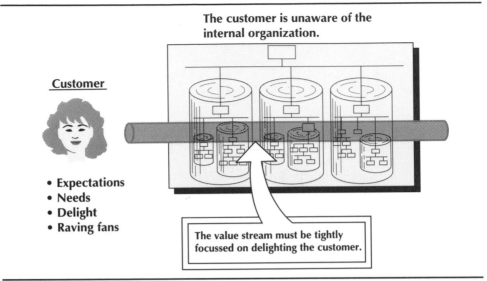

The customer is unaware of the internal organization.

Customer

- **Expectations**
- **Needs**
- **Delight**
- **Raving fans**

The value stream must be tightly focussed on delighting the customer.

Each individual customer experiences only certain aspects of the enterprise. These may be tangible, such as the taste of a food product, or intangible, such as the image of the food product. The enterprise, to customers is only a "black box," a mechanism that somehow produces what they want. Most customers are not interested in the processes inside the black box. They only experience results and judge their experience on the basis of their own unique set of needs, expectations, and beliefs at a given moment. Given this dynamic subjective judgment, value can only be defined from the customers' perspective. Value consists of the aggregate set of judgments that the market makes about the enterprise's products and services.

Organizational change must not simply focus on the "wiring" of the black box. Real customer-based value judgments are the criteria for deciding which internal work is effective and which ought to be eliminated in value-stream reinvention. In most of today's enterprises, no one person *owns* the entire value stream; no one person manages the set of activities that deliver value to the customer. After redesign the new value stream needs to focus narrowly on the customer, and one individual should be responsible for the value of the value stream as experienced by its customers.

Types of Customers

An organization may have many types of customers with different needs. The value-stream teams should be designed to focus on groups of customers who

Exhibit 10.2

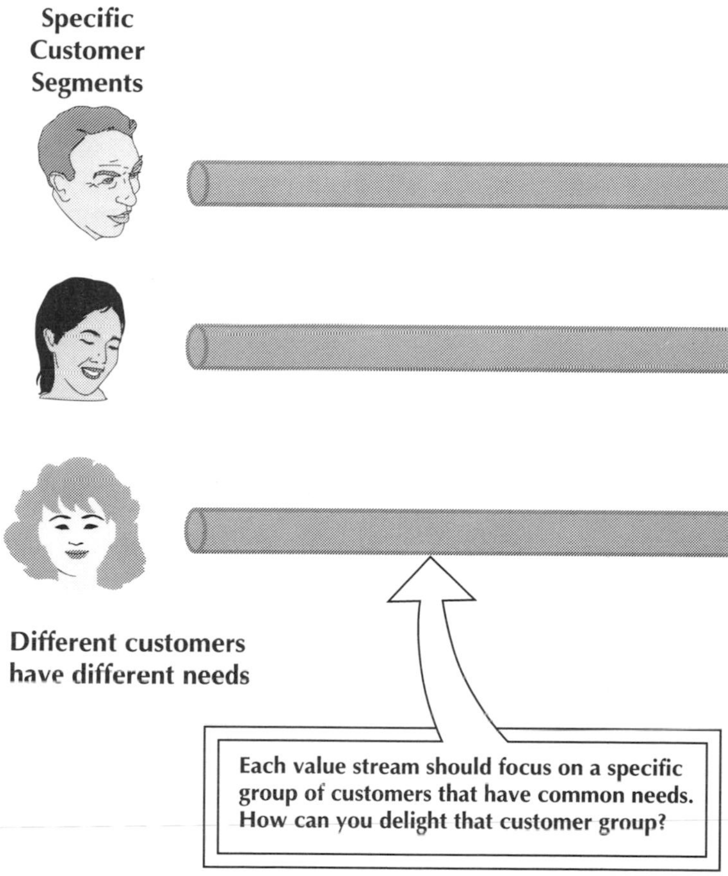

**Specific
Customer
Segments**

**Different customers
have different needs**

Each value stream should focus on a specific
group of customers that have common needs.
How can you delight that customer group?

have similar needs. For example, a travel agent has business travelers and tourists who want to explore new places. What would delight these two groups would be quite different. An insurance company may insure physicians; they have different needs from those of other people insured.

Even when different value-stream teams concentrate on different customer groups, *each customer is unique* and needs to be treated as such. The team must pay attention to each customer individually, not customers in general. The mass market of earlier decades has changed to a world in which each customer wants something special. Products or services are configured to individual customer needs. Delivery times match customers' just-in-time manufacturing plans.

The value-stream team (or individual) should deal directly with the problems and wishes of the customer. Whether a firm sells insurance, financial services, cars, magazines, or airline seats, it should know enough about its customers to tailor its product offerings to individuals. An airline can know that a frequent flyer likes a window seat. A telemarketing firm can answer the telephone with the customer's name. Insurance companies can customize their products to specific customer needs.

Customer needs must be considered as a whole; one unmet need is a weak link in a chain. It is essential that all of the customer's needs be met when a value stream is reengineered; value-stream reinvention considers all of the customer's interactions with the value stream. In the 1980s American auto makers made significant strides in improving product quality only to learn that competitors were providing improved service practices to delight customers. Meeting only the minimum needs of a customer may cause the loss of that customer.

Beyond-the-Call-of-Duty Awards

Employees who interact with customers in any way should be challenged to create raving fans. They should be encouraged to take actions beyond the call of duty to provide exceptional service.

In one store a customer wanted a particular present for his mother, but the store did not have the item. The store employee phoned competing stores, found the item, picked it up at lunch time, gift wrapped it, and phoned the customer to say he was personally delivering it to his mother. He created a raving fan.

Some companies have established a program for giving employees BCD (beyond the call-of-duty) awards. Candidates for such an award need careful monitoring and examination. When part of the award is lunch with top management, the message sent to all employees is that top management considers BCD behavior important. Customers may be made aware of BCD awards and asked to help nominate potential candidates. This makes customers aware of BCD stories and lets them know that the company is really trying to please them.

Raving-Fan Recipe

Ken Blanchard's and Sheldon Bowles's recipe for creating raving fans has three steps.[2]

1. *Decide what you want.* Create a vision of the service you want to deliver to delight the customer. Focus it narrowly on what you can do excellently.
2. *Discover what the customer wants.* Identify the customer's vision. Relate it to your own vision. Enhance the customer's vision or expand your own of what you will deliver as appropriate. Do not advertise more than what you will deliver.
3. *Deliver the vision plus one percent.* Deliver the vision consistently with no slips—but improve it repeatedly.

Unipart is a British company that makes components for cars. It was part of government-owned British Leyland and was privatized in 1986 with many shares being bought by employees. Unipart's factories would not have been competitive outside British Leyland's umbrella. Britain's financial community wanted Unipart to close down its factories and merely to distribute auto parts. However, Unipart's new management set out on a mission to improve the factories dramatically by fully empowering the workers.

Seminars were held for employees as part of the empowerment program, which began with a quote from Japan's Matsushita.

> We are going to win and the industrial West is going to lose. There is nothing you can do about it because the reasons for your failure are within yourselves. With your bosses doing the thinking while the workers wield the screwdriver, you are convinced deep down that this is the right way to run a business.

The employees set out to show the Japanese not only that they were empowered but that they could outsmart anyone in delivering results to customers. The turnaround produced a 19,000-percent increase in Unipart's privately traded employee shares.[3]

Among the programs started by Unipart was one that gave awards to employees or teams who went *beyond the call of duty* to service the customer. Customers knew about the program and could nominate anyone who they thought might deserve this award. Employees also nominated candidates. After careful examination award winners received two framed share certificates and a gold pin, and they attended a lunch with most of Unipart's top executives.

One award winner had been preparing to deliver an oil cooler to the Jaguar factory when he discovered that it was defective. It was late on a Friday, so he took the unit home with him. He worked on it for most of the weekend and delivered a fully working cooler at 8:00 A.M. Monday morning. More and more workers went "beyond the call of duty," until awards were given at the rate of four a month and every worker was looking for opportunities that might afford recognition.

Often a customer becomes a raving fan because an employee does something special for that customer—something not in the procedures manual. The value-stream team that deals with corporate customers should set itself the goal of creating raving fans.

The Importance of Customer Focus

When people at work do not focus on the needs of the customer, they invent all manner of procedures with no direct value. They are not asking, How do we delight the customer? or How do we give the best service? Instead they ask, How do we conform to such-and-such rules? or How do we hand the job over quickly to the next department? or How do we hide information to make next quarter's numbers look good? or What memos should we write to protect ourselves?

Internal procedures grow like weeds in a garden. They take on a life of their own. People ask, How do we improve the weeds, rather than How do we remove them?

Overstaffed organizations drift into introspection and corporate politics. They invent excessive controls. They spend increasing energy on internal matters rather than on pleasing the customer. The more this happens, the more difficult it is to change. There is an old saying: "The Devil makes work for idle hands." What are needed are lean value stream teams narrowly focused on meeting and surpassing customer needs.

The worst possible situation would be having no customer. Going through some border stations when driving from the United States of America to Canada takes longer than going through Checkpoint Charlie did in Berlin at the height of cold war. The border staff has no "customer." Guavas are not really looking for criminals. Smuggling from the United States of America to Canada is inconsequential. When asked what they are concerned about, guards say, "Enforcing the rules." The border guards at Checkpoint Charlie, with machine guns, were excited about their jobs. The Canadian border staff have nothing to be excited about. To give themselves some feeling of importance, some guards resort to harassing travelers to demonstrate their power. If such bureaucracy were eliminated the huge national deficits could be decimated.

Who Is the Customer?

Usually it is obvious who the customer of a value stream is but not always. In an insurance operation is it the insurance agent with whom the company normally deals? Should it be the person or firm insured? Would the insurance company operate better if it dealt with the ultimate customer directly? Should it collect information from ultimate customers and interact with them in designing products?

> Few organizations have given their employees a stronger customer focus than the Disney theme parks. Patrons of Disney's parks or their affiliated hotels sense the friendliness of the staff in greetings and hospitality. Disney refers to its customers as "guests," spelled with a capital *G*.
>
> At Disneyland employees are called "cast members." The employee orientation handbook is called *We Create Happiness*. It explains its philosophy
>
>> Producing the Disneyland Show for our guests requires more than 12,000 performers and more than 400 roles . . . You already know you've been Cast for a Role, not hired for a job, and you'll work

either On Stage presenting the Show, or Backstage preparing and supporting the Show. As Cast Members, we're Hosts and Hostesses to our guests (not customers) and they're an Audience, not a crowd. We don't have rides, we have Adventures and Attractions, each carefully "imagineered" to provide family entertainment unparalleled anywhere in the world.[4]

All elements of Disneyland and Disney World including the park design, "cast" training, maintenance, transportation drivers, security staff—even its vast internal laundry—focus on the guest. All try to bring about the slogan on the Disneyland sign: The Happiest Place on Earth.

Airlines have a *logistics* value stream for which the customers are the mechanics who maintain aircraft. Giving the mechanics the components and support they need, *where* they need them, is complicated because the airplanes travel around the world. At what airports should preventive maintenance be done? How is maintenance done when failures occur or warning lights go on in faraway cities? Although the customer in this case is the mechanic, the captain is responsible for flying the plane and deciding whether to fly. The ultimate customers are the passengers. The answer to How do we delight the mechanics? may far from delight the captain and crew. The captain is often frustrated by delays created by minor problems that cannot be repaired quickly because parts are not available. The flying public wants to avoid being delayed or stranded in Jakarta. The highest goal of all is aircraft safety.

The question Who is the customer? is further complicated by the fact that routine or preventive maintenance must be done at an airport equipped for that task. Repairs may be needed at any airport to which the plane flies. Most failures require light maintenance, such as changing an instrument; some require heavy maintenance, such as replacing an engine. Most maintenance is done by the airline's own mechanics; some is third-party work. The plane must be inspected by the airline's own inspectors and by external inspectors.

When failures take the plane out of service for a time, equipment and flight crews have to be rescheduled. The passengers may be put on other planes. A failure can cause delays that ripple around the world, triggering complex rescheduling of operations. Reinventing the logistics value stream can thus have complex side effects that must be considered.

The customers of the logistics value stream include the following:

Primary customers—mechanics/inspectors
Secondary customers—customer-service managers
First users of the product—Flight crews
Ultimate customers—passengers

An airline-logistics value stream is far more complex than most. Some airlines have done a thorough job of rebuilding this value stream to make major changes in information systems and to forge links between maintenance and marketing. The maintenance planners usually do not know what marketing does, and marketing does not recognize the need to put aircraft into the right station for overnight work. Maintenance needs involvement in the early stages of marketing planning. Selecting the best cities for overnight work is critical, with different stations specializing in different types of aircraft. The types of aircraft that can be repaired at a particular overnight station should not be changed often so as to minimize the costs of retraining and moving material. Logistics support requires cross-functional teams with skills drawn from multiple departments and vendors, and the teams need information systems with worldwide links.

Ask the Customer

In trying to decide what the customer needs, it is essential to ask the customer. It is amazing to observe how often this is not done. In the mid-1980s it was fashionable to build expert systems. These were often developed by the brightest and best IT professionals but fell quickly into disuse. The users did not "buy in" to the concept. A rule emerged: Get user buy-in first before starting to build it.

Customer opinion is obtained in a variety of ways:

- Marketing executives and salesmen like to ask customers what they want. This can help to build closer personal relationships with customers.
- Focus groups may be used to explore ideas from customers.
- Consultants talk to customers because then customers do not hold back on their true feelings.
- Informal contact may occur on golf courses or airplanes.

The first commercial system to use on-line data transmission to a computer with disk storage was American Airlines' original passenger-reservation system. The idea that passenger records should be stored on-line and accessed from across the country seemed outrageous when it was suggested. The idea was hatched when an IBM marketing executive happened to sit next to an important customer, the president of American Airlines, on a long flight. By the end of the flight, the potential for a nationwide on-line passenger booking system had been sketched out.

Similarly the Wal-Mart innovation that large suppliers maintain their own inventory of certain items on Wal-Mart shelves, was dreamed up by Sam Walton and a Proctor and Gamble executive on a fishing trip.

Asking customers what they want from a new value stream demonstrates a desire to work closely with that customer. The new system may require the customer to change in certain ways. The readiness to accept that possibility should be established early.

Breakthrough Ideas

Although it is essential to ask the customer what he wants from the new value stream, it is important to understand that customers rarely produce breakthrough ideas. Usually they ask for incremental improvement or something slightly better than what they have now. They tend to say "I want the delivery on time" rather than "I want it in 24 hours, not 24 days" even though 24-hour delivery could help them greatly. They do not think it reasonable to ask for breakthrough performance. Customers often do not know what they want until they see what they can get. They do, however, know what they do *not* want; that is why it is important to ask them.

Market research is useless when done for a new concept. In IBM's great growth era Thomas J. Watson did not ask customers whether they wanted mainframes, disk drives, teleprocessing, etcetera. IBM invented the new machinery with new applications and then worked out how to sell them. In the 1960s many customers, thinking that data processing was *batch* processing, said that disk drives were a useless gimmick and that they did not need data transmission because the mail was cheaper. But IBM had a vision of how corporations would change. At the same time, the telephone industry (before competition) asked its customers what new technology they needed, and the customers said, "More of the same." When the first packet-switching networks were built, the telephone industry failed to anticipate the need for packet switching, visual-display units, or high-capacity data circuits.

IBM rejected the Xerox patents when they were offered at a very low price. Arthur D. Little advised that even if IBM captured 100 percent of the techniques (such as carbon paper for copying documents at that time), it would not repay the investment needed to get into the copier business. Ironically Xerox reversed the situation twenty years later. After the Xerox Park Research Center had devised personal computers, the mouse, and most of the features that now characterize the Macintosh line, Xerox top management concluded that nobody would want computers on the desk; it still thought of computers as being like mainframes.

The Sony Walkman when it was first proposed seemed a wildly eccentric idea. It was pushed through by Morita, the head of Sony, himself. Market research would have concluded that there was no demand for a Walkman. Morita's view was that the mass public never need be separated from its favorite music. The decision to build something when the customers do not know that they want it, needs to be made by a person attuned to the customer and what would delight the customer. It must be made by a customer-oriented, not a technology-oriented, person. Many computer applications, built painfully and laboriously, when shown to their intended users were responded to by "What did you build that for?" The engineers were having fun without being attuned to customer needs. Today, in an era of overengineering, engineers dream up clever features that customers do not use. They make products complex and, hence, difficult to use. Elegant simplicity and a fine sense of what will delight a customer are important.

Quality Function Deployment

Quality function deployment (QFD) is a technique used for analyzing customer needs and relating them to actions that satisfy those needs. It employs a matrix of *needs* and *satisfiers*. The technique is useful in TQM (total quality management), procedure redesign, and value-stream reinvention.

Often the desires of customers are known to the sales force but do not find their way into the design of products or the actions of a value-stream team. A design is frequently not right the first time and has to be modified. QFD is concerned with making the product or process meet customer needs as closely as possible.[5]

The first step in QFD is to identify all the market expectations that can be found. This information is drawn from sales people, customer interviews, focus groups, and market research. Each general requirement broken down into more-specific requirements, may be further analyzed. This process produces prioritized list of requirements.

The second step is to list the potential *satisfiers,* or features, that could be built into a product or service. Again, each category of satisfier may be subdivided.

A matrix that maps the customer requirements and product or service features is then created. Exhibit 10.4 illustrates such a matrix. In the intersections, symbols indicate the affinity between customer needs and potential features.

Some of the potential features may be self-contradictory, for example a camcorder does not need both floating-lens and electronic-image stabilization; trousers do not need both a belt and suspenders. Correlations, both positive and negative, may be added to the list of features, as illustrated at the bottom of Exhibit 10.3. Similarly the customer requirements may be self-contradictory or inconsistent. For example, in the car industry "reduced emissions" may be in conflict with "increased acceleration." This correlation may be indicated on the side of a diagram as in Exhibit 10.3, through a means similar to the "roof" on the matrix.

The matrix can be adjusted until it reflects the translation of customer requirements into product features. The matrix may be used also to show competitive assessments or target values. The goal of this technique is to make sure that no customer requirements are missed when designing a product, service, or value stream, and to prioritize the possible features.

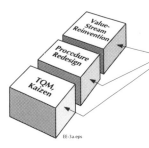

QFD uses a matrix linking an analysis of customer needs to the actions that should occur to satisfy those needs.

Exhibit 10.3 Diagrams used in quality function deployment (QFD)

A matrix maps a hierarchy of customer requirements against a hierarchy of product or service features. Customer requirements are on the left; the product or service features are along the top:

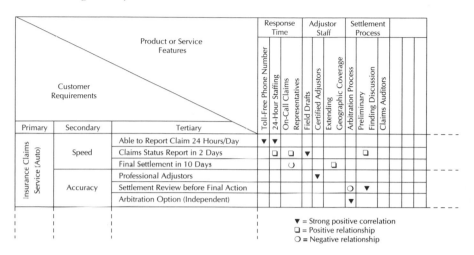

Some of the customer requirements and possible features may be self-contradictory. The above matrix may have a "roof" added to it showing positive and negative correlations among features:

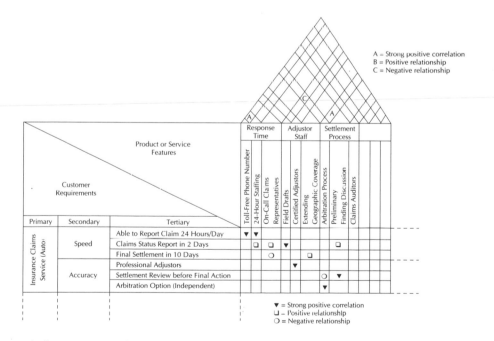

Similarly positive and negative correlations among the customer requirements may be shown.[6]

Zero Defections

It is much more expensive to win a new customer than to retain an old one. American Airlines estimates that persuading new customers to choose American is five times as expensive as persuading old ones. Other companies have quoted similar ratios ranging from 3 : 1 to 10 : 1.

The consultant Bain & Co. has a loyalty-retention practice. Fred Reichheld, the founder of this practice, estimates that in regional banks, a 14-year customer is worth 85 percent more in profits than a 10-year customer, because over time customers' balances grow and they take out new house and car loans.[7] Boosting customer retention 2 percent can have the same effect on profits as cutting costs 10 percent.

A key goal of value streams that deal with the customers of a corporation should be to retain those customers. *Zero defects* is an important goal in manufacturing; *zero defections* should be an important goal in customer service.

The defections of customers are easy to count and record statistically. Just as statistical quality control made the quality movement take off in manufacturing, so statistics about customer retention should be an important measure in customer service.

If near-zero defections is a goal of a value stream, the team should devise various actions to obtain early warning of possible defections and try to prevent them. If a customer decides to defect, the team should be ready with special offers and skills to persuade the customer to stay.

References

1. Ken Blanchard and Sheldon Bowles, *Raving Fans* (William Morrow: New York, 1993).
2. Blanchard and Bowles.
3. Jeffrey Ferry, *The British Renaissance* (William Heinemann, Ltd.: London, 1993).
4. Brad Stratton, "How Disneyland Works," *Quality Progress,* July 1991
5. Lawrence P. Sullivan "Policy Management Through Quality Function Deployment, *Quality Progress,* June 1988.
6. *Enterprise Engineering Techniques, Pocket Guide* (James Martin & Co.: Reston, Va., 1994).
7. *The Quality Imperative,* A Business Week Guide (McGraw Hill: New York, 1994).

11

Sewer Pipes, Not Stove Pipes

Most corporations are organized vertically—with multiple layers of management in functional silos, using stovepipe computer systems designed for a department or function. Value streams, on the other hand, are horizontal—using cross-functional teams that integrate the work needed to deliver results to a customer (internal or external).

Enterprise Engineering causes us to think of an enterprise in terms of its value streams, identify the customers for each value stream, and work out what would most please that customer. The goal is then to deliver those benefits to the customer as simply and directly as possible.

When we think of the entire enterprise in terms of its value streams, it is clear that the management structures of most corporations need to be fundamentally reorganized—horizontally, not vertically (Exhibit 11.1). We need sewer pipes, not stovepipes.

Some corporations have made this transition, but it is not easy. AT & T Network Systems Division reorganized its entire business around value streams and sets budgets by value stream. Xerox reorganized itself with multidisciplinary teams that work on end-to-end processes instead of vertical functions. Lexmark International, the printer division of IBM, removed 60 percent of its managers and created cross-functional teams worldwide. It became profitable in a way it never had been in IBM.

Value-Stream Teams

To deliver results directly requires a value-stream team narrowly focused on satisfying the customer (or internal end user) of the value stream. The teams should be small and should have the requisite skills and information. Sometimes one person can do the work for a customer. The value-stream team (or person) can call for help from specialists when necessary, but most value-stream teams can handle most situations themselves.

Jobs that previously required handing work over to different departments are now done by the tightly knit value-stream team. A value-stream team is a natural grouping of people who together can complete a whole piece of work.

The value stream should be designed to deliver benefits that customers need as simply and directly as possible.

This sounds like simple common sense, but it is light years away from what is actually happening in traditional enterprises.

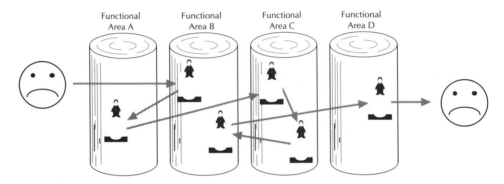

Such teams can be organized in a variety of ways. Designing the right team for the task is a critical part of value-stream reinvention.

Most teams stay together on an ongoing basis, becoming skilled at dealing with a particular type of customer. They go through a learning cycle of continuous improvement. Some teams are created to do one task and then disperse. For example, a team may be assembled to design a special product, deal with a particular problem, or create a new process.

Value-stream teams carry out work that used to be done in functional departments. The team does not contain *representatives* of these departments; it has the skills to do all the value-stream work *itself* (although it may call on specialists for exceptional tasks). Many functional departments lose their reason for existence and need to be wound down. Most of the checking, tracking, reconciliation, and imposing of controls previously done in functional areas disappears. The value stream is designed with its own controls and integrity checks, most of them focused on ensuring that the customer is satisfied. Work which does not add value is eliminated wherever possible.

Sitting at a desk doing paperwork is boring. Doing repetitive tasks on a production line is inhuman. A value-stream team interacts with a customer and is challenged to delight that customer. The team sees results. It gets excited about getting excellent results. The team is not trying to please a manager, play political games, or process 100 documents per hour; it is trying to delight the customer. Doing this involves an endless amount of learning. The team can never fully master customer satisfaction; there are always new challenges. Value-stream

Exhibit 11.1   Corporations organized horizontally, not vertically

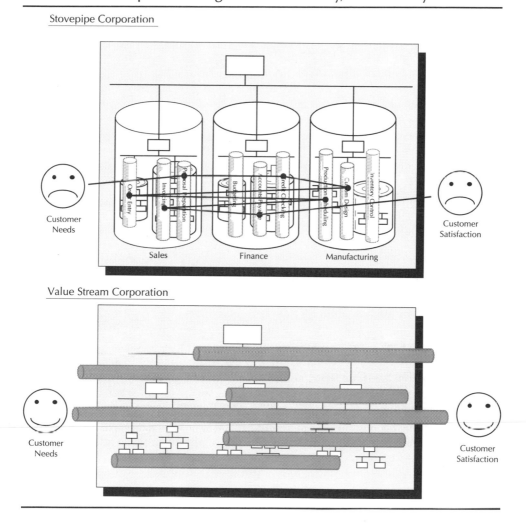

teams share many of the challenges and excitement of entrepreneurs. Being an entrepreneur is very different from being an invoice clerk or a person who bolts on 2 thousand widgets per day.

One of the reasons we can organize work for teams is that we now have a high level of automation and information technology. Routine tasks, such as putting globs of jam on cookies all day, can be automated. Information can be called up on a computer screen. Goods can be checked against central purchase orders with a computer no matter what loading dock they arrive at. The team can look at customer history on a screen. Expert systems can guide employees. A person buying aviation fuel in Hong Kong can interrogate an oil-futures computer in London.

Traditional work has required repeating tasks over and over again. A person trained to fill in purchase orders, calculate beam loadings, or check customers' creditworthiness does not know or care about the overall value stream. In a team, the individual shares responsibility for the whole value stream, not just part of it. He thinks about how to delight the customer or how to achieve excellence or originality, and has a basic familiarity with all the steps in the process. He is challenged to use his ingenuity. People are no longer employed as robots. Machines do repetitive work; people do work that needs thought, ingenuity, outrageousness, love, wit, and human care.

Targeted Teams

A value-stream team has a clear target. It sets out to delight its customer. The clarity of the goal is important.

Fitzhugh, when Secretary of the Army, gave the following description of the Pentagon:

> Everybody is somewhat responsible for everything and nobody is completely responsible for anything. So there's no way of assuming authority, or accountability. There is nobody you can point your finger to if anything goes wrong, and there is nobody you can pin a medal on if it goes right, because everything is everybody's business. . . . They spend their time coordinating with each other and shuffling paper back and forth, and that's what causes all the red tape and big staffs . . . nobody can do anything without checking with seven other people.[1]

Some corporate head offices are similar.

The value-stream team is the opposite. Each person knows exactly what the team is expected to achieve and must act quickly and concisely. The team constantly tries to improve its performance and serve its customers better.

The value-stream team has to "jell." Team members have to develop respect for one another, know one another's talents, and like to call on one another to address a situation collectively. They have a common goal and need to be motivated to drive hard for that goal. It makes sense to have a collective team bonus related to achievement of a clearly measurable target.

A "jelled" team usually has fun. It enjoys its ability to address problems in concert, with different team members peeling off periodically to execute a particular task. When a jelled team is hell-bent to achieve a single clear goal, it can do so with great energy.

Integration of Work, Not Division of Labor

For two centuries efficiency experts have tried to make work processes efficient by division of labor. Henry Ford–style production lines divided work into highly repetitive actions. "Industrial efficiency" experts timed every repetitive human action and tried to minimize its duration. In service work different people did the repetitive tasks of data entry, billing, processing invoices, handling customer queries, issuing drivers' licenses.

In the age of automation, we should do the opposite. Repetitive tasks can be done by machines. Both products and work are being redesigned to minimize repetitive human tasks. Products are redesigned to have parts that machines can assemble. Instead of screws to be tightened by human beings, parts are designed to be clipped together or automatically welded. Amazingly, machines in Hewlett-Packard can assemble a complex computer, with none of the defects found in human assembly, in a total time of four minutes.

Hammer and Champy state that business reengineering really has to do with reversing the industrial revolution.[2] Value-stream reinvention rejects division of labor and uses teams who focus on customer needs. Only in this way can corporations achieve the speed, flexibility, quality, responsiveness, and service that today's customers demand.

Corporations that replace division of labor with value-stream teams have to reject most of the paradigms of earlier industrial-organization—multiple levels of middle management, authorization and control structures, traditional promotion paths, functional division, stovepipe computer systems. Instead of work's being fragmented it is integrated. The entire corporation needs reinventing. It is now clear what a value-stream corporation should look like, although the details will change rapidly. The problem for most management is that they are stuck with a corporate paradigm invented many decades ago. Nations that were the industrial leaders of the twentieth century have enterprises that are now obsolete. They are inflexible and unresponsive, lack customer focus, have high overheads, and are caught in bureaucracies that are difficult to change and that paralyze innovation. New fast, fluid, flexible corporations focusing on the customer can rapidly overtake traditionally organized corporations that do not scrap the old structure and reinvent themselves. Exhibit 11.2 contrasts division of labor with integration of work.

Integration of Work

Value-stream teams combine many jobs into one. The value-stream team must have the ability to execute the entire value stream. There are no throw-it-over-the-wall-its-your-problem hand overs, no assembly lines, no bottlenecks as work passes to different functional areas. The value-stream team must be able to make decisions. It must be empowered. The team member does not pass work up the management chain for approval. The team rule is just to do it! Employees must be trained to take responsibility for tasks that allow an employee to meet customer needs or to be part of a team that does so. The job becomes broader in scope and more interesting.

At some General Motors plants there were as many as 183 job classifications. GM built a new car factory in California that had only 4 job classifications because

Exhibit 11.2   Division of labor, fragmented work done by different people

Routines	*Problems*
Hand overs	Miscommunication
	Arguments about who is responsible
Demarcation expenses	Excessive controls
Labor-management relations	Strife
Rework	Items that fall through the cracks
Delays	Items that sit in queues or "in" baskets
	Major delays introduced by reworking
Traditional staffing	Overstaffing
Excessive resources	"Just-in-case" hoarding at multiple points
Low quality standards	No one team responsible for quality
Poor customer service	No one team dedicated to delighting the customer

Results of integration of work:
A team responsible for every aspect of pleasing the customer.

teams of workers learned to do many types of work. At the NUMMI plant (New United Motor Manufacturing, Inc.), built in cooperation with Toyota, GM hopes to learn the secrets of Toyota's fabled productivity. Decision making is not separated from work, as in traditional management, but is now part of the work. (Usually that is where it should be because only the people who do the work have detailed knowledge about it.) Having a team with all the knowledge and information systems to finish the job greatly reduces overhead costs and time. It enables the organization to be more responsive to customers (internal or external). The team can anticipate problems, helping to eliminate nasty surprises and "things falling through the cracks." It saves sending jobs back for rework or reconciliation—so time-consuming and expensive.

Some value streams involve work that is geographically scattered. Maintenance of aircraft requires worldwide logistics. Supplying a supermarket chain requires continentwide control. Even a simple task such as installing a home telephone requires work in several places. Today's electronics allows team members to work well together when distance intervenes. Magazine editors in different countries can debate the layout of color pages that they can manipulate together on their computer screens. Doctors can interact with a distant specialist. At Digital Equipment Corporation the designers who created the complex mechanisms of Digital's cleverly developed network software were on both sides of the Atlantic. They worked together in the most intricate way at powerful work stations. Today's electronics is essential to the reengineering of work.

Value-stream teams sometimes need help from someone who is not a member of the team. This should be the exception rather than the rule. It should be done to secure specialized knowledge for a particular case. For example, a clinic may have to refer a patient to a specialist. A building-design team may have to call in a heating engineer.

Sometimes an external person joins the team for one task. The video group may hire an outside writer. A design team may hire a computer specialist. The outsider becomes part of the team for the task in question—perhaps for a number of tasks.

Advertising is often done after a product or service is created by an outside organization. It makes sense, however, for promotion to be part of the design value stream. In an early stage of the design the advertisers' skills should be used. The designers can then integrate the most appealing advertising qualities into the product rather than just into the commercials.

Benchmarking

The main image that many people in the West had of the Japanese in the 1970s and 1980s was of swarms of dark-suited men with tape recorders and cameras, photographing everything, even the washroom signs. The Japanese took apart Western products and studied them in meticulous detail. Meanwhile in most Western corporations a negative attitude toward things not invented here prevailed. Westerners, who joked about the Japanese and their cameras, were overtaken by the Japanese. The Japanese *learned* about good products and practices at a faster rate.

The negative attitude toward things not invented here is antilearning. Today everyone has much to learn about how to do things better. This is particularly true as we move rapidly into the era of fundamental value-stream reinvention, in which there is a huge difference between the best practice and average practice.

It makes sense for employees and change agents everywhere to compare their operations with the best practices. The term *benchmarking* is used to describe a process of hunting for the best practices and comparing one's own operation with those. Charts may be drawn comparing one's own practice with the best, as in Exhibit 11.3.

Sometimes corporations that have achieved a major competitive advantage from reengineering do not want to tell their competition about it. The study of best practices in noncompeting corporations can be very useful. Many corporations can achieve similar reengineering benefits with similar processes, such as purchasing, simultaneous engineering, just-in-time stocking, and so on. Corporations in different businesses can learn from each other's approaches to managing cross-functional teams, removing production problems, and so on. Besides looking at the same type of operation in the same industry, much can be learned by drawing comparisons between different techniques in different industries. The facilities manager at the Convex Computer Corporation studied Disney World facilities management. This looked suspiciously like a boondoggle, but few corporations are better at facilities management than Disney. The lessons learned at

Exhibit 11.3   Benchmark comparisons

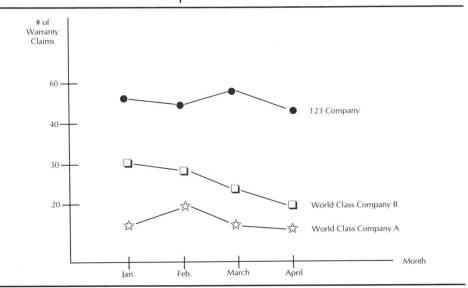

the theme park enabled Convex to make many improvements, including slashing electrical breakdowns in its factory by 80 percent.[3]

> Xerox appears to have nothing in common with L. L. Bean, the mail-order house, but L. L. Bean had a reputation for filling orders very efficiently, so Xerox studied L. L. Bean's order-filling process.
>
> L. L. Bean was "picking" parts for orders three times faster than Xerox. Some of the reasons were simple. For example, L. L. Bean stocked high-volume items close to packing stations. Its workers maintained and studied work-flow charts to learn how to lessen the motion required or to speed up their process.
>
> The study enabled Xerox to improve their mailing of copier parts greatly.

When improvements, including those discovered by benchmarking, are not coordinated, one change sometimes undermines another. A change made by purchasing in order to manage suppliers better, for example, may have results that harm manufacturing efficiency. For this reason benchmarking tends to be most effective when it is part of the design of an entire value stream.

The practice of benchmarking is clearly valuable to industry as a whole, so at the American Productivity and Quality Center in Houston, the International Benchmarking Clearinghouse was set up. It maintains a database of best practices and how-to guidelines. In its network bulletin board members can post appeals for benchmarking partners. Many companies pay annual dues to the Clearing-house.

References

1. Fitzhugh on the Pentagon, quoted by Just Ward, "Soldiers-Part II," *The Atlantic Monthly*, November 1970.
2. M. Hammer and J. Champy, *Reengineering the Corporation* (Harper Business: New York, 1993).
3. *The Quality Imperative*, A Business Week Guide (McGraw Hill: New York, 1994).

12

Sacred Cows and Barnacles

Sacred Cows

Most organizations have sacred cows. People say "You can change most things but you can't change *that!*"

From the start a group doing Enterprise Engineering should list the sacred cows. It should ask, What are those deeply entrenched views which the popular wisdom says cannot be changed? Often these become clear when interviews are conducted with employees. They say, "This is the way we do things here."

Most sacred cows are aging beasts that were important in an era long since gone. They need to be put to rest, or they will prevent important actions. A first step is to identify the sacred cows and shoot them.

Some basic principles are important: Quality is job number 1, or The customer is king, or Development must be fast, fluid, flexible. It is necessary to distinguish the principles valid in a new value-stream enterprise from those no longer valid, such as Pay is related to length of service. The sacred cows that need to be axed are views such as those in Exhibit 12.1. Reengineering calls for new rules.

Sometimes the sacred cows are explicit. Written rules state standards that must be followed, forms that must be filled in, what signatures are needed on requisitions, and so on. Sometimes the sacred cows are implicit, not written in a rule book but widely believed—for example: only certain managers can make certain decisions; contracts must be for short terms; there must be multiple vendors for each item and aggressive price haggling; the vendor is an antagonist; inventory managers pad the inventory "just in case." IBM once had a rule that one could not put alcohol on expense accounts when entertaining customers. A storm of memos erupted because the Waldorf Astoria served a dessert of pears in wine at a company dinner.

Sacred-cow views about vendors have prevented corporations from forging valuable new relationships with vendors. Wal-Mart had a different view. They decided that for some goods Proctor and Gamble could manage the Wal-Mart inventory better than Wal-Mart.

Some IT organizations have standard "methodologies" for software development. The British government has SSADM; the U.S. Department of Defense has 2167A. The software-development process desperately needs reengineering to make it fast, fluid, flexible, and of high quality. The rules of 2167A have prevented

Exhibit 12.1   Sacred cows

- Certain standard forms must be filled in. Documentation must follow mandated guidelines.
- Salaries higher than a certain level need approval of the parent company.
- Purchasing any item for more than $500 needs a requisition with several signatures.
- Every purchase requires competition among, and aggressive negotiation with, many vendors.
- Each item must maintain a minimum inventory level "just in case."
- Pay is related to length of service or to position in the hierarchy.
- Only Board members may own stock options.
- Authors must sign exclusive contracts.
- Professors on tenure are secure for life.
- Certain operational decisions must be made by the Board.
- Work duties must be demarcated (carpenters cannot change light bulbs).
- Problems must be left to the lawyers.
- (Sometimes the most dangerous:) Nothing must interfere with the cash cow.

consideration of most reengineered methods. A rule says that DoD software must be built with the language Ada even if generators are used so that no programmer writes code. For many years Ada compilers were inadequate, and good Ada CASE (Computer-Aided Software Engineering) tools could not be found. The sacred cow called Ada cost U.S. taxpayers literally billions of dollars.

The Canadian government had a rule in the early 1980s preventing it from employing foreign consultants. The prime minister of Ontario asked me to come to Ottawa to consult. While his Hollywood-like limo waited to pick me up at the airport, the immigration authorities blocked my entry on the grounds that foreign consultants were taboo. The affair escalated until it was the subject of the political cartoon in Canada's main newspaper.

Superstitions

Sometimes a sacred cow is not sacred to top management any more, but to lower-level employees it is inviolate. Much education and persuasion is needed to make employees think differently. Rod Atwell, the Managing Director of Mercury, the British telecommunications company, referred to such beliefs as "superstitions."

> Mercury conducted a corporatewide effort to reinvent itself, called "Imagine," in 1994. It conducted training classes for almost all of its 10 thousand employees so that they could help in the reinvention. Although Mercury was not much more than a decade old, its employees already had deeply ingrained superstitions. They thought that only directors could sign certain checks and argued, incorrectly, that this "must" be true. Many authorizations were thought to be "required" that were not required at all. Employees regarded certain customers as hostile competitors. In the fluid world of the 1990s, the same corporation could be a supplier, customer, and competitor.
>
> In some cases long delays were caused by Superstitions. When these were swept away, Mercury could respond to customers much faster. It cut the time to install a circuit for a new customer from 60 to 2 days.

Control Procedures

Many control procedures that have grown up in organizations were instituted to prevent mistakes. Often they have little effect on mistakes but cause lower-level employees to pass decision making upward. That is the opposite to what is needed: to have empowered employees or teams tackling work in a trustworthy manner, organized in such a way that mistakes rarely occur and will be spotted immediately.

The rate of change is such that solutions that worked a year ago may not work today. The controls of yesteryear are of almost no value. What is needed are value-stream teams paying attention to the needs of today and largely implementing their own controls to ensure that their customers' needs are met. This places responsibility unambiguously where it should lie.

When teams doing work require sanctions from higher up, there are many ill-effects. First, it slows down decision making often seriously. Second, it removes decision making from where the action is, from those actually doing the work who have first-hand, up-to-date, relevant knowledge. Third, the person doing the job has "ownership" of it reduced. Fourth, it increases work and provides reasons for employing too many people. Fifth, it leads to a minor industry of control evasion.

Nothing encourages the hoarding of unused office supplies faster than a system that tries to save money by making it difficult to replenish office supplies. Instead of trying to save office supplies, it would be better to save the expensive time of employees.

A subsidiary of the National Education Corporation makes training materials on a difficult, fast-changing, complex subject area. It did so with a ruling from on high that nobody could buy books. If this ruling saved a few dollars, it did endless damage to the resulting product. The company also had a rule about hiring. To hire someone with a gross compensation of more than $75 thousand needed special permission from the parent company. To hire someone with a compensation of more than $100 thousand needed approval from the Board of the parent company. The approvals could take months; and by the time they came through, good candidates had taken jobs elsewhere.

The requirement for supplies and good employees is something that an executive at a central location cannot know about and should not involve himself in.

The value-stream reinvention should minimize the need for controls, checking, and reconciling different pieces of paper. Controls should never cost more than they are worth. Checking should be done as events happen, where possible, because then mistakes are easy to correct. A wrong shipment should be detected on the shipping dock and sent back. Computers should be used to catch design errors as they are made if possible. The value team should do its own checking and reconciliation; these should not be done by some other department at some other time.

No-Lay-Off Rule

Value-stream reinvention is often concerned with getting better results with fewer employees. Some European and Japanese corporations with no-lay-off rules will have difficulty making the needed changes. Overstaffing causes corporate introspection, politicking, growth of unnecessary regulations, and power struggles. People create work for other people.

To manage an overfat company with a no-lay-off policy, new business must be sought vigorously and reengineering done rapidly. Turn the bureaucrats into value-stream teams with clear, aggressive goals. Remove management layers. Send the head-office staff into the field. Change the compensation plans so that pay relates to achievement of value-stream goals, with lower salaries and high bonuses. Drive for advanced technology that enables reengineering. Dump the stovepipe systems. Close offices and give salesmen portable computers. Remove the trappings of comfort. Set outrageous goals and have fanfares for teams that meet them. Create a new corporate vision and build excitement about achieving it. Allow the nonperformers to choose employment elsewhere. Those who cannot stand the heat will get out of the kitchen, but most employees will grow to like the new sense of adventure. People rise to the challenge of delighting value-stream customers.

> A sacred-cow rule in IBM was that under no circumstances did the company lay off employees.
>
> In bad times, to preserve this rule, IBM had waves of early-retirement programs in which it gave people an option of "retiring" at a relatively young age with an exceptionally generous financial package. After 1985 what happened repeatedly was that the good people who were confident of success elsewhere left, and the less-desirable employees stayed in the nest. It was a sure way to weed out the best, the most aggressive, the most entrepreneurial—the people whom IBM most needed. When Lou Gerstner, the CEO from another planet, finally brought down his ax and fired 35 thousand, the loyal stay-with-mother employees who knew no world but IBM were shattered. The no-lay-off rule had helped build employee loyalty and worked charms when IBM was growing; but when IBM went into decline, it made the company's problems steadily worse.
>
> What works well in an era of growth can be a disaster in an era of decline, and can make the decline much worse. The sacred-cow rule should have been relaxed when IBM first needed large reductions in its number of employees.

Compensation

In some enterprises the compensation structure is sacred. This is true in most government organizations, where nobody can interfere with the orderly hierarchy of pay grades.

It usually makes sense to have team bonuses for value-stream teams, sometimes with a substantial proportion of employees' pay being in the form of bonuses. Executives need to be motivated and compensated for long-term success, not short-term, so stock options or other forms of long-term incentive compensation are highly desirable.

> In 1981, before Jack Welch began the transformation of GE, the corporation (rather like the government) had 29 pay levels. These subsequently were reduced to a few broad bands, with extensive use of bonuses.

> In 1981 only one GE employee in 800 received stock options. By 1992 one in 35 received stock options. After the transformation 50 percent of the compensation of the top 400 GE executives was in the form of incentives.

Maryann Keller, a lifelong car-industry analyst—comparing the car industries of Germany, Japan—and the United States, comments, "No one seems willing to topple the sacred cow of Germany's overpaid, underproductive work force."[1] German workers work 700 hours less per year than Japanese workers.

In the United States, in a decade when corporations tried to move from vertical to horizontal structures, the ratio of top-management compensation to worker compensation changed from about 30 to about 150. Newly empowered employees often feel that it should have changed in the opposite direction. In Ben and Jerry's the highest pay is only seven times that of the lowest pay.

Craftsmanship Cows

Craftsmanship has been very important in achieving quality and will always be so. However, there are some old forms a craftsmanship that have been swept away by newer technology or processes. We no longer have hand weavers, scribes with copperplate script, or manual typesetters.

Craftsman are usually reluctant to concede victory to more-mechanistic processes. Printers rebelled against computerized typesetting. Old-fashioned craftsmanship sometimes becomes a sacred cow that nobody dares to run out of town.

The European car industry believed that craftsmanship was the key to making a luxury car. The automobile executives in Europe in the mid-1980s had said that there could be no such thing as a prestige Japanese car. By the 1990s Japan's Lexus, Accura, and Infiniti were demonstrating that luxury car manufacturers were going to have to fight for their lives.

In the late 1980s Jaguar took 700 labor hours to assemble a car. Japanese luxury car companies took 20 to 40 labor hours. Jaguar justified its 700 labor hours on the grounds that special craftsmanship was the key to quality, but this craftsmanship had not given Jaguar a reputation for reliability. Maryann Keller comments in her study of the car industry that John Egan, the knighted chairman of Jaguar, thought that Jaguar was on a path to extinction but made no real effort to lower the 700 labor hours per car—nobody could interfere with true craftsmen. Ford bought Jaguar, reduced the assembly time to 150 labor hours (still high), and improved the reliability. Before long, Rolls-Royce, Lotus, and Lamborghini were up for sale.

A study of the world's car-assembly plants, conducted at MIT, concluded that the main difference between luxury cars and mass-market cars is a thicker gauge of steel, extra coats of paint, better material for upholstery, better fittings, and many additional components.[2] The luxury car can be assembled with the same robots, identical paint booths, and similar assembly techniques. There is a big difference for both luxury and mass-market cars among three styles of manufacturing: traditional mass production, Japanese-style lean production, and European-style "craft" production. The Japanese luxury-car plant required a quarter of the effort of the average European plant and assembled cars with far fewer defects. In most cases the Japanese plant produced a more diverse set of products than the European plant.

The white-smocked workers in the European luxury-car plants explained to the MIT researchers that they were "craftsman . . . proof of our company's dedication to quality." They were adjusting off-standard parts, making difficult pieces fit together, fine tuning parts that needed adjustment, correcting previously incorrect assembly, and so on. To the lean factory engineer all this is waste caused by failure to design parts that are easily assembled and failure to catch and correct the cause of problems as they occur.

The recommendation of the MIT researchers was crisp and emphatic:

> Our advice to any company practicing "craftsmanship" of this sort in any manufacturing activity, automotive or otherwise, is simple and emphatic: *Stamp it out.* Institute lean production as quickly as possible and eliminate the need for all craftsmanship at the source. Otherwise lean competitors will overwhelm you."[3]

Jaguars are stylish cars with a real touch of class, but the view of lean manufacturers is that if the car and assembly process were designed correctly, they could be assembled in 20 labor hours, not 700.

One finds a similar situation in diverse types of work. Programmers resist the automation of programming. Programming is a difficult, error-prone, work-intensive task. Some programmers become true craftsmen who do painstaking design of programs and write neat, efficient code. Like composers they become enamored with the elegant code structures they create. Today, however, a computer can *generate* code in various ways. A systems analyst can design a graphical user interface, moving components around a screen with a mouse, and generate code for it. The logic and database access can be generated from diagrams with CASE (computer-aided software engineering) tools. Code can be constructed from preexisting objects or building blocks.

Code-generation tools have existed for ten years and have steadily improved. They cannot generate all types of code but are widely used for building the systems that process the basic transactions of commerce. Nevertheless, programmers unnecessarily write an enormous quantity of code by hand when they could use generators. The U.S. Department of Defense alone spends several billion dollars per year on manual coding of administrative systems. The programmers claim that they are craftsmen who write better code than that which generators produce. In reality generators produce code that is much more reliable, completely free of syntax errors, and much easier to modify. Code can be generated in a fraction of the time that is needed for manual programming. This saves money—but, more important, it allows the code to be put into use earlier, its misconceptions discovered earlier, and improved ideas implemented earlier. The fast cycle time leads to faster evolution of systems and learning about what systems work best.

The recommendation of professionals skilled with the latest tools and methods is similar to that in car manufacturing: "Our advice to any company practicing 'craftsmanship' of this sort is simple and emphatic: *Stamp it out.* Institute lean production as quickly as possible."

Craftsmanship is extremely important—more important today than it has ever been because we are entering a knowledge society with rich and complex products and services—but it is folly to do error-prone manual operation of something that can be automated or processed more reliably with fewer labor hours. Craftsmanship is needed in the design of the process, the invention of better products, and for creativity, ingenuity, human communication, art, style, inspiration, and those aspects of work in which human talent is unique in an age of machines.

Cash Cows

A particularly dangerous situation can arise when a cash cow becomes a sacred cow. A product or service has become exceptionally profitable, and the development investment needs to keep it going is low compared with the earnings it generates. Management, naturally, wants to keep milking its cash cow. Anything that would interfere with that capability is fiercely resisted. Whereas top management can be persuaded to change its attachment to most sacred cows, it supports the cash cow to the death. Change agents may oppose every other sacred cow in Exhibit 12.1, but if they attack the cash cow they are out.

The reason this is dangerous is that the cash cow can die unexpectedly. Discontinuities come with surprising speed (see Chapter 25) and have wrecked corporations.

The Hollywood stars of silent movies were legendary and untouchable, but they were swept away along with their studios when sound came. Microchips did the same for mechanical cash registers, calculators, etcetera. The defense industry was largely unprepared for the sudden collapse of the Soviet Union. A much simpler and more common change is a switch in public buying habits that suddenly makes an old cash cow keel over. International Harvester predicted a profit of $302 million in 1982; in reality it lost $1.64 *billion*. When the demand for its cash-cow products dried up, it was not ready with alternative products. Even more devastating was the sudden crash of IBM (see case study).

Barnacles

Bureaucracy grows like barnacles on any organization, slowing down the hull speed. Periodically the barnacles need to be removed. Some organizations have grown barnacles for so long they are like the Great Barrier Reef.

Northcote Parkinson describes how the British Navy declined rapidly between 1914 and 1928. In 1914 it had 62 capital ships in commission, in 1928 less than 20. During the same period the size of the Admiralty went from 2,000 to 3,569 officials, however, and the member of dockyard officials and clerks went up by 40 percent. What had been a magnificent navy at sea changed to a magnificent navy on land.[4] Nobody used Enterprise Engineering in the Admiralty.

The Crash of IBM

The prima donna of all cash cows was IBM's 390 mainframe. The 390 was probably the most profitable machine in all human history. Since its introduction it had made profits of roughly $4 billion *per year* (along with its software). It produced a 70-percent return on investment. In much of the 1980s IBM had higher profits than any other corporation, and two-thirds of it came from the mainframe and its software.

By 1992 the payroll previously prepared on a $5 million mainframe could be done on a $50,000 work station. This change had been predicted by IBM's technology models five years earlier. In various ways history's greatest cash cow had become obsolete. However it was difficult to argue with a $4 billion a year profit. The cash cow had become a sacred cow.

Many items in IBM's product line, including its complex architectures for networking and distributed computing, were designed to support the 390. The natural desire to keep milking the cash cow caused IBM to develop products that supported mainframe revenue and avoid those that might take revenue away from the mainframe.

IBM spent more on research and development than any corporation in history. Before it crashed it was spending about $7 billion per year—much more than the Star Wars program at its peak. Tragically, many of the powerful technologies produced by IBM's research and development never reached the marketplace. The reason was often that they were too powerful and might kill the cash cow.

An example is an extraordinary computer produced in 1975 and code-named *ServiceFree,* a small, inexpensive, highly reliable, astonishingly fast computer. It ran at 80 MIPS (millions of instructions per second) whereas the fastest IBM mainframe of that time ran at 1.6 MIPS (a somewhat unfair comparison because the mainframe instruction set is more powerful). ServiceFree ran programs ten to twenty times faster than the mainframe. By any standards ServiceFree was an extraordinary machine for its day. With it a competing company could have taken the industry by storm.

In 1975 IBM management did not want a computer that was incompatible with the IBM 370 mainframe. ServiceFree was buried, and so were other advanced machines produced by IBM research.

In 1987 IBM was flying high. *The Economist* commented that IBM Chairman John Akers looked as if he had won the best job in American business. Akers said he would increase company sales to $185 billion by 1994.

Five years later *The Economist* said, "IBM is now an object of pity. Its fabulous prosperity has been washed away."[5] The stock-market valuation had fallen from $106 billion in 1987 to $27 billion. IBM's 1992 results were, when announced, the largest annual loss of any corporation in human history—$4.97 billion. (Shortly after, GM exceeded IBM's record!) At that time some of IBM's competitors were thriving—Intel, Compaq, Apple, Sun, Hewlett-Packard, and Microsoft. Never before in corporate history had a giant so large and so respected fallen so precipitously.

Some commentators have claimed that there was no way out of the mainframe dilemma, but this is not correct. *IBM's major customers will spend more money on new-world computing in the mid-1990s than they did on computing in the mid-1980s, when IBM was so profitable.* The reason is that most employees will have computers on their desks acting as nerve endings in enterprisewide nervous systems, with high-capacity networks, huge databases, and many new applications built for the new value streams of Enterprise Engineering. Reengineering corporations, to survive the 1990s, need massive automation.

IBM should have been leading the cybercorp charge rather than nursing its sick cash cow.

Organizational Interaction Chart

A goal of value-stream reinvention is to minimize the interactions that take place in a organization. The interactions between separate groups are time consuming and often go wrong.

Exhibit 5.7 (in Chapter 5) is an *organizational interaction chart*. It shows what happened when the procurement process was reengineered at a large utility. The lines between the boxes each represent a hand over (the handing over of work from one department to another). The hand overs caused major delays and costs. They had grown steadily over the years as more approvals and reviews had been established, each for what seemed like a good reason at the time. As is always the case, the division of work caused miscommunication. When inconsistencies were detected, it was time consuming to backtrack and correct them.

The process was redesigned so as to empower business units to interact directly with the vendors and not have to seek authorization for everything they

Exhibit 12.2

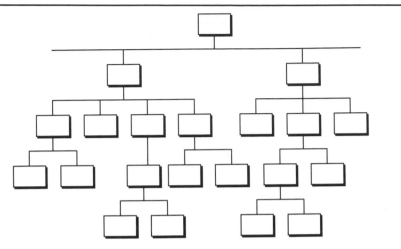

In hierarchical organizations
- Information flow is slow and painful.
- Management layers filter information.
- Turf defense becomes more of a priority than optimizing productivity.
- Managers think that information is power and oppose database systems that share information.

Often the only efficient solution is to rebuild the enterprise, making managers responsible for satisfying customers with end-to-end value streams.

bought. They passed information to accounting; engineering and construction helped to determine what should be purchased; but the main interaction was between the business unit and the vendor. Value-stream reinvention lowered the costs of procurement dramatically.

People create work for other people. Overstaffing inevitably breeds unnecessary controls, hand overs, and complexity. Value-stream reinvention is concerned with scrapping this complexity. Drawing an organizational interaction chart helps to identify and eliminate unnecessary interactions.

Removal of Work Which Does Not Add Value

Clearly, having every employee make the greatest contribution possible to the corporation maximizes profits. It should be a corporate habit to look at every employee and ask How could this job be redesigned to contribute more?

When organizations create maps of the work steps they execute, they are often astonished to find that there are multiple redundancies and that many steps do not add value. Many steps are net negative. Value streams should be designed so that no work step costs more than its value.

It is common to find that the expense of purchasing an item is $100 because of paperwork and controls. If the item costs $50 that does not make much sense. The Department of Defense gained notorious publicity when hammers and toilet seats were reported as costing $1,000. The cost of software in DoD frequently exceeds its value. The press makes a fuss about the cost of hammers yet has never mentioned the staggering cost of software or nontangible systems because these are not obvious.

The redesign illustrated in Exhibit 5.7 cut costs dramatically by allowing business units to buy all items below a certain price (99 percent of items) without approval cycles and internal paperwork. For most approvals, invoices, and internal paperwork disappeared. For some goods the vendors automatically replenished the inventory. The type of diagram in Exhibit 5.7 is called an organizational interaction chart. It is useful for showing the interactions and how they can be changed. Value-stream reinvention should eliminate much of the paperwork flow, hand overs, and delays, and should drastically simplify the process.

The cost of sending everybody and his dog copies of reports, memos, and directives costs much more than the price of copying. The unnecessary paperwork wastes people's time. Many executives state that their efficiency depends upon the speed with which they dispatch most of their mail to the garbage can.

Self-Reliant Value-Stream Teams

A value-stream team works well if its goals are clear, it is highly motivated to meet those goals, and higher management avoids interfering with it.

It has been suggested that the Roman Empire grew so large and survived so long because it had no planes, trains, and telephones. After an emperor appointed a provincial governor, he watched the appointee's chariot and baggage train clatter off in a cloud of dust and knew that he had to trust him. He could not phone the governor or check progress on a computer screen. When there was trouble, the governor had to solve his own problems. He was in charge of his own value streams. He did not have to ask permission from Rome when he took action; there was no way to do that. There was no bureaucratic chain of permission up through the layers in one functional silo, across the great divide into another functional silo and then down again. Top management could not second-guess the governor's decisions. When a triumph or disaster occurred, the top executives in Rome did not know about it until months later, when a messenger came panting up the Via Appennina. It is difficult to imagine the Empire working well if the top management in the days of Claudius and Caligula had had IT. While Rome was snarled in murderous politics, the faraway managers did their jobs, motivated by the prospects of future glory.

Avoidance of Politics

Corporate politics are a menace. The only enemy should be the competition. When people have enemies *within* the enterprise, the enterprise suffers. Corporate politics tend to grow in stovepipe organizations when people concentrate on their own vertical function rather than the cross-functional process of pleasing the customer. Politics is a sign of an overstaffed, overmanaged, functionally oriented enterprise. When an enterprise is reengineered into value teams each tightly focused on pleasing its customers, there is little time for politics. If a value-stream employee plays politics rather than focusing on the customer, this is obvious. His colleagues and manager say to him, "Cut it out Fred; pleasing our customer is too important to waste time on playing political games." Quickly confronting each person who plays politics preempts an escalation of plotting and time wasting. This is much easier to do in the urgency of well-focused value teams than in functional hierarchies. If all the energies are directed toward the value-stream customer, there is little left for internal struggles.

References

1. Maryann Keller, *Collision* (Doubleday Currency: New York, 1993).
2. IMVP (International Motor Vehicle Program) at MIT, a survey of the world's car factories, has produced many publications, which are available from MIT, Cambridge, Mass.
3. James P. Womack, Daniel T. James, and Daniel Ross, *The Machine That Changed the World: The Story of Lean Manufacturing* (Harper Perenniel: New York, 1991).
4. C. Northcote Parkinson, *Parkinson's Law* (Ballantine Books: New York, 1957).
5. *The Economist*, 1992.

13

Reinvention of Work Flow

Reinvention of Work Flow

Work should be done in whatever sequence finishes it quickly. A value team in control of its own activities can decide the most efficient way to do things. This is very different from passing work from department to department, each of which deals with it in its own good time.

Simultaneous Activities

Often tasks can be completed in parallel time lines. Fred can get going on this job while Kenichi does so-and-so and Marisa does that work. Sally makes sure that it all fits together. The top of Exhibit 13.1 shows six tasks being done sequentially; the bottom shows them being done concurrently. In the lower version the work is finished in about a third of the time.

Today complex tasks such as design work or software development are done simultaneously using computers connected to a common database or repository. Computer-aided design (CAD) and Computer-aided software engineering (CASE) tools employ a shared repository and help ensure that separately developed pieces fit together. Work-group software, in various forms, allows people to work on reports, proposals, designs, and so on, sharing one another's work.

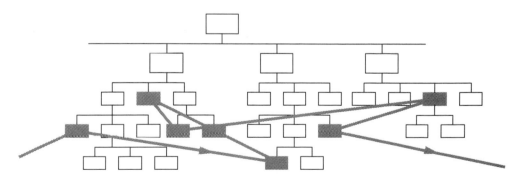

Exhibit 13.1   Tasks carried out simultaneously to take less total time

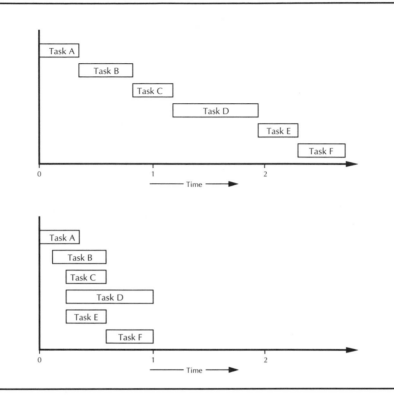

Parallel tasks are given names such as *simultaneous engineering* and *concurrent engineering*. Some car companies have shrunk the time taken to bring a new car to market from 5 years to 3—and in a few cases to 2½. The following activities are done simultaneously:

- **Design of the car**
  - market research
  - design in response to customer satisfiers
- **Design of its components**
  - integrated components
  - common electronics system
  - minimum assembly work
- **Design of the manufacturing process**
  - robotics assembly
  - products designed for ease of manufacturing
  - car designed for ease of assembly

- **Design of supplier system**
  - suppliers on-line to the factory
  - just-in-time delivery
- **Design of service**
  - car and components designed for minimum service
  - field-service network design
- **Design of marketing**
  - dealers on-line to the factory for fast delivery of custom-built covers
  - design of the market image
  - design of marketing campaign, advertising, brochures

Apart from resulting in being more responsive to customers or being first with a product to market, parallel work has other effects.

When something is wrong it is discovered relatively early. In Exhibit 13.1, for example, suppose Task E goes wrong. In the parallel version of the work, it is detected early in the schedule and can be corrected early. The longer the cycle time, the more important saving time is. Development of computer systems often takes two or three years. Suppose that the time scale in Exhibit 13.1 is years. When E is found to be wrong, B, C, and D have to be changed. The sooner the problem with E is detected, the better. In the upper version of Exhibit 13.1 one delay might severely delay the completing date.

The external environment, or customer needs, may change during the process and cause major rework. The probability of this occurrence is diminished when the elapsed time is less. The entire work process should be designed to minimize the probability of the need for reworking at the end of the cycle. Less rework means less cost and delay.

Triage

Triage is a word with a grim history. It refers to the categorization of battle victims to determine which are worth saving. In value-stream reinvention, it refers to the categorization of work items or transactions. Not all items need be handled the same way. Some require only a simple procedure; others need more-elaborate procedures. *Triage* means having alternative versions of a process.

In the past, procedures have grown complex because they have been steadily added to, to accommodate every possible case. This has resulted in simple cases being handled with complex procedures. A disease of bureaucracy is the steady growth in complexity of form filling and procedures. It makes sense to use simple procedures for straightforward cases.

Of particular importance in value-streams reinvention is the goal of automating procedures if possible. It may not be possible to automate all transactions of a given type because some need human attention. The viewpoint of triage would suggest categorizing transactions into those that can be handled automatically and those that cannot. Not all transactions need pass through complex procedures just because a few must.

Banks requiring a process for mortgage renewal should ask: Which cases can be handled automatically? Which can be handled semiautomatically with an expert system? and Which need a slower process of human investigation and approval?

A case manager may divide customer situations or transactions into those that are handled automatically by computer, those that the case manager can handle, and cases for which the case manager needs to call on specialist advisers.

Obtaining city approval for renovating a home takes a year in some cities, although it requires only two hours' work. The job is handled with a process intended for skyscrapers and sits waiting in a pile with the massive-construction projects.

There is no need for most people to have to renew their driver's license every three years or so. Britain issues a driver's license that is valid for life, until age 70. Only exceptional cases need go through a renewal process. This saves time, money, and annoyance.

The cost of processing small claims in insurance companies is high. It makes sense to have a simple procedure for small claims. It might pay to let the insurance agent handle small claims. Computers categorize insurance customers by their claims histories. A customer with a small claim, who has no previous claims or no evidence of false claims, might be paid automatically, without investigation, where this lowers costs. The customers would be made happy by the immediate no-questions-asked payment.

IT organizations have *methodologies* for developing applications. The methodologies become standardized processes designed to work with complex applications. With the U.S. Department of Defense's 2167A methodology, trivial systems take two or three years to build. Some systems that could be created quickly with spreadsheet tools are fed into a clumsy, bureaucratic procedure of mind-numbing slowness. It makes sense to *use simple tools for simple systems.*

Specialists who apply highly professional skills are often overworked or in short supply. Triage would direct to them only the cases that really need those specialists. Simple contracts can be handled quickly by paralegal staff with computers; only difficult ones need be sent to time-consuming lawyers. Paramedical staff can screen patients and send an overworked medical specialist only those cases that really need such expertise.

Bypassing the Middleman

The world is full of middleman organizations: real-estate agents, stock brokers, travel agents, executive search firms, and a diversity of organizations that link buyers to sellers. Computer networks make it possible to bypass the intermediary organization. This can have several advantages. First, fees are cut. Second, the process is speeded up. Third, it is often easier to avoid the dialogue with the

Exhibit 13.2   Appropriate electronic systems that make it possible to bypass the intermediary

Uses of notebook machines:	Bypasses:
Send fax or electronic mail.	the mail room or postal service
Buy direct from the factory.	retailer, distributor, whole-saler, pur-chasing department
Obtain sales information from a super-market chain.	market research company
Analyze and buy stocks.	stockbroker
Do banking.	branch bank
Make airline booking.	travel agent
Make theater and sports bookings.	ticket agent
Send purchase orders.	purchasing department or mail room

agent. Fourth, the intermediary organization's list of clients is limited, a computer system's extensive. Fifth, interaction between buyer and seller is often more satisfactory without agent intervention. Sixth, an operation of limited geography may become global in scope because computer networks are worldwide. Last, and often most important, electronic linkage of the parties may allow complete logistical reinvention.

For example, professional and executive search firms take 60 to 120 days to locate and prescreen prospective candidates. If each industry had a database of professionals and executives, with on-line résumés, prospective candidates could be found very quickly. Instead of being limited to those people known to the search firm, global searches could be done by computer. Digital video interviews of highly paid executives and professionals could be accessed computer before candidates were called for face-to-face interviews.

In many industries it is becoming clear that human intermediaries are slow and inefficient. They sometimes monopolize or distort communication channels rather than opening them up. Electronic systems are most efficient in relatively structured transactions such as locating parts, potential employees, stock brokerage, and real estate. A value team should employ such systems if they help, possibly bypassing the purchasing department, personnel department, and corporate mailroom.

Although traditional intermediaries can often be bypassed, new forms of out-sourcing often make sense. A corporation should focus on its core skills and value streams, those that differentiate it from its competition. Mundane activities, or activities in which it has less than world-class competence, may be out sourced. This viewpoint is causing a reevaluation of the relationships needed between corporations and their trading partners.

Value-Stream Executive Information Systems

Most executive information systems have been built for managers of traditional functions. They give no information about value streams. Most managers have no information about how long it took to fill customer orders or other information about end-to-end processes. The functionally oriented systems provide information that cannot be integrated to facilitate monitoring of value-stream performance. Managers do not know how good or bad their value streams are. They have little information that might help them set targets for improvement.

As we build value-stream teams, we need value-stream information systems. Each value stream has goals. We need measurements for how well the goals are being achieved. Value-stream information systems for high management may not be the first systems built as an organization reengineers itself, but they should be created as value-stream management settles into regular operation.

Boards of directors often create demands for better customer service, faster product development, fewer rejects, better customer retention, and so on. They rarely demand information systems that measure these things. Part of value-stream reinvention should be the building of systems that show how well the value-stream teams are achieving their goals.

Lean Manufacturing

Henry Ford invented mass production, and from his concepts evolved the largest industry in humanity's history so far. Mass production set the style for factories in other large corporations after World War II. While these corporations were generating immense wealth in the West, however, the seeds of a new revolution, referred to as *lean manufacturing,* were growing in Japan. It allowed cars to be built with lower costs and higher quality, and quickly spread to most manufacturing in Japan. In the 1980s lean manufacturing was spreading around the world. Many of the old mass-production corporations appear obsolete but have had great difficulties transforming themselves into lean operations.

Taiichi Ohno of Toyota was mainly responsible for lean manufacturing. Toyota in the 1950s was short of the capital that would permit it to compete with the car factories of the West. Ohno reinvented the flow of work to permit building cars with small inventories of parts.

As the Japanese lean manufacturing lowered costs, it enabled the Japanese to compete aggressively. In the 1980s, GM calculated that it was costing Toyota $2,578 per car less than GM to make a small car.[1] In 1979 Xerox was shocked when Japan's Canon, Inc., sold midsize copiers in the United States for less that it *cost* Xerox to make a similar machine.[2]

Ohno's system was elegantly simple. Parts arrived in containers at the location where they were needed. When the contents were used up, containers were sent back as a signal to send more parts. Empty containers were sent where they came from—the previous step in the production process or to the supplier. If the supplier did not reuse the container, a tag was sent back. With this system the parts could be made to arrive in a timely manner, so inventory costs were kept low.

Today computers are used. The different steps in manufacturing can be linked electronically, telling the supplier when to deliver the next batch.

The just-in-time system squeezed down inventory costs. Ohno set out to squeeze out any other form of waste—space, time, money, or manpower. There were no buffers in Ohno system, so every worker had to understand his own critical role in keeping the system running. Problems had to be solved quickly, or the system would stop. Every problem was recorded and analyzed thoroughly to try to prevent its recurrence. *Kaizen* was vital to the practical evolution of Ohno's system.

Computerized Choreography

It took Toyota many years to perfect its lean-manufacturing operations. Everything in the factory needed to work together. The system needed careful choreography, a delicate balance between aspects of the process. Today the choreography is aided by computers. All teams, including those of suppliers, can observe the progress on their screen to ensure that their own activities occur on time.

An assembly plant is like a complex theater performance with the actors coming in on cue, the scene changers operating the stage machinery, and hundreds of lights being adjusted with perfect timing. A chassis floating down from above meets a power-train trundling along the floor. Parts are bolted, and a master cylinder is welded by a robot. The brake lines move into position at the right moment to connect them. Every person checks the work of the person ahead. Defects are found immediately, if possible, so that the cause of the problem can be quickly pinned down and corrected. It is everybody's job to make the choreography work as smoothly as possible.

Lean, just-in-time operations with computerized choreography can be applied to many aspects of business, not only assembly plants. Most of the world's distribution systems have too many warehouses, too much product sitting in warehouses, too-long delays, and insufficient coordination. Airlines have put much thought into choreographing their worldwide operations, maintenance scheduling, and crew scheduling. Only with complex computing can they reschedule and rechoreograph when breakdowns occur, storms delay flights, airports close, or crew members become sick.

Identifying Problems

Business processes have a diversity of problems. When the value stream is reinvented, problems should be identified and solved. Sometimes problems are un-

Exhibit 13.3   Problems inherent in a manufacturer's distribution process

Work Problems	*People Problems*
Parts out of stock	Lack of trust
Hoarding of parts "just in case"	Lack of motivation
Inventory in "black holes"	Lack of meaningful jobs
Too many back orders	Lack of strategic goals
Misplaced parts ("Whose is this?"	Lack of communication
"Why is it here?")	Lack of understanding of the overall
Incorrect labeling	process
Transit delays	Lack of meaningful jobs
Cost of excessive handling	Lack of training
Slow delivery	Lack of expertise in the right place
Slow pick-up	Information hoarding
Excessive paperwork	

stated; people think they are a law of nature. Problems may be categorized as work problems and people problems, as shown in Exhibit 13.3.

In 1988 the U.S. food distribution industry had about $80 billion worth of products sitting in stores and warehouse.

Some stores and supermarkets introduced electronic systems for responding more efficiently to consumer demands. They monitor shelf stock with scanners and do computer-aided ordering with orders going electronically to manufacturers. In one supermarket chain, product leaves the warehouses for stores within 12 hours, on average, and this is being driven down to 3 hours.

> *With today's electronics, the warehouse should be a switching yard, not a holding yard.*

There is no need for three levels of storage-retailer, distributor, and factory warehouse. With electronic systems either the factory or distributor warehouse can be eliminated in many organizations.

CAO (computer-aided ordering) uses scanners to help determine what has been sold and to cross-check that with what is on the shelves. This information is often used with a forecasting technique based on historical sales of the product. Computer placing of orders is based on what has been sold and what is expected to sell.

CAO systems ought to be combined with EDI systems (electronic data interchange), which send orders electronically to vendors. When goods are received at stores, this should trigger electronic payment to the vendor's bank.

> David Jenkins, CEO of Shaw's Supermarkets, East Bridgewater, Massachusetts, called such systems ECR (efficient customer response). Customer orders in stores automatically trigger reordering from manufacturers. The whole process, including payment to manufacturers, is paperless. It provides fewer "out-of-stocks," serves customers better, and cuts inventory costs. When he retired, Jenkins lambasted the food industry for its waste and inefficiency in not moving quickly enough to redesign its distribution procedures.[3]

A goal of the value-stream reinvention ought to be to solve people problems by creating small teams motivated by intensely focusing on customer needs. Many work problems can be solved by avoiding the throw-it-over-the-wall-its-your-problem handovers of functionally oriented work. Many are solved with information systems that span the entire value stream. Some problems need special attention for which unique solutions must be devised.

Fishbone diagrams and multiple-*why* questioning (described in Chapters 15 and 16) should be employed in the analysis of problems. Exhibit 13.4 shows two fishbone diagrams breaking down the cause of problems in a maintenance value stream.

A Value-Stream Laboratory

When a value-stream is reinvented, it often needs much testing and refinement before it is put into live operation. A "laboratory" environment should be used for testing, refining, and demonstrating the new processes.

When interactive computer applications are designed, they should be prototyped before detailed construction is begun. IT has learned slowly from painful experience that prototyping is very important. Intended users of a system working with the prototype always request changes. It makes sense to build GUI (graphical user interface—such as Macintosh or Windows) prototypes at an early stage of planning the requirements for the system. The prototype reveals misconceptions and logical flaws. Equally important, it causes the intended users to challenge the requirements and, often, to suggest other functions for the system.

In a similar way, a new value stream should be prototyped. The work of the value-stream team should be simulated. Many inventions or suggestions for improvement are likely to come out of this simulated operation; the process is likely to reveal omissions, misconceptions, or impractical aspects of the design.

The new value stream may require new computer systems. Usually these are built in a client-server fashion.[4] Today's tools enable us to build GUI prototypes *very* quickly. Such prototypes should be used by a simulated value-stream team as early as possible.

If it is important to prototype conventional computer applications, it is far more important to prototype new value-stream operations because there is far

Exhibit 13.4 Two of a set of fishbone diagrams showing problems in a maintenance value stream

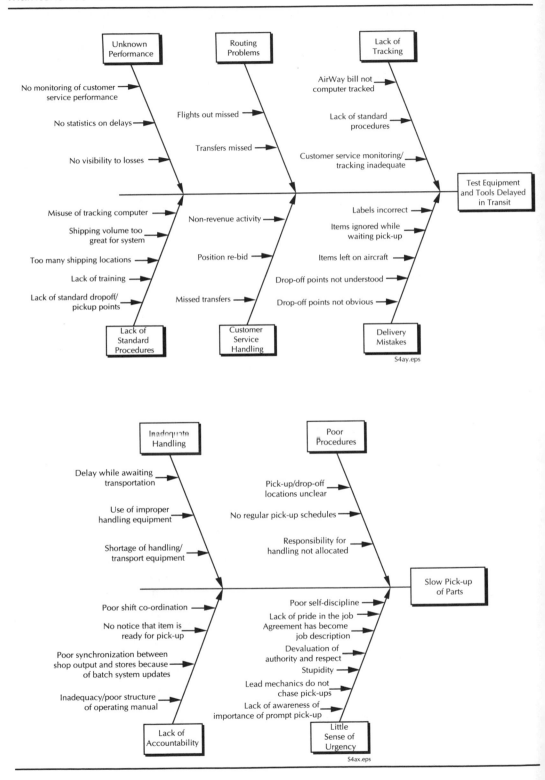

more to learn and far more that could go wrong. The value-stream ideas are new, so there are many potential ways for improving them.

A room should be set up as a value-stream laboratory, equipped to simulate the new value-stream work. Various subprocess components may be tested, and then integrated, as they come together. The development team produces proto-types, and then release versions, of all of new subprocesses that constitute the new value stream.

Through multiple validation cycles, an organization learns whether the new approach is right and steadily refines it. The various stakeholders of the new value stream should be introduced to it in the laboratory environment—the cus-tomers or end users of the value stream, directly affected employees, IT staff, and possibly suppliers, agents, or other trading partners. All should help validate the parts of the new value stream that affect them.

The reactions of people using the new systems should be videotaped. Video-tapes help to pinpoint flaws that need correcting, misconceptions, opportunities for improvement, and aspects of computer-screen usability that need improving. The videotapes may be used to demonstrate the new process to potential users and may be made an important part of training courses.

The laboratory environment can demonstrate how the new value stream "feels." Its stakeholders can be invited to "experience the future." Their comments are likely to provide important feedback and lead to refinements. The risks of the new approach are often made clear in this environment so that the risks can be carefully managed.

Often the laboratory demonstrates the enthusiasm and excitement of new value-stream teams, and this encourages executives, including the CEO, to sup-port the initiative. The various stakeholders should be made to feel that they have some "ownership" of the new process because they contribute ideas to it.

Usually the value-stream prototypes cause significant improvements to be made.

References

1. Maryann Keller, *Collision* (Doubleday Currency: New York, 1993).
2. *The Quality Imperative*, A Business Week Guide (McGraw Hill: New York, 1994).
3. Michael Garry, "Industry Control: Moving Ahead," *Progressive Grocer, January 1993.*
4. *Methodology for Client/Server Development* (James Martin & Co.: Reston, Va., 1994).

Part III

Continuous-Process Improvement

TQM,
Kaizen

Part III focuses on change methods at the base of the Enterprise Engineering arrow: continuous improvement of processes, and the quality movement.

14

*Kaizen**

The massive resurgence of Japanese industry since 1960 has to a major extent been a result of management philosophy called *kaizen*. Management author Masaaki Imai quotes comments that there are three main religions in Japan: Buddhism, Shintoism, and *Kaizen*.[1] Many intelligent Japanese practice all three!

Kaizen has no equivalent word in English, so it is desirable to use the Japanese word. Roughly it conveys the idea of everybody improving everything all the time. The Japanese *kaizen* culture has been translated in the West into the TQM (total quality management) and ISO 9000 (International Standards Organization) movement, but *kaizen* has somewhat different implications. The term CPI (continuous-process improvement) more closely describes *kaizen*, but *kaizen* refers to continuous improvement of more than just processes. There can be a succession of small improvements to products, services, customer support, relationships with suppliers, relationships with unions, software systems, human relationships and so on. In spite of the great importance of *kaizen*, most Western management books do not even have the word in their indexes.

Constant Improvement

Kaizen means continuous improvement involving everyone—top management, managers, and workers alike. If you constantly and relentlessly make small improvements to products, the process of making products, marketing, selling, keeping customers happy, and corporate activities in general, over time the corporation becomes very good at what it does. Japanese industry evolved various methodologies for *kaizen*, with detailed techniques for constantly achieving improvements.

> *The* **kaizen** *concept is crucial to understanding the differences between the Japanese and Western approaches to management. If asked to name the most important difference between Japanese and Western*

*pronounced *ky'zen*

*management concepts, I would unhesitatingly say, "Japanese **kaizen** and its process-oriented way of thinking versus the West's innovation- and results-oriented thinking."*

*In business the concept of **kaizen** is so deeply ingrained in the minds of both managers and workers that they often do not even real- ize that they are thinking.*[1]

—Masaaki Imai, in *Kaizen*

Imai comments that most of the articles written on Japanese management have prompted confusion, each scholar having his exclusive explanation of the secret of Japan's management success—often implying that such success is impossible in the West. *Kaizen* can work just as well in the West as in Japan. Many Western companies have practiced it well, adding substantially to their profits and share value. Converting a traditionally managed corporation to a *kaizen* corporation requires a major shift in corporate culture, however, which takes time and ongoing drive from top management.

The success of kaizen has little to do with national factors. To a large extent it is common sense.

Kaizen strategy involves everyone in the organization—top management, middle management, supervisors, shop-floor workers, support staff. All are motivated to search constantly for improvements, to seek out and solve problems large and small, and to pay constant attention to pleasing the customer. Defined procedures for doing work are referred to as standard operating procedures (SOP). As soon as a new standard operating procedure is established and employees are trained to do it, the procedure is a candidate for change—for improvement. Everybody is motivated to improve, improve, improve—all the time.

If you continue improving something for a long time, eventually it becomes very good. If you improve it by 1 percent each week you will achieve a 14-fold improvement in 5 years. (Compound interest works wonders).

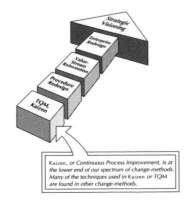

Kaizen, or Continuous Process Improvement, is at the lower end of our spectrum of change-methods. Many of the techniques used in Kaizen or TQM are found in other change-methods.

Kaizen is Learning

Kaizen is a form of enterprise learning vital to the modern enterprise. The results of everybody learning all the time how to do things better are recorded so that others can be trained to use the techniques. Much more learning can come from the people who do the work than from external designers or efficiency experts. The person who works with a machine all day, every day, understands its use better than head-office experts. A corporation with a *kaizen* culture encourages everybody to learn all the time.

Kaizen culture deliberately searches for things that can be improved. Any problem represents opportunities for improvement. A popular term in Japanese industry is *wanusa-kagen,* which refers to a thing that is not really a problem but that nevertheless can be improved. It is usually the worker, not the supervisor, who notices the *wanusa-kagen.* Workers are trained to notice them.

Japanese quality authorities use several words, such as *kaizen* itself that do not translate directly into English. We need a term in order to discuss it. Perhaps a *wanusa-kagen* should be called a *"refinement-candidate."* Where the term *problem* sounds too negative, it might be called a *"kaizen* candidate." The effects of *kaizen* are so impressive that the word *kaizen* should be a basic term in management vocabulary everywhere.

At one of Matsushita's plants in Japan, the waitresses in the cafeteria noticed that tea consumption varied widely from table to table. The same people tended to sit at the same tables so the waitresses started serving different amounts of tea to different tables, depending upon anticipated consumption. They saved half the tea leaves and were given a medal for this.[1] *Kaizen* has to do with everybody's learning how to improve everything.

P-Criteria and R-Criteria

Many Western executives tend to focus more on *results* than on refining the processes. It is not uncommon to hear "These are the numbers you must achieve. I do not care how you do it, but deliver these numbers." Salesmen are motivated to meet their quotas regardless of anything else. Managers are told to meet budgets. Executives are driven to make profits or increase shareholder value. In publicly held corporations, there is intense pressure to achieve quarterly results, causing a short-term rather than long-term focus.

Enterprise Engineering focuses on the *processes* for doing work, with the view that if the processes are made as good as possible, the results will be good; if the processes work poorly, in the long term the results will be poor.

Masaaka Imai distinguishes management applying R-criteria (results-oriented criteria) and P-criteria (process-oriented criteria). R-criteria are concerned with sales, profits, return on investment, share price, etcetera; P-criteria are concerned with process improvement, problems in processes, defects, defect rates, quality circles, time management, skill development, just-in-time techniques, team activities, suggestion systems, and *kaizen* in general. Both P-criteria and R-criteria should be used by every level of management (Exhibit 14.1). Measurements, motivation, and rewards should relate to these criteria.

Much Western management until recently has primarily focused on R-

Exhibit 14.1

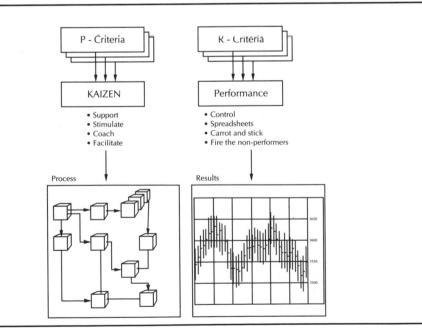

criteria. Japanese management has devoted much more of its effort to P-criteria and rewards for process improvement. It is desirable to establish what measures and rewards can be applied to P-criteria, which generally have a longer-term outlook.

A human organization with no discipline for improvement tends to deteriorate, as a house with no maintenance does. Bureaucracy sets in, and nobody questions the efficiency of procedures. Individuals have private agendas. People acquire their own turf and devise ingenious ways of protecting it. Redundant activities evolve and unnecessary work is done. There is little focus on changing the process to serve the customer better. In some shops or service organizations one has the impression that employees are having a great time but that the customer is a nuisance who spoils their day. As soon as a corporate edifice is built, it starts to deteriorate.

The deterioration can be stopped either by *kaizen* efforts for continuous improvement or fundamental redesign. When processes are modeled or analyzed as part of a procedure-redesign effort, astonishing redundancies and inefficiencies are discovered. This is especially true in organizations with no *kaizen* or TQM culture.

Kaizen improvements involve small changes to standard operating procedures. Each changed procedure must be made to work in a disciplined fashion. *Kaizen* strategies believe that standard operating procedures are made to be changed. They are stepping stones on a road of continuous improvement. As soon as a quality circle has solved one problem, it moves on to a new problem.

Japanese businessmen are sometimes astonished when they revisit a Western factory after many years and find that nothing has changed. Factories rarely stay unchanged in Japan because *kaizen* implies constant change. Engineers and managers in Japanese plants are warned; "There will be no progress if you keep on doing things the same way all the time." If you buy a Japanese camcorder and then compare it to another made six months later, you will discover that the later model has many improvements. Imai comments that *kaizen* strategy means that "not a day should go by without some kind of improvement being made somewhere in the company. Ask any manager at a successful Japanese company what top management is pressing for, and the answer will be *kaizen*."[1]

The costs of semiconductor lasers for use in compact-disc players dropped as follows:

> 1978: 500,000 yen
> 1980: 50,000 yen
> 1981: 10,000 yen
> 1982: 5,000 yen
> 1985: 2,000 yen

Compact-disc players using semiconductor lasers went through hundreds of small improvements, increasing quality and reliability, and decreasing manufacturing costs.

Kaizen applied to product design as well as to process improvement has sometimes resulted in dramatic new possibilities. With semiconductor lasers in Japan, there was a relentless ongoing search for improvements in materials and production engineering. This led to chemical-vapor techniques, for depositing chemicals in very thin layers, and molecular oxidization. The improvements led to power reduction and lower manufacturing cost.

A good *kaizen* cheerleader can build a high degree of enthusiasm in people for the constant improvement of their work processes. At the 3M factory in Weatherford, Oklahoma, they used the term "measles" to describe *kaizen* infection. You have to get it yourself before you can pass it on to anyone else. The measles spread through Weatherford.

A supervisor of one workshop referred to the supervisor of the next workshop as his "customer" and had a policy of never passing defective work on to the next stage. The *kaizen* policy pervading the plant facilitated just-in-time techniques and led to the elimination of process steps and equipment inventories were cut to a quarter—sometimes even less. Defects were greatly reduced and plant efficiency increased.

Kaizen is a culture that needs to permeate an organization from top to bottom. It is only likely to take root and thrive if top management is committed to it and spends time to ensure its pervasive use. It's payback is not immediate. The reward comes from the cumulative effect of many improvements—from processes and products that are repeatedly improved. Aimed at a precise target such as reducing defects in a given product, it can result in a quick payback, but a large one comes from establishing a deep-rooted culture throughout the entire enterprise. Such change may take years of determined effort. *Without determination from top management the culture tends to fizzle out.*

Major reengineering must be designed for constant change and improvement, rather than as a single major redesign. Production-shop floors should be designed so that processing units can be moved easily. In some shops the machinery layout is improved almost weekly to adjust to changing needs. Software should be built to accommodate changes and improvements in procedures easily. This is the opposite of much software today, for which maintenance is a nightmare and to which change is avoided. Instead, we need *kaizen*-capable systems, designed for ease of change and constant improvement.

Quality, Productivity, and Kaizen

A Union of Autoworkers' local chairman in Michigan was quoted in the *Wall Street Journal* as saying "What is quality? I mean, I have a hard time getting my arms around it."[2] The term *kaizen* avoids this danger of misinterpretation. It means the culture of constantly improving anything that can be improved.

"There is a very little agreement on what constitutes quality."

Masaaki Imai, the Japanese *kaizen* authority

Any serious discussion of quality soon finds itself entangled in such issues as how to define quality, how to measure it, and how it relates to benefits. There are as many definitions of quality as there are people defining it, and there is no agreement on what quality is or should be. The same is true of productivity. Productivity means different things to different people. Perceptions of productivity are miles apart, and management and labor are often at odds over this very issue.

No matter what the substance of quality and productivity, the moment we start talking about **kaizen,** *the whole issue becomes breathtakingly simple. Nobody can dispute the value of improvement, since it is generic and good in its own right. It is good by definition. Whenever and wherever improvements are made in business, these improvements are eventually going to lead to improvements in such areas as quality and productivity.*[1]

The PDCA Cycle

Continuous improvement needs a cycle of activities referred to as a PDCA cycle—plan, do, check, act (Exhibit 14.2). This process was first advocated by W. Edwards

Exhibit 14.2

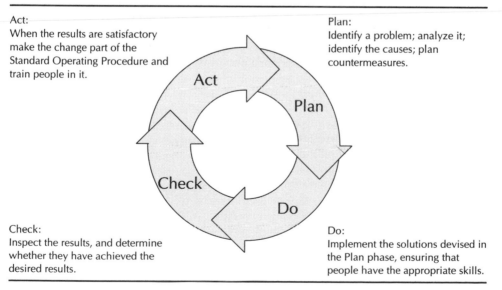

Act:
When the results are satisfactory make the change part of the Standard Operating Procedure and train people in it.

Plan:
Identify a problem; analyze it; identify the causes; plan countermeasures.

Check:
Inspect the results, and determine whether they have achieved the desired results.

Do:
Implement the solutions devised in the Plan phase, ensuring that people have the appropriate skills.

Deming, decades ago.[3] It is one form of enterprise learning that should pervade all processes in the enterprise.

As soon as such a change has been made, new improvements are sought. The new standard operating procedure may quickly go through another PDCA cycle. *Kaizen* means continuous change. Each new standard operating procedure is regarded as a platform on which further improvements will be sought. Exhibit 14.3 shows steps in the PDCA cycle.

The "Do" part of the cycle often needs a PDCA cycle itself to implement and adjust the changes until they work well. Making changes often introduces a crop of small problems that have to be solved.

Do: Implement the solution

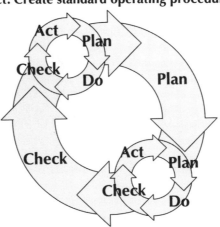

The "act" phase may also have a cycle of its own. It takes effort to standardize and stabilize a procedure. Multiple adjustments may be needed as the procedure is standardized and employees are taught to do it.

Act: Create standard operating procedure

Exhibit 14.3 Steps in the PDCA cycle

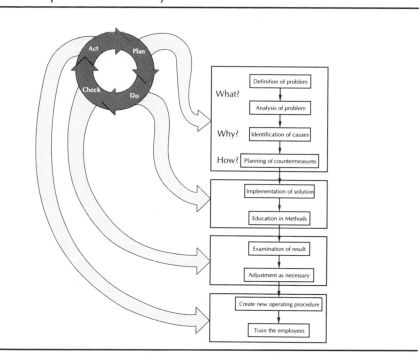

Kaizen possibilities should be expressed in quantitative, not qualitative, terms. Only through quantitative expression can be it be decided what is worth spending on the improvement and whether the improvement efforts have been worthwhile.

The new standard operating procedure exists only to be challenged, revised and replaced by better standards. Thus the PDCA cycle goes round and round. Masaaki Imai comments: "While most Western workers see standards as fixed goals, Japan's PDCA practitioners view standards as the start for doing a better job next time."[1] This is changing. The change-methods of Enterprise Engineering are concerned with multiple different types of enterprise learning—all the ways in which an enterprise can learn. The enterprise needs much more than *kaizen*, but *kaizen* should pervade everything.

The Journey to Zero Defects

A deliberate ongoing effort to eliminate defects has had impressive results in some corporations.

Solectron, a San José manufacturer, cut defects from 100 parts in a million to 2 and at the same time reduced manufacturing costs and cycle time.

Eastman Kodak cut defects in the plastic tips for its blood-analyzer machines from roughly 2.7 in a thousand to just 2 in the 6 million produced from 1987 to 1991.

To achieve such progress, every defect must be detected and its cause determined as quickly as possible. Corrective action must eliminate not just the defect but the cause of the defect. Where this has been done constantly for years, defect rates have been reduced to very low levels. It is essential to detect the defect as it is made if possible. If it is detected when it is made, the person who made it and knows the cause can correct it. Catching defects long after they have been made is not satisfactory because then it may be difficult to find the cause.

New technology can often make it possible to catch errors at their source. Word processors can catch spelling mistakes, for example. Software design tools can detect many design errors when the designer makes the error; it is then easy to correct the error and the designer learns not to do it. Manufacturing processes should be designed whenever possible to catch defects at the source.

Technology can also be designed to *prevent* defects. It if is possible for a worker to install a part upside-down, the part should be redesigned to make this impossible. Each assembly step should be made foolproof as far as possible. When workers detect defects as they are made, they can often devise ways to stop the problems from happening in the future. An ongoing succession of such improvements leads to near-zero defects.

An overriding lesson from the evolution of quality is that there is no quick solution. Quality comes from thousands of improvements, many of them small, most of them suggested by the people who operate the process. Everybody, therefore, must participate in continuous-process improvement and make this a never-ending goal.

Kaizen Is a Vital Value-Stream Goal

A vital goal in implementing a redesigned value stream is to apply *kaizen* (TQM) to the new value stream even if it is not used in the parent enterprise.

When a value stream is reinvented, a new attitude toward work is put into place. Individuals have to learn a new way of working, with a new culture. Part of this culture should be that *everybody improves everything all the time.* Problems should be continuously sought out, analyzed, and solved. The value-stream workers must be directed to make all the suggestions they can for constant improvement. They should take the initiative for making improvements and should participate in improving the operating procedures recorded in manuals, computers, training courses computer-based training, and expert systems.

The sweeping changes of value-stream reinvention bring many new problems. The new value-stream teams must be determined to tackle those problems systematically and constantly to improve the new value stream.

A corporation with no TQM, or one that has had difficulty implementing TQM, should introduce TQM one value stream at a time when that value stream is reinvented.

A Change in Culture

For *kaizen* to be woven into the fabric of the entire enterprise implies, for most enterprises, many changes in management, procedures, information systems, and enterprise culture. It is always easier to change the culture of a small enterprise than a large one. There have been many examples of large Western corporations trying to introduce *kaizen* and failing—like a surgical transplant that does not "take." Some corporations have failed to reap benefits from a corporatewide TQM program, and some have backed away from it. This represents a failure to manage a change in corporate culture (discussed in Part VI).

> I worked in a company that reengineered its television production process. After the transition the entire production team constantly tried to improve the process. The lighting expert would show the teleprompter operator how to adjust his machine better. The teleprompter operator would talk to the actors and would redraw items displayed on the teleprompter if that could help them. The camera operators would pick up coffee cups on the set and adjust the positions of objects on the set. Previously the attitude had been "You do your job and I'll do mine."

On the other hand, some very small corporations have achieved highly visible benefits. Small laundries, village groceries, car repair shops, and graphic arts firms have understood *kaizen* and set out to improve quality and delight the customer. They are a pleasure to do business with.

Curt Reimann, who heads the Baldrige Award program at the U.S. National Institute of Standards and Technology, states that quality programs seem to take an extra year to implement for each additional layer of management. Corporations that have already shrunk their middle-management layers move faster. Small and start-up corporations have no difficulty practicing *kaizen*.

Kaizen-Capable Computing

There are many books and training courses on *kaizen* and the Western implementation of it, TQM. A curious aspect of these books and courses is that (at least when this was written) they almost never mention computers or IT, in spite of the modern corporation's being an organism of people and IT. A reason sometimes stated for this is that it is difficult or impossible to change software, and *kaizen* calls for a culture of constant change.

The modern enterprise needs to be able to change computerized procedures as fast as it can change human procedures. It needs *kaizen*-capable computing.

This means that the software must be built for adaptability. Constant improvements are as essential in the information systems as in everything else. The software must be fluid—changeable in days, not years. This would not have been possible ten years ago, but today the automated tools for developing computer systems allows it to be changed quickly.

In 1991, the large Volkswagen plant in Wolfsburg, Germany, announced that it would start a program of *kaizen*.

A small *kaizen* room was set up near the cafeteria. The company established a department for improvement proposals. At first, employees who submitted proposals were given a pocket calculator. An attempt was made to establish payment for suggestions, but this did not work out because there seemed to be no objective way of evaluating their worthiness. The various departments worried that jobs might be eliminated or delegated elsewhere. The fiefdoms had little motivation to make *kaizen* work. Maryann Keller, writing about Volkswagen's battle with Toyota, comments, "*Kaizen* became another good idea that the organization could not implement because it did not know how to adapt."[4]

By contrast, many small companies have been transformed by *kaizen*. A local cleaning firm, for example, quickly established a culture in which all employees set out to delight the customers, and the effect was immediately visible to customers. Small companies succeed in implementing *kaizen* quickly; big companies often fail to manage the culture change.

In 1993 Volkswagen brought in a tough new production chief, José Ignacio Lopez de Arriortua who vigorously drove worker participation. Volkswagen established 5-day brainstorming workshops at which participants were asked to find ways of improving efficiency and were empowered to make changes. In 1994 Lopez stated that adopting worker suggestions had saved millions of marks. Productivity in manufacturing operations in 1993 improved 21 percent and in administration 23 percent. When Volkswagen involved suppliers and dealers in its workshops, supplier productivity improved 60 percent and dealer productivity 34 percent. About 24 thousand workers took part in the workshops in 1993 and 60 thousand in 1994. Volkswagen claimed to be the first to set up these workshops in dealerships.[5]

I needed to rent a car in England to get to a business meeting. One of the big-name car rental companies agreed to deliver the car to my location, and I gave instructions on how to get there. The driver delivered the car three hours late, so the meeting could not take place that day. The company's excuse was that the driver got lost. When I asked why he got lost, the company explained that it was impossible to enter directions for how to get a location into the computer, so the directions were not recorded. I suggested that the software should be modified so as to solve this problem. The suggestion was greeted with total contempt: "It takes years to change software, and anyway we couldn't ask the IT department to do it—they are too busy." Their tone implied that the customer was seriously out of line to make such a suggestion. In contemporary British fashion, they indicated that the customer should know his place and not criticize a state-of-the-art computer.

Modern software enables designers to build and change GUI (graphical user interface—like that in the Macintosh) screens very quickly and to record new information items. With the right software, directions for how to find a location could be added to the car-rental system overnight. We can design systems for fluidity and constant change so that *kaizen*-style improvements can be made constantly.

Users of spreadsheet software frequently add new items at will. They can constantly improve their spreadsheet applications in a *kaizen*-like fashion. Similar flexibility is now available in major IT systems, with many users employing easy-to-use GUI dialogues.

Software built with COBOL or traditional programming techniques is very difficult to modify. Systems not easy to change have put users into a procedural straitjacket. Modern-style computing requires software that is both easy to use and easy to change. The best tools for building GUI client-server systems achieve this.

When a change is introduced in one branch office, it may be confined to that office until the new procedure has its wrinkles ironed out. When it works smoothly, it is introduced to the other branch offices. A change-control process is needed for developing and polishing a new procedure in one location and then spreading it to other locations. This applies to both the human and software aspects of the procedure. The changed software design should be stored in such a way as to make it easily implementable elsewhere.

Business people have policies and rules that describe how to deal with certain situations. The more automation spreads, the more rules are encapsulated in software. This means that they must be explicit, precise, and agreed upon.

In most business-computer systems the rules are buried in code in a nonexplicit way, so if a rule changes it is extremely difficult to change the code. Worse, it is even difficult to know what programs contain the rule. It may be virtually impossible to extract the rule from the programs by examining the code. The rule is arbitrarily tangled up in spaghettilike code. Too often, business people want to change a policy without changing software.

With the best of today's development tools, software is built in a fundamen-

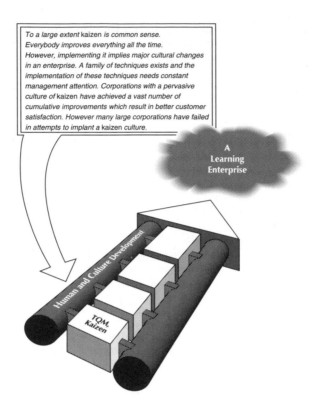

tally different way. The rules are made explicit in the planning and design, and code is generated from the rules. When a rule is changed, the code can be generated. Business people are then free to reinvent the rules. The software can handle the change. *Kaizen* applies to business rules.

The ability to translate policies and rules directly into software has the potential of changing the way organizations are run. Just as a plant controller can turn a valve and adjust a manufacturing process, so business people should be able to modify rules of the business and make direct changes in the software used for running the business. They should be able to simulate the effect of rule changes and make adjustments.

A businessperson traveling with a notebook computer may have on it a model of a complex process, including the rules for running the process. Just as he can experiment today with spreadsheets, so can he experiment with his business model. He can adjust the rules or adjust the work flow, trying to make improvements.

Reengineering the System Development Process

The days of rigid procedures programmed in COBOL, which cannot be changed, are gone in efficient IT shops. Business management needs to understand that this improvement in development technology makes *kaizen* applicable to software use. The requisite IT tools, methodologies, and training must be put into place. *Kaizen*-style improvement of computer systems is an essential part of Enterprise Engineering.

> **We must build kaizen-*capable* IT.**

To make the building of systems fast, fluid, and flexible—so that it is *kaizen*-capable—requires fundamental reengineering of the system's development process.

References

1. Masaaki Imai, *Kaizen, The Key to Japan's Competitive Success* (McGraw Hill: New York, 1986).
2. Patterson, "Two GM Auto Plants Illustrate Major Role of Workers' Attributes," *Wall Street Journal*, August 29, 1991.
3. W. Edwards Deming, *Out of Crisis* (MIT Center for Advanced Engineering Study: Cambridge, Mass., 1982).
4. Maryann Keller, *Collision* (Doubleday Currency: New York, 1993).
5. *Hong Kong China Daily News*, June 1994.

15

TQM and the Quality Revolution

The Drive for Quality

In the late 1980s a feverish drive for quality started to sweep through the Western world. This drive gained momentum in the 1990s and brought irreversible changes in corporate processes, structures, and management. The quality drive was first a reaction to Japanese success in building better products at lower prices but later became a passion in its own right. Quality is a key to competing successfully.

In some corporations a drive for quality caught fire and then flamed out, but across industry as a whole the achievement of quality is growing rapidly. Corporations whose quality drives fail are an endangered species. Trade barriers are coming down; the planet is shrinking. Corporations worldwide are copying whatever is successful, so there are too many competing products. Global competition will turn white-hot, and only the best will survive. Quality is the price of entry to global competition.

The achievement of high quality is regarded by some CEOs as very expensive. If the drive for quality is done right, however, it has two by-products: higher productivity and fewer errors leading to lower cost. The search for quality should be a search for ways in which quality, productivity, absence of errors, and low costs can be achieved with the same technique.

The Western quality drive is encapsulated in the acronym TQM (total quality management). TQM is a form of enterprisewide *kaizen*. It involves everyone in an enterprise in continuous-process improvement, using principles of the previous chapter. Managers and workers set out to make continuous improvements at every level. Problems are sought out and systematically dealt with, with a PDCA cycle (Exhibits 14.2 and 14.3). Suggestions are actively solicited. Quality is everybody's job. The word *total* in TQM implies that it relates to the entire enterprise and should be driven by the head of the enterprise.

Delighting the Customer

A dominant focus of TQM (as with other Enterprise Engineering change methods) is to delight the customer. To achieve this, changes may be made in product design, manufacturing processes, speed of responding to orders, order-entry customizing products, after-sales service, and so on. Computerized links to customers may be particularly important in improving responsiveness and speed of interaction. It makes sense to link TQM to value-stream reinvention and value-stream customers everywhere.

The customer of a process is not necessarily the ultimate customer of the corporation, but sometimes the ultimate customer is too far removed for a worker to visualize his needs. The worker or team may carry out a process and deliver the result to another worker or team. This next worker, in this case, should be thought of as a customer. If an auto worker thinks of the person working next on the car as his customer, problems are personalized. He does not want to deliver something faulty—for example, with bolts not properly tightened—to this "customer." A famous phrase in Japan is "The next process is the customer." Design engineers should think of the manufacturing people as their customers. Computer-systems developers should think of the system users as customers. Clerical staff should think of document users as customers. Each should interact with these internal customers, trying to understand their needs, and have a dialogue that enables them to deliver the best result.

The more each employee thinks about his unique role in "delighting" the customer, the more successful TQM is. Besides continuously improving the product, its features, reliability, human-factoring, style and price, the supplier needs continuously to improve service and support. Customer requirements should be constantly examined and responded to. Problems should be analyzed quantitatively and solved, with successive improvements of the solution.

The most important goal of TQM is to delight the customer, with excellence in products and support, and constant attention to customer needs.

Some Western companies have been remarkably successful in achieving real and lasting improvements by adopting the quality ethic. We mentioned Xerox's dramatic reversal of fortune. Despite this success, Xerox executives understand that the job is not finished and will never be.

> Nothing ever stands still—not our competitors and not technology. Quality improvements must be a continuous and inexhaustible process. We learned that every time we improved; so did the competition. We also learned that every time we improved, the customer expectations increased. And they should. And thus we are in a never-ending spiral of increasing competition and customer expectations.[1]

The Origins of TQM

The ideas of statistical quality control were put to use in World War II. It was desperately important to change factory production in order to produce the weapons needed. Professors W. E. Deming and J. M. Juran learned and preached the methods from which TQM evolved. The methods were introduced by the U.S. government to improve the rate of military equipment coming off the assembly lines. By applying appropriate measurements to the manufacturing and assembly process, possible failure conditions were detected, and the source of errors located and corrected, before a failure could result.

After World War II more than half of the world's gross production came from one country—the United States. This had not happened since the days of ancient Rome and will probably never happen again. Much of America's industrial competition had been bombed into oblivion. The United States then enjoyed a monopoly in many markets. Customers had a limited choice; they had to buy the available product. So commercial enterprises in the United States ceased to be interested in the ideas of Deming and Juran.

Deming and Juran went to Japan, where they found enthusiastic acceptance of their gospel. The Japanese understood that the quality ethic could be applied to everything that a company does—a total quality approach. They also saw that the success of the approach was dependent upon the involvement of everyone in the company, from CEO to janitor, and that the improvement process should be continuous. By achieving high quality standards the Japanese were able to gain considerable market share from the other industrial nations. Deming and Juran became fierce rivals in Japan—the high priests of the quality movement.

In the 1970s jumbo jets and globalization intensified international competition. The Japanese use of TQM matured and made Japan exceptionally effective. As competition increased in the 1980s, particularly from the Japanese, a far greater range of goods became available, and customers began to demand products that met their precise needs. Satisfying the customer became a competitive imperative for any company that wished to remain in business.

In the late 1980s, the West got the quality message. Deming, when he was almost 90, and Juran, four years younger, came into great demand in the United States. TQM became fashionable in the West, ironically to protect it from the success of Deming and Juran's teachings in Japan.

At a 1990 conference in Tokyo, Juran averred "made in the U.S.A." will again become a symbol of world-class quality. Even if the United States does not quite catch up with Japan, it will come close: "When 30 percent of U.S. products were failures, versus 3 percent for Japan, that was an enormous difference. But at failures of .3 percent and .03 percent, it'll be difficult for anyone to tell."

When the whole world achieves very low defect rates, the competitive edge will lie with basic research, originality of design, style, and service—something the West may be better at than Japan.

Quality Circles

A *quality circle* is a small group of employees that meets regularly on a voluntary basis to perform quality-control activities within its areas. It carries out this work continuously as part of a corporatewide program of quality control, individual development, and overall improvement. Quality circles typically focus on such areas as cost and defect reduction, safety, and productivity. They usually have a localized scope—for example, they may concern themselves with improvements within one workshop. Such programs teach employees how to analyze and solve quality problems with minimal management supervision.

Quality circles have been important in achieving quality and productivity in Japan. Japan calls them QC circles (quality-control circles). Their role in Japan has sometimes been exaggerated. They generally account for 10 to 30 percent of overall quality-control effort in Japanese companies. Roughly 10 percent of Japanese workers are involved in quality-control circles. There are more than 300 thousand QC circles in Japan. A typical QC circle has 6-to-10 members. A nationwide organization conducts regional and national conferences, where QC circle leaders exchange know-how.

Quality circles in some companies are more flexible than the textbook version.

Unipart, a British auto parts company that narrowly escaped being closed down during the Thatcher era, used to be a moribund strikebound part of government-owned British Leyland. Rather than close it, it was spun off as a partially employee-owned independent company with a vigorous employee empowerment program and became very successful.

The born-again company created its own type of quality circle, which it called OCC (our contribution counts) circles. Unipart believes that its OCC circles are more powerful than the typical American quality circle and more flexible than Japanese quality circles.

Any employee can establish an OCC circle to solve any problem or address any specific business improvement. He can sign up any member of the company who he feels is needed, even the top executive. The circle is dissolved once the problem is solved. The person who calls the circle organizes its meetings and sets the agenda. Trained facilitators teach circle leaders how to run the circle.

A lifelong shop-floor worker, with a strong rural accent, Melvin Thornton was concerned about a recurring moisture leak that caused tiny spots of paint to leak into fuel tanks. A better stopper was needed to keep moisture out of the tank. He convened an OCC circle with five shop-floor colleagues, and they designed a stopper that worked well and was inexpensive because it could be made of scrap metal.[2]

At that time the chief executive, David Nicholas, returned from a visit to Japan and brought back a stopper designed in Japan to solve the problem. He had ordered 500 of these stoppers from Yachiyo. Melvin Thornton hit the roof. He protested that the rules of the OCC circle were that nobody could stop the circle leader's finishing the project. A meeting took place with senior managers to compare the two solutions. The OCC circle explained why its members thought their solution was better than the Japanese one.

The entire shop floor watched the affair because a country-bumpkin shop-floor worker had confronted the chief executive. The OCC circle won. It became clear that worker empowerment really meant something if Melvin Thornton could win a confrontation with the chief executive.

The Sanwa Bank, one of Japan's largest banks, has 2,400 QC circles involving 13 thousand employees, many of them tellers and clerks. They are concerned with quality of service to customers, customer satisfaction, reduction of errors, how to gain new accounts, and lesser topics such as saving electricity, routing mail more efficiently, saving stationery, and reducing overtime work. They improve employees' familiarity with the services the bank offers.

A Systematic Suggestion Scheme

TQM, and other forms of *kaizen*, make major use of suggestion schemes, actively soliciting suggestions for improvement from workers, supervisors, teams, and managers.

Most workers have much know-how about the work process. They can be ingenious in making improvements and finding ways to solve problems, a skill wasted in companies not having some form of *kaizen* program. *Kaizen* encourages workers to use their brains as well as their hands. Employees are systematically rewarded for good suggestions. In Toyota, in Japan, workers provide 1.5 million

Exhibit 15.1 TQM critical success factors

Many corporations have improved their competitive position with TQM. Those who succeed exhibit a common set of critical success factors:

- Leadership and participation of key executives
- Training for all employees
- A team approach, in an open and sharing culture
- A long-term view
- A quantitative approach—application of statistical methods
- Focus on the customer and the delivery of excellence

These and other factors are measured against world-class standards for those who wish to compete for the coveted Malcolm Baldrige or Deming award for quality.

---

suggestions a year, and astonishingly 95 percent of them are put to practical use.[3] Rewards paid to workers are in proportion to the benefits measured after the suggestion has been put into practice.

Some companies set quotas for the number of improvements its employees suggest. Canon tells managers each to identify more than 200 tasks for improvement and foremen 100 tasks. Each supervisor posts a *kaizen* Project 100 sheet in his workshop. Each time an improvement is thought of, it is written on the sheet. In some plants foremen are told to set aside the half-hour between 11:30 A.M. and noon as *kaizen* time. There can be no phone calls or meetings during this half-hour, only thought or discussion about *kaizen* actions.

Just as many companies have an awards ceremony for salesmen, Canon has an awards ceremony for employees' suggestions (Exhibit 15.2).

Nine Types of Waste

Canon identifies nine types of waste (Exhibit 15.3) and trains its employees to eliminate them using *kaizen* techniques and its suggestion scheme. Canon estimates that it saved $100 million in 1983 and a similar amount in other years. It is worth substantial effort to achieve such savings.

Problems are Opportunities

To the practitioner of TQM *(kaizen)*, every problem is an opportunity for improvement. He seeks out problems like a hunter searching for deer. He then analyses the causes of the problem and creates solutions.

The cause of a problem is often buried several layers deep. Many questions have to be asked to uncover the cause.

Exhibit 15.2   Canon's annual awards

Canon gives annual *kaizen* awards at a ceremony somewhat less glitzy than Hollywood's Oscar.

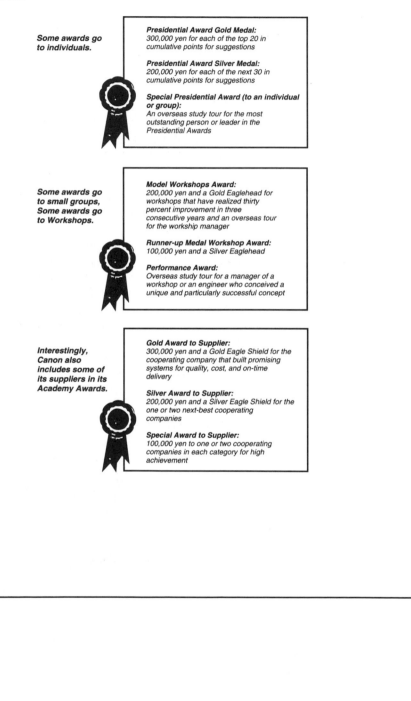

Some awards go to individuals.

Presidential Award Gold Medal:
300,000 yen for each of the top 20 in cumulative points for suggestions

Presidential Award Silver Medal:
200,000 yen for each of the next 30 in cumulative points for suggestions

Special Presidential Award (to an individual or group):
An overseas study tour for the most outstanding person or leader in the Presidential Awards

Some awards go to small groups, Some awards go to Workshops.

Model Workshops Award:
200,000 yen and a Gold Eaglehead for workshops that have realized thirty percent improvement in three consecutive years and an overseas tour for the workship manager

Runner-up Medal Workshop Award:
100,000 yen and a Silver Eaglehead

Performance Award:
Overseas study tour for a manager of a workshop or an engineer who conceived a unique and particularly successful concept

Interestingly, Canon also includes some of its suppliers in its Academy Awards.

Gold Award to Supplier:
300,000 yen and a Gold Eagle Shield for the cooperating company that built promising systems for quality, cost, and on-time delivery

Silver Award to Supplier:
200,000 yen and a Silver Eagle Shield for the one or two next-best cooperating companies

Special Award to Supplier:
100,000 yen to one or two cooperating companies in each category for high achievement

Exhibit 15.3   Nine types of waste in production (identified in Canon)[4]

Waste Category	Nature of Waste	Type of Economization
Work in process	Stocking items not immediately needed	Inventory improvement
Rejection	Producing defective products	Fewer rejects
Facilities	Having idle machinery and breakdowns, taking too long for set-up	Increase in capacity utilization ratio
Expenses	Overinvesting for required output	Curtailment of expenses
Indirect labor	Excess personnel resulting from a bad indirect-labor system	Efficient job assignment
Design	Producing products with more functions than necessary	Cost reduction
Talent	Employing people for jobs that can be mechanized or assigned to less-skilled people	Labor saving or labor maximization
Motion	Not working according to work standard	Improvement of work standard
New-product run-up	Making a slow start in stabilizing the production of a new product	Faster shift to full line production

The Five *Whys*

One technique for finding the cause of problems is to ask why? multiple times until the root cause emerges. At Toyota one is expected to ask why five times.[5]

Leadership

TQM needs to be driven from the top in an enterprise. The company's senior leaders need to create clear quality values and to put into place the system for achieving quality goals—the measurements, suggestion schemes, quality circles, kaizen culture, and the ingredients of TQM in Exhibit 15.7.

Sometimes numeric targets for quality are established by top management. Motorola set a goal that there should be no more than 3.4 products in a million, on average, with a defect. (3.4 in 1,000,000 is six standard deviations in a normal distribution. It is referred to as six sigma quality). IBM, following Motorola, set a multi-year goal to improve software quality to no more than 3.4 bugs per million lines of code.

Managers throughout the company need to have regular involvement in visible activities concerned with quality performance, awards ceremonies, and personal recognition of quality achievement.

Exhibit 15.4 Five Whys

FIVE WHY's

1. ***Why did the machine stop functioning?***
   There was an overload and the fuse blew.
2. ***Why was there an overload?***
   The bearing was not sufficiently lubricated.
3. ***Why was it not lubricated sufficiently?***
   The lubrication pump was not working sufficiently.
4. ***Why was it not working sufficiently?***
   The shaft of the pump was worn and rattling.
5. ***Why was the shaft worn out?***
   There was no strainer attached and scrap metal got in.

If "Why?" was not asked 5 times, the fuse or the shaft might be replaced.

The problem will occur again unless a strainer is attached.

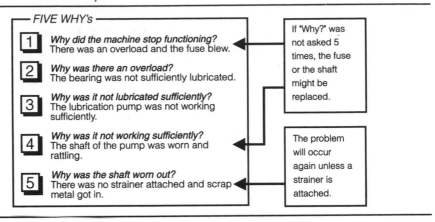

Exhibit 15.5 Five Whys

FIVE WHY's

1. ***Why can't the I.T. Department build the applications we need?***
   Because it has a 3-year backlog.
2. ***Why does it have a large backlog?***
   Because application development takes a long time.
3. ***Why does it take a long time?***
   Because it takes much work to code and debug COBOL.
4. ***Why is COBOL used?***
   Because nobody has developed skills with code generators.
5. ***Why has nobody developed these skills?***
   Because insufficient money is spent on I.T. education.

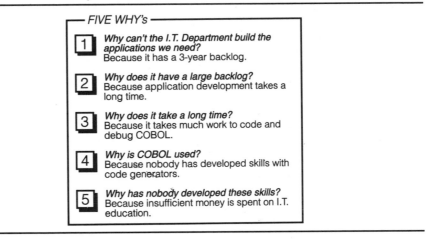

Exhibit 15.6 Five Whys

FIVE WHY's

1. ***Why will the supplied part not fit?***
   Because it is out of tolerance.
2. ***Why?***
   Because a suppliers machine will not hold tolerance.
3. ***Why?***
   The machine operators cannot be adequately trained.
4. ***Why?***
   Employees keep quitting to look for other work.
5. ***Why?***
   Because the work is noisy and unchallenging.

Solution: Reduce the noise. Challenge the workers to continuously improve the work process.

The ultimate cause is often an organizational problem.

Exhibit 15.8 lists roles necessary at different levels for TQM.

Motorola provides a dramatic illustration of what is possible when quality is pursued relentlessly.

In 1987 it had six defects in each thousand components it produced. It set a goal referred to as *six sigma* (See next chapter)—that there should be no more than 3.4 defects in a million components. By the end of 1992 it had driven defects down to 35 per million on average and to six sigma for some products. It continued on its journey to six sigma, and Motorola Chairman George Fisher considered setting an even tighter goal of 60 defects per billion.

Some companies complain that high quality is expensive. However, Motorola's quality drive succeeding in lowering the cost of manufacturing, partly because the correcting of defects is expensive.

To achieve close to zero defects, a corporation requires high quality from its suppliers. Motorola set a requirement that its suppliers apply for the prestigious Malcolm Baldrige Award for quality. Motorola would hold special coaching classes for its suppliers. Some suppliers balked at applying for the Baldrige Award, saying they did not have the time, and forfeited sales to Motorola.

When patients in hospital have operations, 2 percent on average (in the United States) have postoperative wound infections, very unpleasant for the patient. The inflamed incision needs cleaning with sutures over the abscess and packing the wound with gauze, which is painful and expensive, needs more days in hospital, and at worst can result in death.

The Intermountain 520-bed LDS Hospital at Salt Lake City used TQM techniques and succeeded in reducing its postoperative wound infections from 1.8 percent to 0.4 percent of their operations.[6]

A study showed that only a few hundred of America's 6 thousand hospitals have made a start with TQM techniques.[6]

International Quality Standards

Before TQM spread in the West, the Japanese Industrial Standards body created a standard for quality (JIS Z 8101–1981). It defined quality control (QC) as: "a system of means to economically produce goods or services that satisfy customer requirements." The Japanese standards states:

> Implementing quality control effectively necessitates the cooperation of all people in the company, including top management, managers, supervisors, and workers in all areas of corporate activities such as market research and development, product planning, design, preparations for production, purchasing, vendor management, manufactur-

Exhibit 15.7   The ingredients of TQM

Top management drives TQM culture	Small teams
KAIZEN attitude pervades the entire workforce	Qualitative analysis of problems
Focus on delighting the customer	In-depth analysis of problem causes
Constant improvement of the work process	Statistical quality control
Systematic suggestion scheme, with awards	Benchmarking
Quality circles	Information systems designed for continuous improvement
Quality Function Deployment	TQM linked to other aspects of Enterprise Engineering 287

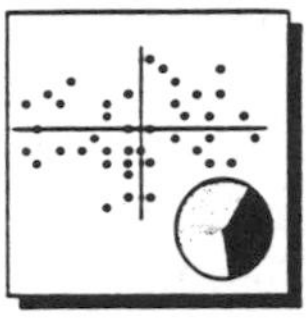

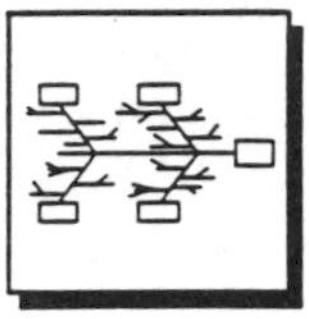

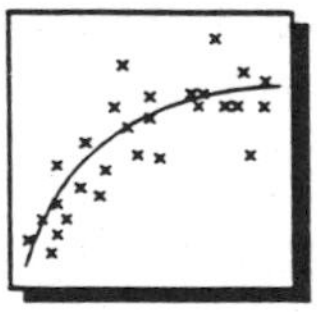

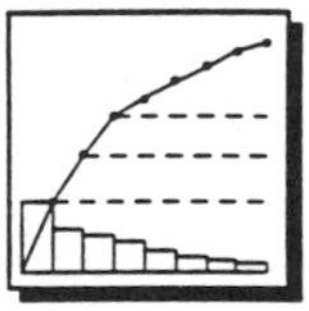

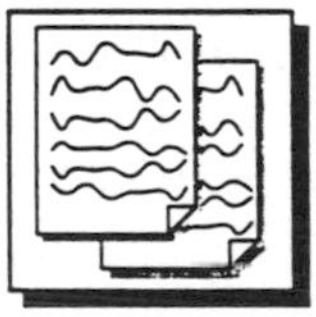

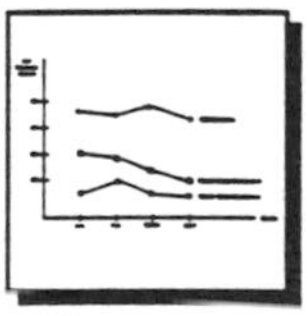

Exhibit 15.8   TQM Roles

Top Management

- Be determined to introduce TQM as a corporate strategy.
- Allocate resources for TQM.
- Realize TQM through policy development.
- Build *kaizen*-capable system, including *kaizen*-capable IT.
- Ensure that TQM is used to help value-stream reinvention succeed.

Middle Management

- Deploy and implement TQM programs and policy.
- Audit the use of TQM.
- Upgrade standard operating procedures.
- Make employees TQM conscious through intensive training.
- Help employees develop skills for problem solving.
- Ensure that TQM is used to make reinvented processes succeed.

Supervisors

- Formulate plans for *kaizen* and provide guidance to workers.
- Improve communication with workers and sustain high morale.
- Support quality circles.
- Support the suggestion scheme.
- Provide *kaizen* suggestions.
- Support and participate in facilitated workshops.
- Ensure workplace discipline in following improved procedures.

Workers

- Participate fully in the suggestion scheme.
- Participate in quality circles.
- Participate in facilitated workshops for improving the work processes.
- Engage in continuous self-improvement to become better problem solvers.
- Enhance job skills.
- Adopt a policy of delighting the customer.

ing, inspection, sales and after-sales services, as well as financial control, personnel administration, and training and education. Quality control carried out in this manner is called Company-Wide Quality Control (CWQC) or Total Quality Control (TQC).

Six years later the International Standards Organization published a set of quality standards, ISO 9000 (see Exhibit 15.9). The standards have been widely accepted and adhered to in Europe and elsewhere. Many thousands of European supplies have ISO 9000 certification. Many buyers make this certification a prerequisite for purchase. Some laws relating to machine safety and product liability relate to ISO 9000 conformity, which could help defend products against liability claims in European courts.

The Malcolm Baldrige Quality Award

As the quality movement swept through the United States in the late 1980s, the Government established a prestigious award for corporations that excel in quality—the Malcolm Baldrige Award (Exhibit 15.10). For the first years the award was presented by the President of the U.S.A. in person. In three years there were requests for 180 thousand copies of the Application Guidelines.[7] Even corporations that were not serious contenders for the award found that following the guidelines improved their operations; they helped to establish quality as a state of mind.

The award examination addresses all key requirements of TQM. It focuses not only on results but on the processes and conditions that lead to results. It offers a framework for continual process improvement:

- Quality is defined by the customer.
- The senior leadership of businesses needs to create clear quality values and build the values into the way the company operates.
- Quality excellence derives from well-designed and executed systems and processes.
- Continuous improvement must be part of the management of all systems and processes.
- Companies need to develop goals, as well as strategic and operational plans to achieve quality leadership.
- Shortening the response time of all operations and processes of the company needs to be part of the quality improvement effort.
- Operations and decisions of the company need to be based upon facts and data.
- All employees must be suitably trained and developed and involved in quality activities.
- Design quality and defect-and-error prevention should be major elements of the quality system.
- Companies need to communicate quality requirements to suppliers and work to elevate supplier quality performance.[7]

The Deming Prize

The Deming Prize was created in Japan nearly four decades before the Baldrige Award was in the United States. The Deming Prize requires an application of

Exhibit 15.9 The ISO 9000 Standards

The ISO 9000 Standards

ISO 9000 is a series of five standards for developing Total Quality Management and a Quality Improvement Process, for the Geneva-based International Standards Organization.

- ISO 9000 establishes basic definitions and concepts. It offers guidelines to help select and use the other documents, ISO 9001 through ISO 9004.

- ISO 9001 outlines a model for quality assurance in design, development, production, installation, and servicing.

- ISO 9002 outlines a model for a quality assurance in production and installation.

- ISO 9003 outlines a model for quality assurance only for final inspection and testing.

- ISO 9004 provides guidance to organizations on applying total quality principles. It is similar to the Malcolm Baldridge National Quality Award guidelines

ISO 9000 has been adopted by many countries as their own national standard. Most countries have assigned their own numbers to the standards as shown.

To be certified a company must demonstrate that it is committed to quality. For example, to comply with the requirements of ISO 9001, a company must show that it controls the quality of its products at all stages from the initial design to after-sale support. Qualified assessors are used to certify that each company meets the rigorous standards of ISO 9000 before certification is given.

The U.S. Department of Defense is replacing its quality standard MIL-Q-9858A with ISO 9000. Conformance will be required for sales to DoD.

Many thousands of European suppliers are certified to the ISO 9000 standard. Some buyers insist that suppliers meet ISO 9000 standards as a condition of purchase.

COUNTRY	STANDARD #
Australia	AS 3900
Austria	OE NORM-PREN 29000
Belgium	MBN X 50-002-1
China	GB/T 10300.1-88
Denmark	DS/EN 29000
European Community	EN 29000-1987
Finland	SFS-ISO 9000
France	NF X 50-121
Germany	DIN ISO-9000
Hungary	MI 18990-1988
India	IS: 10201 PART 2
Ireland	IS 300 PART O/ ISO 9000
Italy	UNI/EN 29000-1987
Netherlands	NEN-ISO 9000
New Zealand	NZS 5600: PART 1-1987
Norway	NS-EN 29000:1988
Russia	40.9001-88
South Africa	SABS 0157: PART 0
Spain	UNE 66 900
Sweden	SS-ISO 9000: 1988
Switzerland	SN-ISO 9000
Tunisia	NT 110.18-1987
United Kingdom	BS 5750: 1987: PART 1 ISO 9000/ EN 29000
USA	ANSI/ASQC Q90-1987

up to 1,000 pages, as opposed to about 75 for the Baldrige Award. Winning the prestigious Deming Prize is an immense job. An NEC subsidiary that won it, for example, submitted 244 thousand pages of directives, plans, and reports.[8] This enormous amount of work did pay off, however, in improved quality translating into improved profits.

Winning the Baldrige requires about three times as much detail as ISO 9000 certification. It has been said that ISO 9000 is just the bare bones of quality.

The Baldrige Award and the ISO 9000 standards have had a major effect on encouraging Western corporations to improve their quality so that they compete better. Winning the Baldrige Award and ISO 9000 certification, however, does not guarantee success. Some winners have had disastrous corporate problems after winning. Much more is needed to run a company well than TQM. TQM is only one technique on the spectrum of change methods that Enterprise Engineering must address.

Exhibit 15.10

The Malcolm Baldrige National Quality Award is an annual Award to recognize U.S. companies that excel in quality achievement and quality management.

The Award promotes:

Awareness of Quality

Understanding of the Requirements for Quality Excellence

Sharing of Information on successful Quality Strategies.

Three Eligibility categories of the Award are:

Manufacturing Companies,

Service Companies, and

Small Businesses

Up to two Awards may be given in each category each year. Recipients are expected to share information about their successful quality strategies with other U.S. organizations.

Companies participating in the Award process submit applications that include completion of the Award Examination. The Award Examination is based upon quality excellence criteria created through a public-private partnership. In responding to these criteria, applicants are expected to provide information and data on their quality processes and quality improvement Information and data submitted must be adequate to demonstrate that the applicant's approaches could be replicated or adapted by other companies.

The Award Examination is designed to serve not only as a reliable basis for making Awards but also to permit a diagnosis of the applicants overall quality management. All Award applicants receive feedback reports prepared by teams of U.S. quality experts.

Award recipients may publicize and advertise receipt of the award and will receive recognition for sharing information about their successful quality strategies.

THE U.S. MALCOLM BALDRIGE AWARD

"Photograph courtesy of the National Institute of Standards and Technology, Office of Quality Programs, Gaithersburg, Maryland, 20899. Photograph by Steuben."

References

1. David Kearns and David Nadler, *Prophets in the Dark* (Harper Business: New York, 1986).
2. Jeffrey Ferry, *The British Renaissance* (William Heinemann: London, 1993).
3. Eiji Toyoda, Chairman of Toyota Motor Co., quoted in Masaaki Imai, *Kaizen: The Key to Japan's Competitive Success* (McGraw Hill: New York, 1986).
4. Imai, *Kaisen.*
5. Ibid.
6. *The Quality Imperative,* A Business Week Guide (McGraw Hill: New York, 1994).
7. The Malcolm Baldrige National Quality Award, managed by United States Department of Commerce National Institute of Standards and Technology, Route 270 and Quince Orchard Road, Administration Building, Room A537 Gaithersburg, Md. 20899.
8. *The Quality Imperative.*

16

Statistics and Problem Solving

For some problems there are obvious solutions. TQM tackles less-simple problems by investigating them in depth and collecting and analyzing statistics. Statistical quality control insists that data and statistics be used, rather than hunches, to help ensure that the right problems are addressed and the best solutions found. Relevant aspects of a process such as yield, cycle time, defect rate, productivity, etcetera are plotted against time or plotted for each batch. Exceptional values can be observed on the plot and overall variance computed. It makes sense to enter the relevant data into a personal computer spreadsheet tool that can print clear charts to help in clarifying the problem.

The diagrams for analyzing a problem, categorizing its causes, planning countermeasures, and checking the results, are used as a team cycles through the PDCA loop (Exhibits 16.1 and 16.2).

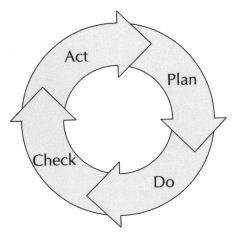

Exhibit 16.1 Three types of charts commonly used

First—statistical charts are drawn showing the nature of the problem, its frequency of occurrence, and its severity. Histograms, bar charts, pie charts, scatter diagrams, control graphs, and other graphs may be used.

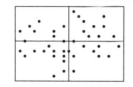

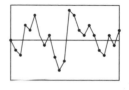

Second—a cause-and-effect diagram is drawn, showing a breakdown of the causes of the problem. Sometimes this is called a fishbone graph.

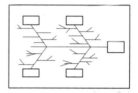

Third—a Pareto diagram is drawn, showing the relative importance of the different causes of the problem that are on the fishbone diagram.

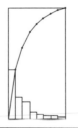

Example: The Telephone Problem

Consider a company whose potential customers phone in. It is desirable for the callers to receive a good impression. The operators who take the calls are trained to be pleasant as possible. Nevertheless, the telephone sometimes rings many times before an operator answers. This may irritate a potential customer or create a bad impression. Surveys indicate that if the phone rings more than five times before it is answered, the person often does not call again.

Exhibit 16.3 relates to a half-hour period during which 46 calls are received. Most are answered promptly, but 17.4 percent are answered after five rings. Worse, 6.5 percent ring off before the call is answered—they are lost.[1]

This is clearly a problem that needs to be solved. Figures for the rest of the day indicate that some times are worse than the above half-hour. This is made clear on charts such as Exhibit 16.4.

Exhibit 16.2   Diagrams for statistical quality control used at various stages of the PDCA cycle

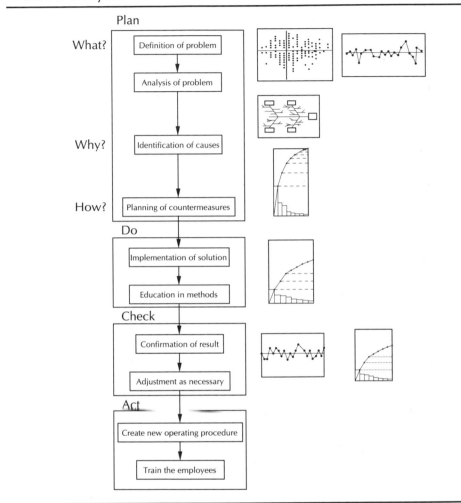

Cause-and-Effect Diagrams

As with most problems there could be multiple causes. Therefore, a cause-and-effect diagram is drawn. Four overall factors specified in Exhibit 16.5 may contribute to the delay.

The group dealing with the problem explores the possible causes and fills in a cause-and-effect diagram like that in Exhibit 16.6.

This form of diagram is called a fishbone graph. In Japan it is sometimes called a Godzilla-bone graph; that name is not used in the West because this is serious! The diagram is a hierarchy and can equally well be represented with

Exhibit 16.3   Time: 11:30–12:00 a.m.

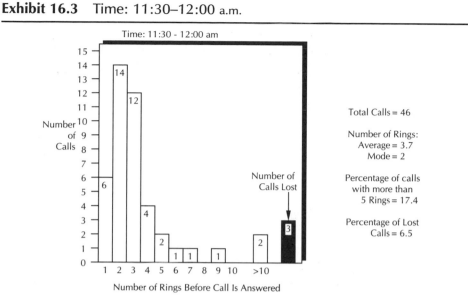

Time: 11:30 - 12:00 am

Total Calls = 46

Number of Rings:
Average = 3.7
Mode = 2

Percentage of calls
with more than
5 Rings = 17.4

Percentage of Lost
Calls = 6.5

Number of Calls Lost

Number of Rings Before Call Is Answered

Exhibit 16.4

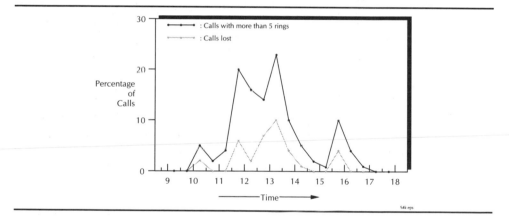

: Calls with more than 5 rings

: Calls lost

Percentage of Calls

Time

Exhibit 16.5

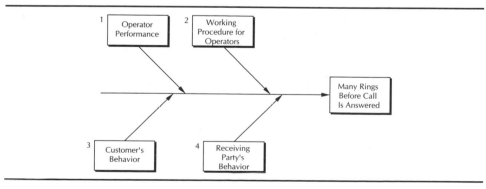

Exhibit 16.6   Analysis of the causes of a problem (Ishikawa diagram)

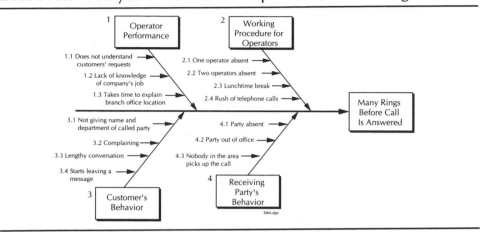

the hierarchical outlining tools that exist in software, such as Microsoft Word or Persuasion. Such programs makes it easy to manipulate the cause-and-effect list, and can automatically number the items.

Pareto Diagrams

Of the possible causes on a cause-and-effect diagram some may be major contributors to the problem; others not. A Pareto diagram shows how frequently the different causes occur. In the above case the telephone operators keep a tally sheet during certain time periods to show how frequently the causes occur. Each time the cause occurs a dash is marked on the tally sheet. The relative frequency is plotted on the following Pareto diagram.

This shows that the most common cause is number 2.1 from the fishbone graph (Exhibit 16.6)— *One operator absent.* The next most frequent cause is number 4.2—*Party out of office.*

After analyzing the causes of the problem and measuring their frequency, the team knows where to direct its efforts in solving the problem. Causes easy to correct should be corrected immediately. Some must be corrected because they are a major contributor to the overall problem. Various corrective actions are taken, and the number of Pareto diagrams is redrawn to show the effect.

The operators are now rarely absent. The biggest problems are that the party is out of the office and that nobody picks up the call there. Because of this a rule can require parties leaving their desks to notify the operator. Cause number 1.2 (operator's lack of knowledge of company's job) is still a problem, so a list can be compiled to help the operators.

Exhibit 16.7

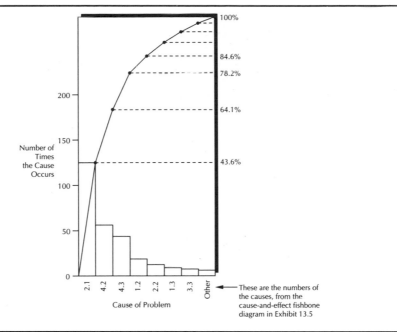

Exhibit 16.8

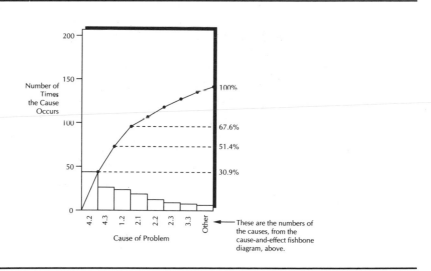

Exhibit 16.9

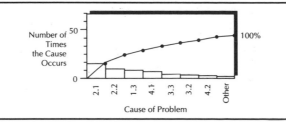

Exhibit 16.10   The normal density function

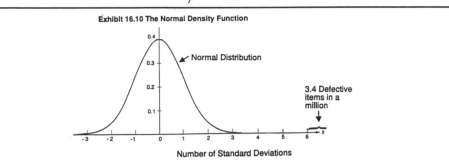

The Pareto chart after implementing these improvements is as follows.

The group has thus eliminated one cause after another of the problem, with the guidance of the statistics collected.

The diagrams shown here should be pinned on the wall—in the work area, in this case the telephone operators' room—and a goal should be set to lower the bars of the Pareto chart as much as possible by making continual improvements.

Statistical Quality Control

When components are manufactured, there is a certain amount of variation from one unit to another. If the variation is larger than a certain amount, it will cause problems. Measurements are made and plotted statistically so that if they drift too much the problem can be detected and action taken to correct it. Employees are taught to understand the trend graphs and quality-control charts. In nonmanufacturing work, elapsed time, error rate, mistakes, number of customer complaints, and other measures can be examined statistically so that relentless steps can be taken to improve quality. Deviations from acceptable limits are examined with techniques such as fishbone diagrams and Pareto charts. Many corporations train employees to monitor quality continuously. Many courses teach techniques of statistical quality control.

Design of Experiments

We have emphasized that, in order to keep ahead of its competition, a corporation needs to experiment, not just in a remote laboratory but in the workplace. Workers on the factory floor, quality circles, and value-stream teams should conduct experiments in order to find fundamentally better ways to do things.

Sometimes a problem has many possible causes. We often guess the cause and correct that, but the true cause may lie elsewhere. We can find the true cause by experimenting. We need to design experiments that help us distinguish among the different factors that might cause the problem.

A statistical technique called design of experiments (DoE) has been used for decades in fields such as agricultural research to discover what mix of fertilizer, crop rotation, seed varieties and planning methods provides the best yield. A Japanese engineer, Genichi Taguchi, learned how to apply DoE to improve product quality in manufacturing.[2] Taguchi's method produced a relatively quick way to test a large number of possible causes of defects or variations in quality and to rank them statistically in terms of their impact. Instead of seat-of-the-pants experimenting, which we often do, Taguchi's disciples experimented systematically and located the variables that required attention first. Dorian Shainin, an American, developed a simpler and more accurate version of DoE that is used widely in Motorola and elsewhere.[3] Simple, disciplined design of experiments can be applied to the continuous improvement of both products and processes in many types of work.

When problems need to be solved, often the most plausible ideas are used without any testing. Workers and their managers accept feasible conclusions and make changes. Often a large amount of money is spent on the changes without experimentation. DoE techniques systematically evaluate the effects of different variables and determine which are important. Variables thought to be important frequently are not, whereas others are critical.

In the past, corporations have attempted to improve overall quality by tightening all specifications. DoE techniques can reveal that only certain specifications are critical. Sometimes a specification previously seen as crucial is found to have very little effect. A chef in a good restaurant may insist on using only the most expensive ingredients, but careful experiments reveal that, although certain ingredients need to be the best, others do not matter. By concentrating on the ingredients that matter, the chef can save money. The same is true in many processes. We should focus attention and effort on the factors that truly make a difference. The most effective general concentrates his forces on the few significant battles.

DoE techniques might reveal that cheaper materials are adequate for certain components, whereas other components need the best materials. Cheaper materials may be found to work well under certain temperature conditions, or if the design is changed, for example. A goal of DoE is to save money as well as produce a better product. It replaces casual tinkering with planned experiments.

Six-Sigma Quality

In many processes zero defects would be ideal, but this quality level is not quite attainable. The term *six-sigma* quality is used to mean that an average of 3.4 items in a million has a defect. The term originated in Motorola, where a target was set for the small electronics devices of no more than 3.4 defects in a million.

Sigma is the Greek letter used for a standard deviation in statistics. In a normal distribution 3.4 items in a million are more than six standard deviations away from the average. Hence the term *six-sigma quality*.

References

1. This illustration is derived from an example at the Ricoh Company, Ltd., which is published in *"The Quest for Higher Quality—The Deming prize and Quality Control"* (Ricoh Company, Ltd.: Japan, 19?).
2. "Case Study: Taguchi's Design of Experiments," *Productivity*, Vol. 10, No. 2, February 1989.
3. Keki R. Bhote, "DoE, The High Road to Quality," *Management Reviews*, January 1988.

17

Failures in TQM Programs

In today's corporations quality is essential, both in products and processes. Increasingly it is the price of survival. *Kaizen* is practiced with great benefits in almost all competitive companies in Japan. The continuous *learning* that comes from TQM offers a major competitive advantage. Some authorities have argued that it is the *only* source of sustainable competitive advantage.[1] In the long run a successful quality program is not an option for corporations doing business with today's intensifying global competition.

Nevertheless, many Western corporations have found their TQM programs a failure. Many have backed away from TQM because they failed to derive any lasting significant benefit from the program. In March 1992 a study carried out by Arthur D. Little showed that only 36 percent of the 500 companies surveyed considered adoption of TQM significantly to boost competitiveness. Studies by McKinsey & Co., Ernst and Young, A. T. Kearney, and Rath and Strong showed similar results. For every TQM success story in the United States, there are two corporations that have failed in using TQM to achieve significant or even "tangible" improvements in quality, productivity, competitiveness, or financial returns.[2]

Given the vital importance of quality, this finding is alarming. It is essential to know why quality programs fail and how to correct the causes of failure.

Reasons for Failing

There are many reasons for disappointing TQM results, but these are the common causes:

- Lack of top management leadership and commitment
- Expectations of quick results
- Lack of true employee empowerment
- Failure to recognize the need for culture change
- Limited scope of application
- Emphasis on the internal rather than the external customer

The failure of some companies to achieve benefit from the adoption of TQM is a result of the way it was implemented rather than the approach itself. What is needed is top-management commitment to a corporatewide *kaizen* culture that is expected to have long-term rather than short-term benefits and that applies to everything and everybody.

A *kaizen* culture does not require a large investment but does require ongoing effort and commitment. In order for the *kaizen* spirit to survive, management must make a conscious and continuous effort to support it. Management by slogan and periodic fanfare does not grow a *kaizen* culture.

Oren Harari, analyzing the reasons for TQM failure, concludes that TQM is not synonymous with quality. "Quality is about unbending focus, passion, iron discipline, and a way of life for all hands. TQM is about statistics, jargon, committees, and quality departments."[2] TQM is often implemented badly.

> **Quality is sacred; TQM is not.**
>
> —Oren Harari of the Tom Peters Group

Bottom-Line Payback

The companies that have implemented TQM well have achieved a major bottom-line payback.

The U.S. Government Accounting Office (GAO) studied in detail the effects of TQM in 20 Baldrige Award winners.[3] The average annual performance improvements of these companies are impressive, as Exhibit 17.1 shows. Their annual increase in market share was 13.7 percent at the time of the Baldrige Award. The improvements in Exhibit 17.1 come from good management in general and should not be attributed solely to TQM; however, the TQM program was a major contributor.

The GAO noted that *a TQM strategy does not produce quick results.* It took an average of 2.5 years, with a range of 1-to-5 years for 20 companies studied to realize initial benefits. The benefits continue to grow if quality programs are maintained over a long period, as Japanese *kaizen*-based companies have shown.

While the 20 Baldrige Award winners studied by GAO have had major benefits from TQM, many other companies have not. Brian Usilaner, the project leader of the GAO study, described two approaches to TQM that he called "Big *Q* and Little *q*."[4]

Big *Q* and Little *q*

Big *Q* programs integrate TQM into the fabric and strategy of a company, with full top-management support. To do this demands fundamental changes in corporate culture with an emphasis on empowered teams of employees continually seeking improvements in everything. This TQM culture continues to produce results on a long-term basis.

Exhibit 17.1   Average annual improvements achieved by 20 Baldrige Award winners

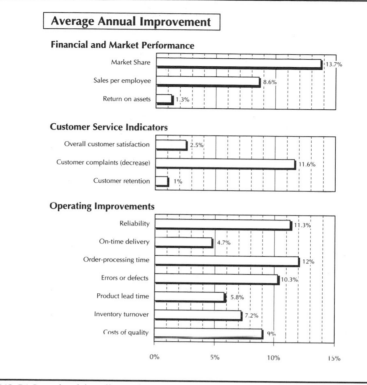

—from a US GAO study of the effects of TQM.[3]

Little q programs emphasize training, tools, and techniques, but do not make fundamental changes in the culture. They often have short-term slogan blitzes but no change in corporate structure. Top management gives lip service but little energetic support. As shown in Exhibit 17.2, Little q often fades after some initial results, where as Big Q brings long-term ongoing improvements. Little q "hits a wall" after two or three years, after which improvements cease.

Commitment of Top Management

All 20 of the companies GAO studied could not stress enough the need for top management to drive the TQM strategy. TQM needs top-management leadership, visibility, and sustained commitment over the long haul. The study commented, "If a number could be set on the amount of time senior management directly spent on quality activities, it was about 20 percent."[4]

Top-management attitudes to quality programs might be categorized as un-involved, supportive, and active. The *uninvolved* CEO lets somebody else handle quality issues. The *supportive* CEO allows the investment in TQM, encourages TQM consultants, and occasionally attends quality-related meetings. The *active* CEO is passionate about quality and makes this known; he allocates time and attention to quality issues; he makes sure that quality is on the agenda at planning and strategy meetings. The active CEO makes everyone know that TQM is not just another management program but a permanent change in the organization and way of life of the enterprise. It changes the design of teams, the organization of the production line, the relationships with suppliers. It is integrated into all the strategic and operational planning.

Active commitment of all senior management is needed to register on the Big Q curve of Exhibit 17.2.

Reward Systems

Successful quality efforts have well-established reward and recognition systems for all employees who achieve quality improvements. Companies have spent time and effort developing such systems. In particular, management compensation must relate to quality, as it does at Ford, Federal Express, Motorola, and others.

An Ernst and Young study that pointed out the failure of about two-thirds of TQM efforts found that less than 20 percent of organizations in the auto, banking, computer, and healthcare industries had senior-management pay affected by de-fect rates, quality-performance measures, or customer-satisfaction measures.[2]

Fads and Wall Posters

In some companies quality campaigns have been treated like a drive to raise church funds. There are speeches, wall posters, slogans, cartoons, and fairground ring-the-bell scales. The quality drive is treated as though it were a quick fix to existing procedures. Many employees regard it with cynicism and know that soon there will be a different campaign.

A true quality turnaround cannot be achieved with a quick fix. It needs a culturally pervasive change in the way work is done. Like any culture change it takes time and meets resistance. It is an emotionally disruptive process that changes an organization from the core out. It needs new teams who become ex-cited about working in new ways. It demands sustained care and attention from management. When the culture change is achieved, it becomes a way of life.

Too many seminars say that TQM can be achieved without this gut-wrenching upheaval. It is sold as a neat, easy set of techniques with training classes and charts.

Exhibit 17.2   Reasons some TQM programs fail and others succeed

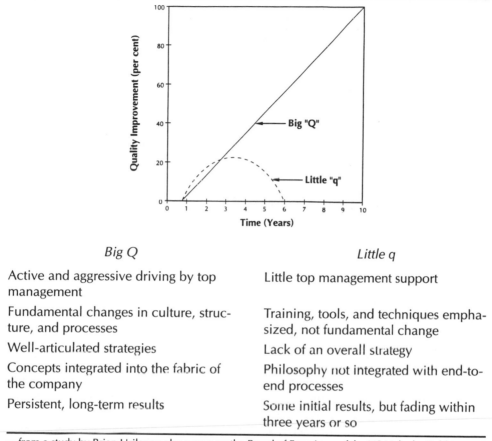

	Big Q	Little q
	Active and aggressive driving by top management	Little top management support
	Fundamental changes in culture, structure, and processes	Training, tools, and techniques emphasized, not fundamental change
	Well-articulated strategies	Lack of an overall strategy
	Concepts integrated into the fabric of the company	Philosophy not integrated with end-to-end processes
	Persistent, long-term results	Some initial results, but fading within three years or so

—from a study by Brian Usilaner who serves on the Board of Examiners of the US Malcolm Baldrige Award[4]

Bureaucracy

TQM, like other techniques, can be turned into a bureaucracy in which rules, charts, and measurements take on a life of their own. As the bureaucracy grows (and it is never *called* a bureaucracy), the quality-assurance staff multiplies and creates more statistics, more techniques that must be adhered to, more sign-offs, and reams of paperwork.

Florida Light and Power won the Malcolm Baldrige Award in 1989. It achieved some particularly interesting innovations in quality. For example, Florida has 80 days of thunderstorms on average each year, and lightning causes service interruptions. The company developed a computer-based lightning tracking system to anticipate where problems might occur and positioned crews at these locations to speed up recovery. It set out to halve the number of minutes of service unavailability. However, the quality department at Florida Light and Power grew to 85 full-time individuals monitoring 1900 quality teams with detailed statistics. The quality review system took on a life of its own. It grew large and expensive without corresponding gains in customer-perceived quality. Management eventually slashed back the quality bureaucracy, shrinking it from 85 individuals to 6.

When a culture of quality pervades a work force, it should not need quality police with endless paper sign-offs and statistics. The pressure to achieve certain statistics often causes stress and depression, and employees concentrate on fudging the numbers. True quality is reflected in every employee's taking pride in doing the best job possible and in finding ingenious ways to solve problems and make improvements. True quality is shown in pride in work, not statistics and form filling. Statistics can show where to focus effort in solving problems.

True quality requires the people who do the work to "own" the process and be excited about improving it in any way they can. It relies on constant feedback from the customer so that customer-perceived problems and wishes are dealt with. It needs the determination of every member of each team not to let the team down.

Paradoxically, ISO 9000 certification, and to a lessor extent the Baldrige Award, have resulted in a cynical attitude toward quality. Companies cannot bid for various government sales, especially in Europe, unless they have ISO 9000 certification, so they ask, "How do we get certification as quickly as possible? What forms do we have to fill in?" If the form asks, "Is the quality program driven by top management?" they fill in "Yes." That was easy; what's the next question? ISO 9000 certification becomes an exercise in bureaucracy rather than a careful, long-term effort to change the culture of all employees.

As any craftsman knows, true quality is perceived in subtle ways that defy numeric measurement. Max de Pree, the respected ex-CEO of the Herman Miller furniture company, emphasized the need for a "covenant" between a company and its employees in which the company constantly helps and encourages the employee to learn and the employee constantly helps the company to improve. De Pree commented, "Managers who only understand methodologies and quantification are modern-day eunuchs."

The Quality Czar

Many companies have appointed an executive in charge of quality. Particularly important in the skills of the quality czar are the abilities to persuade, cajole, plead, sell, close an agreement, and the other skills of a successful salesman. The quality czar needs mover-and-shaker skills. The basic QA (quality assurance) knowledge may be added to by sending the quality czar to a course on selling.

Such courses teach how to listen to customers—the employees who need to be persuaded about quality.

Often, however, the quality czar is more statistician than salesman. There can be good reasons for not using a QA professional as the quality czar. The technical side of QA can be fairly easy, compared with the difficulties of convincing people to accept the culture of quality and do something about it. The more technical and purist about QA the leader is, the more he needs training on selling and human sensitivity.

Inward-Looking TQM

TQM ought to be looking hard at the customers and how to please them. However, in many corporations it has become a program with an internal focus in which little attention is paid to the customer.

The approach is preoccupied with the processes, as indeed it should be, but sometimes this focus inward is done at the expense of attention outward toward the market and its changing needs. GE used to describe it as having its face toward internal management and its back toward the customer.

The TQM measurements are often concerned mainly with internal performance, counts of defects, productivity, absence of rework, and not with the constantly shifting perceptions and preferences of customers or the potential enhancements in products or services that have a growing effect on competitiveness. The internal focus might result in higher quality in products that are out-of-date, unexciting, uncompetitive, or irrelevant. The Baldrige Award reinforces the internal preoccupation by allotting 750 or so possible points out of 1000 to internal-process improvement and only 250 or so to the actual *results* of the quality efforts.[2]

The emphasis on internal-process improvement is important and would only be harmful if it were done at the expense of external focus on customer needs. If the company becomes more efficient but less responsive, less flexible, or less interesting, it will lose market share in spite of its efficiency. Oren Harari quotes a manager as saying that before his firm's TQM investment they produced "poorly made products that customers don't want." After TQM they produced "well-made products that the customers don't want."[2]

Requirements for Big *Q*

The GAO study concluded that companies that have made the most progress with TQM have the following characteristics:

Active Top Management—CEO and top management drive the principles of quality throughout the corporation. They constantly revitalize quality strategies.

Delighting the Customer—There is a central focus on listening to the customers—not only meeting current needs but anticipating future needs and developing innovations to delight the customers.

A Culture of Quality—The corporation's culture is adjusted to support the philosophy of quality. This requires empowered teams and removal of autocratic management. The processes and systems must be aligned with quality principles.

Quality Involving Everybody—Quality-improvement efforts should extend to the lowest levels of the organization. The philosophy of quality should be understood by everybody. Everybody must be appropriately trained and know that improvement never stops.

Management by Fact—Quality efforts need better systems for gathering, analyzing, and using data about the company's performance and customer needs. The data must be made easy to understand.

Involving Suppliers—Suppliers must be made full partners in the quality-improvement process. A corporation and its supplier may climb a joint learning curve. Suppliers not committed to joint quality must be replaced.

Success in these six aspects of quality is needed for Big Q (as in Exhibit 17.2).

TQM versus Mozart

Tom Peters describes a scene from the film *Amadeus* when he talks about TQM.[2] Mozart sits at the piano and plays a Salieri score with absolute precision before Emperor Joseph II. The music is uninspiring. But then Mozart begins to improvise, and suddenly he makes the music magnificent and emotional. The mechanically perfect rendering, Peters says, is zero-defects TQM music.

Zero-defects quality is the admission ticket today. Without it Mozart would not have played to Emperor Joseph II. But to achieve greatness, we need flair, excitement, and originality. Statistical quality control has nothing to say about Mozart. The winners in products and services today are those with sizzle and inspiration. Sony camcorders, Italian silk scarves, good Parisian restaurants, BBC television, and Macintosh computers have much, much more than zero-defects quality. We might distinguish between *TQM quality* and *inspirational quality*. TQM quality is, in a sense, minimal quality—the prerequisite to being in business. Inspirational quality is needed for world-class leadership. Customers want products that are useful, ingeniously designed, special, clever, bedazzling. Zero-defects quality represents only part of the package.

Unfortunately, intense focus on TQM, ISO 9000 or the Baldrige Award has seduced many companies into thinking that zero-defects TQM defines quality. Some cynics use the expression "six-sigma buggy whip" to refer to a product that has six-sigma quality but is obsolete. Many movies marshall the best cinematography that armies of skilled technicians can produce, but the script is pathetic. It is easy to concentrate on the mechanics and not the inspiration.

Mozart's music or Tolstoy's writing could not have been created by empowered teams and quality circles trained in statistical quality control. Inspiration usually comes from a unique individual. There are many unique individuals around, but we often build bureaucracies that shut them out. If Shakespeare worked for CBS, he would probably produce nothing worthwhile. We need corporate structures that encourage virtuosos to stretch their talents. Often the virtuosos are not good team players. Teams with TQM may implement what virtuosos design. Teams may be designed to pass work to unique specialists. In some corporations today, all the emphasis is on rather boring, regimented teams; there is no place for wild ducks that refuse to fly in formation. Inspirational quality is missing.

TQM, in some corporations, has been blamed for lack of innovation, inspiration, and creativity. Oren Harari, expressed it well:

> TQM attempts to make quality happen via an analytically detached, sterile, mechanical path. What's often missing, frankly, is emotion and soul. Go out and look at all the sincere individuals diligently following the step-by-step processes they've learned in the TQM ... training classes, and ask yourself: "Where's the love of our product and our customer? Where's the joy of the pursuit of excellence? Where's the passion in the doing and the creating? Where's the *fun* in being here? ... Where's the *thrill* in accomplishment?" If you can't find evidence of these, you probably won't find real quality either.[2]

References

1. Richard d. Spitzer, "TQM: The Only Source of Sustainable Competitive Advantage," *Quality Progress*, June 1993.
2. Oren Harari, "Ten Reasons Why TQM Doesn't Work," *Management Review*, January 1993.
3. *Management Practices: U.S. Companies Improve Performance Through Quality Efforts*, U.S. General Accounting Office, GAO/NSIAD-91-190, May 1991.
4. Brian Usilaner, "What's the Bottom-Line Payback for TQM?" *Engineering Management Journal*, Vol. 5, No. 2, June 1993.

18

TQM vs. Revolution

Quantum Leap before TQM

Chapter 3 spoke of many computer systems that have been built, and are being built today, that are the wrong systems. They automate an old procedure, when the real value of IT is that it makes possible dramatically different end-to-end processes. The same is true with TQM.

Most TQM effort is being expended on traditional processes, when what is really needed is dramatically different processes. Part II explored how corporate value streams need to be fundamentally reinvented. The reinventions are quantum-leap changes, which can be traumatic and risky but are badly needed. The reason for the reinvention is to address the needs of customers better. Often the speed of response is dramatically increased and customer service greatly improved. To achieve this improvement, the organization has to be torn apart and rebuilt. It needs discontinuous change, not the continuous change of *kaizen*. It is revolution, not evolution. Even value-stream reinvention is not right unless it is an implementation of the strategic vision to be discussed in Part V. In Europe most ISO 9000 effort is harmful because it is applied to processes which should not exist and tends to sanctify those processes.

> *TQM ought to be applied to reinvented value streams, not the old value streams.*

There would have been no point in applying TQM to the Soviet economy of 1991. What was needed was a revolution in the way the economy worked. Most corporations need a revolution in their management structure and the way their end-to-end processes work. TQM should be built into the basic fabric of the post-revolution processes.

As we reinvent value streams, we should reinvent them with teams designed to make ongoing *kaizen* efforts as effective as possible. The radically new value stream should make the best possible use of IT and the best possible use of *human* quality capabilities. Even if a corporation does not have a culture of TQM, the teams that operate the new value stream should be created with TQM built into their training and their instinctive way of functioning.

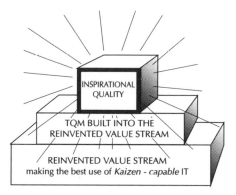

When end-to-end value streams have been totally reinvented with kaizen-capable IT, and TQM is the basic grammar of the new value-stream teams, then real quality can begin—inspirational quality, the search for ways to astonish and delight the customer, Mozart, not Salieri.

New knowledge often comes from research and experimentation. Quality circles sometimes experiment in a casual way. Making worthwhile breakthroughs often requires broad-ranging research and skillfully designed experiments, sometimes with a substantial budget. Chapter 31 explores why research and experimentation should often be done by people involved in the work process rather than by a remote research lab. Much of the experimentation concerned with improving work processes should be done by value-stream teams.

TQM vs. Quantum-Leap Redesign

It is important to contrast TQM or *kaizen* with clean-sheet redesign. *Kaizen* is concerned with continuous improvement of an existing process. Value-stream reinvention is concerned with scrapping existing processes and replacing them with fundamentally different processes.

TQM or *kaizen*, if it is managed well, is low-risk and pragmatic; a large number of improvements can see major results. A culture of quality in which every employee seeks to improve everything is becoming the price of long-term survival. In most corporations, however, a discontinuous break with the past is needed.

Some changes, by their very nature, cannot be incremental. They need the introduction of a fundamental change—a break with the past. If the European Union decided that British vehicles must drive on the right of the road as in Europe, Britain could not elect to make the change incrementally, first with the buses driving on the right, then trucks, and then cars. The clean-sheet innovations described in Part II could not have been achieved with *kaizen* alone; they require a different level of fundamental reinvention.

Western corporations have tended to be good at large-scale innovation but have often neglected the need for continuous small-scale improvements. Japanese companies tend to favor a gradualist approach to improvement; American companies tend to favor a great-leap-forward approach. Great leaps forward are dramatic and demand attention; *kaizen* is undramatic, with results that are usually not visible immediately. Champions of great leaps forward estimate their return-on-investment, and sometimes the ROI is irresistible. Because *kaizen* is continuous, with a continuous stream of small improvements, however, its long-term effects can be spectacular. Exhibit 18.1 contrasts TQM *kaizen* and clean-sheet reinvention.

Japan is very much a collectivist society. People tend to behave in ways that are collectively acceptable. Rugged individualists are rare. A common saying about people is "the nail that sticks out is hammered down." America, on the other hand, is full of nails that stick out. The folklore represented in Western movies is filled with rugged individualists, pioneering new territory. The frontiers to be conquered today are in corporations. The Wild West is Silicon Valley (or whatever replaces it). America is the land of the entrepreneur, the innovator, the cyber-cowboy, the champion of new ideas. Today's dramatic changes in business need pioneers. Much of Enterprise Engineering is concerned with quantum-leap innovation.

However, quantum-leap redesigns of processes are much more likely to succeed if *kaizen* is also applied to them. The radically changed procedures need much adjustment and fine-tuning if they are to work well; new procedures generate swarms of new problems. There are many refinement candidates. Value-stream reinvention works much better if the new process is constantly refined. A brand-new house is likely to need many improvements to it when it is first occupied. The same is true of new business processes. Many small inventions are needed to make it work well. The implementors must seek out, analyze, and correct the new problems that arise.

A business process tends to deteriorate slowly, like a house, if attention is not paid to improving it. Wrinkles in procedures grow that do not make sense to the overall business. In one of New York's largest stock-brokerage houses the auditors discovered excessive bills from Federal Express. On investigation they found that these were for items going from New York to New York. Federal Express flies them via its hub city of Memphis, so they were making a 2400-mile round trip to cross Manhattan. Worse, some were addressed from one floor to another of the same building! It was faster to send mail by Federal Express than via the snarled-up mailroom. An organization with a *kaizen* culture would have improved its mailroom procedures rather than adopting an it's-not-my-problem attitude.

Exhibit 18.2 shows quantum-leap redesign. Without *kaizen*, its new procedures tend to deteriorate. With *kaizen*, they steadily improve.

The redesign of procedures is often technology oriented. There is great scope for new technology to improve business processes fundamentally. However, pro-

Exhibit 18.1 Comparison of TQM/*kaizen* with clean-sheet reinvention

	TQM/Kaizen	*Clean-Sheet Revention*
	Small steps—gradual, constant	Great leap forward—abrupt, radical
Intended result	Small, steady improvement	Quantum-leap improvement
Frequency	Continuous	On-off
Effect	Undramatic	Dramatic
Starting point	Existing processes	Clean sheet
Span	Often narrow	Sometimes broad, cross-functional
Effect on current processes	Improve	Scrap and rebuild
Approach	Collectivism—group effort	Individualism—strong, innovative leadership
Participation	Everybody	Few champions, IT, strong leadership
Resistance to change	Low	High—specific actions needed to overcome resistance
Implementation	Mainly from the bottom up	Mainly from the top down
Effect on people	Supportive, skill building	Traumatic change, exciting innovation
Spark	Know-how of current processes	Technological breakthroughs; new theories; innovative thinking
Risk	Low—no danger of major failure	Some major failures
Change management	Need for *kaizen* culture	Needs skilled planning and change management
Investment	Low initial investment, major effort to sustain ongoing TQM	Large initial investment
Return of investment	Difficult-to-compute ROI, high long-term payoff	Aims at high ROI
Evaluation	Measurement of employee participation, number of defects	Measurement of end result, ROI, decrease in cycle time

Exhibit 18.2   *Kaizen* and quantum-leap redesign

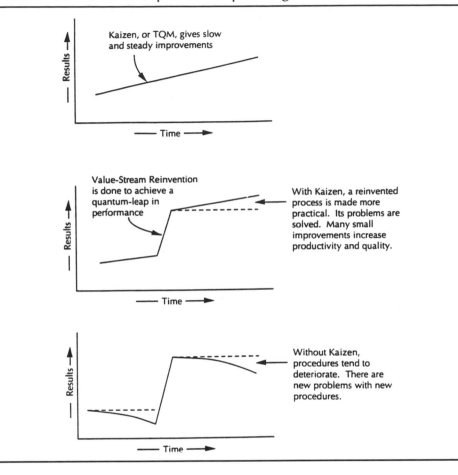

cess redesign must also be people oriented. It means investing in people. It requires virtually everybody's personal efforts. The winning formula is technology-oriented redesign linked to people-oriented building of empowered teams and a culture of *kaizen*. Fundamental changes created by the use of new technology need people-oriented *kaizen* to deal with the new problems they introduce. Technology-oriented change without people-oriented determination to solve problems is usually a failure.

Kaizen ought to be an umbrella concept that relates to all or is used in conjunction with all management techniques (Exhibit 18.3). One of its implications in a world increasingly dependent on IT is that IT systems must be built that are adaptable to continuous improvement. That is not true with many IT systems today. They are often difficult to modify and lock their users in a straightjacket of unchangeable applications. *Kaizen*-capable systems are necessary.

Exhibit 18.3 *Kaizen* as an umbrella concept

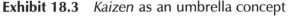

KAIZEN

- Procedure Redesign
- Value-Stream Reinvention
- Customer orientation
- TQM (Total Quality Management)

- QC (Quality Circles)
- Training
- Suggestion system

- Productivity improvement
- Robotics
- I.T. platform evolution

- EDI (Electronic Data Interchange) evolution
- Software designed for continuous improvement

- Just-in-time techniques
- Continuous-flow manufacturing
- Zero defects
- Small group activities
- Quality improvement
- Cooperative labor-management relations
- Product improvement
- New product development
- Relationships with suppliers
- Relationships with customers
- Business modeling
- Repository-based development
- SWAT teams
- Enterprise redesign

A culture of *kaizen* should be applied to all of the management techniques in modern industry. If the culture change necessary to achieve the quality revolution has been brought about in a corporation, the corporation is much better positioned to succeed with radical innovation.

Nearly all major innovations that determine the direction of future product and process development originate in Western firms. Japanese firms display their strength in incremental innovations in fields whose general contours have already been established.

While initially the performance characteristics of a product are the deciding factor in competition, mass production leads to a second deciding factor: the cost of the product. After its first appearance major innovations no longer occur frequently. From then on, the center

stage is occupied by incremental innovations aiming at product re-
finements and at improvements in the manufacturing process.[1]
Kenichi Imai & Akimitsu Sakuma of Hitotsubashi University

Masaaki Imai, in his classic book on *kaizen,* states that management has two major components: standard operating procedures and improvement.[2] The higher the level of management, the more its time is concerned with improvement.

Of the improvement activities, most are *kaizen*—multiple small improvements to existing processes. A small proportion are new innovation.

Imai comments that the *kaizen* part of the above diagram is largely missing in many Western companies. He draws the following chart to represent the breakdown in the West:

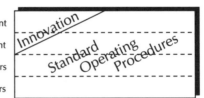

Kaizen has now spread in many Western companies in the form of programs for total quality management, however, and many Western companies are doing more clean-sheet innovation than their Japanese counterparts:

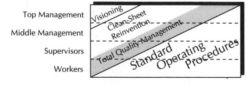

Most business procedures need to be fundamentally reinvented—partly because of new technologies such as information superhighways, EDI (electronic data interchange), image processing, smart cards, and the plunging cost of computer power; and partly because people can be organized, motivated, energized, and put to work much better than in hierarchical structures, and partly because better relationships can be built between separate organizations. Continuous-process improvement and quantum-leap change need to support each other.

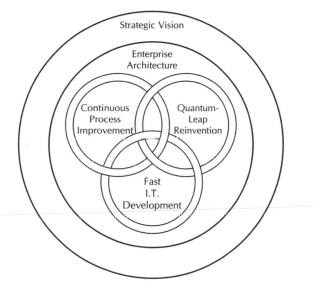

Both need appropriate information technology with systems that are far more flexible than those of the past. As this is applied to an entire enterprise, there needs to be a sense of enterprise architecture (discussed in Part VI). The overall enterprise design needs to be done with a top-management strategic vision (see Part V).

We have emphasized that there is a spectrum of change methods for implementing corporate evolution and revolution and that these change methods need appropriate methods for IT development and for organizational and culture change.

Beyond TQM

TQM/kaizen is the basic grammar of the future corporation. It should be the basic way every process and every employee operates. But TQM by itself does not provide top quality any more than spelling and grammar produce good writing. A corporation needs bedazzling products, innovative design, intense focus on customer needs, flexibility and speed to adapt to fast-changing requirements, and reinvented intimate relationships with suppliers, contractors, agents, retailers, etcetera. No corporation can have top quality if its processes are obsolete. Value-stream reinvention is needed, and reinvented value streams must be steeped in the culture of **kaizen.**

Once a corporation has the right value streams, implemented in the right way, and a pervasive, instinctive, **kaizen** *culture, true quality can begin. True quality needs inspiration and flair; it needs virtuosos; it needs employees who love their work; it needs wild ducks; it needs the joy that comes from achieving excellence; it needs management that encourages the virtuosos, knowing that it now has the right corporate culture in place. It needs strategic visioning to determine how core capabilities should be invested in to make the corporation unbeatable.*

Multicorporate TQM

We should catch defects *when they occur* insofar as possible and correct not merely the defect but the *cause* of the defect. We should correct it as quickly as possible so that it causes no more trouble. Sometimes the cause is not in our own corporation; it is from a supplier or service provider. To please its customer, the supplier or service provider ought to correct the cause of the trouble immediately. To achieve this, a supplier may have a resident engineer at the site of its customer or at least have the mechanisms in place for rapid response.

The cause of the problem may be patched quickly, but true correction may require quality circles, new ideas, perhaps new design. The new ideas may come from the supplier, but often they come from its customer, who is affected by the problem. The customer, in fact, may have many good ideas about how to improve the supplied product or service. Conversely, the supplier often has good ideas about how its customer can use what it supplies in better ways.

The implication of this is that the supplier and its customer, or trading partners in general, should climb a *joint* learning curve. In the constant search for improvements, each can contribute specialized knowledge. Cooperative learning is much better than single-company learning.

Value streams often span trading partners. They are part of an extended enterprise. This multicorporate value stream needs inventing so that it works as smoothly as possible; then TQM should be applied to the joint-value stream.

Experimentation often results in the most innovative learning. The multicorporate relationship should be established so as to foster joint experimentation.

References

1. K. Imai and A. Sakuma, *Economic Eye* (Kiezai Koho Center: Tokyo, 1983).
2. Masaaki Imai, *Kaizen: The Key to Japan's Competitive Success* (McGraw Hill: New York, 1986).

Part IV
Procedure Redesign

Part IV focuses on the reengineering of procedures within the existing management structures, in a manner more cross-functional than kaizen but less traumatic than scrapping and replacing entire value streams.

Procedure Redesign

19

Nontraumatic Redesign

When value-stream reinvention is undertaken, the activities that constitute a value stream are not merely improved; they are replaced with something new. This necessitates major organizational upheaval and restructuring—often a traumatic change resisted by people whose jobs are reinvented, by the custodians of old computer systems, and by middle managers who are swept away. Such change can be vital and can bring major improvements in competitiveness, but it often fails—because of cultural problems, because of information-technology problems, and because the executives responsible lose their nerve. It needs tough management and a good understanding of cultural change (see Part VI).

A middle ground between the gentle continuous change of *kaizen* and the scrap-and-replace upheaval of value-stream reinvention is the discontinuous redesign of procedures, often major redesign involving radically changed information systems without the major organizational changes needed for value-stream reinvention. We refer to this as procedure redesign.

The Difference between Procedure Redesign and Value-Stream Reinvention

In much literature the term *business-process redesign* has been used without distinguishing between procedure redesign and value-stream reinvention. There is a fundamental difference:

- Value-stream reinvention is concerned with an entire end-to-end value stream and is entirely focused on the satisfaction of the customers (external and internal) of that value stream. Procedure redesign relates to existing procedures, narrower in scope.
- Value-stream reinvention demands a clean-sheet approach. It requires scrapping and replacing the entire value stream, not improvement of existing procedures. As such it drastically changes jobs, and management.
- Procedure redesign requires the modeling of an existing procedures so that it can be changed. Value-stream reinvention usually avoids modeling what already exists because it fundamentally replaces what exists.

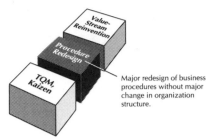

Major redesign of business procedures without major change in organization structure.

- Value-stream reinvention sets "outrageous goals"; it aims at 10-times, not 10-percent, improvement. Procedure redesign usually has more-modest goals and is not capable of 10-times improvements.

The Difference between *Kaizen* and Procedure Redesign

Procedure redesign is different from *kaizen* in the following ways:

- Procedure redesign is broader in scope than *kaizen*. It usually spans multiple departments, functional areas, and divisions and often spans separate corporations.
- Procedure redesign requires a higher level of analysis. It often requires the building or modification of major information systems.
- Procedure redesign is not limited to incremental improvements; it involves major redesign.
- *Kaizen* requires that a process be at a relatively stable state from which continuous process measurement and procedural tweaking can take place. Procedure redesign may relate to new procedures.
- *Kaizen* is everybody's job; management needs to build a pervasive *kaizen* culture carefully. Procedure redesign does not require corporatewide culture change.

Some TQM specialists say that TQM incorporates what we describe as procedure redesign. There are many different variants of TQM from different authorities, and some would involve the redesign of wide-ranging procedures. More commonly TQM sets out to improve the procedures that are the purview of one department or team. Procedure redesign is concerned with wide-ranging, cross-functional procedures that extend beyond the horizon of existing departments or teams.

Procedure redesign can result in the design of cross-functional teams with the existing management structure. Sometimes it results in the changing of procedures spanning a wide range without the creation of a single team whose work spans that range. The redesigned procedure may span separate enterprises, for example, without creating a team of workers culled from those enterprises.

The Risk of Suboptimizing

Often the right course of action is total reinvention of value streams, but executives search for alternatives because of value-stream reinvention's major impact on jobs and organizational structure. Middle management searches for alternatives because value-stream reinvention replaces middle management.

A CEO should make certain that lower executives are not using procedure redesign as a comfortable alternative when the best course of action is value-stream reinvention. They often attach the name "business reengineering" to something that is in fact procedure redesign and that avoids both the trauma and the benefits of reinventing the value stream.

Organizations often bend over backward to avoid the radical redesign of organization structures. They will use automation, motivation, employee empowerment, mission statements, management reorganization, downsizing, and the current year's buzzwords, before resorting to value-stream reinvention. The results are of little consequence when what is really needed is replacement of an inefficient value stream. In some situations procedure redesign is valuable; in others it is like replacing the deck chairs on the *Titanic* with automated recliners. Increasing the use of computers often does little more than immortalize a badly designed value stream. One reason given for avoiding a necessary value-stream redesign is often that stovepipe computer systems are so expensive and difficult to change. This is not a good reason in the long run.

The detailed modeling that is used for procedure redesign is impressive. It gives the modelers a good feeling of professionalism. But it disguises the fact that the end-to-end value stream should have been scrapped and replaced, often with something much simpler, more straightforward, faster, and less expensive.

All Three Are Needed

TQM, value-stream reinvention, and procedure redesign are not mutually exclusive. On the contrary, all three are desirable. They should be mutually reinforcing. If a culture of *kaizen* is in place, value-stream reinvention or procedure redesign are much more likely to succeed. As we have stressed, a reinvented value stream should have its own built-in *kaizen*. When a reinvented value stream becomes operational, it may need major improvements. The new value stream may become the target for procedure redesign. A detailed model of the new value stream may be built and polished.

Evaluation of the Three Alternatives

When a corporation sets out to redesign a business process it may consider three alternatives: continuous improvement *(kaizen)*, procedure redesign, and radical value-stream reinvention.

Exhibit 19.1

Alternative 1 requires the following actions:

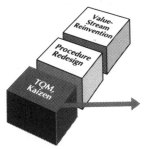

- Implement low-cost process improvements.
  Reduce levels of authorization.
  Reduce the assets managed.
  Simplify the budget process.
  Use electronic funds transfer.
  Expand use of corporate payments card.
  Simplify tracking and expense procedures.
  Simplify purchasing procedures.
- Purchase an accounts-payable package.
- Develop an expense-tracking system.

Alternative 2 requires the following actions:

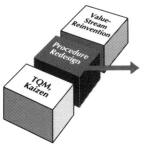

- Implement low-cost improvements (listed in alternative 1).
- Purchase an integrated software package that incorporates the following value streams:
  Accounts payable
  Purchasing
  Asset management
- Implement redesigned procedures linked to the new software package.
- Develop an expense-tracking system.

Alternative 3 radically changes the procurement value stream in the following actions:

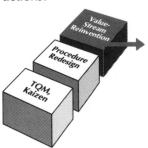

- Introduce end-to-end value-stream management.
- Implement low-cost improvements (listed in alternative 1).
- Introduce on-line ordering (electronic-data interchange).
- Eliminate invoices (payment on receipt acceptance).
- Simplify and automate payment.
- Eliminate most purchase orders through blanket order contracts.
- Decentralize purchasing actions to users.
- Simplify and automate travel expense.
- Simplify and automate asset management.
- Develop integrated value-stream system to support the radical change.

Exhibit 19.2

Alternative 1 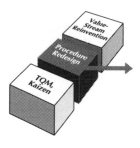		***Pros*** • Simple to implement • Minimal investment cost • Lowest-cost alternative • Safe solution	***Cons*** • No large-scale problems solved • Improvements in performance only minor • No value-stream management • No reduction in time to respond to customers • No meeting of targeted cost savings

Alternative 2

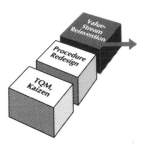

Pros	***Cons***
• Simpler technical solution • Less risk • Less implementation cost than alternative 3 • Short-term solution	• Less flexibility • Limited customer satisfaction • Less user functional than alternative 3 • Possible creation of redundancy • Greater operating cost than alternative 3 • Network and connectivity problems • Limited technical solution set • Difficulty providing integrated databases

Alternative 3

Pros	***Cons***

• Greater customer satisfaction
  Simple process
  Timely response
  Flexible approach
  Reduced material cost
• Leveraged use of technology
• Elimination of redundancy
• Lowest operating costs
• Improved quality
  Reduced errors
  Reduced reconciliation
• Integrated database
	• Highest development cost
	  Additional implementation costs
	  Human resources
	  Policy procedure changes
	  Forms redesign
	  Reorganization expenses
	• Layoffs required

One large enterprise set out to redesign its procurement activities. It identified a value stream which included purchasing, payment of vendors, and inventory management. Each of these activities had many problems which needed to be solved. The design team charted the problems with fishbone diagrams and set goals for the business process redesign.

The design team examined in detail three possibilities:

Alternative 1—continuous improvement of the existing procedures
Alternative 2—redesign of the procedures, with a high level of automation, within the existing functional structure
Alternative 3—radical reinvention of the value stream

Exhibit 19.1 shows the actions needed for the three approaches. The team evaluated in detail the pros and cons of the three approaches.

A chart was drawn up listing the problems and showing the extent to which each of the three solutions solved them.

Exhibit 19.2 shows an assessment of the pros and cons of the three approaches. Such an assessment is desirable to help top management decide whether to embark on the upheaval of radical change. In this case, alternative 3 (value-stream reinvention) achieved sufficient major ongoing benefits, warranting the added cost and risk of taking that route.

The cost and risks of radical rebuilding of value streams are worth incurring only if the expected payoffs are substantially higher than those that could result from continuous-process improvement or procedure redesign.

20

Counterintuitive System
Behavior

In many corporate situations, an individual, no matter how hard he tries, can make things happen only to a limited extent. As in driving across a city in a rush-hour traffic jam, he cannot achieve fast results. The system, represented by the city streets or the corporate organization, exhibits a behavior of its own. To speed up rush-hour travel across the city would require fundamental redesign of the system. The corporate system represented by corporate policies and procedures not only puts a limit on the speed of achieving results; it sometimes has the opposite effect of what was intended. Procedure redesign is concerned with understanding and changing the system.

As commented earlier, organizations have complex webs of interrelated activities that have behavior patterns of their own. Often these behavior patterns are contrary to the intuition of managers who make decisions and create policies. It is only too common to observe policies whose ultimate effects were quite different from those intended. The system seems to have an agenda of its own.

The fault is not in ourselves; it is in the system.

Webs of Activities

An activity in one place has effects elsewhere that cause other activities. There is a complex web of interrelated activities—an elaborate structure of activities causing other activities.

In an enterprise an action in one place causes an action in another place, possibly after a time delay. A factory orders more material; several weeks later the material arrives. A sales manager lowers a product price; some time later its sales volume increases; this requires increasing the production rate; but production cannot be increased beyond a certain level without establishing a second shift, which is expensive. These collections of interconnected activities can be referred to as a *system*. The enterprise has a certain behavior determined by its system, referred to as *systemic behavior*.

Webs of activities might be easy to understand if they were linear, but they are not. They are filled with feedback loops.

Long-Span Activity Webs

Where a web of activities takes place fairly quickly, managers observe it, learn about it, and try to improve it. Where the web has long time delays or causes effects in remote places, managers cannot directly observe the effects so often do not learn about them. We refer to webs of activities that span long distances, involve more than one organization, or have long time delays as *long-span activity webs*.

It is becoming increasingly common for an action and its results to be far apart. Long-span activity webs are becoming far more common because of the trends towards globalism, intercorporate operations, tighter relationships with trading partners, and corporate complexity.

Activity webs sometimes span separate enterprises. Customers buy goods from retailers; this causes retailers to place orders with distributors; distributors then order shipments from a manufacturer; the manufacturer consequently plans its production schedule; the manufacturer's marketing executive decides how much to spend on advertising; the advertising changes the rate at which customers buy goods; and so on.

An enterprise requires people taking actions and making decisions. The outcome of these actions depends to a large extent upon the activity webs and systemic behavior. The result of an activity may not be immediate. Most managers associate an activity with short-term results, not results in the distant future. For example, a decision to eliminate features from a product in order to lower its production cost may bring short-term profits but long-term sales loss. A national decision to improve security by building new weapons causes potential adversaries to build new weapons in response, which in the long term reduces security.

When activity webs result in long delays, cause effects in remote places, and involve feedback loops, they cause unexpected behavior—the consequences of management actions that managers do not expect.

Counterintuitive Consequences

Much of the skill of managers is based on what they learn from experience. They observe the results of their actions and learn from them. However, there are certain results that they cannot observe because these results take place far away or far in the future. The intuition of managers is trained by experience, but that experience excludes effects distant in time or space. Activity webs that span long distances, involve more than one organization, and extend over long time periods are often not learned about by experience and so can produce counterintuitive results. A manager does the obvious thing, but it may not produce only an obvious outcome.

Local autonomy often results in decisions that are disastrous for the organization as a whole. Sometimes corporations find themselves in downward spirals that vigorous corrective actions only seem to make worse. The managers are trapped in a pattern of systemic behavior and do not comprehend the mechanisms at work. To get out of the downward spiral, they need to change the system. *Kaizen* does not work in such a situation; a fundamental change in the system is needed. Sometimes this can be achieved with relatively straightforward redesign of procedures, using information technology to eliminate time delays or the negative effects of distance.

System Dynamics

Counterintuitive behavior was demonstrated by Jay Forrester in his seminal book *Industrial Dynamics*.[1] When he modeled webs of activity with a computer to simulate the behavior of corporations, he demonstrated that webs of activities cause various counterintuitive results in corporations. Decision makers intuitively expect their actions to have a certain effect, but actually they cause a different one. Decision makers are often pleased with the good short-term effects of their decisions and unaware of the harmful long-term effects. Often a corporation's well-intended policies create a harmful web of activities. If managers had understood the systemic behavior, they would have acted differently. Decision makers often focus on symptoms and take actions that produce short-term benefits but long-term problems.

Forrester's work is referred to as "system dynamics." Forrester expanded his system-dynamics work on corporations to include government issues. He illustrated how many issues (such as urban decay, unemployment, and ecological problems) are characteristics of systems that are counterintuitive to decision makers. The problems are often aggravated by well-intentioned policies that cause a complex system to behave in ways that are not understood.[2,3]

Peter Senge and his colleagues at MIT have studied and simulated systemic behavior in corporations. Senge refers to the understanding of systemic behavior as "the fifth discipline."[4] He believes that most managers and corporate decision makers do not understand corporate systemic behavior. The widespread development of such understanding will change the way we engineer our enterprises.

Senge illustrates that controls that managers put into place to deal with problems often have a limited effect on corporate behavior. The system perspective tells us to look beyond individual mistakes or bad luck to understand important problems, beyond personalities and events, into the underlying *structures* that shape individual actions and create the conditions likely to result in certain types of events.

*The system causes its own behavior. When placed in the same system,
different people tend to produce similar results.*

Oscillations in a Distribution System

Senge describes the simulation of a retail-wholesale distribution system and illustrates how it can develop oscillations and overstocking of an extreme nature. The simulation, done in classes at MIT's Sloan School of Management for over twenty years, is referred to as "the beer game."[5] Retailers respond to customer orders for a speciality beer by placing orders with a wholesaler. Wholesalers respond by placing orders with the brewery.

In the Sloan School simulations, classes are divided into three groups to play the roles of retail, wholesale, and brewery managers, respectively. Each group is instructed to manage their inventory the best way possible and to place appropriate orders so as to maximize their profits. What happens generally astonishes participants. The seemingly intelligent, clever decisions, far from maximizing profits, produce disastrous results.

What "the beer game" demonstrates is extraordinary. It has been played by thousands of players, of enormously diverse backgrounds, in five continents, the players ranging from students to seasoned business people with years of experience in production-distribution systems. In all cases the "intelligent" decisions to run the simulated business well result in a build-up of excessive inventories of beer that cannot be unloaded, and there are wild oscillations. The fault lies not in the intelligence of the decision makers but in the structure of the system. If thousands of diverse players all generate similarly catastrophic results, the system must be at fault.

The simulation starts with a situation in which the order rate from a retailer's customers has been constant for a long time—4 cases of beer per week. Suddenly, the order rate doubles to 8 cases per week and remains constant at this new level:

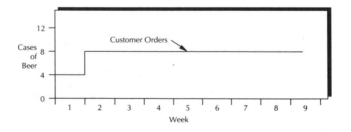

One might expect the retailer and wholesaler to adjust their orders in an equally regular fashion. What actually happens is that the simple change in customer behavior triggers wild overreaction in the system.

The retailer observes the sales increase in week 2 and so doubles the weekly order he places with the distributor, from 4 to 8. There is normally a delay of 4 weeks between the retailer's placing an order and the distributor truck's delivering it.

The distributor's truck arrives once a week, and each week the retailer gives the truck driver a new order. The retailer usually maintains an inventory of 12 cases, which provides a comfortable 8-case surplus in the store. In week 2 the inventory falls to 8; in week 3 it falls to 4. The retailer orders 12 cases in week 3 and telephones the distributor instead of merely filling in the truck driver's weekly order form. Responding to this the distributor delivers 5 cases in week 4, so the inventory falls to 1. Alarmed, the retailer orders 16 cases in week 5:

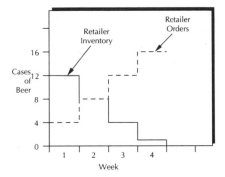

In week 5 the retailer runs out of stock, and his customers are asking for 8 cases per week. The distributor delivers 7 cases, responding to the higher orders, but 7 is not enough. Many of the customers are loyal and leave their phone numbers promising to buy beer when it comes in.

In week 6 only 6 cases are delivered—half of what was ordered four weeks before. The delivery man says they are backlogged. In week 7 and again in week 8, only 5 cases are delivered. The retailer has kept his order rate at 16, but in week 8 he orders 24 because only a fraction of his earlier orders are being delivered:

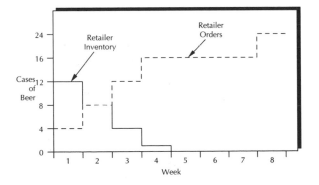

The wholesale distributing firm serves a large city and its surrounding area. It places orders for beer with the brewery. It serves many retailers, all of whom have increased their orders in a way broadly similar to that above.

The wholesaler places orders by the gross each week when the brewery truck arrives, and again it is four weeks before the truck delivers the order. Before the rise in customer orders, the wholesaler ordered four gross week after week after week. That was enough to maintain an inventory of 12 gross.

In week 4 the wholesaler starts to receive higher orders from the retailers. These continue in the following weeks, and by week 6 the wholesaler's inventory has dropped to zero. The wholesaler increases his orders to the brewery:

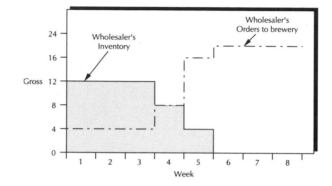

The wholesaler telephones the brewery, and in week 6 the brewery manages to make extra shipments from its warehouse. In week 7 it makes larger shipments but exhausts its limited warehouse stock. In week 8 the wholesaler is expecting to receive still larger shipments but is horrified to find that the brewery delivers only 4 gross. It takes several weeks for the brewery to increase its production volume. The wholesaler's backlog is rising alarmingly, so in weeks 8 and 9 the wholesaler orders 30 gross:

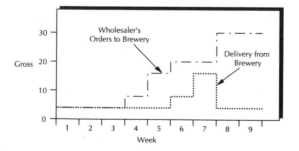

The wholesaler telephones the retailers, asking them to be patient. The retailers' backlog of orders is growing rapidly—so they again increase their order rate.

The brewery can ramp up production only slowly, but in week 10 it delivers 8 gross to the wholesaler. The wholesaler's backlog of orders is still rising, so he increases his weekly order rate to 40 gross. In week 11, the brewery's delivery rate goes up to 12 gross. The wholesaler now has more than 100 gross in unfilled orders from retailers. In weeks 12 and 13, the backlog climbs still higher; the wholesaler pushes the order rate to 60. Large shipments finally start to arrive in weeks 14 and 15:

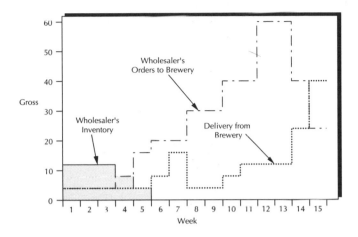

In weeks 14 and 15 the wholesaler ships all the beer he receives to make up past orders. The retailers, suddenly overstocked, reduce their orders to zero. In weeks 16, 17, and 18, the wholesaler receives deliveries of 55, 60, and (again) 60 gross, in fulfillment of his earlier orders, and is alarmed to see his inventory suddenly grow tremendously with the retailers ordering nothing. The wholesaler drops his order to zero correspondingly.

If this sudden build-up of inventory is expensive for the wholesaler, the situation at the brewery becomes far more traumatic.

In the brewery it takes time to prepare for a major increase in production. By week 8 it becomes clear to the brewery management that major action is needed. By week 10 the order rate is 10 times higher than the traditional order rate. The brewery staff works overtime, and a second shift is established. By week 14 the brewery is still well behind its order rate.

By week 16 the brewery has caught up and is now prepared to manufacture at a greater rate; but to their total surprise, the orders drop to zero.

The beer-drinking customers continue to buy this beer at double the old rate for several weeks and then drift back to the old level:

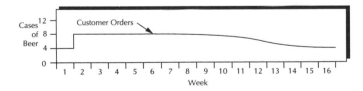

By week 16 the wholesaler has an inventory of more than 200 truckloads, and the retailers are still ordering nothing. It will take about a year to work off the overstock. Many wholesalers, in a similar state, will order almost nothing from the factory during this time.

The beer being brewed keeps adding to the factory inventory and is unsaleable. Production must be cut back or stopped.

There will be severe layoffs, and the factory may have to be closed. The surge in sales, which should have been good news for the beer factory, causes a tragedy.

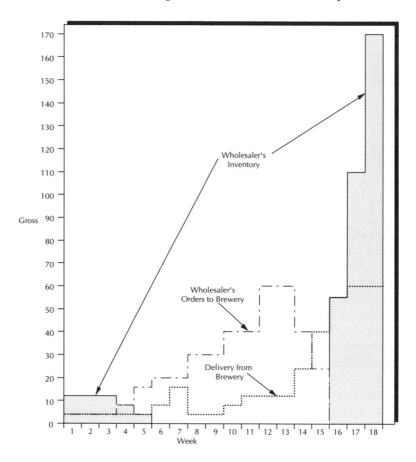

Lessons from the Story

Senge describes how this beer-distribution simulation has been played out thousands of times in classes and management seminars, with young people, old people, people of all different cultures, often with seasoned managers and sometimes with executives from retail-wholesale operations. Every time the simulation is played out the same crises ensue. Almost all players end up with large inventories that they cannot unload. The effect on the brewery is catastrophic.

Many real-life examples of crises in production-distribution systems exist in which a small change in customer demand has caused excessive overstocking, wild oscillations, and severe losses. In the semiconductor industry it has happened multiple times. Changes in demand have resulted in massive losses, sometimes crippling semiconductor companies. In 1985 the prices of memory chips doubled, tripled, and quadrupled.[6] Retail chain stores have been particularly prone to boom-and-bust cycles. There are many different examples of webs of activities in other areas with built-in delays that behave in a similarly counterintuitive way.

Senge describes three lessons from the beer-distribution simulation.

First, *systems cause their own crises*. Different people trying to maximize profits produce similar results. The cause of the problem is not external forces, such as customer behavior, and not mistakes by individuals; the cause is the system. The systemic mechanisms need to be redesigned.

Second, *human decision making, whose effects are subtle, is part of the system*. We translate perceptions, goals, rules, and cultural behavior into action, and the actions often have counterintuitive effects.

Third, *leverage comes from new ways of thinking*. It is easy to redesign the beer-distribution system so that it behaves well, but often this is not done because the cause of its behavior is not understood. We fail to understand that it is the design of the system behavior that is causing instability.

Redesigning the System

Once we realize that the problems are caused by the structure of the system, we can change the structure. Often a major change in behavior can be brought about by a relatively simple change. Major leverage can result from an inexpensive change. This is usually the case when webs of activities have delays that cause counterintuitive behavior.

Delays are a major cause of systemic problems. The overstocking of beer in the above example is made worse by long delays. If the wholesaler delivered the retailer's orders in one week, not four, and the factory responded to the wholesaler in one week, much less overstocking would take place. In general, the shorter the delays in a system, the less prone it is to extreme overshots or oscillations of high amplitude.

Lack of good information is another cause of systemic problems. The wholesaler in the story receives orders from the retailer, and the brewery receives orders from the wholesaler; neither has direct information about what the customer is ordering. If both the brewery and the wholesaler could see the changes in customer orders as they occur, neither would overstock beer to the extent that they do. Both are misled by the system into thinking that the increase in sales is much higher than it really is. Both think the problem is caused by wild swings in buying patterns when in fact these have not occurred. If the brewery and the wholesalers had access to the retailers' information, the catastrophic swings would not occur. An outsider seeing the whole picture would think that the extreme inventory build-ups are ridiculous. They occur, as in so many corporations, because of bad information.

Both of these problems can be dealt with by better use of information technology. The brewery and wholesalers should have systems that provide information about the customer orders directly. This knowledge ought to pass electronically from the retailer to the wholesaler and brewery production planner. In worldwide organizations such as Benetton, information about customers' buying patterns goes immediately from the retail stores to the central computers in Italy, which are used to plan production and distribution. Benetton pulled way ahead of its competition because it built such a system.

Information systems should be designed to minimize delays. Instead of the retailer giving his orders to the wholesaler's truck driver once a week, and the wholesaler giving them to the brewery driver, they should be sent electronically. The wholesaler and brewery systems should be designed to respond to orders as quickly as possible. There will then be less overordering to compensate for delays.

Information technology enables us to build systems that respond fast and transmit relevant information to decision makers as soon as the information is available. Both of these characteristics help to lessen systemic problems.

Throughout corporations today, one finds numerous examples of not getting the right information to the right people at the right time.

What the Canadian firm in the case study on page 72 should have done when it found its market share eroding is to build a system in which details of customer orders are transmitted from dealers, worldwide, to the factory, when the orders occur. The factory should have been designed to respond quickly to changes in sales switching from making snowmobiles to sea scooters and vice versa, to help ensure that orders were not lost.

As with the beer story, major defects in the system could have been corrected with information technology.

These are examples of procedure redesign. They do not need the high-risk changes in management that are needed for value-stream reinvention or business reengineering. Change can be nontraumatic. The change in the Canadian company was urgently needed because of the rate of market loss. Situations that demand rapid change occur often. When speed is essential, it may be desirable to outsource the building of the necessary IT (information technology) systems to an organization with the skill to build them quickly.

IT Actions Needed

Three actions that can be achieved with IT systems help to eliminate oscillations and counterintuitive behavior such as that in the beer-distribution system:

- Eliminate delays where possible.
- Get the right information to the right people at the right time.
- Simplify the system and its human interactions.

Delays in the web of activities cause oscillations. The retailer, distributor, and factory warehouse build up stock because they know that it takes a long time to fill their orders. If the delivery time of four weeks were cut to one week, the overstocking would become less extreme. Electronic systems make possible *just-in-time* inventory stocking, *continuous-flow* manufacturing and distribution, and in general fast response to fluctuating situations.

Erratic or suboptimal behavior is often caused by decision makers' not having the right information. Electronic systems should provide the best information available. Information is often channeled in an organization instead of being given to a decision maker who needs it. The flow of information needs to be changed. In the beer-distribution system, if the wholesaler and factory had known the current volume of orders placed by customers with retailers, they would not have overstocked as in the simulation.

Thrashing in activity webs is caused by bad information. Far-reaching webs of activities tend to have bad information because of time delays and long distances. Information systems can span the distances and deliver information rapidly. They can often be designed to do that with relatively simple reengineering.

Thrashing and suboptimal behavior is often made worse by unnecessarily complex systems or webs of activities. Enterprise Engineering is concerned with simplifying procedures. Information technology makes it possible to eliminate intermediate stages in processes. All opportunities to do this should be sought out.

In the beer-distribution system, for example, it is not necessary to have three levels of warehouses—retailer, wholesaler, and brewery. The brewery can ship directly to the wholesaler (eliminating the brewery warehouse) or directly to the retailer (eliminating the wholesaler warehouse). The retailer can communicate electronically with its suppliers and sign a contract requiring them to keep the shelves stocked even though customer orders fluctuate. Many such changes have swept the supermarket and distribution industries.

The factory needs the best information possible to plan its production schedules. In traditional retailer-distributor-factory networks, production planning is based on old information badly distorted by the retailers and wholesalers trying to protect themselves. The best information would be to have point-of-sale data transmitted electronically to the factory as in Exhibit 20.1. For every decision and planning process the enterprise engineer should ask "What is the best possible information?" Systems and enterprises should be reengineered to make timely use of the best information.

In some supermarket chains products leave the warehouse 12 hours after arriving, on average, and this is being driven down to 3 hours. The warehouse used to be regarded as a *holding yard*; now it is regarded as a *switching yard*. Robotic warehouses are used to achieve fast turnaround of goods in the warehouse.

Exhibit 20.1

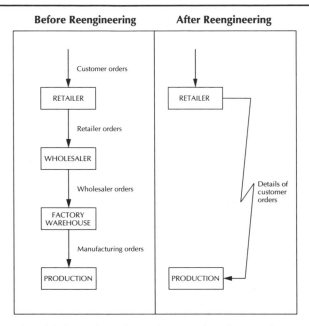

Information should flow directly and immediately to where it is needed, by-passing intermediate stages.

Sales are monitored electronically at cash registers with bar scanners, the sales are cross-checked with shelf-inventory counts using bar scanners. This information is transmitted immediately to distribution warehouses and often to suppliers. There is electronic ordering and electronic payments.

Many companies need to reengineer their distribution logistics. When retailers, wholesalers, and factory warehouses are considered part of one system, major simplications can be made, and often one level of warehouse can be closed down.

Jim Keebler was brought in to run distribution at Hill's, a manufacturer of special dietary products for pets. His philosophy was that distribution, factory warehousing, and marketing should not be separate, isolated functions; they are part of a linked process. That linked process needed reengineering as a whole.

Unlike other pet-food manufacturers, products made by Hill's are not sold in grocery stores but by veterinarians, pet shops, and special pet-food stores. Hill's sells food for sick animals, dogs and cats on diets, police dogs, and a few orangutans.

Hill's had four factories that manufactured pet food to fulfill warehouse orders. The warehouses received orders for wholesalers and shipped products to wholesaler service centers. The wholesalers, in turn, received orders from pet shops and veterinary clinics.

Keebler mapped out the operation and concluded that many tasks could be eliminated, thereby saving considerable time and money. The end result was a continuous flow system to supply vets and pet shops and the elimination of factory warehouses. Hill's now ships directly from the plants to 48 service centers that are owned either by Hill's or by independent distributors. Many steps in inventory management were eliminated.

Before the reengineering, market executives worked on promotions to move factory inventories. Now the marketing efforts are focused on customer need and demand. Keebler comments, "We reversed the polarity." The tension is now a *pull,* based on what's happening in the marketplace. Before it was a *push;* the company would make forecasts, fill the warehouses, and push the product on its wholesalers.[7]

The restructuring saves about 20 days' worth of inventory and about $7 million per year in logistics costs. It cut the order cycle time from 2 months to 2 weeks, enabling the factory to react more quickly to changes in demand and hence to avoid overstocking and inventory build-up. The new process reacted to customer needs in a way that served the customer better.

Leverage

Long-span webs of activities create surprising problems in many types of enterprise interactions other than distribution systems. It is desirable to redesign the behavior so as to minimize the problems. Well-focused changes can often make large, lasting improvements. Sometimes small changes can have a major effect. No matter how clever the human decision makers, they cannot make a flawed system behave well. A flawed system needs fundamental changing, often with information systems that span functional areas or electronically link separate corporations.

The term *leverage* is used to imply that a small change in a process can produce a large effect. It is desirable to search for high leverage, which can often be achieved with information systems that move information to decision makers with electronic speed. Computerized systems can eliminate the delays that cause systemic oscillations. Often it is advisable to change the flow of information and the place where decisions are made.

High-leverage changes are usually not obvious to the corporate players because the systemic behavior that requires them is not understood. It is desirable to map out the systemic behavior, and possibly simulate it, in order to understand how it can be changed.

Often the interactions that cause systemic problems span separate functional areas in an enterprise or sometimes span separate corporations. Many executives understand their own functional area but not others. Often corporate rules and politics prevent interaction with other functional areas. The separate fiefdoms for research, marketing, manufacturing, and distribution tend to prevent managers from thinking about the patterns of systemic behavior that need redesign. Stovepipe IT systems hide, rather than solve, the true cause. High leverage often comes from cross-functional or intercorporate redesign using information technology.

As "downsizing" became popular in IT in the early 1990s, much money was spent to create departmental systems. These were built with some understanding of how one department worked but often no understanding of the problems caused by far-reaching webs of activities. *Such systems tended to cast into concrete the wrong procedures.*

If a procedure or a value stream is redesigned without an understanding of far-reaching activity webs and their behavior, it will cause harmful side-effects. Enterprises often build IT systems to automate existing procedures without understanding the problems inherent in these procedures.

A major message of Enterprise Engineering is:

> **Do not automate until long-span activity webs have been redesigned so that technology can solve the problems inherent in their procedures.**

References

1. Jay Forrester, *Industrial Dynamics* (MIT Press: Cambridge Mass., 1961).
2. Forrester, *Urban Dynamics* (MIT Press: Cambridge, Mass., 1969).
3. Forrester, *World Dynamics* (MIT Press: Cambridge, Mass.).
4. Peter M. Senge, *The Fifth Discipline* (Doubleday Currency: New York, 1990).
5. Ibid.
6. Steven Burkey and Ken Siegmann, "Memory-Board Prices Surging in the Wake of Chip Shortage," *PC Week*, March 1, 1988.
7. "How Hill's Reengineered Its Logistics Network," *Traffic Management*, November 1992.

21

Dangerous Feedback

Historians will look back at the nuclear command-and-control systems of the Cold War era and say we were lucky to have survived.

The United States, ever suspicious of the Soviets, built a worldwide nuclear alert system to detect Soviet planes, submarines, and missile launches. The far-flung radars and detectors funneled information into the NORAD computer center deep in the granite of Cheyenne Mountain. The Soviets, ever suspicious of the United States, built a similar system.

The U.S. system had five levels of nuclear alert: DEFCON 1, 2, 3, 4, and 5. DEFCON 5 is the normal state indicating no hostile activities. DEFCON 4 is the lowest level of alert in which weapons systems are activated: missile silo doors open, B-52 nuclear bombers take off, and so on. DEFCON 1 is highest level of readiness, the brink of all-out nuclear war in which many thousands of nuclear warheads could be immediately launched. The United States escalated to DEFCON 2 during the Cuban missile crisis and DEFCON 3 during some other crises. At each level there are multiple different readiness steps.

The system, especially in its earlier decades, was plagued with false alarms triggered by false radar readings and computer errors. On one occasion a war-game tape was loaded erroneously and made a simulated all-out Soviet attack appear real. False alarms were usually rectified quickly, but not always. Sometimes Strategic Air Command nuclear bombers would take off. The Soviets would detect this and immediately put their system on alert. Both sides watched each other intensely with electronic surveillance. When the United States saw the Soviets ratchet up their alert, the Americans would become more alarmed and would take action to enhance readiness, which the Soviets would detect and ratchet further. There was thus a mutually reinforcing set of steps that increased tension.

If there was no political crisis neither side expected the mutually reinforcing alerts to lead to war. However, if the same escalation occurred during a period of war in the Middle East or during an intense crisis like the Cuban missile crisis, then it was always possible that the other side could be serious. The computers on one side or the other might be telling their commanders that the best option was some form of preemptive strike. Fortunately, nothing as tense as the Cuban missile crisis happened between 1962 and the time of the Soviet dissolution.

If a crisis were to escalate to the brink of nuclear war, it is likely that the leaders of the two sides would become so paralyzed with fear that one or other may become incapable of rational action. Khrushchev at the height of the Cuban missile crisis sent a rambling six-foot-long telex that suggested a level of mental stress under which wild actions might be taken. Stalin was mentally incapacitated for a time when Hitler invaded Russia.

In 1914 an escalation of mutually reinforcing military responses plunged the workd into a war that no country wanted. The rulebooks of military and political behavior constituted *a system that had inherent instability built into it*. No politician alone started World War I; it was the fault of the system. The system was later described as "a war waiting to happen." The nuclear systems of the 1970s were similarly a war waiting to happen, and we were lucky that no crisis became deep enough to trigger it.

Mutually reinforcing hostilities occur in business also. Company A sues Company B. Company B counter-sues Company A. Company A's lawyers encourage a hostile response. Company B's lawyers fan the flames of hostility. The process escalates, and in the end everybody loses, but the lawyers feel they have done a good job.

In an attempt to prevent crises and mutually reinforcing alerts leading to war, a "hot line" was set up between the American and Soviet leaders. In an extreme crisis a hot line would probably have been insufficient, so a crisis control center was proposed in which professionals from both sides would monitor events and try to defuse a potentially dangerous crisis as early as possible. In business it makes sense to defuse escalating hostilities before they get out of control. A crisis control center would not be manned by lawyers or generals.

Price wars periodically break out in the airline industry and escalate until all parties make a loss. Price wars sweep through other industries too, and in most countries antitrust laws prevent any mutual agreement to limit price drops. Price competition is essential to capitalism.

Positive Feedback

The foregoing situations are examples of *positive feedback*. Positive feedback is a chain of cause-and-effect relationships in the form of a loop that causes a change in one element in the loop to effect a change in another, which causes the original element to change more in the same direction. An increase in A causes an increase in B, which causes an increase in A. For example:

Positive feedback often has good effects rather than bad. For example, Exhibit 21.1 shows positive feedback causing ongoing growth of the cellular-phone industry. Companies that understood the interactions in Exhibit 21.1 and made it their business in the 1980s experienced spectacular growth.

Exhibit 21.1 Positive feedback driving ongoing growth of the cellular-phone business

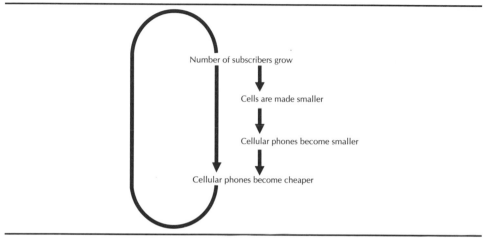

Number of subscribers grow

Cells are made smaller

Cellular phones become smaller

Cellular phones become cheaper

Positive feedback often causes exponential growth. The growth doubles in a certain time period and continues doubling. The more it grows, the more it is capable of growing. It continues to grow exponentially until other forces limit the growth. The capability of microchips grew exponentially for three decades, for example, enabling ongoing growth in power of computers.

When exponential growth encounters an unmoveable limit, that limit can be approached very rapidly. For example, a patch of weed on a pond doubles in size every day. As more weed grows, that weed also doubles. It will choke the entire pond in 100 days. By the start of day 97, not much change can be noticed; it still occupies only 6.25 percent of the surface, a narrow band around the perimeter. In three more days it has reached its limit and destroys the pond. (Exhibit 21.2)

Negative Feedback

Negative feedback is a widespread phenomenon. It is used to adjust continually a variable to a desired value (Exhibit 21.3). In engine governors it regulates the engine speed. A person driving a car is exercising feedback control over it. A missile honing in on a target is steered using negative feedback.

We usually do not think of negative feedback as having harmful effects. It is generally used to keep something on target. When long delays occur, however, negative feedback causes oscillations.

Exhibit 21.2

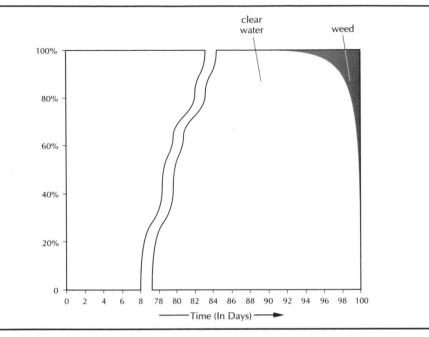

Exhibit 21.3 Feedback

Positive Feedback
When an element changes, this causes effects that in turn cause the element to change further in the same direction.

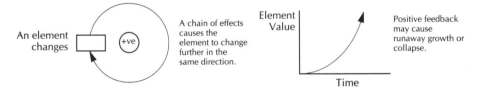

Positive feedback is sometimes referred to as a "vicious circle" or a "virtuous circle"

Negative Feedback
When an element changes, this causes effects that in turn cause the element to change in the opposite direction.

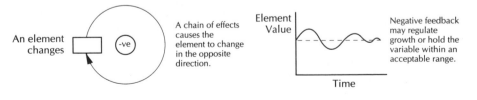

Negative feedback causes oscillation if there are delays in the feedback

Exhibit 21.4   Quick-response and slow-response feedback

Quick-Response Feedback—room temperature controlled by a thermostat.

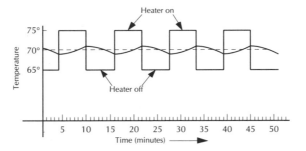

Slow-Response Feedback—room temperature controlled by a man stoking a log fire.

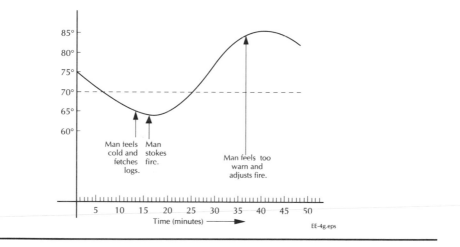

Exhibit 21.4 illustrates the difference between quick-response and slow-response feedback. The thermostat maintains the room at almost constant temperature, whereas the person permits large swings in temperature to occur by not acting quickly or often enough. He waits until he feels cold and then loads logs on the fire, but it takes some time to bring the temperature back to 70 degrees. It is characteristic of a human controller who realizes that an error has become large to overcompensate. The cold person loads too many logs on the fire in an attempt to correct the error quickly, thereby causing the temperature to swing too high.

This is how oscillations occur around the desired state. They may be small and of no significance, or they may be large, wasteful, and damaging. At worst, oscillations can steadily increase in magnitude until the system becomes unstable.

We may cause major damage to the earth's ecology because of the delays inherent in the global system. Damage to the ozone layer occurs ten or twenty years after we release chlorohydrofluorons (CFCs) into the atmosphere. After we detect the damage, it takes years before nations agree to enforce appropriate controls. After the enforcement of controls, the old CFCs remain active for decades, slowly damaging the ozone. Even if we behave perfectly now, the ozone layer may become much worse.

Environmental dangers tend to fellow this pattern. Nobody takes action to stop them until they have gone too far and are very difficult to stop. Similarly harmful feedback loops that are not understood until too late have wrecked corporations.

Nature is full of feedback systems. A lake has a few fish in it. In April they produce hundreds of babies. The next year, the pond is teeming with fish, and they produce thousands of baby fish. The next year, there are tens of thousands. Not all of these babies can grow into adults because there is not enough food, so the older fish start eating the babies, and the only ones that survive are those with a place to hide. The pond develops a cycle of population growth and die-back.

Recent management theory has become concerned with such systemic behavior. The system we work in is often not clear to us because we are part of it. The fish in the pond do not know why their population grows and dies back.

Multiple Interactions

In business there are many feedback loops. Some of them are subtle and may take months or years to play out their effects. Often, there is not one feedback loop but multiple causality paths that interact with one another. The patterns of interactions tend to have a behavior of their own which, as illustrated in the previous chapter, may be counterintuitive to decision makers.

- A company making educational products persuades its customers to sign long-term contracts for receiving new products at a discount. When many customers have long-term contracts, financial executives decide to increase profits by trimming back the production of new products. For a time this improves the financial picture, and the company is very profitable. The business is managed so as to maximize the profits. The customers perceive the cut-back, however, and do not renew their contracts. A collapse in expected contract renewals causes disastrous cash-flow problems.
- Department A adjusts its budget numbers unrealistically, trying to obtain a large slice of the pie. Other departments react to this by similarly adjusting their budgets. Department A, determined to increase its share, further adjusts its budget. The other departments follow suit. Higher-level management is led to believe in a completely unrealistic set of numbers.
- A highly successful real-estate developer makes large profits and borrows to the hilt for aggressive expansion. The area becomes overbuilt, and the

market turns bad. The developer is stuck with high costs on long-term projects and massive loans that it cannot repay. The developer goes bankrupt.

- A car manufacturer planning a new model approaches many potential suppliers, aggressively trying to drive the price down. Suppliers deliberately bid low in order to win a contract that will provide business for many years, knowing that they will have to raise the price later. This causes many cost increases for the car manufacturer, which may make it difficult to make the new model a success. The suppliers keep their true costs secret; hence there is much less detailed communication between the supplier and manufacturer than there should be about mutually beneficial design changes. Such problems have been overcome in Japan by much closer cooperation between suppliers and manufacturers, starting at the early design stage of the car.

- The trend toward downsizing of computers started in the mid-1980s. Small computers became more and more powerful and inexpensive. The payroll that was done on a $5 million mainframe could be done on a $50 thousand work station. Corporations began to take work off the mainframe—very slowly at first, the way the growth of pond weed began. Massive mainframe earnings paid for IBM's way of life and constrained many of its other activities. The decline in mainframe sales was like the pond-weed curve, however, and in 1993 IBM shocked the world by announcing what was then the largest loss in the history of human enterprise—almost $5 billion.

Corporate Learning

Corporate learning, like learning in life, is to a large extent based on experience. We take action, observe its effect, and learn from that how to improve performance. This describes how we learn to drive a car, conduct a meeting, or run a factory shop floor. It describes most *kaizen* activities. It describes how a child grows to adulthood and how the adult becomes "savvy." However, it only works when we can clearly associate an action with the results of that action. It depends upon our observing cause and effect, and we can do that only when the effect is close in time and space to the cause. In complex systems the cause and effect are often not close together in time and space. In that case, we do not easily associate them and so cannot learn by observing their interaction.

> *The way we think about reality is fundamentally different from the nature of reality in systems whose cause and effect are separated.*

Learning based on the *observable* results of our actions is limited in what it can teach us. Managers, policymakers, and system designers need to understand far-reaching causality webs, the type of behavior they cause, and the techniques for lessening problems with them.

If managers learn thoroughly from observable experience, they have "street smarts" but may also have a learning disability. Their insight and intuition have not been trained on long-span effects. The organization exhibits behavior that is *counterintuitive*. Often the counterintuitive behavior is of large magnitude. In many cases it has caused severe corporate decline. Management wrestles with a situation that refuses to behave as expected. As we reengineer enterprises, we need to analyze long-term causality webs and their counterintuitive effects.

Actions That Are Needed

There are important actions that should be taken to limit the harmful effects of the interactions described in this and the previous chapter. These actions are a valuable part of process reengineering:

> *Reduce delays in systems.* Counterintuitive systems are those having long delays. We should use computers and telecommunications to reduce the delays. This is being done in many ways—just-in-time techniques, continuous-flow manufacturing, point-of-sale information collection transmitted to inventory managers and distributors, worldwide sales information transmitted to production planners, travel-agent computers on-line to airline load managers, etcetera.
>
> *Link causes and geographically distant effects.* Dangerous feedback occurs when cause and effect are far apart so that decision makers do not associate them. A decision that looks good locally may have distant harmful effects. We can build information systems that link causes and distant effects. Decision makers can then observe relationships between the cause and remote effect.
>
> *Make cause-and-effect relations visible.* When the effects of an action are felt far away or at a different time, the effects are often not visible. We must make far-reaching effects visible to the decision makers by transmitting and gathering the relevant information. We can create spreadsheets or displays that show causes and effects that are separate in space and/or time. Decision makers can analyze the cause-and-effect relationships with spreadsheets or other tools.
>
> *Combine responsibility for cause and effect.* In hierarchical organizations an action taken in one part of the organization is often entirely isolated from the results of the action that affect a different part of the organization. When value streams are reengineered, a team should be responsible for actions and their results. If the results occur far away, the team should be linked to those results with information technology.
>
> *Stop positive feedback before it becomes dangerous.* Positive feedback which could cause escalation of problems, or growth and collapse, should be stopped before it does harm. Similarly, negative feedback should be pre-

vented from causing large oscillations. The process should be reengineered so as to prevent harmful escalation or overswings.

Simulate the system dynamics. Process modeling should be effected with a computer so that managers or staff can learn with models rather than reality. The models shrink time and space greatly and allow endless experimentation with the model.

Facilitate learning about system behavior. Managers and decision makers need to be taught about systemic behavior. We can create examples of typical systemic patterns and train managers to look for them, recognize them, and understand the behavior. Although rarely done today, this is likely to become a valuable form of training for management and decision makers. Senge describes ten common archetypes of systemic behavior that are counterintuitive unless an executive's intuition is trained to recognize them.[1]

Build closer interactions among trading partners. Harmful feedback often exists in the interaction among trading partners. To overcome its effects, closer relationships should be built between manufacturers and suppliers, retailers and distributors, and so on. A vendor may have on-line access to a customer's information computer. Information from retailers' bar-code readers may be transmitted directly to manufacturers. A manufacturer and vendor may cooperate closely in product design. Just-in-time relationships may be built between suppliers and manufacturers or between manufacturers and retailers

Fast, computerized interaction, special relationships and contracts, and agreements to exchange information can eliminate overswings and harmful delays.

Stop building stovepipe systems. Most systems built today have a narrowly focused viewpoint, such as that of one department. The work of the department may be optimized and automated, but this does not correct feedback that goes beyond the department; it may make it worse. In the beer-distribution activities discussed in the previous chapter, the retailer, distributor, and brewery could each have its own highly efficient computer system, but this would not stop the harmful overswings. Computers sometimes increase overswings—for example, with stock market crashes with computerized program trading.

It is necessary to build systems with an understanding of the long-span interactions. Stovepipe systems make it more difficult to optimize long-span interactions. Most enterprises today are building the wrong systems. The pressure for downsizing encouraged the building of localized stovepipe systems.

Enterprise Engineering demands a nonparochial viewpoint. If a corporate vision, or a vision for a reengineered process, is established without an understanding of far-reaching webs of cause and effect, it will be a flawed vision.

We often tend to focus on the symptoms of problems rather than the underlying systemic structure. We can repair or improve the symptoms, but this has only a short-term effect. Failure to deal with, or even understand, the underlying cause may make matters worse in the long run. There are many examples in business of managers giving aspirin when the patient has cancer.

Reference

1. Peter M. Senge, *The Fifth Discipline* (Doubleday Currency: New York, 1990).

Part V
Strategic Visioning

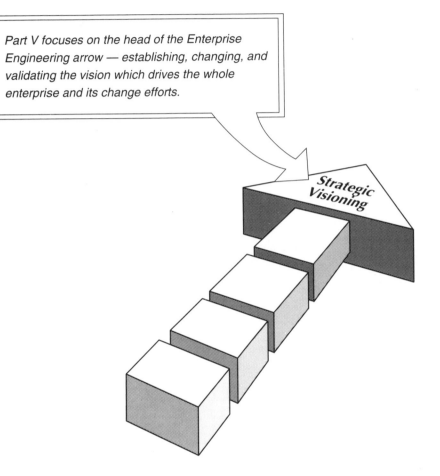

Part V focuses on the head of the Enterprise Engineering arrow — establishing, changing, and validating the vision which drives the whole enterprise and its change efforts.

Strategic Visioning

22

The Strategy Revolution

The arrow at the top of the Enterprise Engineering diagram relates to top management's vision and strategy of the enterprise and where it is going. The other components are an implementation of that vision.

If the strategic vision is wrong, excellent implementation of the other parts of the arrow will do little good. A rocket with a faulty steering mechanism is in trouble, no matter how well engineered the rest of the rocket is.

There are many books and articles on corporate strategy. This book does not compete with them. Instead it is concerned with the overall changes in strategic vision that must result from the increasingly dynamic nature of competition.

The strategic vision of the enterprise affects everything else. It should help determine the architecture of the enterprise and help create lower-level visions for each value stream. It should translate into vision statements that help to excite and energize employees. Of the components of Enterprise Engineering, strategic visioning is the one that is *unique* to each enterprise. It is greatly dependent on the views of the chief executive and his advisors. At the highest level, every enterprise has different problems and unique solutions. Nevertheless, there are aspects of strategic visioning that should be done in every enterprise, and there are methodologies for doing them.

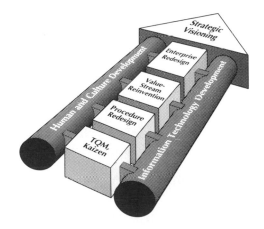

Planning vs. Visioning

It is vital to separate the notion of strategic visioning from that of strategic planning.

Most successful strategies are visions, not plans. The vision reflects holistic insight and creative ideas about the business and its directions. It requires imagination and inventiveness. Planning, on the other hand, is done with computerized spreadsheets and tools for collecting, understanding, and manipulating masses of data. Strategic planning often gets in the way of strategic thinking because executives engaged in planning often focus on the manipulation of numbers rather than creating a fresh vision.

Formal planning relates to the investigation and rearrangement of existing categories, such as products, markets, and strategic business units. Visioning is not about exploring existing categories but *inventing new ones*. Planning does not forecast discontinuities; strategic visioning must be alert to discontinuities because they can be very dangerous. Planning tends to preserve the existing mental models of executives; visioning is about changing those models. Strategic visioning often leads to a fundamental change in the basic *architecture* of a corporation. Strategic planning usually operates within the existing architecture.

Russell Ackoff of the Wharton Business School commented:

> A good deal of corporate planning I have observed is like a ritual rain dance; it has no effect on the weather that follows, but those who engage in it think it does. Moreover, much of the advice and instruction related to corporate planning is directed at improving the dancing, not the weather.[1]

The rise of Japan has been led by a number of great corporations with great strategic thinking. Kenichi Ohmae, Japan's leading management guru, has studied this phenomenal success in great detail. He observes that many of the best Japanese corporations have no big planning staffs and no "gold-plated" methodology for strategic planning. Instead, they have a strategist of great natural talent—often the founder or chief executive. "Often—especially in Japan where there is no business school—these outstanding strategists have had little or no formal business education, at least at the college level. They may never have taken a course or read a book on strategy."[2]

The key to successful strategy is *insight*. Insight is creative and intuitive, and often challenges the popular wisdom. Strategic insight needs innovative holistic thinking. It requires the creative synthesis of many aspects of the situation in the head of one person, or sometimes a tightly knit team, who must be able to communicate insights persuasively. Ohmae comments that great strategists have "an idiosyncratic mode of thinking in which company, customers and competition merge in a dynamic interaction out of which a comprehensive set of objectives and plans for action eventually crystallizes." The resulting plans may not make sense from the analyst's point of view, as Nicolas Hayek's drive to make Swatches did not (Exhibit 22.1) or Akio Morita's drive to make a product (the Sony Walkman) that no customers said they wanted. Market researchers would have said No to many of the strategies that produced world-changing products. Spreadsheets do not indicate the need for something entirely new.

Successful business strategies are not the result of rigorous analysis but a holistic mental process that is creative and intuitive. Einstein once said, "I never discovered anything with my rational mind." Instinctive strategic thinking is found in great entrepreneurs who link it to a sense of mission and determination to make it succeed. The strategist uses analysis only to test the ideas that emerge,

Exhibit 22.1

The most impressive examples of a vision that fundamentally changed an enterprise are usually the vision of one person. Sometimes the vision of one person has changed an entire industry.

Until the mid-1970s Switzerland dominated the world's watch industry. In a few years in the late 1970s it was battered by Japanese competition based on cheap quartz and microelectronics technology. By 1983 its share of the world market had plunged below 15 percent and was rapidly heading down. More than half of the Swiss manufacturers went under, and creditor banks took over the country's two largest watchmaking groups, SSIH and ASU, intending to close them down and sell the brand names to the Japanese.

In 1983 a group of Swiss banks sought the advice of an un-Swiss-like Swiss, Nicolas Hayek, on how to save the Swiss watch industry. Hayek had an American father, a Lebanese mother, and a hairy, grinning face with a childlike exuberance. He created the vision of the plastic Swatch, short for "Swiss watch," telling the sceptical Swiss on Swiss television that they could again be no. 1 in watchmaking.

Switzerland was one of the world's most expensive labor markets, and the conventional wisdom said "make watches abroad in cheap-labor countries." Hayek's view, however, was that the Swiss were brilliant at automation. They invented clockwork; they could build clockwork factories. The Swatch was designed with half the number of parts of Japanese quartz watches. Parts were built directly into the plastic casing, designed for *automated assembly,* entirely in Switzerland.

The plastic watch featured bright colors and trendy designs. Some designs were "must buys" for teen-agers, some for children, some for high fashion, some for smart business people. Concorde passengers were given Concorde Swatches. In eight years over 100 million were sold.

Hayek led a group of investors and bought the two largest watchmaking groups from the banks. He effectively gained one-third control of the Swiss watch industry. Switzerland once again controls more than half of the world's watch industry and the hairy Hayek is a billionaire (in dollars).

to reject many of them, and to evaluate what is needed to make the good ones a market success. Success, according to Thomas Edison, requires one percent inspiration and 99 percent perspiration—but without the one percent inspiration there is no hope of greatness.

Ohmae comments, "Great strategies like great works of art or great scientific discoveries, call for technical mastery in the working out but originate in insights that are beyond the reach of conscious analysis."

Strategic planning is something that should happen once the *vision* is created. Planners can collect information about the vision, populate spreadsheets, estimate resources and costs, explore alternatives, and generate charts. Planning can take a vision and work out how to make it operational.

Good-bye to Stability

Corporate strategy is being revolutionized. The reason for this is that everything is changing faster. Competition is becoming much more volatile. Product life cycles are shrinking. As the fickle world of corporate competition changes, windows of opportunity become shorter, and "owning" a market segment becomes more difficult. The key to success is being able to change and innovate fast.

The increasing rate of change is caused by technology and by the reengineering of business to take advantage of technology. Exhibit 5.6 showed examples of how value-steam reinvention causes dramatically shorter response times. Reengineering changes the logic of competition, making it more dynamic; and this in turn, means that corporate strategy must change. The successful corporations are those that can move faster than their competition.

Electronic networks, media, and computer systems often extend worldwide, contributing to the rise of a *global* economy. Barriers between national and international markets are being removed. Cheap-labor countries are becoming massively industrialized. It is much easier than it was to build a reengineered factory in Mexico or India. Malaysia has become the largest exporter of memory chips. Places such as South Korea and Singapore have grown at an explosive rate. China, with over a billion people, may grow equally fast.

When competition was relatively static, strategy could afford to be static. The world used to have well-defined national and regional markets, durable products, and stable customer needs. General Motors could become the world's largest corporation while paying little attention to the car market outside North America. Strategy, when products were relatively stable, consisted to a large extent of building market share in clearly defined market segments. Today the world is being increasingly flooded with copycat products and new designs. The strategist can make *no fixed assumptions* because any assumption may be invalidated overnight.

The more volatile the business world becomes, the more important it is to emphasize strategic visioning separately from strategic planning.

How Do You Build a Tiger?

Management literature everywhere today states that the *successful corporations will be those that are fast, fluid, and flexible*. The winners can change direction instantly, introduce new products faster than their competition, and adapt immediately to new customer needs. However, it is even more important to emphasize that *corporations will not be successful unless they are good at something*. As global competition intensifies, they have to become *very* good. The corporation that introduces new products or services that are faddish, trendy, or gimmicky, but that does not aim for an underlying excellence, will be quickly swept away. Corporate excellence takes a long time to build.

The paradox for today's strategist is how to be fast, fluid, and flexible when the skills needed for survival take a long time to build.

A tiger in the jungle is fast and nimble. It can react immediately to new threats and attack new prey with terrifying speed. The skill of the tiger, however, developed over millions of years of evolution. Herein lies the challenge of today's strategist: How do you build skills that enable you to be a tiger? What skills would be difficult for competitors to emulate but would enable you to move faster and better? How do you create a game that the customers will want to play but whose price of entry is too high for competition?

Strategic Skills

The following two chapters discuss *core competencies* and *strategic capabilities*. These are skills that can be applied to multiple products and services, or that enable a corporation to move rapidly into the high-return-on-investment sector of an industry. A corporation needs these skills to be unique or very difficult for competition to emulate.

Unique capabilities take a long time to build and require substantial investment; otherwise competition can easily copy them. They must be such that they enable the corporation to move faster than its competition in pleasing customers. The strategist needs to ask: What are we exceptionally good at, and how can this skill be made better? Do we have the right skills? What skills would place us in an unbeatable position?

Often a strategic capability is a value stream (Part II). The next chapter distinguishes between *core competencies* and *strategic value streams*. The strategist should ask, What value streams should we build to an unbeatable level of excellence? A strategic value stream should be a top-priority candidate for reengineering.

> *A value stream identified as strategic should have its goals thought out carefully. It is concerned not just with delighting its customer today, but with building a long-term capability to delight the customer. That capability should be difficult for the competition to emulate.*

Carver Mead is a visionary who repeatedly pushed for revolutionary change in the microchip industry. Lynn Conway and Carver Mead conducted a campaign in the early 1980s to introduce revolutionary chip-design methods into both academic and industrial organizations. Their approach has much in common with how a corporation should produce a knowledge infrastructure for aggressive learning.

Conway began the change process at MIT.

> Our method was to project ourselves ahead ten years, then write the chip design book as though reflecting back upon a decade. Then we would let the people in the community critique it, and let the book itself become the focal point for the creation of methods.[3]

She produced the visionary book and then prototyped the breakthrough ideas in her classes at MIT as well as experiments at Xerox PARC to accelerate learning and gain enthusiasts. Finally, she used ARPANET, the forerunner of Internet, to broadcast these results and create widespread awareness of methods that would transform the chip industry. This sequence, in a nutshell, symbolizes the change processes needed in advanced corporate learning. A future vision stimulates radical learning within the enterprise by defining strategic gaps beyond today's organizational capability. These radical demands in turn stimulate inventive reengineering of the fundamental infrastructure of the enterprise. Finally, the new ways invented to close the strategic gaps are implemented by systematic, methodological learning throughout the enterprise.

The learning processes used in such an organization-change sequence must be learned themselves. This is not a classroom project—the enterprise must learn by doing. It must begin to practice these processes and methods in order to change. Once it begins, the enterprise's learning infrastructure grows out of these change processes, and in a sense the knowledge infrastructure *becomes* these learning processes. The change processes of Enterprise Engineering need to move an organization toward systematically growing a knowledge infrastructure and at the same time energize the enterprise to close its strategic gaps. Thus, Enterprise Engineering is a continuously maturing set of processes for both learning and managing enterprise change for long-term success.

Five *Whys* for the CEO

The strategist should ask not only What ought we to be uniquely good at? but also What are we bad at? and What needs urgent improvement? A conversation with the CEO can quickly reveal what he is worried about. Chapter 15 discussed asking five *why* questions to identify the true causes of problems. Exhibit 22.2 shows five *whys* in action—in a conversation with the CEO.

The conversation in Exhibit 22.2 reveals the urgent need to establish a proce-

Exhibit 22.2 Five *why* questions that CEOs should be asked about all problems

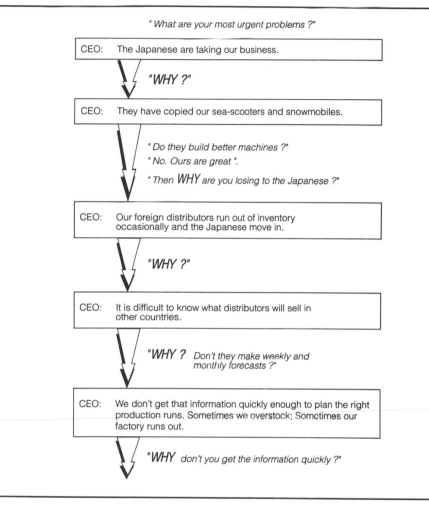

" What are your most urgent problems ?"

CEO: The Japanese are taking our business.

"WHY ?"

CEO: They have copied our sea-scooters and snowmobiles.

" Do they build better machines ?"
" No. Ours are great ".
" Then WHY are you losing to the Japanese ?"

CEO: Our foreign distributors run out of inventory occasionally and the Japanese move in.

"WHY ?"

CEO: It is difficult to know what distributors will sell in other countries.

"WHY ? Don't they make weekly and monthly forecasts ?"

CEO: We don't get that information quickly enough to plan the right production runs. Sometimes we overstock; Sometimes our factory runs out.

"WHY don't you get the information quickly ?"

dure for obtaining forecasts from distributors quickly. The company in question did not have a computer network to its distributors. It could quickly implement such a network, worldwide, so that details of sales and forecasts would go directly to the computers used for manufacturing planning.

Surprisingly often there is a solution that can be implemented quickly to problems of major concern to the CEO. Often problems that the CEO perceives as serious relate to a value stream that is inadequate in some way. That value stream is a high-priority target for value-stream reinvention.

All strategists should have repeated "five-*why*" conversations with top management.

Long-Term Investment

Corporations that are exceptionally profitable or have exceptional growth rates for a long period have core competencies or capabilities that take years to build up. Top management needs to understand the requirement for substantial, year-after-year investment in the strategic skill. They need to commit themselves for the long haul.

Sony spent twenty years doing research and acquiring skills that today enable it to produce world-beating video-camera products. Sony introduces innovations to these products amazingly fast. Its rate of change is made possible by its underlying core competencies and value streams. Some corporations have an unbeatable capability because of an extremely elaborate computer system built for a redesigned value stream. American Airlines obtained great strategic value from SABRE, Benetton from its worldwide network, American Express from its authorizer system, Canon from its lens-design system, and so on. Airlines with computerized load-management systems try to maximize revenue from their flights in a brutally competitive industry by introducing fare change and special deals at an astonishing rate.

Ongoing investment in a strategic skill may have little short-term payoff but a large long-term payoff. The pressure for short-term results sometimes makes long-term investments difficult. In Japan there is less pressure for quarterly results than in America, and they are often more patient with the slow, long-term building of core capabilities. Some Japanese corporations that did not seem world-class in the 1960s and 1970s grew steadily in capability until they dominated world markets in the 1980s.

Honda in the early 1950s was a modest manufacturer of a 50-cc engine designed to be attached to a bicycle. It steadily built its expertise in engine design and manufacturing, moving to motorbikes, lawn mowers, outboard motors, and cars, until it eventually challenged the world's largest car manufacturers. It would be very difficult for a Western company to compete with Sony today in its main markets, because of Sony's core competencies built over many years.

A key strategy should be the building of skills or processes that give a corporation world-dominating capability and recognizing that this requires long-term investment. Paradoxically, the ability to be fast, fluid, and flexible requires constancy in the long-term development of know-how.

Innovation

As business becomes increasingly global and the world increasingly flooded with copycat products, the key to growth is innovation. Corporations that stay ahead are those that innovate to put them ahead of the pack. They need exciting new products, brilliant ideas, and revolutionary processes.

The most innovative corporations generate many hundreds of product ideas for each one that comes to fruition. They learn by experimentation. Companies that are short of ideas tend to implement anything they have and often sink considerable money and effort into a poor idea.

Many large corporations have forgotten how to innovate. They have a culture of continuous improvement rather than breakthroughs. They are caught by surprise when technology discontinuities occur. Computerized planning is often planning without innovation. A corporation needs innovative thinking if it is to hold its own. It needs to head off the beaten track of its deeply rooted thought patterns.

The traditional view has been that strategic thinking is done by a handful of bright people at the top of an organization. New ideas can spring up anywhere, however, and often the most valuable come from people who work with the customers and understand their problems firsthand. As we increasingly build value-stream teams, we should encourage those teams to think about how their value streams ought to change in the future. There should be a dialogue about strategy between the top-level strategists and the creative members of value-stream teams. This is especially so as corporations reengineer *strategic* value streams.

> **Strategy, like everything else, should not be dictated blindly from the top; it should be contributed to by bright people who are close to the action.**

The successful corporations of the future will be those that constantly innovate, constantly experiment, and organize themselves to pursue new ideas. As Chapter 31 describes, they may operate like a laboratory, with people in many areas participating in research, experimentation, and the search for better ideas.

Successful innovation is strongly affected by the corporate vision of what it would like to achieve and by the corporate architecture. Valuable innovation is strongly inhibited by compartmentalization. Innovation requires the willingness to combine ideas from unconnected sources; it requires the ability to integrate across different parts of the enterprise. If employees are boxed into one department or segment of the corporation, much of the scope for innovation is lost. It is necessary to see problems as wholes, related to longer wholes. Rosabeth Moss Kanter, in a detailed study of what enables corporations to innovate concludes: *"Segmentalization inhibits innovation at every step of the solution-search process."* [4]

Instead of segmentalization, one needs the *boundarylessness* advocated by Jack Welch, who transformed GE. Kanter comments:

> Companies where segmentalist approaches dominate find it difficult to innovate or handle changes. Changes threatens to disturb the neat array of segments, and so changes are isolated to one segment. In searching for the right compartment in which to isolate a problem, those operating segmentally are letting the past—the existing structure—dominate the future. The system is designed to protect against change. [5]

The use of value-stream teams is a major attack on compartmentalization and results in greater innovation. However, creating value-stream teams is only one way to remove boundaries. The boundaries between value streams need to be removed. Open intercommunication is needed throughout the entire enterprise. Kanter found this to be a characteristic of the most innovative corporations.

Some innovation comes from a problem searching for solutions; some comes from a solution searching for problems. The latter is often powerful and valuable but tends to be suppressed if the innovation is boxed into one department.

Strategic Stagnation

When corporations grow old, they become set in their ways. Organizations age much faster than people. Nevertheless, great strategies come from instinctive, creative, holistic thinkers who challenge their world in innovative ways. The thinking of a natural strategist can be deeply at odds with the ingrained culture of the corporation.

Kenichi Ohmae says that the instinctive strategist is dying out in both Japan and the West—or is being pushed aside by rational, by-the-numbers, analytical planners. Today's large institutions, he observes, are not organized for innovation. They are oriented toward TQM and incremental improvement: "Advocates of bold and ambitious strategies too often find themselves on the sidelines, labeled as losers, while rewards go to those more skilled at working within the system."[5] He feels that in large Japanese companies promotion is based on tenure; there is no fast track for brilliant performers. Startling innovation will not help your career and, if it goes wrong, could damage it.

Large corporations everywhere tend toward strategic stagnation unless the CEO takes deliberate action to reverse this. The instinctive strategist, at odds with the culture of his large corporation, often leaves and becomes involved in a start-up corporation. The strategists of today who will be in the history books are people such as Bill Gates, Steve Jobs, Anita Roddick (of the Body Shop), Ted Turner, Nicolas Hayek (the Swatch impresario), Ross Perot, Luciano Benetton, and Richard Branson (of Virgin Records and Virgin Airways). None of these would have survived long on the planning staffs of most large corporations.

Discontinuities in Technology

Strategic stagnation is much more dangerous now than it was ten years ago. We are moving into a world of very fast change and brutal competition. Much of the fast change comes from changing technology. The evolution of technology is not a smooth journey but is characterized by wrenching discontinuities. Transistors replaced vacuum tubes; chips replaced transistors; electronic gadgets replaced mechanical gadgets; biological techniques for creating pharmaceuticals replaced many chemical techniques. When discontinuities occur, they cause wrenching dislocations. Leaders become losers. A strategic capability or core competency may become obsolete. Some of the very best corporations, such as IBM, have been shipwrecked by technology discontinuities.

The ability to anticipate and manage technical discontinuities is a critical part of strategic visioning. They often take root without appearing dangerous until it becomes too late. As many entrepreneurs know, they provide great ways to attack established industries.

Top-Management Radar

As business becomes more dynamic and unpredictable, it becomes more important for the people who steer the corporation to have a good radar. The waters are uncharted, but management would like warning of rocks ahead.

Chapter 25 discusses technical discontinuities, Chapter 26 the uses of scenarios for attempting to make top management aware of dangers and opportunities. Given the capability to change an enterprise, it is important to ask a fundamental top-management question: What should the enterprise become?

Every organization has an implicit architecture, inherited from the past, based on old paradigms largely unseen but continually guiding it. Strategic visioning questions this foundation. It rethinks the paradigms, beliefs, and basic architecture of the enterprise. Management must be willing to take on the "founder's" role anew, while it continues to deliver results today. This is a challenge that many management teams refuse to consider. Nonetheless, the onrushing changes in the external world demand this kind of thinking about the foundations of success.

Whereas value-stream reinvention applies clean-sheet thinking to a value stream and how it should operate, there is no "clean sheet" for the enterprise as a whole. Top management is constrained to make changes while keeping the existing enterprise running. Executives have to drive the car at the same time as they reengineer it. Nevertheless, it is important to ask deep and fundamental questions about what the enterprise *ought to be*, how its environment and customer needs are changing, and how it can capitalize on its core competencies.

Often the best way for a corporation to challenge its conventional wisdom is to use outside consultants in the strategic-visioning process. They bring fresh view points, different methods, and a knowledge of dangers that lie ahead.

Sometimes the question about what the corporation ought to be leads to the conclusion that it should remove one line of business and acquire new lines. In the mid-1980s all television sets were similar. There seemed little scope for product innovation. Television sets could be mass produced in factories of cheap-labor countries. Jack Welch had set as the goal for GE that each of its businesses should be the best or second-best in the world; if this goal was not achievable, it should be sold because it had a lower probability of surviving the decade ahead. GE was the largest television manufacturer in the United States but was unlikely to become no. 1 or 2 worldwide. Welch exchanged GE's television business for a manufacturer of medical-imaging machines. Medical-imaging technology was one in which GE had a good chance of being a world leader because this field needed a high level of innovation.

In 1987 General Electric was America's largest manufacturer of television sets and video cassette recorders in the United States. However, Jack Welch, the legendary CEO who transformed GE, sold GE's consumer electronics company to Thomson S.A., the largest French electronics company, in exchange for the Thomson CGR manufacturer of medical-imaging machines. The U.S. press howled with rage. The *Los Angeles Times* said that Welch had "sold an American birthright," throwing in the towel to the Japanese.

Welch believed that only businesses at the top of their fields would survive the 1990s because of worldwide competition's intensifying and technology's accelerating. He established a rule that any GE business that was not no. 1 or no. 2 in its field must either be made no. 1 or no. 2 or be closed or sold.

GE's television company was no. 1 in the United States but no. 4 in terms of the world television market. Welch argued, "There's no room for third-tier players. In TVs we were at the end of the whip: We'd have a good year; then all of a sudden TV would cost us $40 million."[6] Being the no. 1 American manufacturer did not guarantee worldwide success. Welch said that his rule must apply internationally. In the 1990s, globalization must be taken for granted and the measure of corporate success must be *worldwide* market share.

From the business point of view, the move was successful. It helped GE to move its highly profitable medical-systems company (GEMS) into a strong global position and to divest its TV business, for which future profits were in question. GE was better able to lock in profits in the more intellect-intensive business of CAT scanners, X-ray machines, and medical electronics than in TV and VCR manufacturing, which were easily copiable in cheap-labor countries.

Global market share will be increasingly important as the trends to globalism strengthen further.

References

1. Russell Ackoff, *Creating the Corporate Future* (John Wiley & Sons: New York, 1981).
2. Kenichi Ohmae, *The Mind of the Strategist* (Penguin Books: New York, 1983)
3. George Gilder, *Microcosm* (Touchstone, Simon & Schuster: New York, 1989).
4. Rosabeth Moss Kanter, *The Change Masters* (George Allen & Unwin: London, 1984).
5. Ibid.
6. Noel M. Tichy and Stratford Sherman, *Control Your Destiny or Some One Else Will* (Doubleday Currency: New York, 1993).

23

Core Competencies

Competencies and Capabilities

In an influential *Harvard Business Review* article in 1990, Gary Hamel and C. K. Prahalad stated, "The most powerful way to prevail in global competition is still invisible to many companies."[1] Top executives in the 1990s, they said, will "be judged on their ability to identify, cultivate and exploit the *core competencies* that make growth possible."

A *core competency* is a competency with a key technology or skill that can be used in many products. Once a corporation has mastered a set of core competencies, it can introduce, faster than its competition, diverse new products that employ these competencies. A core competency is something which a corporation does better than its competition, which competition cannot emulate quickly, and which can be used in many products. Canon, for example, built core competencies in precision optics, lens design, imaging, microprocessor controls, and precision mechanics, enabling it to diversify from cameras into video cameras, fax machines, laser printers, copiers, and image scanners. Hamel and Prahalad argued that core competencies should be the central building block of corporate strategy. The term *core competency* spread through the literature on corporate strategy. Executives set out to identify and build the core competencies of their organizations.

Two years later in the *Harvard Business Review*, George Stalk, P. Evans, and L. E. Shulman argued that core competencies are "not the whole story."[2] They used the term *capability* and argued that corporations are successful because they have an end-to-end capability that enables them to perform better than their competition. Senior managers, they said, should see their business in terms of one or more *strategic capabilities*. A capability is a value stream—an-end-to-end set of activities that delivers results to a customer (internal or external). A strategic capability is a value stream critical to competing, performed at a level of excellence difficult for competing companies to copy. Once a strategic capability is identified, top management should invest in it and build it to a level of excellence that enables the corporation to do better than its competition and to build barriers to competition.

Core competencies and *strategic capabilities* are different but complementary entities in corporate strategy. Whereas a core competency is a technological or production skill at a point on a value stream, a strategic capability is an entire value stream. Both emphasize "behavioral" aspects of strategy, and both require redesign of the corporation itself. Both change the concept of corporate architecture.

A key part of strategic thinking is to ask: What core competencies and strategic capabilities do we have? What can we do better than competition? What core competencies and strategic capabilities should we be building to a high level of excellence so that we can please our customers and build barriers to other corporations competing with us? How should we exploit our core competencies and strategic capabilities in new ways?

This chapter discusses core competencies. The following chapter discusses strategic value streams.

Core Competencies

A core competency is the mastery of an *enabling technology or skill* used in multiple products. Sony, for example, mastered miniaturization, creating or acquiring tiny components such as super-flat motors, disk-drive mechanisms, control chips, reliable microswitches, high-density read-write heads, and small batteries. From these components, it could build many products and so created the Sony Walkman industry. More than 160 variations of the Walkman were introduced between 1980 and 1990.[3]

Black and Decker set out to create common elements from which it could build many power tools. Nearly $20 million was allocated to this effort.[4] In 1970, Black and Decker products used more than 30 motors and 60 motor housings. Each of hundreds of power-tool products had its own unique armature. Black and Decker developed a hexagonal copper-wire-wrapped motor field with standard electrical plug-in connections. By varying the length of the motor field, power could be achieved ranging from 60 to 650 watts. The company designed standard motor housings and controls, and did research to constantly improve its motors. This core competency enabled Black and Decker to reduce product costs to such a level that its number of competitors declined from 20 to 3. Its market share rose from 20 percent to a dominant share.[5]

Microsoft changed its software-development methods to use object-oriented techniques. The goal was to build a library of software objects, each with a clearly specified behavior. Subtypes of these objects have the behavior of the parent object but also have some identifying behavior of their own. An object can have subtypes, subtypes of subtypes, and on on. Some objects may be highly complex because they are built out of other objects. This use of reliable objects of proven behavior enable Microsoft to build software of ever-increasing complexity at a much lower cost than by coding it line by line.

Once standard core technologies exist, a diversity of products can be created from them. Core competencies take a long time to develop, but once they exist new products can be introduced at a rapid rate.

Canon was a much smaller corporation than Xerox when it took Xerox by storm in the early 1980s, and its main business was cameras, not copiers. Canon had carefully thought out how it could build multiple product lines from a common set of core competencies. It entered, and sometimes dominated, diverse markets that used the competencies. It repeatedly excelled in the camera and video-camera market by using more advanced lens design than its competition. When it came close to destroying Xerox, it had spent a fraction of what Xerox had spent on copier research.

Unlike many Western corporations, Canon's separate business units had to share core competencies, which often meant they shared or exchanged the people knowledgeable in these core competencies. *Competency carriers* were deliberately rotated among the camera business, copier business, and other businesses.

In the view of Prahalad and Hamel, today's corporations should be designed around core competencies. Strategic business units must be designed to share core competencies. When the strategic-visioning process identifies the core competencies, some of these may be obtained by acquisitions. The human-resource organization should track those employees who are *competency carriers,* guide their careers, and ensure that they are exchanged or employed by the separate business units. Those people critical to core competencies are a key *corporate* asset that must be deployed strategically. It is tragic to observe how often in Western corporations employees who are the core-competence carriers have been fired.

The central planning of core competencies enabled corporations such as Canon, Sony, NEC, Casio, and Honda to expand business unit activities much faster than corporations with entirely separate business units.

Exhibit 23.1 compares growth in the 1980s of NEC and GTE. NEC planned its strategy around core competencies, and GTE did not. NEC in the 1970s articulated a strategy based on anticipated convergence of semiconductors, computing, and telecommunications.[6] It set out to build and acquire the "enabling technologies" that would make it dominant in these converging fields, so it eventually became the world leader in semiconductors and a first-tier player in telecommunications products and computers, bridging the gap between telecommunications and office automation.[1] NEC constituted a committee of top managers to oversee the building of the core competencies needed to achieve this goal. Prahalad and Hamel comment that it shifted enormous resources to strengthen the set of core competencies that were employed across its separate businesses. It entered into more than a hundred strategic relationships aimed at building its competencies rapidly and at low cost.[1]

GTE was originally much better positioned than NEC to capitalize on the marriage of telecommunications and computing, and top management widely discussed this convergence. However, GTE senior line managers managed independent business units, which delayed the building of shared core competencies.

The central planning of core competencies is at odds with the otherwise-valuable strategy of creating business units, each responsible for its own testing. A deliberate plan to build diverse products with the same core competencies is far more powerful. Prahalad and Hamel state that "too many companies have unwittingly surrendered core competencies when they cut internal investment in

Exhibit 23.1

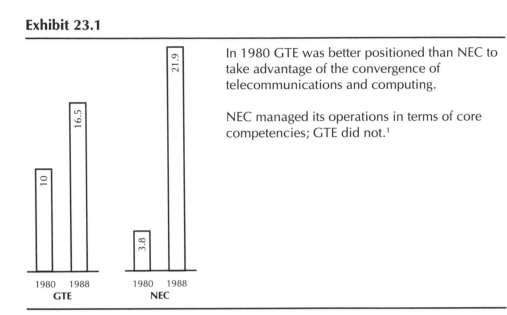

In 1980 GTE was better positioned than NEC to take advantage of the convergence of telecommunications and computing.

NEC managed its operations in terms of core competencies; GTE did not.[1]

what they mistakenly thought were just 'cost centers' in favor of outside suppliers."

Vertical Inflexibility

Many large enterprises in the 1960s and 1970s sought total vertical integration. Executives were taught to optimize, in financial terms, every step in their operations and to reduce every expenditure. The belief in the logic of optimization caused large corporations to try to extend the chain of manufacture so that they controlled every step. They could demonstrate theoretically that large savings accrued from controlling and integrating every stage in the long chain of manufacturing. They sought to own component manufactures as well as final assembly, distributors, and sometimes even raw materials.

The drive for vertical integration in the giant chemical company ICI led it backward into oil and forward into the manufacture of textiles. This seemed the logical pursuit of optimum profit. It sought tightly controlled vertical optimization. Massive capital went into owning and integrating every stage of the manufacturing chain.

The problem was that this led to inflexibility. A massively capitalized vertical group tries urgently to *sell what it can make* rather than to *make what it can sell*. When markets change, it is difficult to respond quickly in a tightly integrated vertical conglomerate.

Sir John Harvey-Jones, ex-chairman of ICI, writes: "Albeit unwittingly, we had created for ourselves the highest possible risk profile."[7] ICI put more and more capital into vertical integration; but the more they did this, the more difficult it was to react to major shifts in the marketplace. Harvey-Jones explains,

> I have been seared by the experience of verticalization and I believe that the current experiences of other companies who have followed this approach should be a salutary warning to every one of us. It was not just the risk profile of what we had erected; it was also the fact that owning every stage of the operation lost us flexibility and time.[7]

As the rate of change inevitably increases, loss of flexibility and time will become even more damaging. Instead of owning all the corporations in the food chain so that they can be controlled, it makes sense to have close partnerships with corporations with the intricate integration that today's electronics make possible. If something goes wrong or if the market needs change rapidly, partners can be changed if necessary. A partnership supplier, knowing that a switch of partner is possible, will try extra hard to delight the manufacturer with which it has a special relationship.

General Motors and Ford were companies that sought total vertical integration. Japanese car manufacturers built relationships with suppliers for joint design of components and just-in-time delivery of components and suppliers. The Japanese partnership approach worked better than the Detroit own-the-entire-food-chain approach. Similarly, IBM sought the maximum wholly owned integration, whereas Hitachi and Fujitsu grew vigorously with many partnerships. Japanese car and computer companies were specifiers and assemblers, to a large extent, rather than vertically integrated monoliths.

Canon and Sony identified the core competencies necessary for their strategic vision and set out to achieve the highest level of excellence in these competencies. They realized that the most cost-effective way to accomplish that was not usually to do all the research and development themselves but to identify technologies that they could buy or have access to by means of a partnership with another corporation. The technologies that were critical to their products could change suddenly, so they needed the flexibility to switch partners quickly, if necessary. The goal was not vertical integration but rather to have assured access to the critical technologies most cost-effectively, with the ability to switch technologies or add new technologies fast when necessary. Wherever it might reside, they wanted world-dominating skill with the core competencies.

A problem with the own-the-entire-food-chain approach is that it becomes like the Soviet Union in miniature. In principle, each subsidiary should run itself as efficiently as possible. In practice, there are internal power struggles and politics rather than the relentless discipline of the marketplace. When decisions migrate upwards in a massively integrated company, the higher levels of management become like the Kremlin. They mitigate a loss in one area by making changes in another. They defend the changes they make, creating their own games rather then listening to the subtle voices of the marketplace. Rather than attempt to own the whole food chain, it makes sense to have flexible, cost-effective access to whatever makes available the highest level of skill in the core competencies.

References

1. Gary Hamel and C. K. Prahalad, "The Core Competence of the Corporation," *Harvard Business Review,* May-June 1990.
2. George Stalk, Philip Evans, and Lawrence E. Shulman, "Competing on Capabilities: The New Rules of Corporate Strategy," *Harvard Business Review,* March-April 1992.
3. S. Sanderson and V. Uzumeri, *"Cost Models for Evaluating Virtual Design Strategies in Multicycle Product Families"* (Rensselaer Polytechnic Institute, Center for Science and Technology Policy: Troy, N.Y., 1991).
4. A. Lehnerd, "Revitalizing the Manufacture and Design of Mature Global Products," *Technology and Global Industry: Companies and Nations in the World Economy,* ed. B. R. Guile and H. Brooks (National Academy of Engineering Press: Washington, D.C.: 1987), pp. 49–64.
5. Marc H. Meyer and James M. Utterback, "The Product Family and the Dynamics of Core Capability," *Sloan Management Review,* Spring 1993.
6. C. K. Prahalad and Gary Hamel, "Strategic Intent," *Harvard Business Reiew,* May-June 1989.
7. Sir John Harvey-Jones, *Managing to Survive* (Heinemann: London, 1993).

24

Strategic Value Streams

Unique Capability

A value stream is much broader than the "competencies" discussed in the previous chapter. A *core competency* generally refers to exceptional skill with a critical technology that can be applied to multiple products. One or more value streams may also be critical. A *strategic value stream* is a unique capability which enables a corporation to move faster or better than its competition. It is a capability that competing firms cannot emulate easily.

As the competitive world changes ever more rapidly, the capability to respond quickly to changing needs depends strongly on the design of the relevant value streams. The value-stream teams, seeking to delight their customers, should be constantly alert to changes in customer needs or wishes. Value-stream teams involved in design or manufacturing should be constantly seeking innovation.

A traditional value stream, which clunkily passes work from one functional area to another as in Exhibit 24.1, cannot move quickly. Because there is no "owner" or manager of the traditional value stream, it rarely moves with decisiveness and precision. Of all the value streams in a corporation, certain ones will provide strategic capability. These should be identified as part of the strategic-visioning process, and if they have not been reengineered as discussed here, that should be done with high priority.

Different corporations in the same business may regard different value streams as strategic. They have different areas of excellence. Stalk et al describes the competition between K-mart and Wal-Mart in the United States.[1] At the end of the 1970s, Wal-Mart was a small niche retailer in the South, whereas K-mart was America's king of discount retailing with 1,891 stores and revenues of nearly $14 billion. By the early 1990s, Wal-Mart was the largest and highest-profit retailer in the world. Its growth was concentrated in half the United States, so it had ample room for further growth.

As in most corporate success stories, many things contributed to Wal-Mart's success. The press talked much about Sam Walton's charismatic personality and staff in the stores who greeted customers, but this alone would not have enabled Wal-Mart to grow so impressively. A key capability in Wal-Mart was its logistics system for getting the right goods to the stores at the right time with minimum

Exhibit 24.1

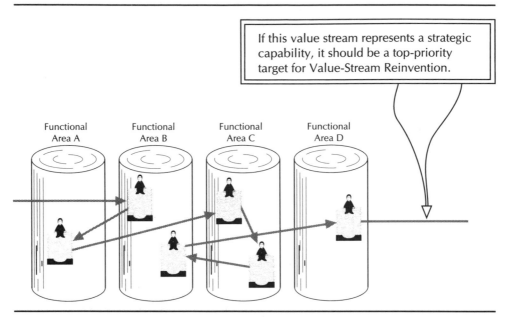

cost—the inventory-replenishment value stream. The value stream was reinvented with a clear goal: *Get goods on the shelves of the stores at a lower cost than
competition can.*

Wal-Mart built a system called "cross-docking" in which goods coming into
a warehouse are selected, replaced, and dispatched quickly to stores. Cross-
docking enabled Wal-Mart to buy whole truckloads of goods, and so pay lower
prices, but quickly dispatched these goods to stores without much inventory-
holding cost. The system needed a continuous flow of information from every
point of sale to the distribution centers and to Wal-Mart's 4,000 vendors. An elaborate computer network choreographed the rapid movement of goods, making
sure that stores had the goods customers wanted to buy but that the holding costs
were minimized. Wal-Mart replenished goods on its store shelves far faster than
the industry average, achieving lower holding costs and bulk discounts. Rather
than centrally *pushing* goods to the stores, which stores then *push* to their customers with advertising and special discounts, Wal-Mart's computerized logistics allowed customer purchases to *pull* the right goods to the stores. The computers
provided store managers with detailed information about customer behavior
from across the system so that they could make informed decisions about what
to stock.

Wal-Mart allocated shelf space to certain key suppliers such as Proctor and
Gamble so that *they* were responsible for filling these shelves. This guaranteed
these suppliers good shelf space to use in whatever way they thought best. Wal-

Exhibit 24.2

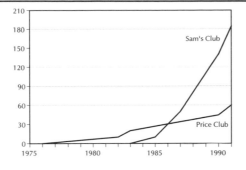

Source: Boston Consulting Group

Because of the exceptional capability of its computer-choreographed inventory-replenishment system, Wal-Mart was able to move into a new retail sector, warehouse clubs, and quickly beat the industry leader, Price Club.

Mart did not pay these suppliers for the goods until after the customers paid, so Wal-Mart could have a *negative* inventory-holding cost.

Wal-Mart fine-tuned the system, constantly inventing improvements to its strategic capability in inventory replenishment. It used this capability to move aggressively into new retail sectors. Wal-Mart created Sam's Club, for example, to move into the area of warehouse clubs, which sell products in bulk at a deep discount. Exhibit 24.2 shows how it overtook the industry leader Price Club quickly after entering the business.

To make the strategic value stream unbeatable by competition may require the development of highly complex technology. Wal-Mart made its distribution value stream unbeatable because its elaborate computer network linked bar scanners in its stores to central computerized planning of inventory. Immediate information about sales was transmitted to key suppliers. Detailed estimates could be made jointly with suppliers about sales patterns, to help get the right goods in the right quantities to the stores. Software enabled the mechanisms for distribution to be elaborately choreographed as events happened. This software to do this had to be built; it was not available in off-the-shelf packages.

In many other corporations software that is difficult to build has helped to create an unbeatable strategic value stream.

Capability Predators

George Stalk et al use the term *capability predator* to refer to a corporation that has built a strategic value stream to a level of excellence that is not quickly copiable and then uses it to move aggressively into new areas.[1] The example of Wal-Mart's moving into warehouse clubs illustrated in Exhibit 24.2 is an example of a capability predator.

Different types of capabilities can provide predator opportunities. Canon's manufacturing excellence made Xerox struggle for its life in the early 1980s. Toyota's development of lean manufacturing enabled Toyota and then other Japanese companies to move aggressively in the car industry.

Banc One asked the strategic question: What capabilities would enable Banc One to perform better than other banks? It observed that small local banks can serve a community in a personal way, having deep roots in that community, but large national banks such as Citicorp have powerful information systems and highly competitive cost structures. It concluded that it should have both of these capabilities. If it used centrally designed automation to give local bankers all the information and support they needed, local bankers could spend their time building quality relationships in their community.

As with Wal-Mart and many others, building the information systems to support the vision was tough and expensive. At Banc One it cost over $100 million. Banc One partnered with EDS to build the system (see case study) EDS paid much of cost of this, hoping to sell it to other banks. Banc One did not worry too much about other banks having access to the software because they believed that most banks would not compete effectively with it because they would not build the human expertise with the community that Banc One emphasized. The human part of the human-technology partnership is what creates true winners.

Most banks know remarkably little about their customers. Customer records with incompatible data structures exist on multiple computer systems, some for transactions, some for savings, some for house mortgages, and so on. Different systems record different types of loans. There is often no way to know whether a business tycoon is overextended on credit. Donald L. McWhorter, president of Banc One Corp, based in Columbus, Ohio, had a different vision: "We're in the information business, not the transaction business."[2] He wanted computer systems to pull together *all the relevant information about a customer.* This would help avoid bad loans and would provide many opportunities to do cross-selling, provide better customer services, and target marketing campaigns.

McWhorter wanted to reverse decades of banking tradition. Instead of focusing on transactions, he wanted his bank to know everything there is to know about a customer. This was thought to be a vital strategic capability that needed elaborate new computer software. Armed with such a system, bankers could spend their time deepening their relationships with customers.

To build a strategic capability well beyond that of the rest of an industry takes dedicated effort and investment over an extended period. The computer systems needed to implement McWhorter's vision took several years to develop and cost more than $100 million. A central system had 10 million lines of code and networked personal computers in a branch automation system acting as interfaces to the central system. The new system replaced 17 fragmented incompatible systems. Banc One teamed up with EDS to build the software with a contract in which EDS paid about 80 percent of costs in return for being able to sell the software to other banks. EDS grilled 300 bank employees to find out what information they wanted from the future system. The new system delivers a complete customer profile. It can produce a profile of an entire household or of all the customers who work for a given employer. It can store as many as 12 thousand pieces of information about a customer. It has substantially increased the accuracy of basic customer data.

Good bankers should know much about their local community, but often banks that have deep connections in their community lack the state-of-the-art systems and economies of scale of large national banks. Banc One's vision of itself was that it "out-locals the national banks and out-nationals the local banks."[1]

Banc One gave local bankers exceptional power in their region, encouraging them to build community relationships. Equipped with the system, bankers spent less time on paperwork and more quality time with customers, knowledgeably selling them better services. When Banc One had this capability and its technology working well, it could take over other banks and make them more profitable by using Banc One's hardware, software, and know-how. It set out on a acquisition binge.

In 1991 this core capability enabled Banc One to have its most profitable year ever—earnings were up 25 percent.

Local bank presidents in Banc One could run their operations in their own way, setting prices, making credit decisions, and serving their community with the canniness and flexibility of the best small banks. The central organization provided the automation support and constantly learned how to improve bank practices. They paid attention to reengineering the bank processes, reinventing its value streams, and spreading the best processes among the affiliate banks. Banc One set out to achieve the best mix of local employees and central support. Local bankers spent time learning how to serve their community better; central management spent time learning how to automate, reengineer, and constantly improve the processes.

Once Banc One had established these capabilities, it could take over banks and improve their profitability by putting its information systems in place and intensively training the officers of the acquired bank. It set out on a search for banks to acquire.

Benetton expanded around the world at astonishing speed once its network, systems, and robotic warehouses enabled it to hit the accelerator. Microsoft built software for building software and established an ever-growing library of software and software objects. Using this core competency it relentlessly improved its software development life cycle until this strategic capability helped make it a feared predator in the software industry. Visa International spent $50 million building a worldwide system for its card-processing value stream, which it believed would enable it to outgrow its competition (Exhibit 1.1).

The American movie industry developed processes, technology, and special-effects capability to make it an entertainment "predator" causing the rest of the world to complain about U.S. "cultural imperialism" and Europe to single out movies for exclusion from the critical GATT trade agreements of 1993.

Although excellence with a strategic value stream may enable a corporation to be a "predator," weakness in a strategic value stream can cause a corporation to lose market share. A company whose product is excellent found much of its business slipping away because its competition had developed relationships with dealers and were out-maneuvering it. The company needed to regard its dealer-support value stream as strategic and fundamentally reengineer it.

> Some spectacular corporate successes have resulted from identifying a strategic capability and reinventing it so that it is far better than in any competing corporation; it has "predator" capability. To build a capability that is unbeatable is no easy task. The corporation often encounters major problems and requires tough, persistent leadership. Big ideas require big money and require unwavering determination.
>
> Fred Smith, the creator of Federal Express, invented a way to deliver packages across the United States faster than any services that then existed. Instead of using commercial services whose schedules were designed for passenger traffic, he wanted to acquire a dedicated fleet of jets that would ship all packages via a central hub, for which Memphis seemed the right location. Smith, at the age of 28, raised $91 million in venture funding for this audacious idea. Several hundred trained employees were needed, along with the jets and the Memphis hub, before the operation could start.
>
> The new business lost over $40 million in its first three years. Various "experts" said that the market was too small for Smith's operation. Some investors tried to remove Smith and creditors tried to seize assets. Under pressure which would have cracked most leaders, Smith managed to maintain morale, demonstrate the potential market, and somehow mollify investors and creditors while spending large sums on national advertising to build market share. He realized that he had to advertise directly to users, not to mailroom managers who traditionally bought delivery services. Eventually Smith's extraordinary fortitude paid off. By 1988 Federal Express had annual revenues of $3.8 billion.
>
> Similar long-term fortitude characterizes the implementation of many other corporate reinventions, but far more often a potentially excellent reinvention is lost because its champion loses his nerve.

Linking Core Competency to Value Streams

Core competencies are chosen so that they may be shared among business units or used in several products. A number of value streams may share core competen-

Exhibit 24.3

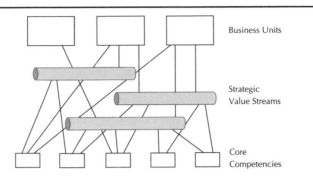

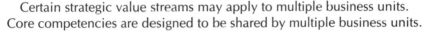

Certain strategic value streams may apply to multiple business units.
Core competencies are designed to be shared by multiple business units.

cies. Value-stream teams for product design should share core competencies in technology. Value-stream teams for administrative operations may require unique computer systems to make a core capability unbeatable. Sometimes a strategic value stream may be used by multiple business units or help a corporation to move rapidly into new business areas.

The architecture of the enterprise should be designed for appropriate sharing of core competencies and value streams (Exhibit 24.3).

Startling New Successes

Reuters changed from a news service to a financial-services company and expanded much more rapidly than its competition. Exhibit 24.4 gives other examples of surprising moves into different business areas. All of these are examples of corporations with strong core competencies or strategic value streams which they put to use in a different way. Reuters used its worldwide electronic network for delivering news to deliver financial services.

Occasionally core competencies become a liability. A corporation may be extremely good at something that is obsolete. The culture may be so emotionally entwined with the obsolete core competency that it is difficult to change. Some computer companies in the early 1980s were highly successful because they had a core competency of designing and building extremely complex mainframes. When mainframe sales declined precipitously in the early 1990s, the mainframe-oriented culture of these corporations made it difficult to move to a world of personal computers and local area networks. Outsiders can help a corporation to overcome its emotional entanglements with a proud competency whose time is past. Sometimes the strategic capability of a small company cannot be expanded easily as it grows into a large company. The key capability of a company of several hundred people may relate to companywide interaction among brilliant innova-

Exhibit 24.4   Some enterprises have rethought what they ought to be in startling ways. The following are examples of corporations identifying a core competency or strategic capability and putting it to use in a different way

- Kao is Japan's leading manufacturer of soap and household products. In 1986 it diversified, selling a surprisingly unrelated product—floppy disks. Analysts were highly dubious about Kao's entering such a different area, but by 1992 Kao had become the world's largest producer of floppy disks, outselling Sony and Verbatim. Kao's scientists produced skin-care products that are based on surface science and lubricant technology. This core competency was applicable to the surface technology of the floppy disk drive head.
- British Oxygen used its know-how in transporting liquid oxygen to diversify into a chilled transport service; it handles, for example, almost all the chilled transport for Marks and Spencer.
- Shell predicted roller-coaster changes in oil prices and established an electronic oil-futures trading service.
- Benetton diversified into selling insurance policies and mutual funds using the same innovative yet low-risk management strategies that had fostered the growth of its clothing empire.
- Canon diversified from leading in camera manufacture to office equipment. It used its core competencies in optics, imaging, and microprocessor controls to build copiers, laser printers, image scanners.
- Nokia, an ancient forest-products company in Finland, moved aggressively into cellular telephony and quickly achieved the world's second largest sales of cellular telephones way ahead of the giant telephone companies (see Exhibit 24.6).

tors, but this culture cannot easily be expanded to a large, geographically dispersed company.

In 1992 when Jorma Ollila was appointed CEO of Nokia, the company was in deep trouble. For more than a century Nokia had been a producer of pulp and paper in the heavily forested country of Finland. It made other mundane products such as rubber boots and electrical cables. In the 1980s it diversified into manufacturing television sets but failed; it made small computers but sold its computer division to ICL (owned mainly by Japan's Fujitsu). In 1989 its CEO committed suicide. To compound its troubles, the Finnish economy was hurt badly by the collapse of the Soviet Union. Nokia underwent terrifying losses in 1991 and 1992. Then 41-year-old Jorma Ollila became CEO.

Nokia had a mobile-phone division. Mobile phones achieved a higher penetration in Finland than most countries because of Finland's vast empty spaces. Ollila set out to focus on mobile telephony and data transmission and to downgrade most of the rest of Nokia. He concentrated on a new generation of cellular phones based on digital rather than analog technology and aggressively marketed these products worldwide. Nokia stayed lean and mean, buying most of the technology from the outside. Nokia produced a featherweight phone, which it advertised worldwide as "the most portable phone." As well as marketing in industrial countries and far outstripping the Japanese at their own game in Japan, Nokia targeted countries such as China, where almost no homes have phone lines and digital cellular technology allows telephone services to be provided cheaply.

Nokia became number one in Europe and second only to Motorola in the United States. It quickly rose to become the world's twelfth-largest telecommunications manufacturer, with revenues of $2.25 billion in 1993 and a 20 percent profit on its phone manufacturing.

The giant telephone companies largely missed the boat in the race for pocket cellular phones. Conventional wisdom was that size was critical in the capital-intensive telephone industry. Nokia demonstrated that in new markets such as cellular phones, speed was more important than size.

Nokia's extraordinary turnaround demonstrates how different the 1990s is. Small corporations or subsidiaries can streak past the giant corporations with slow-moving hierarchies. Lightning speed is possible in global markets with innovative products, built with purchased components and out-sourced know-how.

Strategic Learning Laboratory

A value stream can be operated like a learning laboratory. It is managed so that the value-stream team does research, performs experiments, and constantly searches for innovations that can improve its capability (Exhibit 24.5). A strategic value stream operated in this way can become a critical capability that is hard for competitors to imitate. It can form a basis for repeated innovations that provide sustainable competitive advantage.

In reality, most strategic capabilities today are more like those in Exhibit 24.2. They meander across multiple departments and functional areas. The strategic capability is a small part of many people's jobs rather than the explicit job of highly focused teams. Because the strategic capability is scattered almost randomly among different departments, no one executive is in charge of it. To invest in the capability and improve it enough to make it a major competitive resource would mean investing in many functional areas. This might be difficult to justify in normal accounting terms. Internal accounting and control systems miss the strategic nature of the scattered activities. For these reasons most corporations do not focus closely on a strategic capability; they fail to develop and exploit the capability as they should.

Once the capability is identified as a value stream, it becomes clear that value streams should be operated by cross-functional teams and should be redesigned

Exhibit 24.5

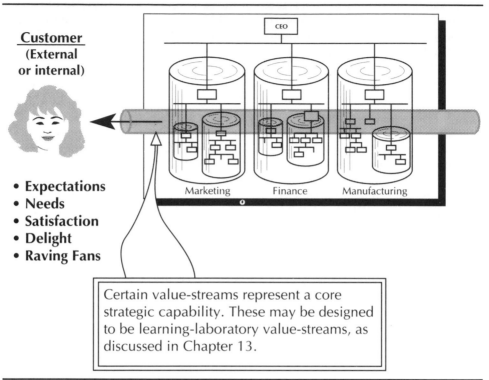

- **Expectations**
- **Needs**
- **Satisfaction**
- **Delight**
- **Raving Fans**

Certain value-streams represent a core
strategic capability. These may be designed
to be learning-laboratory value-streams, as
discussed in Chapter 13.

to achieve the strategic goals as directly as possible, using technology to maximize
the effectiveness of the value-stream team.

To become unbeatable with such capabilities requires constant flow of new
ideas, experiments, and research. The value-stream teams should be constantly
scanning journals and product catalogs for new ideas, thinking about how to use
them to improve the core capability. It is much quicker and cheaper to *buy* most
technology than to develop it in-house. Value-stream teams should be talking
to inventive information-technology professionals and constantly exploring the
possible use of evolving resources such as smart cards, Internet, image processing, cellular data transmission, and so on.

Strategists should think in terms of strategic value streams using core competencies and establish a learning-laboratory environment in which the teams identified as strategic can experiment and search the world for improvements. Often
technology or skills should be obtained by corporate acquisitions or partnerships
in order to build the core capabilities to an unbeatable level.

Once strategic value streams have been reinvented, the value-stream teams
should provide major input to strategic thinking. Thus strategic thinking is not
solely the province of senior management. It can be strongly contributed to by
strategic value-stream teams. Such teams are often more alert to changing needs

than top management and are more aware of possible innovations that are desirable. Value-stream teams can provide a major resource in helping to anticipate and initiate trends and to implement innovative new games ahead of competitors. Strategy, of course, should be contributed to by bright people who are close to the action.

Out-sourcing

Sometimes a component of the value stream is carried out in a different corporation. For example, the logistics value stream for moving goods from a central warehouse to retail outlets may employ an external trucking company. K-mart moved out of trucking because it was cheaper to use a subcontracted fleet. At the same time, Wal-Mart built its own trucking fleet, eventually owning nearly two thousand trucks. Wal-Mart believed that being fully in charge of the end-to-end process for replenishing its store shelves was a strategic capability. Quick replenishment with low inventories was critical to saving costs and offering low prices to customers. Wal-Mart wanted its trucks to have computers on board and be part of an intricately choreographed logistics system, a key factor in enabling Wal-Mart to grow rapidly at the expense of K-mart.

Some corporations out-source the building of computer applications. This may make good sense for bread-and-butter applications or for fast implementation of reinvented value streams; but for software needed by a strategic capability, a key requirement may be the ability to modify that software very rapidly. It is better to have the capability to do this in-house with speed and certainty. A corporation should be fully in charge of its core strategic capabilities whenever possible, recognizing that this often requires close links to partnership corporations.

When a corporation's strategic capability includes suppliers or other partners that cannot be owned, it should forge special relationships with those partners, with special contracts. The trading partners may be asked to change their own business processes, for example. They obtain some benefit for this change, such as guaranteed business or better payment terms. The special relationship may need computer-to-computer links to the trading partner or video-conferencing links.

Although it is essential to manage the strategic capabilities in-house, it may make sense to out-source capabilities that are not strategic. If bread-and-butter activities are contracted out, management can focus the corporate talent on those activities that make a competitive difference. Most of the corporate energy can be directed to core capabilities.

Management at the CEO Level

Much value-stream reinvention needs to be driven by the CEO because it crosses functional areas and requires major management changes in those areas. However, it is especially important that the reinvention of *strategic value streams* be managed at the CEO level. This reinvention strongly affects the core strategic capability.

When some top executives identify a strategic capability and realize that nobody is explicitly managing it, they may set about improving it to enhance its contribution without going through a fundamental reorganization. The strategic capability has pieces reporting to different executives, and matrix management is needed to control the end-to-end capability. This is far from satisfactory. The organization needs to be restructured so that the strategic capability can have an executive in charge of it and can use teams dedicated to delivering the best end-to-end results.

Only the CEO can focus the entire corporation's attention on building strategic capabilities into an ever-stronger competitive weapon. Only the CEO can authorize the cross-functional investments needed to achieve this and manage the upheaval of replacing a fragmented capability with well-managed and well-focused teams. George Stalk of the Boston Consulting Group comments, "A CEO's success in building strategic capabilities will be the chief test of management skill in the 1990s."[1]

A company that is conceived in terms of core competencies, value streams for strategic capabilities, and market-focused business units that share the core competencies and capabilities will be the best equipped to do battle. The CEO and chief organizational architect need to formulate strategy in these terms and design the corporation accordingly.

Summary

In any industry there is a wide range of profitability. Profitability varies far more among businesses within one industry than it does across separate industries.[3] To be at the upper end of the range, a corporation needs assets that are hard to replicate or skills that are hard to imitate. These assets or skills cannot be bought off the shelf; they must be acquired through investment, development, and learning.

Core competencies and strategic value streams that give a major competitive advantage tend to have the following characteristics:

- They take time to develop. Often corporations fail to develop them because they are impatient and do not persist for the long haul.
- To develop them needs substantial investment.
- Their value relates to the quantity and quality of learning that occurs. Everybody should contribute to the learning and be encouraged to search for innovation.
- Building a powerful knowledge infrastructure is necessary.
- A strategic capability generally requires value-stream reinvention. The reinvented value-stream teams should constantly contribute to learning how to make the strategic capability better.

Exhibit 24.6

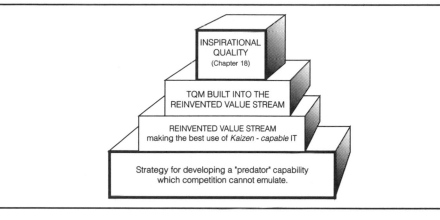

- Most strategic capabilities need the development of major computer systems, often with unique, not off-the-shelf, software.
- Building high-performance teams, rather than work groups, can be critical. Inspirational quality (Exhibit 24.6) is needed.
- Putting the competency or capability to best use needs inspiration, not just routine planning.

The strategist should do the following:

- Analyze his corporation's core competencies and strategic capabilities.
- Examine the core competencies and strategic capabilities of the competition.
- Determine what technology discontinuities might change this assessment (Chapter 25).
- Decide what core competencies need development and investment, and determine what can make them a unique resource.
- Target strategic value streams for reengineering and determine what can make them a unique resource.

References

1. George Stalk, Philip Evans, and Lawrence E. Shulman, "Competing on Capabilities: The New Rules of Corporate Strategy," *Harvard Business Review,* March-April 1992.
2. "Files with Faces" *Computerworld,* Dec. 14, 1992.
3. R. Rumelt, "How Much Does Industry Matter?" *Strategic Management Journal,* December 1991.

25

Discontinuities

Dangerous Shifts

As technology evolves, major discontinuities occur. A new technology replaces an older one. A corporation stuck with an old technology suddenly finds itself in trouble. One reason the average life span of corporations is low is that they fail to manage discontinuities in technology.

NCR, in the early 1970s, announced that it had $140 million worth of newly designed cash registers that it could not sell. NCR stock crashed to less than a third of its price. The CEO was fired. Of 35 corporate officers, 28 lost their jobs and were put on "consultant" status. Dayton, Ohio, was decimated as thousands of workers were laid off. NCR had insisted on sticking with tried-and-true mechanical cash registers while new competition produced cash registers with microelectronics. Mechanical cash registers went from 90 percent of the market in 1972 to 10 percent in 1976.[1]

Japanese firms such as Sony and Hitachi invested more than $8 billion in analog HDTV (high definition television). Japan's state-owned broadcaster, NHK, broadcast eight hours of HDTV programming per day. Europe's government in Brussels caused European firms to spend about $2 million on an equivalent European white elephant. Analog HDTV was suddenly made obsolete by digital television.

Technology is changing at a furious rate. More scientists are at work today than all scientists who have ever worked in all prior human history. Technology has become global and jumps barriers between industries. A glass manufacturer revolutionized telecommunications; a cosmetics manufacturer became number 1 in computer disks.

A set of core competencies can enable a company to introduce new products rapidly. However, a competing company may create technology that makes obsolete the core competencies. The marketplace is full of attackers trying to do just that.

The rate of change of technology is increasing; discontinuities are becoming more frequent—a major reason for the high rate of corporate change that affects all strategic planning. There will be many more NCR stories. Understanding and managing technology discontinuities is a vital but often neglected part of strategic visioning.

The Life-Cycle Curve

Any technology has a life cycle. It starts with new ideas, and money has to be spent on these ideas for some time before anything works well. If the development is successful, the technology rapidly grows in capability. It often grows exponentially for some years. If growth is plotted on log paper with performance on a log scale and time on a linear scale, exponential growth appears as a straight line. Performance might double every year for several years.

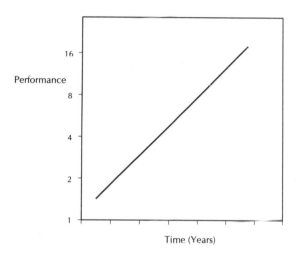

Every technology has limits. The growth slows down and eventually ceases. Plotted (on linear paper), the growth looks like a rising snake:

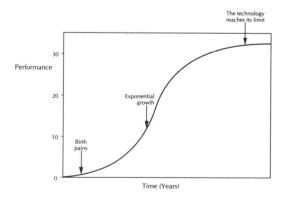

Often as one technology approaches its limits, another technology comes along that will eventually replace it, as in Exhibits 25.1 and 25.2.

Failure to Manage Discontinuities

As technology evolves, discontinuities such as that in Exhibit 25.1 inevitably occur. Corporations often fail to anticipate or manage the discontinuity, which can be surprisingly dangerous because frequently technologies A and B come from different corporations. A gaggle of start-up corporations may be excited about technology B. Sometimes a large corporation is skillfully working out how it can use technology B to attack a corporation entrenched in technology A.

Many corporations have lost an important part of their business through not anticipating and managing such discontinuities. They are wedded to technology A because they have invested a large amount of money in it and it has made them successful. They put up mental blocks against believing that technology B could seriously challenge technology A. In its early days technology B performance is inferior to that of technology A. However, the new technology grows in capability with surprising speed.

Discontinuities occur not only in technological industries but in dull-sounding low-tech industries—for example, containers. Companies making large profits out of glass bottles found much of their business replaced by steel cans and paper cartons from other manufacturers. Steel cans, in turn, were replaced by aluminum cans from other companies. Paper containers were replaced by plastic.

Exhibit 25.1 One technology replacing another, each with a particular growth pattern

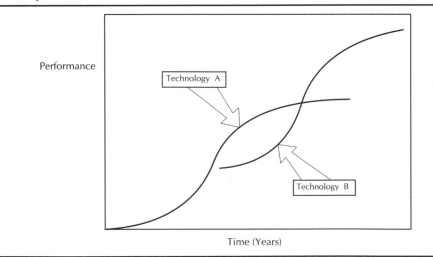

Exhibit 25.2   A succession of technologies, each with its own life cycle, showing the growth of particle accelerators

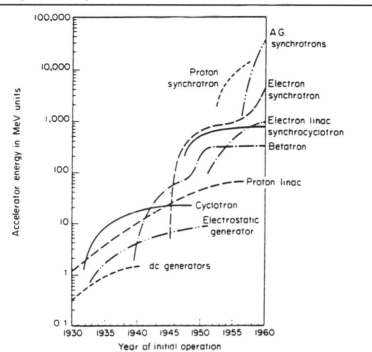

Many industries have a long-term history of one technology replacing another. (From M. S. Livingston).

Richard N. Foster of McKinsey & Co. has studied such discontinuities and concludes that when they occur, corporate fortunes change dramatically. "The leaders in the current technology rarely survive to become leaders in the new technology. Their losses can vary from gentle to total, from embarrassment to humiliation."[2] The leaders-to-losers story is sometimes played out on a grand scale with nations losing entire industries, such as Switzerland losing its mechanical watch industry, Germany losing its camera industry, and the United States losing its video industry.

Foster remarks that although hard statistics are difficult to establish, it appears that when discontinuities strike, leadership switches to a different corporation in about seven cases out of ten. "A change in technology may not be the number one corporate killer, but it certainly is among the leading causes of corporate ill health."

Exhibit 25.3, from Foster's book, shows the turnover in industry leadership that occurred when transistors replaced tubes and successions of semiconductor technology replaced transistors.

Exhibit 25.3   From vacuum tubes to semiconductors

Technological transitions lead not only to the disappearance of individual product lines but to the demise of whole industries.[2]

	1955 (Vacuum tubes)	1955 (Transistor)	1960 (Semi-conductor	1965 (Semi-conductor	1970 (Semi-conductor	1975 (IC)	1980 (LSI)	1982 (VLSI)
1	RCA	Hughes	TI	TI	TI	TI	TI	Motorola
2	Sylvania	Transitron	Transitron	Fairchild	Motorola	Fairchild	Motorola	TI
3	GE	Philco	Philco	Motorola	Fairchild	National	National	NEC
4	Raytheon	Sylvania	GE	GI	RCA	Intel	Intel	Hitachi
5	Westing-house	TI	RCA	GE	GE	Motorola	NEC	National
6	Amerex	GE	Motorola	RCA	National	Rockwell	Fairchild	Toshiba
7	National Video	RCA	Clevite	Sprague	GI	GI	Hitachi	Intel
8	Rawland	Westing-house	Fairchild	Philco/Ford	Corning	RCA	Signetics	Philips
9	Elmac	Motorola	Hughes	Transitron	Westing-house	Philips	Mostek	Fujitsu
10	Lansdale Tube	Clevite	Sylvania	Raytheon	American Micro	American Micro	Toshiba	Fairchild

Reproduced with permission from *Innovation* by Richard N. Foster.

This danger has existed since the Industrial Revolution, but today its incidence is increasing because new technologies are flooding into existence at a furious rate. The death rate in high-technology industries is spectacular, but now high technology is making an impact in most industries. The key value streams are changing as fast as the computer industry or even faster as they move through the discontinuity of value-stream reinvention. Airlines have been dramatically affected by networks to travel agents, load management systems, and computerized logistics. Steel has been dramatically affected by continuous-flow mills. Banc One has become a "capabilities predator" in banking. Computerized logistics systems have played havoc in the distribution industry.

A necessary part of corporate strategy is the understanding of technology life-cycle curves, the limits to growth of technologies, and the discontinuities that are likely to occur. It is not difficult to spot new technologies in their early stages and monitor them. It is essential to take action then, before they become dangerous. However, it is surprising how many companies fail to do this.

The Investment–Life-Cycle Curve

The investment in a new technology produces little or no workable results for a time. Eventually the investment starts to pay off. If the work is successful, results appear at a fast and furious rate. The performance improves steadily until the limits are approached. When the life cycle is close to its limits, further investment produces little benefit. Exhibit 25.4 illustrates this.

We will refer to this curve as the investment–life-cycle curve of a technology. To manage technology-based aspects of change, executives need to understand the investment–life-cycle curve. The slope at center of Exhibit 25.4 is much steeper than the steep slopes in Exhibit 25.1.

In the early stages, because investment produces nothing that works, executives may become impatient or doubtful about the investment. Sometimes, they terminate a development that could have succeeded, or invest insufficient money in it. It needs a major act of faith to believe that the payoff will occur. At the other end of the curve, executives are aware of the success of the technology, may regard it as a core competency, and often continue to invest in it, not realizing that the investment can have little payoff because the technology is close to its limits.

When one technology replaces another, as in Exhibit 25.5, the productivity of development work on the new technology is much higher than that on the old technology that is approaching its limits. It would make sense for a corporation

Exhibit 25.4 The investment–life-cycle curve

The life span of this curve has been two decades or more with many technologies of the past. Today the rate of change is faster. Some technologies have a life span of three years.

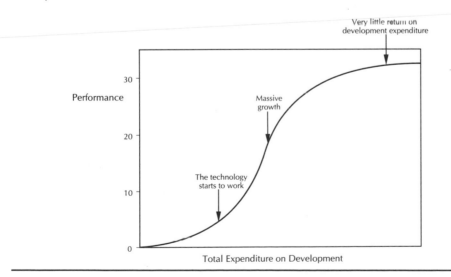

to be spending its development money on the new technology B, but usually the corporation that has been successful with technology A continues to try to improve the old technology.

McKinsey & Company has analyzed technical spending in large companies. Richard Foster observes, "It is not uncommon to find 80 percent of the effort going to the defense of products that are more important for what they have contributed in the past than for what they are going to contribute to the future."[2] Foster says that investments in emerging technologies often have five times the productivity of investments in mature technologies. It does not make sense to spend 80 percent on technology A instead of technology B. Barely 10 percent of R & D funding in pharmaceuticals was going in newer biological techniques for creating drugs, whereas probably more than half the total innovations would come out of that area.

The two life-cycle curves in Exhibit 25.5 are the same shape. Often this is not the case. A new technology may develop faster, its performance much, or perhaps only slightly, better. The situation shown in Exhibit 25.6 is more dangerous to the owners of technology A. They have less warning that technology B is being developed and that it will produce a considerably higher level of performance.

It is often the case that pushing to improve technology A can achieve a small percentage gain, perhaps 20 percent, whereas technology B brings a 200-percent gain, sometimes much more. No matter how well a company does with technology A, it cannot in the long run compete with technology B.

When personal computers were introduced, they vastly exceeded minicomputers in sales. Microwave ovens were a major step beyond conventional ovens.

Exhibit 25.5   Total expenditure on development

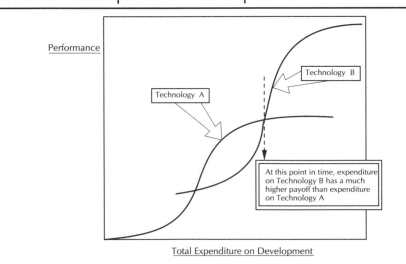

Optical cables transmit thousands of times more than copper cables. Code generators give much higher productivity than manual coding. New technology linked to value-stream reinvention can cut schedules dramatically or increase capability. No other area of management can match new technology linked to value-stream reinvention as a means of improving performance.

Falling Technology Cost

In the early days of a new technology, it is often too expensive and may be dismissed for that reason. Some technologies, however, plunge rapidly in cost. The cost of memory chips, for example, has fallen rapidly for many years. Something far from economical today may become so in the future, so development work should proceed in anticipation of the cost drop. Often the decline in cost is predictable, as it was with memory chips and microprocessor power (Exhibit 25.6).

When the first video recorders were built in the United States and Britain, they were too expensive to consider making into consumer products. It was clear to the Japanese that television recording and playback could be extremely attractive as a home facility, so development work continued for many years in anticipation of major cost reductions. When the price became acceptable to consumers, the Japanese owned the industry.

In a curious reversal of fortune, the Japanese continued to develop analog HDTV on the grounds that digital television was too costly. American and European companies anticipated the drop in cost of digital television and pushed hard

Exhibit 25.6

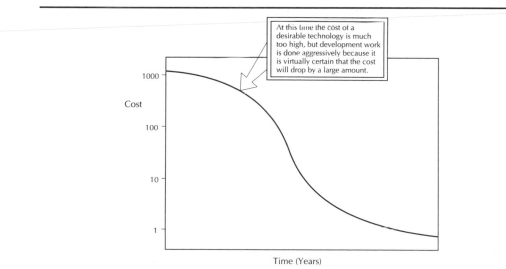

At this time the cost of a desirable technology is much too high, but development work is done aggressively because it is virtually certain that the cost will drop by a large amount.

to develop it until it made analog HDTV obsolete. The drop in cost was predictable, so it is astonishing that the Japanese, driven by MITI, and Europe, driven by the Brussels government, spent so much on a doomed technology.

Draw the S-Curves

Richard Foster describes curves such as those in Exhibits 25.1 through 25.5 as S-curves, because of their shape. He says that in order to understand the issues of limits and discontinuities, management should have S-curves drawn for their technologies. It is difficult to draw them with precision. That does not matter; approximate drawing makes the issues clear.

Understanding the limits of a technology represented by the plateau at the top of the S-curve is important. Once the limits are clear, a corporation can search for new ways to circumvent those limits with new technologies that can open up new opportunities on a grand scale.

Sometimes executives believe that a technology can continue growing in performance for a long time if only the right research is done. They may point out that computers have been increasing in speed for four decades or that telecommunications circuits grew from telegraph speeds to billions of bits per second. What this observation does not reveal is that such long-term evolution has been made possible by dramatic discontinuities in technology. Telecommunications evolved from wire pairs, to coaxial cables, to microwave radio, and then to fiber optics. There is little resemblance among those technologies. Within *one* of them major discontinuities made practical the invention of repeaters and multiplexers, the move from analog to digital systems, speech digitization, cellular telephones, and many other breakthroughs. There were repeated investment life-cycles curves, each with its own limits.

It is important to understand the limits of one's technology. When the curve is leveling off, developers should be taking replacement technologies very seriously.

Sudden Reversals

The history of competition is full of examples of corporations defending an existing technology and believing that all is well until a reversal of fortune comes with surprising suddenness, as illustrated in Exhibit 25.7.

Some high-tech start-up companies experience violent roller-coaster rides. KnowledgeWare, a company making "CASE" tools for software builders, grew from a valuation of zero in 1987 to a stock-market valuation of over $400 million in 1990. Then the technology of KnowledgeWare's business went through a discontinuity. CEO, Fran Tarkington, moved like a quarterback in pursuing the new direction, but the brilliant developers responsible for the original success had left. Those who saw the discontinuity ahead cashed in their chips. KnowledgeWare did a roller-coaster plunge and was taken over.

The corporation using technology A has sales that continue to grow while technology B is slowly struggling into existence. When technology B begins to work, probably in a niche market, it has little effect at first on the sales of technology A. The penetration of technology B is less than the growth in sales of technology A. The corporation having technology A often regards a downturn as a normal fluctuation that needs some change in sales management or advertising, not a switch to an alien technology. However, suddenly technology B becomes more attractive to customers than technology A. Technology A sales drop drastically, and the corporation employing technology B acquires the cash to drive up its steep curve of increasing performance. The sales of the corporation having technology A crash precipitously.

Exhibit 25.8 shows the manufactures of bias-ply tires losing 50 percent of the tire market to radial tires in 18 months. Radial tires came mainly from Michelin in Europe. American manufacturers did not take them seriously until too late. Customers did because radial tires lasted longer. Michelin used its technology B to gain a massive entry into the American market.

When technology B enters slowly into existence, change seems gradual for a while, but then revolution occurs.

Exhibit 25.7

A corporation having technology A may be largely unaffected by the evolution of technology B until a period when much of the market shifts fairly quickly to technology B. The corporation using technology A often has plenty of warning but dismisses it and spends its development budget on its existing technology.

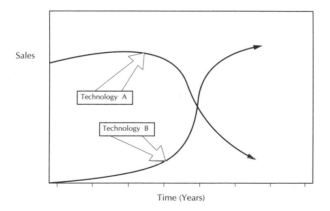

Exhibit 25.8   Tire consumption in the United States

Bias-ply manufacturers lost 50 percent of the tire market to radials in 18 months.[2]

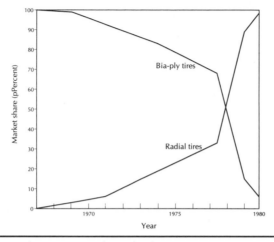

Reproduced with permission from *Innovation* by Richard N. Foster.[2]

Reluctance to Switch

When a discontinuity occurs, reluctance, rather than inability, to change usually causes damage. Corporations that know about technology B and should switch to it by one means or another (including taking over start-ups or buying external expertise in technology B) find all sorts of arguments for not making the switch.

It can be surprisingly difficult to slow down expenditure on the older technology. People are emotionally committed to it. Many do not understand the new technology or are scared that it will make their skills obsolete. Much new education is needed.

The technologies used for programming computers have changed over the years. At the end of the 1980s, code generators, CASE (computer-aided software engineering), and object-oriented techniques came into use. Where these techniques were used well, major improvements occurred in the speed and quality of application development. Most experienced COBOL or C programmers were remarkably reluctant to switch to the new techniques, however. They devised all manner of arguments for continuing to do what they knew well. The Software Engineering Institute, which claimed to be leading the way in software productivity, seemed to know almost nothing about technology B and spent its time advocating that TQM techniques be applied to technology A.

When IBM mainframe sales crashed in 1992, in a way that seemed inconceivable, IBM ran expensive advertisements saying "Millions of people depend upon mainframe technology," and cynics read them as "Millions of people depend upon obsolete technology" (see case study).

Discontinuity: The Crash of IBM

In the late 1980s IBM was confronted with a fabulous opportunity. Since its start, the computer industry had undergone a series of dramatic discontinuities. It was about to go through another. This one would be large-scale, highly disruptive, and powerful in its results. Computer customers everywhere would need a leader that would help establish industry standards and architecture. Corporations needed guidance from a computer vendor they could trust, one dedicated to customer service that would assemble the immensely complex jigsaw puzzle of the new paradigm and make it work. IBM had played that leadership role for four decades.

IBM's models of future computer technology were probably more accurate than those of any other corporation. It had predicted the power and cost of future chips, personal computers, mainframes, fiber optics, networks, storage systems, and so on. It had predicted manufacturing costs and software costs. What it foresaw in 1987 was startling.

Desktop machines would grow in power at a phenomenal rate. They would be linked together with local area networks that would have "servers"— small machines which would become extremely powerful and be able to store quite large databases. The desk machines would display images and move toward multimedia applications. Such capabilities needed local area networks of appropriate capacity. Fiber optics were ideally suited to this. The desk machine must be user friendly, like the Macintosh. The "client" software on the user machine would interact intimately with software on the "server" machine. "Client-server" systems would sweep through the corporate world. Local area networks were spreading everywhere. Users loved the new freedom and power of client-server computing, but local area networks created islands of computing that needed interconnecting. The "client" on the desk needed access to servers anywhere in the enterprise, which in turn required wide-area networking of high capacity. The system introduced highly complex problems of building, managing, and controlling enterprisewide client-server computing. How could diverse local machines be enabled to interact across the enterprise, to find the data or resources they needed, to avoid integrity problems, security violations, and traffic jams? The answer lay in new and complex architecture. This corporatewide client-server architecture became referred to as the new world of computing.

The new world was big money! It was essential for building the corporation of the future. The opportunity to build the new world and lead its customers into it was the largest opportunity in IBM's history. No company was better equipped to do it. The new world needed a leader with the power of IBM. If IBM had taken the lead, starting in 1987 or so, it could have had sales over $100 billion by 1994.

John Akers, the CEO of IBM, said he would increase IBM revenues to $185 billion by 1994, but in January 1993 IBM shocked the world by announcing a loss of staggering magnitude, $4.97 billion—a train wreck of immense proportions.

What went wrong?

The crash was caused by a handful of top executives who had great hierarchical power. To succeed, IBM's top management must come to grips with the severe paradigm shift as T. J. Watson and son had done so well in the past. Unfortunately much of top management was committed to architectures that they had struggled to create with intense emotional energy—the mainframe world, the SNA network architecture, the SAA architecture for linking IBM's machines to common systems. These architectures were immensely complex and expensive. IBM management thought that they gave IBM "account control." Large mainframes and their software were the source of much of IBM's profit. The detailed models of the new world showed a lesser role for mainframes. IBM's SNA network needed replacing. SAA needed replacing. Industry-standard "middleware" was needed, as were new operating systems. The new world needed new machines, new software, new architecture.

The good news was that IBM had world-beating technologies with which it could build the new world. Its best developers understood what was needed and were straining at the leash to build it. IBM was spending $7 billion per year on research and development—more than the rest of the Silicon Valley computer firms in total. Its developers used excellent models of future technology to address the questions:

- What will our customers want from us as the role of the mainframe declines?
- How do we assume unquestioned leadership in the new world of corporate client-server computing?
- What will enable us to beat our competitors in the future as new types of systems sweep through the industry?
- How can we change fast enough and achieve high profits?

IBM's architects found excellent answers to these questions. They spelled out the dangers to IBM as its old-world mainframes and software became bypassed.

They jokingly called the company IDM—International Dinosaur Machines. They described the desperate need for industry leadership that customers would have in the new world and the massive opportunity IBM had to provide that leadership.

Tragically, top management did not change its mental models as the younger developers did. The hierarchy, like all hierarchies, filtered the messages. Certain aspects of the old world were sacred. As in a religious order or on a politically correct campus, certain thoughts could not be expressed. IBM in the decade before its crash became the world's largest commercial example of inbreeding. Inbreeding destroys companies much faster than it destroys royal families. Like Spain after Philip II, IBM's immense success caused its leaders to believe that they knew all the answers: they must do what their predecessors had done.

The story has a lesson for CEOs everywhere: When paradigms shift, a mental model based on past success can be lethal.

False Sense of Security

Often the first wave of products using a new technology is not very impressive, which lulls the company with the old technology into a false sense of security. Technology B products may not have the "industrial strength" of the products with the old technology. More expense is needed to provide high quality or versatility. The products may fit into only a niche in the market. The company selling them is often too small to be regarded as a serious threat. How could the tiny Texas Instruments selling silicon transistors in the late 1950s be regarded as serious competition for the giants Hughes and Sylvania selling germanium transistors? The answer is that silicon was technology B. The first transistors were germanium, but silicon was more reliable and became cheaper; silicon replaced germanium as the basis for the semiconductor industry. Nobody talked about Germanium Valley!

The first product of a new technology may be very expensive. The first electronic calculators were more expensive than mechanical calculators and did not have a printer. It was easy for the vendors of mechanical calculators to believe that they would occupy only a niche in the marketplace. IBM introduced the first computer with magnetic disks in the late 1950s, and IBM's competition regarded disks as a passing fad. Most computer companies pooh-poohed data transmission for the first five years of its life because "it was cheaper to send data by mail."

The first product of a new technology pays for the start-up costs. The second product is often produced faster at much lower cost. The corporation that employs technology A underestimates how rapidly technology B products will im-

Exhibit 25.9

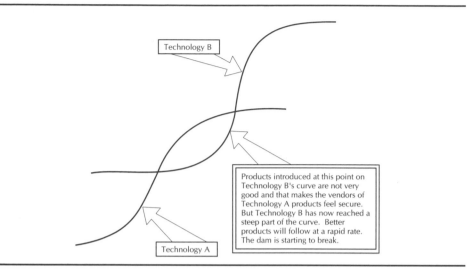

Technology B

Products introduced at this point on Technology B's curve are not very good and that makes the vendors of Technology A products feel secure. But Technology B has now reached a steep part of the curve. Better products will follow at a rapid rate. The dam is starting to break.

Technology A

prove. This may be reinforced by the marketplace's holding back and not buying technology B at first (Exhibit 25.9). The marketplace is often like a herd of sheep, cautious at first and then all moving together.

Protection of Investment

A corporation that has invested much money in technology A feels a need to obtain a good return on that investment. There is pressure not to divert funds to a competing technology that would endanger the investment. Higher members of management, perhaps the CEO, initiated the investment in technology A. They will look bad if it does not produce a good return. They see the protection of their existing business as a top priority. Reallocating resources to the new technology is painful. Many people fight the reallocation overtly or otherwise. Investing in the new technology would probably be seen as doubly risky—first because it diverts resources from the existing business, and second because it is stepping into the unknown. The CEO might be severely criticized by the board and outsiders for taking this double risk. Forsaking the technology a corporation understands, and moving to a technology it does not understand, can be difficult to justify, but it is exactly what a corporation must do when life-threatening discontinuities in technology occur.

This dilemma is the essence of coping with the discontinuity. It requires good understanding of the S-curves.

The Attacker's Advantage

Foster uses the expression "the attacker's advantage" to describe the difference between a firm defending an old technology and one attacking with a new technology. When there is a major discontinuity, the firm attacking with technology B is likely to win in the long run against the firm defending technology A. The stronger the discontinuity, the greater the attacker's advantage.

The traditional military wisdom is that the defender has the advantage. An army attacking a well-established position needs three or more times as many soldiers as the army defending the position. A corporation often believes that it has a similar advantage when defending a well-established position. If the attackers are small corporations short of capital, the defender does not worry much. In fact, even in the military, when a major discontinuity in technology occurs, the attacker having technology B can have a major advantage. Saddam Hussein's army in Kuwait was larger than the attacking army in 1991, but the attacking army won the land war in one hundred hours. The attacker had better technology.

A good attack policy is to avoid alarming the defender so that the defender will continue to back technology A. The attacker may market a niche product that does not worry the defender until the attacker has climbed the steep part of the S-curve. Then it may be too late for the defender to do much.

The defender often creates its own disadvantages by saying that its top priority is to protect existing businesses. The small attacker has no old technology to protect. It can devote all of its resources and intense emotional energy to technology B. If the defender does not attack back, the attacker may climb to the point at which the dam breaks and technology A is swept away.

Often a powerful corporation believes that it can control the pace of innovation in the marketplace. IBM believed that it could control the rate of change from mainframe computers to smaller machines until the precipitous decline of its mainframe sales in 1992. DuPont believed that it could control the rate at which tire manufacturers switched from nylon to polyester tire cord, but tire manufacturers switched at a speed that took substantial business away from DuPont. Both IBM and DuPont had superb research facilities and could have been excellent with technology B. Their mistake was trying to make technology A last too long. When the reversal came, customers called the shots, not IBM or DuPont.

Fast Development

When a corporation identifies a new technology as critical it is important to develop or acquire it as quickly as possible. The slope of the S-curve needs to be as steep as possible. Various studies have compared the cost of accelerated development with the costs of being late to market. In most cases the costs of being late to market overwhelm the costs of accelerated development. It is sometimes worth spending four times as much on development if this achieves early product intro-duction. Hewlett-Packard rose rapidly in the early 1990s to become the second largest American computer company largely because of its emphasis on minimiz-ing the time to develop and introduce new products.

The speed of development can be increased in many ways. Development should be regarded as a value stream to which all the techniques of value-stream reinvention apply. Usually development needs connection to the design of the manufacturing process in order to cut production costs and increase reliability. Development should often be linked also to product marketing, advertising, and market research. The processes for achieving the best product introduction need to be integrated.

To speed up development, the processes should be broken into pieces that can be done in tandem. Each piece should have a short cycle time, if possible, so that if any piece goes wrong it is known about quickly. It may make sense to farm out pieces to contractors or suppliers and to identify components that can be bought rather than developed. IBM, for example, needed to create the first IBM personal computer in the early 1980s with a development time much faster than that for standard IBM products. IBM based its PC on a microprocessor from Intel and an operating system from Microsoft; it bought its monitor from Matsushita, its printer from Epson, and its floppy disk from Tandem. This was highly unusual for IBM, which had a reputation for building all its own components. But getting the PC out early enabled IBM to make it an industry *de facto* standard.

The key to using other suppliers in a joint development is to manage them very tightly, doing prototyping and testing early and thoroughly, and to apply rigorous controls to ensure that the components work together. As with in-house development, the activity should be broken into short steps so that there is early warning of potential problems. Cooperating companies should put specialists at one another's sites.

If software is involved, it should be built with rapid-application development (RAD) techniques,[3] with prototypes being constructed at the earliest possible stage. Complex software should be broken into components that can be built quickly by small skilled teams using automated tools.

The development cycle is faster and more satisfactory when the up-front work of research, understanding requirements, prototyping, and design is done thoroughly. This makes it possible to drive up the steep part of the S-curve faster and lessens the problems that occur.

Continuous-Discontinuity Management

In the past one could identify specific times when a discontinuity in technology had occurred and the attacker had had the advantage over the defender. In the future, technology is likely to change constantly; there will always be discontinu-

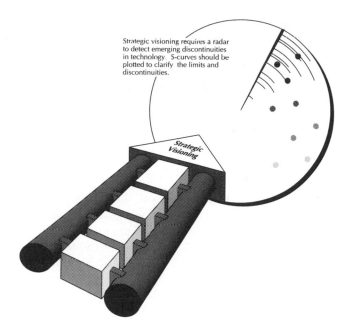

Strategic visioning requires a radar to detect emerging discontinuities in technology. S-curves should be plotted to clarify the limits and discontinuities.

Strategic Visioning

ities in one part of the business or another. This is true in some industries today; it will be true in most industries tomorrow. Technology is becoming more pervasive in all industries and is changing much faster. To counter the constant competitive threats from one part of the world or another, the successful corporation will not *occasionally* move into attacker mode; it will *always* be in attacker mode. Continuous management of technical discontinuities will be essential for survival. The strategic vision must reflect this, and the value streams need to be designed to support it.

To manage a corporation well in an era of ongoing technology discontinuities demands a CEO who communicates well with the chief scientist, chief technical officer, chief information officer, or whoever is in charge of technology change. These executives must be able to translate the needs of the business into the required technology development. The CEO and the CEO's CTO and CIO should be able to examine the S-curves together, agree about the limits, and discuss what emerging technologies are important.

The CTO and CIO must be able to talk the language of the CEO. Often a language barrier prevents the warm mutual understanding that is needed. Sometimes the chief scientist or CTO has little understanding of the needs of the business. The classic development laboratory has been in a deliberately isolated location able to do research unaffected by current business pressures. This is part of the old world of isolated functions that do not communicate well. Today core competence and critical value streams must be related to technology, its S-curves, and the opportunities and threats from emerging technologies. Understanding this pattern is a vital part of strategic visioning.

References

1. Richard N. Foster, *Innovation. The Attacker's Advantage* (Summit Books: New York, 1986).
2. Ibid.
3. James Martin, *Rapid Application Development* (Macmillan: New York, 1991).

26

Scenarios and Mental Models

When the Official Future Is Wrong

If management had a crystal ball, strategic planning would be done better, but no crystal ball exists. Nobody can have a precise view of the future. Instead, planners can create scenarios that give alternative views of the future. Executives are then made to consider what would happen and what actions they would take if each scenario were true.

Most enterprises have an official future, a vision on which their operating plans are based. The official future is a scenario that describes where management thinks the enterprise is heading. Often the official future becomes gospel, and managers feel constrained not to talk about any alternative. Reality almost always turns out to be different from the official future. Unless alternative scenarios have been planned for, the corporation may find itself taken by surprise and unable to cope well with what happens.

The official future is based on a set of assumptions, most usually not verbalized. Peter Schwartz, a leading authority on the use of scenarios for planning, comments: "Most official futures turn out to be mere propaganda; but everybody in the organization subscribes to them almost unconsciously. . . . One of our first tasks as consultants is to flush out the organization's version of the Official Future. We present it as one of a group of scenarios."[1] Usually when the official future is examined with scenarios, it becomes clear that managers have serious delusions. The enterprise is often striving for improbable ends that nobody dared to challenge. Reality will be different.

Wang had an official future in 1985. It showed massive growth. Dr. An Wang, the genius CEO who built the corporation, showed me detailed charts displaying how Wang could overtake IBM in the 1990s. Wang was unprepared for the market changes that pushed it into Chapter Eleven. IBM's official future was also incorrect and dangerous. Both of these companies' top executives might have challenged the assumptions that ultimately wrecked them had serious scenario planning been done.

Scenario planning cannot predict the future, but it *liberates people's insights*. It cannot give an accurate picture of the future, but it leads to *better decisions about the future*.

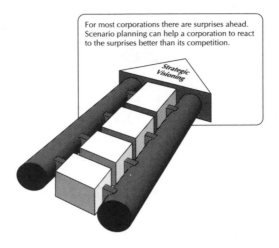

For most corporations there are surprises ahead.
Scenario planning can help a corporation to react
to the surprises better than its competition.

Mental Models

When we make decisions, we have an image of how our world works. Our mental model contains deeply ingrained assumptions, generalizations, and images, based on experience. The decision maker's visions of the future are based on his mental model. Often the managers of an enterprise collectively share a mental model (although they usually do not call it that). This is their *official future.*

A person's mental model is based on experience. As experience lengthens, a manager develops insights and an understanding of what to do in various circumstances. Preconceived notions grow stronger, as he learns from experience.

Most decision makers are not conscious of their mental model. It contains unwritten assumptions, prejudices, and rules. When courses of action recommended to managers contravene their hidden mental model, these courses will not be taken.

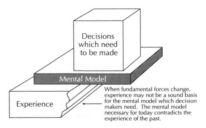

Decisions
which need
to be made

Mental Model

Experience

When fundamental forces change,
experience may not be a sound basis
for the mental model which decision
makers need. The mental model
necessary for today contradicts the
experience of the past.

A learning organization needs to uncover the hidden mental models and examine them. Much management change cannot be achieved unless managers' mental models are changed. Today the corporate environment is changing fast, often fundamentally. When fundamental changes occur, many of the assumptions and rules learned from experience are no longer valid.

A mental model based on experience is harmful when a paradigm shift invalidates that experience.

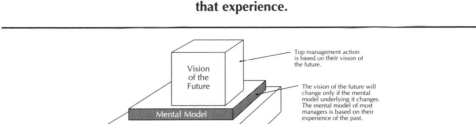

The use of scenarios is one technique for exposing and changing mental models. Scenario builders should have the goal not only of exposing decision making to possible future changes but also of changing the way they think about changes. In other words the goal is to expose and improve the mental model. Improving the mental models of decision makers is crucial to corporate learning. Scenario planners should be constantly helping managers to learn and improve their mental models.

Scenarios should not merely portray events but the reasons, patterns, and systemic structures that underlie the events. With improved models, executives are able to make better decisions about the future. The scenario planning team and the executives must be partners. The changes in assumptions may have to be communicated to many managers.

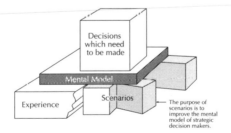

Scenarios at Shell

In 1970 Forbes called Royal Dutch–Shell the "ugly sister" of the seven sister oil companies. It was generally thought to be the weakest of the seven. Ten years later it was the strongest of the seven and, with Exxon, arguably the most profitable.

The new strength of Shell resulted, to a large extent, from its corporate planning activities in London. The London group pioneered the use of scenario planning and helped to change the mental models of Shell's many executives. Because of this, Shell was uniquely prepared for the shocks that OPEC gave the oil industry in the 1970s. Shell became skilled at using scenarios to help executives and planners learn. Instead of planning for one official future, with steady oil prices, Shell planned for and rehearsed what would happen with alternate scenarios. After OPEC had rocked the oil industry with high prices and production cutbacks in the 1970s, Shell management thoroughly planned and was prepared for the collapse of oil prices in 1986.

Pierre Wack was the main advocate of scenario planning in Shell.[2] Oil prices had remained more or less steady between World War II and the early 1970s. The behavior patterns of Shell executives had been established in a world of stable oil prices. The economies of the major nations depended on oil, and it was thought that this fact would keep the price low. To Wack and his scenario-planning group, continuation of this pattern seemed unlikely. American demand for oil was rising fast, and America was beginning to exhaust its oil reserves. OPEC (the Organization of Petroleum Exporting Countries) was starting to show signs of political power. The Islamic countries were beginning to regard the West with bitterness and hostility because they perceived that the West, and especially the United States, had engineered Israel's success in the 1967 six-day Arab-Israeli war. Saudi Arabia and other countries were reaching the limits of usefully investing oil revenues. Business and emotional reasons seemed to dictate that the Islamic countries should would collectively cut back production and charge higher prices for their oil.

Wack presented a scenario to the directors of Shell, predicting an oil price crisis sparked by OPEC. The implications for Shell would be severe. The directors understood that if such a price rise occurred they would have to change their operations in major ways.

However, management took no action. Pierre Wack and his fellow scenario builders were sure that an OPEC shock was coming whose impact would be immense. They watched in horror as Shell management continued business as usual. What happened to Wack has happened to many other corporate futurists. The planners believe a scenario they describe; they have given much time and thought to it, and much of it seems obvious. If it is even partially correct, it is vitally important. But top management takes no action.

The reason management does not act is that it has a mental model of its company, industry, and markets that is based on years of experience. If the scenarios contradict that experience, management pays little attention to them. Pierre Wack's scenarios were contrary to two decades of experience of predictable growth with stable oil prices.

Wack and his colleagues then realized that scenarios that describe events are not enough to change management behavior. Management action conforms to a mental model. Behavior patterns can be changed only by changing the underlying mental model. Wack knew that he must set out to change the mindset of the decision makers. Presenting the scenarios must no longer be simple storytelling; they must be based on an underlying set of assumptions. Alternative assumptions must be tested and their full business consequences explored. Scenario planning must *cause managers to question their own model of reality and change it when necessary.*[2]

The prevailing view of the near future, as in many companies, was that little would change, but the view was based on assumptions that would almost certainly break down. As Wack and his team examined the assumptions behind Shell's official future, they concluded that they were about as likely as cross-country skiing in Hell. Wack's team built scenarios based on new assumptions. They set out to change the executives' mental model and help them think through the consequences of the new assumptions. "Prepare!" Wack told oil refiners and marketers. "You are about to become a low-growth industry." The consequences of a sudden rise in oil prices, and the business actions needed to counter it, were explored in detail. Refinery building would have to slow down. Refineries must be redesigned to use whatever type of crude oil was available. Exploration for oil would have to expand to new countries. Different countries would react differently to an oil price shock, so Shell's operating companies in each country must have the autonomy to deal with that country's reaction.

When the OPEC oil embargo suddenly happened, Shell executives had rehearsed it and were ready. They had forecast energy demand more accurately than their competitors. While competitors increased central control of country operations, Shell did the opposite, giving local operating companies room to maneuver. The country managers were more prepared for the crisis. Wack's team traveled around the world working with hundreds of executives to unfreeze their official-future view and help them reexamine the assumptions in their mental model. Wack stressed that he was not predicting the future; he was improving managers' own ability to make the right choices. Shell steadily refined its capability for scenario planning.

Peter Schwartz comments that the scenario planning at Shell caused it to *ask different questions* about its decisions. Managers challenged the assumptions inherent in their mental models and came to some dramatically different conclusions. Oil prices that had been relatively stable for decades were now on a roller coaster. This meant that there could be a good business in trading oil the way that commodities are traded. Existing traders with a higher level of skill in the futures market could make better deals, for example in selling fuel to airlines, than oil companies. A trading system needs computers with a worldwide network and takes years to set up. Scenario planning caused Shell to build a trading system. By the time the oil price collapsed in 1986, Shell was trading two and a half million barrels a day.[1]

Oil companies have to make decisions of staggering magnitude. The Troll gas field is a vast deposit of natural gas discovered by Shell in the North Sea under water one thousand feet deep. Peter Schwartz describes it. "It was going to take a platform fifteen hundred feet high to get that gas out. That platform and its satellite wells were going to cost six billion dollars. It would be the biggest moving object ever built, the single most expensive machine ever built."[1]

Each oil platform has several hundred people living on it, with its own dormitories, racquetball courts, and hospital. There are so many oil rigs in the North Sea that there are more helicopter flights to them than flights out of London's Heathrow Airport. A North Sea platform takes years to plan and then years to build. During those years the price of gas and oil could change dramatically. If the prices fell, the operation could be rendered entirely worthless.

The small group of people in Shell who decide whether to build North Sea rigs and other oil facilities influence about 8 percent of the world's production of oil. They use scenarios as a tool to help them explore and articulate their decisions. In the 1980s the scenarios helped prepare managers for the major drop in oil prices in 1986. Shell avoided overinvesting in new oil fields when the prices were high and buying oil-related companies at premium prices. After the price fall of 1986, it was able to buy oil reserves at half the price they were six months before.

Telling Stories

In the age of computers, it is common to think that management needs the precision of spreadsheets, charts, graphs, and perhaps fishbone diagrams and pareto diagrams (Chapter 16). These are invaluable tools for operational decisions, but most strategic decisions are too complex, imprecise, and holistic to be expressed with graphs and spreadsheets alone. They need *story telling*.

Stories help us to interweave events. They enable us to express meaning, motives, and possibilities. They suggest why things happen in a certain way. They engage the emotions and have a psychological impact that spreadsheets and fishbone diagrams do not. Scenarios are *stories* that can be crucial to understanding what may happen.

Richard Snyder, the highly successful CEO of Simon and Schuster, met me in the corporation's expensive dining room high above Manhattan and immediately attacked his top computer author with "Computers are totally irrelevant to me." Publishing, he said, requires an intuitive, holistic view of the rapidly changing market; it is like a sailor watching the weather, not a left-brainer watching spreadsheets.

When the space shuttle *Challenger* blew up with a schoolteacher on board, the television image of the explosion shocked the world.

Before the final launch of the *Challenger* NASA engineers were asked if they had anything they wanted to say about the decision to launch. They remained silent although some of them had serious fears about the O-rings.[3] An engineer said privately to his fellow engineers before the fatal launch, "This was a meeting where the determination was *to launch,* and it was up to us to prove beyond a shadow of doubt that it was not safe to do so. This is in total reverse to what the position usually is in a preflight readiness review."[4]

The unvoiced fears about the O-rings were justified. An O-ring, which had been at too low a temperature because of severe weather, leaked, and the crew of seven was killed.

If the designers of the shuttle launch procedures had simulated the procedures with scenarios exploring human behavior, they would probably have discovered a situation in which engineers felt inhibited about voicing concerns. Their engineering caution was overridden by the determination to launch. Scenarios would have used role playing, rehearsing what could happen. NASA management had a pervasive "can do" attitude. Role playing could have revealed that engineers felt that they should not be seen as willing to stop a launch even if they were worried about a problem. The process had built-in organizational defenses that prevented the danger signs from reaching the executives who decided to launch.

The Presidential Commission on the *Challenger* disaster made recommendations to change the launch procedures—but too late.

Three or Four Scenarios, Not More

Authorities such as Pierre Wack, Peter Schwartz, and the late Herman Kahn spent much of their life using scenarios to help change the mindset of executives. Their experience taught them to have a small number of scenarios—typically three, sometimes four. In-depth examination of a small number of scenarios is more likely to change the mental models of decision makers than considering many scenarios. The three or four scenarios are each given an explanatory name and executives talk about the scenarios at ongoing planning meetings. People cannot cope with more than about four stories.

> *To have too many scenarios is confusing; it creates a mental muddle, not a mental model.*

Peter Schwartz says: "At SRI in the early 1970s, we generated thousands of possible futures. We had to use a computer to sort through them. It was silly."[1] He describes how later he used ten scenarios, then seven,[5] for the Environmental Protection Agency and comments "The EPA would have learned more if we had given them just three."

Decision makers must *not* choose one scenario from the set. There is often an irresistible temptation to choose *one*. Industry is littered with examples of executives who chose one plan of action and ignored the others, and this approach was wrong. The whole reason for scenario planning is to be alert to alternatives so as to be ready for them. To be prepared for only one possibility is dangerous.

Sometimes a scenario seems so improbable to executives that they do not want to consider it. In Shell in the early 1970s, the OPEC-triggered rise in oil prices seemed too improbable to executives who had spent their entire careers with stable oil prices. The price collapse in 1986 also seemed improbable.

Schwartz comments that Shell executives were persuaded to consider a scenario that included an unthinkable price drop to $16 per barrel of oil *only because they also had scenarios for rises to $30 and $50 per barrel*. Oil did, in fact, fall to $15 per barrel.

Decision makers can be reluctant to consider a completely gloomy scenario. A mental block against a bad scenario can be dangerous, as when IBM management in the early 1990s refused to believe in a collapse of mainframe sales in favor of small computers. Hewlett-Packard and Sun did believe in it and grew vigorously. The opposite is also true. Executives often refuse to consider a very optimistic scenario. Increasingly today extreme swings, good and bad, occur.

Names That Convey the Story

When exploring alternative scenarios, it is important to give names to the scenarios. A good name can communicate much of the essence of the scenario and so helps people to remember it.

Scenarios are stories, and sometimes they are named after stories that everybody knows, such as "The Boy Who Cried Wolf" or "Napoleon's Retreat from Russia" or "The Guns of Singapore" (all the guns of Singapore were positioned to stop a sea invasion when in 1942 the Japanese invaded by land). The "Take the Money and Run" scenario describes a policy of maximizing profits by cutting all research and development, making the books look good, and then selling the company. Scenario names that relate to stories or powerful images are an important shorthand when executives or planners meet. They talk about the end-game scenario, the trickle-down effect, King Canute management, the Lone Ranger, the King James Version of the methodology, and so on. Before the OPEC price shocks, Pierre Wack made Shell planners think of the years ahead as "the decade of the rapids."

In 1982 the Shell scenario planners asked themselves, Is there a plausible scenario under which OPEC's control over oil prices collapses? They listened skeptically to an OPEC breakup scenario presented with many detailed charts and graphs. For nine years the directors of Shell had spent much emotion negotiating with OPEC and trying to understand OPEC.[2] The presenter summarized the complex scenario with a picture from a child's nursery rhyme book showing a broken egg with human features: "Humpty Dumpty had a great fall." In this scenario OPEC's price mechanism shattered, and the OPEC ministers had no way to regain their former strength. The presenter in a thoughtful voice with a sense of theater intoned, "All the King's horses and all the King's men couldn't put Humpty Dumpty back together again." In meetings thereafter Shell executives talked about the Humpty Dumpty scenario. The image of the broken egg stayed in their minds.

The great change agents of the past have been skilled with metaphors and stories. The parables of Christ, Mohammed, and Buddha survived through startling changes in society. They even survive in an era of network television and Arnold Schwarzenneggar.

Pictures and Legos

Besides picking an evocative name for the scenario, good pictures have a powerful effect in communicating the message. Imaginative metaphors are also valuable. Jim Brown[5] uses the term *lego* to refer to a simple and sometimes colorful metaphor that helps in sketching ideas with general management. Once it has been created, a colorful lego tends to be used repeatedly in management discussions.

An insurance company, for example, wanted to refer to empowered agents' capability for finding insurable situations flexibly in the field. Management latched on to the lego expression "floating crap game" to discuss the implications of this scenario. The term was helpful in executive discussions (but was not used outside the team engaged in these discussions!).

A manufacturing corporation coined the expression "Chinese menu" to refer to the capability of making a diversity of products from a small inventory of parts. This lego referred to the ability of Chinese restaurants to provide a menu of a hundred items from only six pots of food cooking in the kitchen.

Sometimes a diagram is used for the "lego." For example, here is a picture of the Chinese-menu lego:

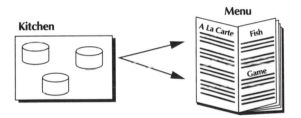

Charles Handy (who is Irish) uses a shamrock lego to represent the idea that an organization should divide work among three types of workers.

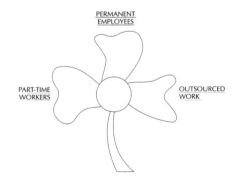

The use of nonpermanent workers affords more flexibility when volumes decline or changes are made, and can give the permanent employees more job security. The use of out sourcing increases the capability to concentrate on core competencies and strategic value streams. This intricate set of ideas can be encapsulated in the simple reference to the visual, "shamrock organization."

Here is a "channel lego" indicating that there are multiple channels—some of high value and narrow scope, other of less value but wide scope.

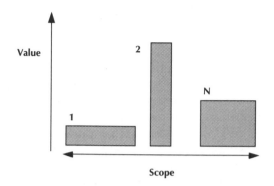

The Enterprise Engineering "rocket ship" graphic device summarizes the statement in one lego that the seven components of Enterprise Engineering are all important and need to be integrated. TQM or business reengineering alone is not enough.

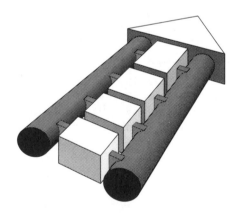

In scenario planning, reinventing value streams, and strategic visioning, the participants should seek out any verbal or pictorial metaphors that help the discussion.

What Is Predictable?

Some facts about the future that are relevant to a decision are fairly predictable; some are completely unpredictable. It is often appropriate to categorize relevant aspects of the future:

Almost certain	Probable	Roulette wheel	Of low probability but important

Some aspects of the future that are "almost certain" are surprising to many executives because they have never thought about them.

There will soon be two billion teen-agers on the planet. At the time of writing, this surprises most people and alarms many. It is "almost certain" because they have already been born. There has been an international baby boom. Many of these teen-agers will be avid consumers of the same films, pop music, Internet offerings, virtual-reality headsets, fashion goods, and global products of the "knowledge society." Whereas the number of teen-agers is almost certain and some aspects of their behavior are probable, other aspects of their behavior are completely unpredictable. Will they use personality-changing drugs such as Prosac or "safe" hallucinatory designer drugs while immersed in virtual-reality software? How will they evolve as a planetary force?

Good use of metaphors and images can have a critical impact on strategic visioning.

An old-line, highly profitable insurance company needed to position itself for long-term change resulting from increasing competitiveness in its market segments. The major difficulty it experienced was the conservative beliefs of senior management—what had served the company well for more than one hundred years would continue to work in the future. In order to stimulate new thinking, the CEO formed a strategic-visioning team and charged members with inventing innovative ways that the company could address its customers in the future.

The team first immersed itself in considering the "voice" of the customer and found, to its surprise, that customers saw the company as fragmented, with many lines of insurance and no comprehensive concern for the customer's overall situation.

The team contrasted shopping on main street with shopping in a modern galleria. In the main-street scenario the customer has to wander through many independent shops, whereas in the galleria a concierge greets the customer, discusses his needs, and guides him to where the needs can be met.

The team told top management that today's company is the main street whereas tomorrow's company must be the galleria. This metaphor encouraged discussions about the future because it circumvented management's complex language of risk assessment and control.

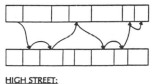

HIGH STREET:
Customer must navigate

GALLERIA:
Concierge greets and
guides the customer

> The strategic direction was changed because senior management could understand the image of the galleria with its concierge. The term "galleria" entered their basic business vocabulary.

Technology is perhaps the single most powerful force causing corporations to change. Many aspects of the future of technology that are almost certain are startling to managers who have not thought about it. Fiber optics will cause the capacity of data networks to expand very rapidly. Optical networks will link the main industrial nations worldwide, handling entertainment as well as information. Memory chips will quadruple in capacity every three years. Processor chips will become more powerful at a rapid, predictable rate. Computers will grow in power even faster because they will be built with not one but many processors. The planet will have hundreds of millions of computers increasingly linked into worldwide networks, which many of the two billion teen-agers will grow up with.

As Chapter 25 discussed, discontinuities in technology are highly dangerous but are bound to happen sooner or later. Scenario planning must be linked to the analysis of technology S-curves.

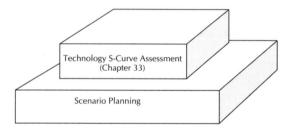

Many aspects of business are, of course, entirely unpredictable. Change is accelerating and as it speeds up new competition arises. Old markets collapse and new ones appear. The game that business is playing needs to be reinvented constantly.

It is the unpredictable aspects of business that give rise to different scenarios. A danger in many corporations is that management is expecting "more of the same" when major discontinuities lie ahead. The goal of scenario planning is to illuminate the possible discontinuities.

If scenario planners create, say, four scenarios, the "almost certain" aspects of the future are the same in each. The "roulette wheel" or "low probability but important" aspects cause the scenarios to be fundamentally different.

Warning Signals

When scenarios are established and rehearsed, the scenario builders should identify the early-warning symptoms that the scenario might be on the brink of realization. This is desirable with both good- and bad-news scenarios.

Early-warning signals might be a shift in attendance at industry seminars on certain subjects, articles in the trade press, announcements of improved technology, a corporate takeover, a drop or rise in price of certain items, jobs-wanted advertisements, a change in commodity-trading futures prices, a change in advertising or staff layoffs by a competitor, industry rumors or "intelligence," and so on.

Scenario planners should work out the warning signals when they create and test the scenario. At that time they are less susceptible to emotional pressures, disbelief, and misinterpretation. Once warning signals are established, it is perilous for executives to disregard them.

The Test of Scenario Effectiveness

A scenario is not valuable unless it changes the behavior of managers or decision

Exhibit 26.1 The process of using scenarios for decision making[7]

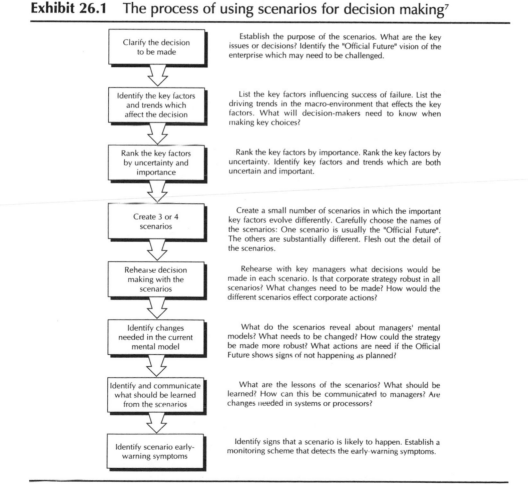

Clarify the decision to be made	Establish the purpose of the scenarios. What are the key issues or decisions? Identify the "Official Future" vision of the enterprise which may need to be challenged.
Identify the key factors and trends which affect the decision	List the key factors influencing success of failure. List the driving trends in the macro-environment that effects the key factors. What will decision-makers need to know when making key choices?
Rank the key factors by uncertainty and importance	Rank the key factors by importance. Rank the key factors by uncertainty. Identify key factors and trends which are both uncertain and important.
Create 3 or 4 scenarios	Create a small number of scenarios in which the important key factors evolve differently. Carefully choose the names of the scenarios: One scenario is usually the "Official Future". The others are substantially different. Flesh out the detail of the scenarios.
Rehearse decision making with the scenarios	Rehearse with key managers what decisions would be made in each scenario. Is that corporate strategy robust in all scenarios? What changes need to be made? How would the different scenarios effect corporate actions?
Identify changes needed in the current mental model	What do the scenarios reveal about managers' mental models? What needs to be changed? How could the strategy be made more robust? What actions are need if the Official Future shows signs of not happening as planned?
Identify and communicate what should be learned from the scenarios	What are the lessons of the scenarios? What should be learned? How can this be communicated to managers? Are changes needed in systems or processors?
Identify scenario early-warning symptoms	Identify signs that a scenario is likely to happen. Establish a monitoring scheme that detects the early-warning symptoms.

makers. Truly effective scenarios change their mental model or the assumptions that underlie their decisions. The Shell scenario of $16 oil, and the assumptions that backed it up, caused Shell to cut costs on the North Sea gas fields. Furthermore, instead of buying oil fields when oil was $30, which the other oil companies did, Shell waited and bought when oil was $15.

> *Scenario planners emphasize that the test of how good scenarios are is not whether they predict the future but whether they change people's behavior. Good scenarios are part of the process of enterprise learning.*

We should ask: Did the scenarios change behavior in the right direction? Did they improve the mental model of decision makers? Decision makers, after they use scenarios, should be able to recognize warning signals or new trends and should know what to do.

The Process of Using Scenarios

Exhibit 26.1 shows a typical set of steps in using scenarios.
It is important to link scenario planning to the other aspects of strategic visioning (Exhibit 26.2)

Exhibit 26.2   Scenario planning
___

Scenario planning needs to link to the other components of strategic visioning.

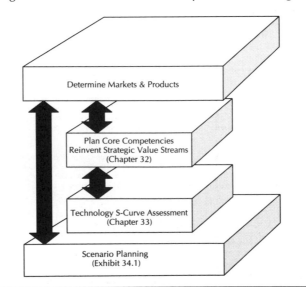

References

1. The term *Official Future* is used in Peter Schwartz, *The Art of the Long View* (Doubleday Currency: New York, 1991).
2. Pierre Wack, *"The Gentle Art of Reperceiving"* (two-part *Harvard Business Review* article): "Scenarios: Uncharted Waters Ahead" (Sept–Oct 1985); "Scenarios: Shooting the Rapids" (Nov–Dec 1985).
3. *Presidential Commission: On the Space Shuttle Challenger Accident* (Government Printing Office: Washington, D.C.), Vol. 95, June 6, 1986.
4. Ibid, 93.
5. Peter Schwartz, Paul Hawken, and Jay Ogilvy, *Seven Tomorrows: Toward a Voluntary History* (Bantam Books: New York, 1982).
6. James Brown, Enterprise Engineering Pioneer at James Martin & Co., Reston, Va.
7. The process is based on Schwartz, *The Art of the Long View* (Doubleday Currency: New York, 1991).

27

The Corporate Gospel

Vision and Excitement

In a great corporation, employees are excited about what they do. There is passion in the air. There is determination to succeed in making a vision come true.

Great corporate leaders create such a vision. They work with the employees to tune and perfect it. They lose no opportunity for communicating the vision to as many employees as possible so that it excites and energizes them. Thomas J. Watson, Jr., of IBM gave employees goose pimples when he addressed them on the corporate vision. "Do you realize how lucky you are to be in this corporation at this time! Imagine if you worked in the coal business!" Watson used every means to ensure that his vision was shared by everyone in his organization.

In the 1950s IBM had a hymn book. At company meetings IBM employees used to sing songs like "Ever Onward" representing Watson's vision. Those days are long since gone in the West, but today some Japanese companies sing their vision. Matsushita employees sing the company song about "sending our goods to the people of the world endlessly and continuously, like water gushing from a fountain." Although today we do not sing it, a company vision should be always present and deeply felt. Great corporate leaders repeatedly emphasize the vision, making sure that it pervades the entire organization.

Hillhaven, a medical services company, produced the vision statement in Exhibit 27.1 that inspired and motivated employees. They thought, That's the type of company I want to work for. It set the style for the management action needed to change the business.[1]

Writers, artists, political workers, and product developers work with passionate intensity to make something happen. Great corporate leaders create a worthwhile goal that inspires employees. Henry Ford envisioned ordinary people owning motor cars. Theodore Vail of AT & T envisioned a country where anyone could speak to anyone else by telephone. Steve Jobs envisioned easy-to-use computers being used by everybody. Steve Jobs's vision of the Macintosh was represented vividly in a famous television advertisement that portrayed IBM's world as the world of George Orwell's *1984* and the Macintosh as the bringer of freedom. This advertisement and the vision behind it inspired and excited employees from factory workers to John Sculley, the CEO.

In the presence of a thrilling vision, pettiness disappears. It is worthwhile to

Exhibit 27.1   Hillhaven

We are committed to the quality of life around us, as individuals and as a company. We are building a new future for the health services industry and for all of the people and communities we serve, creating a future of wellness fashioned from and for humanity.

We are dedicated to instructional dignity. We recognize and appreciate the inherent quality of all human beings, and we are committed to the complete expression of our appreciation in every business, program, project, and interaction we have with every person, every day.

We work with skilled hands that are directed by creative minds that are guided by compassionate hearts.

We understand that nothing is more personal and important than one's health, one's home, one's family, and one's ability to contribute. We accept the challenge of providing the best possible opportunities and choices to all we serve and employ.

We consider it our responsibility to continuously raise the standards of our industry and to seek out better ways to serve.

When **Hillhaven** becomes universally synonymous with

- first-class health services,
- first-class employer,
- first-class employee,
- first-class business leadership, and
- first-class investment,

we will consider ourselves successful.

---

come to work each day and to work hard. When Japanese employees sing their vision, it has to be a vision that excites them. Bill O'Brien, the CEO of Hanover Insurance, observes: "We recognized that there is a burning need for people to feel part of an ennobling mission. If it is absent, many will seek fulfillment only in outside interests instead of in their work."[2] Meaning in work translates into energy.

Criteria for an Effective Vision

James Belasco gives five criteria for an effective vision:

- A short simple statement . . .
- of some value-adding and marketplace advantage
- that positively distinguishes your organization . . .
- in the minds of everyone with whom your organization interacts (customers, employees, suppliers) . . .
- and produces clear, inspiring decision-making criteria[3]

Exhibit 27.2 gives some examples of vision statements.
Watson, chairman of IBM in its great growth period, wrote:

> The real difference between success and failure in a corporation can
> very often be traced to how well the organization brings out the great
> energies and talents of its people. What does a corporation do to help
> these people find common cause with each other? How does it keep
> them pointed in the right direction despite the many rivalries and dif-
> ferences which may exist among them? . . . Any organization, in order
> to survive and achieve success, must have a sound set of beliefs on
> which it premises all its policies and actions. The single most im-
> portant factor in corporate success is adherence to those beliefs.[4]

IBM had three firmly stated basic beliefs:

- We have respect for every individual.
- We want to give the best customer service of any company in the world.
- We pursue all tasks with the idea that they can be accomplished in a supe-
  rior fashion.

Watson constantly talked and wrote about IBM's beliefs. He personally addressed management development and sales-training classes. IBM constantly
changed the nature of its products, but its *basic beliefs* remained constant.

Customers should be able to see the effects of a corporate vision statement.
Customers going to Disney World or its affiliated hotels feel the effects by the
friendly way the staff greets and helps them. A vitally important criterion for a
corporate vision is that it translates into action, and top management knows *how*
it translates into action.

Consensus about the Vision

The vision should come from a wide-ranging debate and consensus among the
managers who implement it. It should not be a commandment handed down
from on high but a statement distilled after multiple iterations from the beliefs of
the managers who have to make it work.

The somewhat-lengthy vision statement of Hillhaven, in Exhibit 27.1, took
almost six months to create. It reflects the consensus of many employees in Hillhaven, a billion-dollar health-care corporation. The employees felt that they owned
the vision statement and were exceedingly proud of it. At one time it was suggested that the statement be sent to an advertising agency to be polished. The
employees were outraged. It was their statement, their vision, and they did not
want an outsider changing the words. The employees truly wanted to live up to
the vision.

Exhibit 27.2 Examples of corporate vision statements or components thereof

Apple

- We will pioneer new directions and approaches, finding innovative ways to use computing technology to extend the bounds of human potential.
- Apple will make a difference: our products, services and insights will help people around the world shape the ways business and education will be done in the twenty-first century.

Akzo (Holland)

We will combine entrepreneurial zeal with prudent management to ensure continued stability.

AA (Britain's automobile association)

To make AA membership truly irresistible.

Bayer AG (Germany)

Our expertise lies in research, service, technology, quality, and efficiency in all our areas of activity. This forms the basis for our success and safeguards the future. We consider it our duty to use this expertise to benefit mankind and to play our part in solving major problems of our time . . .

Burson-Marsteller (Public Relations)

- Burson-Marsteller has embarked on an adventure in communications . . . a journey without end; but one with a distinct destination.
- We seek to build the most exciting counseling and communications organization in the world, adding new dimensions to the meaning of public relations and public affairs.

Federal Express (U.S.A.)

We will produce outstanding financial returns by providing totally reliable, competitively superior, air-ground transportation of high-priority goods and documents that require rapid time-certain delivery. Equally important, positive control of each package will be maintained using real-time electronic tracking and tracing systems. A complete record of each shipment and delivery will be presented with our request for payment. We will be helpful, courteous, and professional to each other and the public. We will strive to have a completely satisfied customer at the end of each transaction.

(continued)

Exhibit 27.2   *continued*

Ford

Quality is Job 1.

Hertz

- Provide a level of service that never fails but meets our customers' needs every time.
- Satisfied customers are our greatest asset.
- Exceed our customers' expectations by delivering the rental experience that is second to none.
- "Get it right first time, every time."

Hershey Chocolate

- Protect and enhance the corporation's high level of ethics and conduct.
- Maintain a strong "people" orientation and demonstrate care for every employee.
- Attract and hold customers and consumers with products and services of consistently superior quality and value.
- Sustain a strong results orientation coupled with a prudent approach to business.

Honda

- Quality in all jobs—learn, think, analyze, evaluate, and improve.
- Reliable products—on time, with excellence and consistency.
- Better communication—listen, ask, and speak up.

IBM in the Watson Era

- Have respect for every individual.
- Give the best customer service of any company in the world.
- Pursue all tasks with the idea that they can be accomplished in a superior fashion.

J.C. Penney

- To serve the public, as nearly as we can, to its complete satisfaction.
- To expect for the service we render a fair remuneration and not all the profit the traffic will bear.
- To do all in our power to pack the customer's dollar full of value, quality, and satisfaction.
- To continue to train ourselves and our associates so that the service we give will be more and more intelligently performed.
- To improve constantly the human factor in our business.
- To reward men and women in our organization through participation in what the business produces.
- To test our every policy, method, and act in this way: Does it square with what is right and just?

(*continued*)

Exhibit 27.2 *continued*

James Martin & Co.

Deliver solutions that simplify complexity.

Johnson & Johnson

We believe our first responsibility is to the doctors, nurses, and patients, to mothers and all others, who use our products and services . . .

Nordstrom

Respond to unreasonable customer requests.

The Scout Association (U.K. Boy Scouts)

To promote the development of young people in achieving their full physical, intellectual, social, and spiritual potentials, as individuals, as responsible citizens, and as members of their local, national, and international communities.

Servicemaster

- Honoring God in all we do.
- Grow people.

Tandem Computers

- All people are good.
- People, workers, management, and company must understand the essence of the business.
- Every single person in the company must understand the essence of the business.
- You must create an environment where all the above can happen.

The vision must be believed in by the entire management, and seen to inspire and influence the basic behavior of employees throughout the organization. The vision must translate into action.

> *The strategic vision should not be a secret guarded by top management but an exciting view of future possibilities that all employees share in and contribute to.*

Translation into Action

The vision statement is of no value unless it is translated into action. Every manager must believe in it and act upon it. Employees must believe in the vision, be

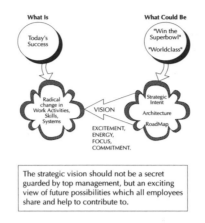

What Is

Today's Success

What Could Be

"Win the Superbowl"

"Worldclass"

Radical change in Work Activities, Skills, Systems

VISION

EXCITEMENT, ENERGY, FOCUS, COMMITMENT.

Strategic Intent

Architecture

RoadMap

> The strategic vision should not be a secret guarded by top management, but an exciting view of future possibilities which all employees share and help to contribute to.

motivated to act upon it, and appraised in terms of how they do so. The vision must be constantly restated and reinforced; otherwise it will become forgotten.

> *The test of a vision is the extent to which it influences the whole enterprise, guiding every decision, large and small.*

Nordstrom, the department-store chain, launched a major expansion program in the Northeastern United States in the early 1990s when that region was in deep recession and other chains were in trouble. Nordstrom's visionary instruction to employees was *Respond to unreasonable customer requests.* Employees enjoyed reacting to problems that customers threw at them and kept a scrapbook of "heroic" acts. They would go so far as to change a customer's flat tire or deliver items to the customer at an airport. They enjoyed creating "raving fans." In the recession, Nordstrom grew at 20 percent per year to sales of $2.89 billion in 1993.

Unless the vision can be translated into guidelines for how work is done, it may have little effect. Grand, abstract visions maybe *too* inspirational. Gerhard Langeler, president of the systems group of Mentor Graphics Corporation warns that a company may end up making "more poetry than product."[5] When vision statements are too grandiose and beyond employees' power, the employees do not "buy" them, and they fail.

Value-Stream Visions

Probably the best way to translate a vision into action is to relate it to value streams. Chapter 10 explained that an enterprise might have a dozen or so value streams. Every enterprise should be mapped into its value streams. When the enterprise vision is established, a vision should be created for each value stream, whether or not the value stream has been reinvented yet.

It is relatively easy to map an enterprise into value streams. When this is done, the vision for each value stream should be stated, at least in a preliminary form. This helps to clarify how the enterprise vision will be translated into action.

When a value stream is reinvented there should be detailed discussion of its vision and mission statements that should be subscribed to by everyone. The final statement should be worded by the value-stream teams themselves but must be discussed with top management and relate to the vision statements for the enterprise and other value streams. Substantial tuning and improvement of value-stream mission statements should occur as the value-stream teams learn to improve their work.

A corporate vision must translate into many team visions. Each value-stream team must be excited about what it can achieve if it pulls out all the stops.

Vision and Advertising

Some vision statements look like advertising slogans. The message that a corporation wants to communicate to the public should usually be part of what it communicates to its own employees:

British Airways: "Everybody's favorite airline"
Burson-Marsteller: "Imagination with substance, execution with style"
Hertz: "You don't just rent a car, you rent a company."
Ford's simple vision statement "Quality is Job 1" pervaded Ford from top to bottom. It led to quality circles, TQM throughout, redesign of products to reduce the number of working parts, and closer relations with suppliers. The internal vision became the external advertising so that customers associated Ford with quality.

Good vision statements may incorporate an advertising slogan but need more than that to inspire and guide employees.

Cynicism

Creating vision statements became a fad, and often they were composed without any detailed thought when top management "walked in the woods" at an annual get-together. In some organizations a new vision statement has produced more cynicism than change. Posters and wallet cards that state the vision may memorialize the lack of any real intent to change. A consultant described being shown a vision statement by upper management—a full-color layout spread with a set of impressive statements about strategic intent and values—and observed that employees were saying: "What a crock! Who are they trying to kid? They went off on a boondoggle, played golf for three days, and this is all they produced."[6]

Many corporate vision statements seem to have a cynical sameness as though they were written by a computerized vision-writing agency.

Hard Vision

Many vision statements tend to be *vacuous* and simplistic. Statements such as "We want to be number one in our industry" or "We will be the preferred supplier to our customers" are of little value.

The term *hard vision* describes a vision statement whose objectives translate into action rather than "soft" generalizations. Instead of saying "We will be the best company in our field," the hard vision says "Respond to credit requests in the minimum time possible" or "Catch all defects at the time they occur and attack their causes."

Hammer and Champy calls for a vision statement that meets the following criteria:[7]

- It focuses on operations.
- It includes measurable objectives and metrics.
- It is really powerful; it changes the basis for competition in the industry.

The vision stated by Federal Express in its infancy has this criterion: "We will deliver the package by 10:30 the next morning." Some authorities distinguish between a vision statement and a mission statement. A mission statement relates to a target or goal rather than an all-embracing set of beliefs. Churchill's inspiring "We will fight them on the beaches . . ." speech was a vision. The directive to invade Sicily was a mission.

The following are statements that include goals or targets:

"We will build software with fewer than 100 bugs per million lines of code."
"We will shorten the product development cycle by 30 percent."
"We will work with the FDA to shorten the drug approval time to 2 years."
"We will drive for six-sigma quality" (Chapter 21).
"By the end of 1993 we aim to provide service on demand—within one day, seven days a week—and to clear all faults within one day" (British Telecom).

It is often more appropriate to associate *mission* statements with the value streams of the enterprise and separate them from the enterprise vision statement.

> *Every value stream should have a vision, and a mission statement which expresses tangible goals. These should relate to the customers of the value stream.*

Vivid Expression

Vivid expression and clarity of wording can help to keep a vision in the mind of team members. When Mr. Honda was expanding his product from motorcycles into the car market, he believed that environmental consciousness would become a major social issue, so he developed engines that would not pollute. Seeking an articulate expression that would stay in the mind, he told his engineers to find a way to take care of their own "piss and shit." This was the expression that got their attention![8]

A Leader's Use of Language

David Potter, historian of the American Civil War, made a striking assertion, "If the Union and the Confederacy had exchanged presidents with one another, the Confederacy might have won its independence." One of Jefferson Davis's principal failures was an inability to communicate effectively with other Confederate leaders and with the Southern people.[9]

Jefferson Davis seemed to speak in platitudes and think in abstractions; Abraham Lincoln used language rich in allegory, parable, fable, and metaphor.

Flawed Visions

Sometimes a vision statement is astonishingly flawed, or dates back to an earlier era. Consider this statement which, according to consultant Ian Mitroff, was a set of implicit guidelines for success, used for many years in General Motors:

- GM is in the business of making money, not cars.
- Cars are primarily status symbols. Styling is therefore more important than quality.
- The American car market is isolated from the rest of the world.
- Workers do not have an important impact on product quality.
- Everyone connected with the business has no need for more than a fragmented, compartmentalized understanding of the business.[10]

Amazing though it may seem today, this set of assumptions served General Motors well for many years. When times changed, however, the vision did not—until many years later. The contrast with Honda's vision statement could hardly be more extreme:

- Quality in all jobs—learn, think, analyze, evaluate and improve
- Reliable products—on time, with excellence and consistency
- Better communication—listen, ask and speak up

Peter Senge uses the GM example to show that an entire industry can have a flawed mental model. He says:

> Entire industries can develop mental models chronically out of touch with reality. In some ways industries are vulnerable because all the individual members of the industry look to each other for standards of best practice. It may take someone from outside the system, such as foreign competitors, with different mental models, to finally break the spell.[11]

According to Senge, Detroit did not realize that its vision statement represented mental models; they thought it represented reality. They should have said, "We have mental models that say customers want style, not quality," and "Workers do not have an important impact on productivity and quality." A statement acknowledged as a mental model can be examined and tested. One is not recognized to be a mental model is not compared with alternative models. Senge comments: "As the world changed, a gap widened between Detroit's mental models and reality, leading to increasingly counterproductive actions."[11]

In the decade before its crash, IBM had a vision statement that was known to every employee:

- To match or beat the growth in all segments of the information industry during the coming decade,
- To exhibit product leadership across our entire product line,
- To be the most efficient at everything we do, and
- To sustain our profitability, which funds our growth.

This statement could have applied to the 1960s or any other decade. By the 1990s, however, the computer industry was fundamentally different: it had an extreme rate of change. The IBM vision statement should have emphasized speed, fluidity, and rapid adaptability to fast-changing markets—but it did not.

New corporations were springing up and growing faster than ever before in history. Some grew to a billion dollars of revenue in five years. McCaw Cellular Communications sold for $12.6 billion six years after it was started by McCaw and his brothers. The world of small machines, hacker networks, and software stores was very different from the staid world of the mainframes. To survive in the computer industry you had to be fast, fluid, and flexible. The Akers-era IBM mission did not emphasize speed, fluidity, and adaptability to fast-changing markets.

The management style that had made IBM so successful in the past had become a liability. Its size, centralization, and high level of discipline cause it to respond too slowly. While IBM was trying to swing around an ocean liner, small, nimble powerboats were racing to its customers.

Summary

The purpose of the vision statement is to inspire employees and make them proud of their work. The overall strategic vision, discussed in the previous chapters, is more complex than that. The vision statement needs a clear focus; a shopping list has no capability to excite people.

As old-style management-gives-the-orders hierarchies have given way to participative management, executives have had to explain their strategic thinking to employees. They may, for example, explain core competencies. Each value-stream team should understand the aspects of detailed strategy that relate to that value stream. Each value stream ought to contribute to the strategic thought processes.

Employees need to recognize that the vision statement is not an empty piece of rhetoric but that it has a detailed strategy to back it up. Management by slogans does not work. Employees must observe the vision translating into action at every level.

References

1. From Randall A. Lipton of the Lipton Group, who helped create the vision statement of Hillhaven.
2. Bill O'Brien, quoted in Peter M. Senge, *The Fifth Discipline* (Doubleday Currency: New York, 1990).
3. James A. Belasco, *Teaching the Elephant to Dance* (Random House: New York, 1990); paperback (Century Business: London, 1992).
4. Thomas J. Watson, Jr., *A Business and Its Beliefs* (McGraw Hill: New York, 1963).
5. G. H. Langeler, "The Vision Trap," *Harvard Business Review*, March-April 1992.
6. From Jim Brown, James Martin & Co., Reston, Va.
7. M. Hammer and J. Champy, *Reengineering the Corporation* (Harper Business: New York, 1993).
8. Maryann Keller, *Collision* (Doubleday Currency: New York, 1993).
9. James McPherson, *Abraham Lincoln and the Second American Revolution* (Oxford University Press: London, 1991).
10. Ian Mitroff, *Break-Away Thinking* (John Wiley: New York, 1988).
11. Senge, *The Fifth Discipline*.

Part VI
Enterprise Redesign

Part VI focuses on re-architecting the enterprise to make it implement its strategic vision as effectively as possible given the many changes required by Enterprise Engineering.

Enterprise Redesign

28

Old-World vs. New-World Corporations

In the last ten years numerous corporations have tried out new types of organization and made diverse attempts at reengineering. From this body of experience an understanding has grown of what a modern enterprise ought to be like. It is fundamentally different from the enterprise of the 1970s. We will refer to the traditional enterprise as "old-world" and the new enterprise as "new-world."

The CEO confronted with the need for reengineering has to decide whether to tackle one important aspect of change or embark on a journey that will eventually change the entire enterprise from old-world to new-world.

New organizations around the world are being built on the new-world model. They will often be able to compete better than old-world organizations, which need to transform themselves, hence the passion for business reengineering. But the transformation is difficult and risky.

Many top executives try to improve the efficiency of a corporation without making major changes to its overall architecture. They downsize, establish teams, redesign processes in existing departments, computerize operations, spread the

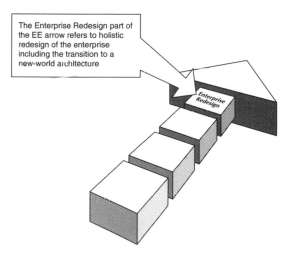

The Enterprise Redesign part of the EE arrow refers to holistic redesign of the enterprise including the transition to a new-world architecture

Enterprise Redesign

use of TQM and achieve ISO 9000 certification. They may aggregate such activities into a corporatewide campaign with a dramatic name. But if the corporate architecture is wrong, there is a limit to what can be achieved. Sooner or later more wrenching changes will be required. The functional fiefdoms have to be replaced with horizontal structures. Employees have to look outward to customers, not upward to bosses. The hierarchy has to be broken up and replaced with value-stream management.

> *Many "reengineering" efforts result not in a new-world enterprise but an old-world enterprise with minor changes.*

Design for Ongoing Change

Once an enterprise has a new-world architecture, rapid change can occur within it. Indeed, a primary goal of new-world architecture is to create an enterprise more adaptable to change than an old-world enterprise. The new-world enterprise is composed of value-stream teams focused on delighting the value-stream customer. Such teams are fluid and can adapt their behavior to changing needs much more quickly than the old-world hierarchy. The new-world enterprise needs new-world IT (information technology), with *kaizen*-capable computing, rapid-application development (RAD), information superhighways, and enterprise IT architectures that facilitate "open" connection. The culture of the new world is one of constant learning and experimentation. The motivation, compensation, appraisals, budgets, union relationships, training, and rewards all need to support this new-world culture.

The problem in most corporations is that their present architecture represents a world gone by, but a seismic upheaval is needed to make the transition from the old to the new world.

One of the largest U.S. property-management companies redesigned itself, thinking of itself as a simple "machine" composed of five core processes that needed to mesh as smoothly as possible. The strategic goal was to increase growth dramatically in the number of properties owned and managed, with an appropriate level of profit.

Prior to redesigning the company, the senior managers had each focused on limited areas of responsibility rather than the success of the whole. The new "business-success model" provided unification so that management could function as a team and focus both on individual responsibilities and the machine as a whole.

The new corporate design simplified managers' problems by giving them a common language about cross-functional processes and their link into a single machine. Each part of the machine feeds the other parts the diagram shows. For example, improving the efficiency of the maintenance process produces

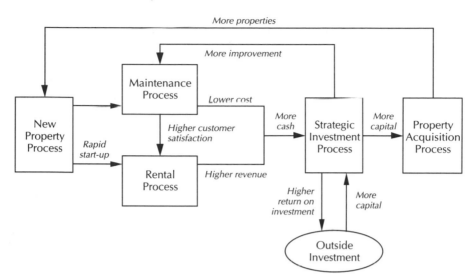

lower costs and higher customer satisfaction, which leads to more rentals and more cash for the strategic-investment process. This provides more capital for the property-acquisition process, and so the machine becomes a vortex with positive feedback stimulating more and more growth.

The key point in the new design is that it aligns the mental models of senior managers and so lessens divisive competition. Each component sees its role in driving the machine as a whole.

Redistribution of Power

At the core of enterprise change is a crucial structural issue: Where does the power reside?

The transition from an old-world to a new-world structure is a major power shift. Traditionally the "golden rule of business" has been "He who has the gold sets the rules." Today, however, shares are often widely distributed, and shareholders often have next to no power. The CEO has power, but increasingly the layers of middle executives are being removed.

In order for organizations to survive in a highly dynamic world, management must give employees the freedom to create. This is the only way to be fast and responsive to the new, global markets and issues. But individual knowledge workers do not have the skill, by themselves, to undertake the complex tasks of the modern enterprise, so work groups, teams, and (where possible) high-performance teams are set up rather like entrepreneurial organizations and provided with resources and autonomy. The traditional fiefdoms need to be replaced with value-stream teams.

As Exhibit 28.1 indicates, managers change from order givers, who tell

Exhibit 28.1   The transition needed in management

Old-World Organization	*New-World Organization*
Managers give orders.	Managers set up self-managing teams.
Managers supervise workers closely.	Managers set directions, build teams, and coach the teams.
	Managers are enablers and facilitators.
Managers oversee fragmented tasks requiring multiple hand-overs from department to department.	Self-managing teams integrate their work to deliver end-to-end results.
Measurements and rewards relate to departmental costs and budgets.	Measurements and rewards relate to results delivered to value-stream customers.
Motivation relates to pleasing the boss.	Motivation relates to pleasing the value-stream customer.
There are few workers per manager.	There are many workers per manager.
Managers "own" information. They collect, control, and integrate information.	Computer-processed information is available to everyone.
Managers protect their turf.	Managers focus on getting people to work together. They manage conflict, focusing on achieving ever-better value-stream results.

people how to work, to direction setters, coaches, and enablers for the empowered teams—trying to ensure that work is redesigned for effectiveness.

This transition is at the heart of Enterprise Engineering (EE). The change methods of EE determine the best teams and clusters and their design, focusing on developing management's role as coaches and enablers of change. They must identify and reinvent value streams, and then enable the reinvented value streams to improve continuously. Enterprise redesign must establish how the new value-stream teams fit into an overall corporate design. The corporate architecture needs a vision, culture, knowledge infrastructure, and computer systems to support value streams.

Changing the Role of Managers

In the new-world enterprise both the role and style of management are fundamentally different from the those in the traditional enterprise. Usually is it much easier to change behavior of workers than of executives. James Champy laments that most reengineered corporations do not have reengineered managers. He comments that workers can usually make the transition but questions how many managers can. The answer, he says, will determine "whether it will take 5 years or 50 years to reverse the industrial revolution."[1]

Managers ask, If the teams manage themselves, what do I do? There is still a vital role for managers; workers may be self-managed but not unmanaged. The role of managers with value-stream teams is quite different from that in the traditional hierarchy. A manager *empowers* the teams, making sure that the right team members are together, that they are measured and rewarded in the best way, that they are motivated, excited, and energized. Managers may help to get the right information to the teams and ensure that obstacles to success are removed. A manager has more people to look after when teams are self-managing. In software development, for example, one manager used to manage one product. Now he can manage multiple concurrent projects because self-managing teams with power-tools permit rapid development.[2] The manager may set up the projects; ensure that the best tools, techniques, and measurements are used; coach the teams; review the results; and make sure that the customers (end users) are happy.

Managers in the new-world enterprise need to be skilled at building teams, putting the right players together, dealing with conflict, and establishing vision that excites and energizes the people. This is very different from the old-world role of the "glue" that sticks together the fragments of work done in hierarchical departments.

Managers no longer "own" information that they collect, control, and integrate. Instead, computer-processed information is freely available to everyone. Managers no longer hide information to protect their turf or to help meet next month's budget. Databases designed for value-stream teams ensure that the team has all the information necessary in its own area. Software enables the team to use this information as effectively as possible. Rather than watching the budgets of balkanized departments, managers need to watch the overall results of value-stream teams. Various measures of the effectiveness of value-streams can be established—speed of delivering results, customer satisfaction, cost per unit delivered, percentage of customers who reorder, defect rate, etcetera.

How Much Do We Need to Change?

Almost every top executive knows that enterprises are in flux and asks, "How much do we have to change?" The unavoidable challenge for leaders is making a clear decision about change.

Exhibit 28.2 shows the playing field for change. Leadership must choose where to be on this playing field. There are beneficial and harmful regions. Maintaining the status quo, or a wait-and-see attitude year after years defers crucial adaptation. Procrastination in the lower region of the playing field eventually results in panic migration to the upper-left, "quick fix," or "panic mode" region, with wasteful, demoralizing effects. Meaningful, persistent performance im-

Exhibit 28.2 How much do we need to change?

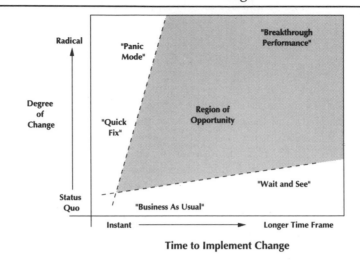

provement occurs when management becomes personally committed to leading to effect change.

The upper right-hand area of the "region of opportunity" provides the greatest promise of results and the greatest challenge to leadership. Many corporations are achieving breakthrough performance by reengineering that frequently involves paradigm shifts concerning the nature of work, markets, and management itself.

The decision to drive for breakthrough performance must be conscious and deliberate if major barriers are to be overcome to reach this part of the playing field. The enterprise's culture is organized to preserve its current behavior and reject paradigm shifts, and existing mental models of executives limit both current performance and the ability to change. Attempting to achieve breakthrough has risks which should be analyzed. Management needs to understand the techniques and consequences of driving for major organization change. Sooner or later breakthrough must be achieved if corporations are to stay competitive.

There is no cookbook for these decisions. They involve assessing the entire playing field and deciding how rapidly the enterprise must make the transition. Move too slowly, and the organization may be bypassed by its competition forever, missing the window of opportunity. Move too rapidly, and the organization may find itself on the "bleeding edge" of change.

Change may occur within the existing structure. Part of the structure may be changed by reinventing one or two value streams. Sometimes a holistic transition of the entire enterprise is planned. Sometimes new-world operations are introduced by establishing "green-field" start-up units, where enterprise designs can be built from scratch.

Exhibit 28.3

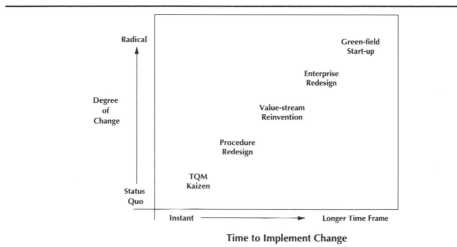

The various processes of Enterprise Engineering differ in time scale and degree of change. They occupy different areas of the playing field. (Exhibit 28.3)

Comprehensive enterprise redesign—the transition from an old- to new-world enterprise—is a long and risky journey that needs the highest level of top-management dedication. Often it is easier to build new operations than to rebuild existing operations. The best course may be to establish new-world factories, new divisions, or new subsidiaries from the start. Ideally they should be in a new location so that the old-world culture, pay-scales, politics, etcetera, in no way restrict the freedom of new-world design. The green-field environment needs to be protected so that it can succeed on its own with no subtle sabotage from the old-world power structure.

Partial vs. Holistic Transition

Most corporations that have practiced reengineering so far, including many that have achieved spectacular results (as in Exhibit 5.6), have tackled one or more specific aspects of the corporation rather than attempting holistic conversion to a new-world corporation. Some have introduced TQM within the old-world organization chart or reengineered a procedure within one function. Some have reinvented one value stream, perhaps a strategic one.

Although the decision to tackle one aspect of change at a time is often pragmatic, the CEO and chief organizational architect should realize that in the long run a holistic transition to a new-world enterprise is needed. Once this quantum change has occurred, less-painful change becomes a way of life. Several principles apply to this holistic transition (Exhibit 28.4).

Exhibit 28.4   Principles of transition to a new-world enterprise

Principle 1.	The enterprise must be dealt with as a whole—all of its business, social, and technical systems must be dealt with in a holistic and integrated way.
Principle 2.	The enterprise can only be changed incrementally.
Principle 3.	The transition to a new-world enterprise requires all seven aspects of Enterprise Engineering (the seven components of the rocket diagram) to be fully integrated.
Principle 4.	The enterprise must develop a learning culture which sees change as an ongoing (not a one shot) process.
Principle 5.	The new-world enterprise has an architecture within which ongoing change is fast and fluid.
Principle 6.	Success is directly related to the involvement, interaction, and buy-in of all levels within the organization. Leaders at all levels must demonstrate their commitment on an ongoing basis.
Principle 7.	It is often easier to evolve by starting new units than by "reengineering."
Principle 8.	The transition succeeds only when the CEO is passionate about it.

Reengineering the Entire Enterprise

A few CEOs, understanding the competitive advantages, have embarked on a journey to reengineer the entire enterprise. Reengineering the enterprise holistically can be complicated and arduous, but with the right management passion and professional skill it has advantages.

First, the corporation will reap the benefits earlier if it succeeds. Second, there can be a concerted corporatewide effort to get all the employees excited and motivated about the "adventure," rather than having some feeling left out and some disempowered by the reengineering of fragments of the corporation. Third, an integrated plan can ensure that all of the pieces fit together, avoiding the interface problems when part of an organization is new-world and part of it old. Fourth, the changes in enabling services can support the entire corporation rather than only a reengineered fragment. This includes such areas as compensation, employee development, new-world IT, culture change, stock options, etcetera. Last, the traumatic upheaval associated with cross-functional reengineering is not dragged on for years as one value stream after another is tackled; it is concentrated in time.

The demands of total corporate reengineering are intense. Enough talent has to be available, and multiple new IT systems have to be built, to tackle multiple projects simultaneously. Out sourcing is risky, but however it is done, it requires a large investment. Each value-stream reinvention is a step into the unknown that inevitably brings its own crop of surprises and problems. When many are tackled at once, the unanticipated complexities may be overwhelming. The different aspects of engineering need to fit together. The intricacies grow geometrically with the number of value streams reengineered. And reengineering always meets with resistance. The more projects tackled simultaneously, the greater the total resistance.

It takes very determined management to tackle the overall corporate transition at once. The planning and design phase of a reengineering project is often much easier than its implementation, so integrating planning and design is often much better than tackling each value stream in isolation. Some value streams are closely related, others largely independent. Manufacturing and purchasing, for example, are closely related, whereas IT-system development and financial control are largely unrelated. Closely related value streams may be designed and perhaps implemented together.

We have emphasized that these are two critical enablers for the EE arrow of change methods, IT development and human and culture development, the two cylinders on the sides of the EE diagram. It may be important to reengineer those before setting about corporationwide transition to a new-world enterprise.

> *A new-world enterprise needs new-world information technology and new-world human-resource management.*

The human-resource organization needs to be ready to cope with retraining, counseling, motivation, new compensation plans, reward systems, appraisals, measurements, and in general the human care and attention required to accomplish radical severe shifts in the work environment.

New-world IT is very different from old-world IT. Instead of difficult-to-change mainframes an enterprise needs a nervous system that reaches everybody's notebook computer or work station, with easy-to-change systems, graphical user interfaces (such as Windows or Macintosh), rapid application development, and databases designed for making value-stream teams as efficient as possible. The value-stream databases and software for value-stream automation can take a long time to develop. Cross-functional client-server applications can be difficult to build.

In some corporations the IT organization has progressed vigorously into new-world IT even though the corporation is not yet ready for corporatewide reengineering. IT has put into place the networks, data administration, business objects, and skills for rapid development, and is able to respond quickly to the true needs of its user community. It can delight its customers. In other corporations IT is stuck in old habits, with old methodologies, and its user community regards it as an unresponsive bottleneck to progress.

The reengineering of the IT function is a critical precursor to corporatewide reengineering.

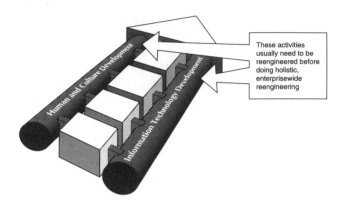

These activities
usually need to be
reengineered before
doing holistic,
enterprisewide
reengineering

New Units

It is difficult to convert a large corporation from old- to new-world IT. However, new corporations can grow from the beginning with new-world structures. The cybercorp revolution will happen in part with new-world corporations springing up and growing vigorously while old-world corporations die, what proportion of each we do not know yet. The death rate will be much faster than human death rate; perhaps ten years from now few old-world corporations will exist in competitive business.

An existing corporation may transform itself by creating new units that have new-world design from the start. This has happened in the U.S. car industry, which has built new-world factories while closing some mass-production facilities that were ensnarled in old-world problems. It has happened in the computer industry, which has built new divisions for new products. IBM sold its old-world printer division, which became a separate corporation, Lexmark, and thoroughly reengineered itself. This reengineering could happen in a new corporation but apparently not within the old IBM.

The strategic-visioning process should deliberately identify opportunities for creating new-world units—factories, divisions, subsidiaries, strategic partnerships, or units that provide services to the parent corporation. New business thrusts should often be new-world units. A corporation may transform itself like an apple tree putting out vigorous new growth where the old wood is sawn off.

The Context of Strategic Visioning

Enterprise redesign is sometimes accomplished without changing the strategic vision of the enterprise. Top executives are accustomed to shuffling the building blocks of the enterprise. Strategic visioning is more fundamental: executives are challenged to rethink the most basic ideas of the business. They reinvent the "game" they are playing rather than the means of playing it. They rethink the values of their founder.

Only a weak form of enterprise redesign can come about without strategic visioning. In many corporations, however, strategic visioning is unlikely to be done first. Our experience is that no more than about 10 percent of top executives are ready to undertake the profound rethinking entailed by strategic visioning, although they often charge ahead to change the building blocks of the enterprise. A horrifying amount of "business reengineering" is done with the wrong strategic vision.

Strategic visioning may result in major changes in the enterprise—plants being closed, takeovers of other corporations, establishment of a new mode of operating. Vertical integration may need to be replaced with more fluid structures. New core capabilities may need to be built that reflect new strategic thinking and that may call for new alliances and technology for coordinating complex new value streams.

Changing from a corporation with massively capitalized vertical integration, such as GM or IBM, to a company with changeable partnerships that enable it to be fast, fluid, and flexible, is especially difficult. The change takes many years and is sometimes fought all the way by executives of the earlier era. It usually requires the sale of subsidiaries. It almost always requires bringing in a new CEO from outside. IBM replaced much of the top management with powerful executives from outside the computer industry. Only in this way could the self-sustaining internal myths be confronted with harsh reality.

Types of Organizational Change

David Nadler and Michael Tushman have done much research on organizational change and have come to a sobering conclusion that all CEOs should be aware of.[3,4] *Strategic* change failed in more than 90 percent of the organizations they studied when it was *reactive*.

Nadler and Tushman categorize change as incremental or strategic. *Incremental change* takes place without changing the values, mode of organizing, and general strategic framework. *Strategic change* has an impact on the whole system of organization and ends up "redefining what the organization is, or changing the basic framework of organizing, including strategy, structure, people, processes, and (in some cases) core values."

Nadler and Tushman also categorize change as reactive and anticipatory. *Reactive change* is forced on an organization in response to an external event or change. *Anticipatory change* is made because of a belief that initiating such change in advance of future events will provide competitive advantage.

Nadler and Tushman combine these two dimensions of change.[5] Exhibit 28.5 summarizes key findings of Nadler and Tushman's research.

Fewer than one in ten *reactive strategic* changes succeed. Strategic changes need to be anticipatory if possible. The reactive strategic changes that do succeed almost always involve a change of CEO and senior leadership, often with the new leadership coming from the outside. This indicates the importance of an ongoing

Exhibit 28.5   Key findings from Nadler and Tushman's research on organizational change[6,7]

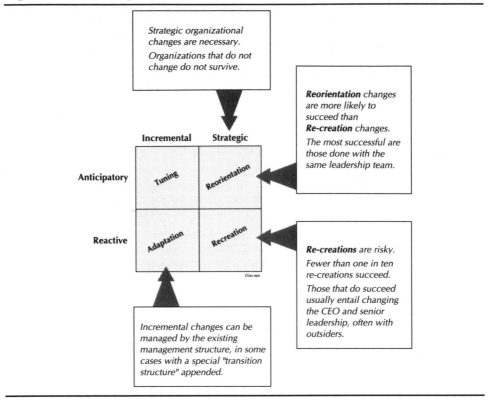

visioning process. To be caught by surprise so that reactive strategic changes have to be made is very dangerous.

The planning of enterprise redesign should take place in conjunction with strategic visioning. New-world capabilities effect the strategic vision, and the strategic vision effects the enterprise design.

A Continuum of Change

Strategic visioning should be a ongoing process, not a one-time project. The future is dynamic and unpredictable, so the top executive team must revisit the enterprise's strategic context repeatedly.

Enterprise redesign should be undergone within the context of strategic visioning. Value-stream reinvention and procedure redesign should be done within the context of enterprise redesign. *Kaizen*/TQM should be a basic part of each reinvented value stream. Exhibit 28.6 shows stages of this continuum.

One successful experience with value-stream reinvention usually creates the desire to tackle other value streams. The situation is a little like remodeling a house—once you change the kitchen, the entire house begins to look old and in need of remodeling. The process and value-stream changes stimulate broader discussions within the organization—about reward systems, structural barriers, poor IT architecture and system delivery capability, etcetera. Top management begins to think about its role in enterprise change and steadily prepares. A success in tackling one value stream encourages enterprise redesign and helps to make it more practical. Success in enterprise redesign encourages top management to implement the changes highlighted in the strategic-visioning process. The process in Exhibit 28.6 is thus not a one-way, top-down, logical sequence, but rather a set of activities that feed on one another, the successes reinforcing the capability of the enterprise to learn and evolve at all levels.

The chief organizational architect needs to be alert to the whole continuum of change processes and to maximize the valuable feedback wherever possible.

As empowerment occurs and the right teams are set up, especially value-stream teams, the capability of harnessing the energy and excitement of employees grows. Change becomes easier to accomplish. The whole organization should focus on how to make major improvements.

A Long Journey

Bringing about the change needed in most enterprises is a long journey (Exhibit 28.7) calling for tough leadership and professional knowledge of Enterprise Engineering. The change is painful to many people, especially in its earlier stages.

One can observe many corporations now having embarked on the journey, and some having completed parts of it. Many others seem unaware that they need to change. Still others are postponing the trauma. Some of the case studies show enterprises bravely setting out to change without understanding the change methods, or without having a clear idea what reinvented value streams ought to look like. They drive aggressively for improvements in productivity or profit but within an architecture that cannot work well.

Certain projects associated with the transition are likely to need implementation as quickly as is practical. There is a constant pressure to increase sales, profits, and productivity. Change goes on repeatedly. However, the changes should fit as far as possible into an integrating vision.

Exhibit 28.6

The continuum of change usually is not a one-way, top-down logical sequence; rather it is a set of activities that feed on one another.

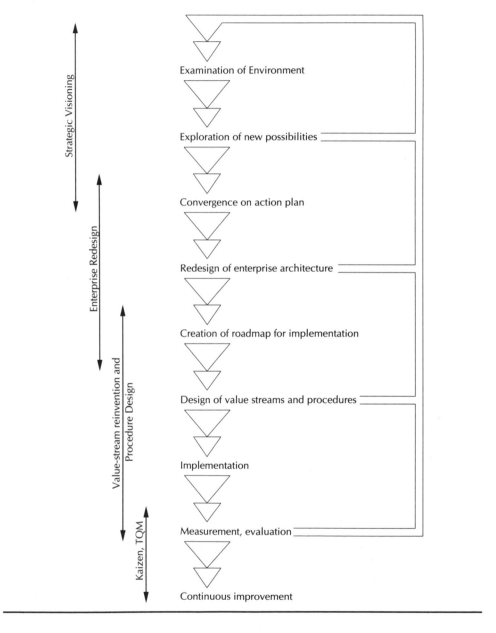

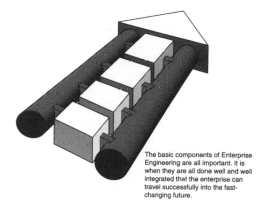

The basic components of Enterprise Engineering are all important. It is when they are all done well and well integrated that the enterprise can travel successfully into the fast-changing future.

The chief organizational architect needs to create a road map for the journey and coordinate the many tasks that have to be accomplished, involving many people over a long period. He must establish a framework within which ongoing change progresses. The roadmap can be adjusted as the experience proceeds.

SmithKline Beecham called its journey the "Simply Better Way." Jan Leschly, chairman of SmithKline Beecham Pharmaceuticals, told managers, "If we don't have fire in our hearts, the Simply Better Way will fail." Robin Cammish, team leader of the Simply Better Way stated, "Implementation of the Simply Better Way throughout SmithKline Beecham won't be achieved in a week, a month, or a year. It will take time and tremendous commitment and focus on the part of the entire organization."[8]

The SmithKline Beecham management directive stated, "If we can gain the commitment of the entire organization behind the Simply Better Way, then all of our jobs will become more fulfilling, we will work more efficiently and effectively, and we will become the kind of healthcare company we want to be—the best."

Many executives focus naively on only one type of change method, such as TQM, business reengineering, or business-process redesign. Top management must be aware of the range of options available.

An EE assessment should start with the strategic-visioning process. It may scan the existing visions in the enterprise, and lay out possible alternatives to these visions. It should then examine a set of possible change processes and their costs, likely benefits, and risks. It should identify which value streams to reinvent, how to undertake this, what procedure redesign can occur within the existing corporate structure, and what changes in corporate structure are needed.

The result should be a road map to the desired future, with projects of different scope and duration being coordinated. The road map provides a framework

Exhibit 28.7   The journey

The change from old-world to new-world enterprise takes time, toughness, professional EE skills, and relentless determination. Many different change projects need to
be planned in an integrated way so that they fit together into one overall architecture.
Change may be tackled a step at a time, one value stream at a time. It is a pilgrim's
journey.

A road map is needed for the journey, with separate road maps for parts of the journey, such as the change in IT. The road map should set realistic targets and timetables. Constant learning will necessitate repeated adjustments to the "living" road
map, which will have a long-term strategic intent and may have some targets for
three years, some for shorter-term breakthrough projects, some for immediate improvement.

The vision of where the business is going may shift repeatedly. Strategic visioning
has its radar on a moving target. The vision of how the enterprise should manage its
processes is more constant, but the radical change needed will take time to complete.
Success depends on the commitment and enthusiasm of everybody in the organization. Employees need to be excited by the vision and understand the road to that
vision. Many managers need to be trained as coaches.

The journey needs clear-headed leaders who understand the change methods, the
culture problems, the IT requirements, and the vision. Like any major change process, its success depends on the constant attention of caring executives determined
to make the journey and deal with the problems and setbacks that occur.

There will be many problems on the way. They need to be constantly dealt with
TQM techniques. *Kaizen* is everyone's job.

for change that its sponsor can use as a rallying point for initiating enterprise
change—an explicit, visible set of change projects that move the enterprise toward a revitalized vision of the future.

Often external events or declining profits force top management to act, but
the greatest success stories tend to occur when top management is not "under
the gun" to change but sets out to improve an already successful operation.

The road map for change will integrate projects on widely differing schedules. Many of the major projects for procedure design or value-stream reengineering last 6 to 24 months. Some may not start immediately but fit into a framework
for change that may span 5 years. The strategic context and vision for what the
corporation will eventually be may look even further into the future. Meanwhile
many daily improvements occur, and TQM activities indicate a stream of changes
that can be made in days or weeks (Exhibit 28.8).

Constancy of Vision

Throughout the journey there must be constancy of vision and leadership. The
successful leaders of organizational change are quite clear where they are going

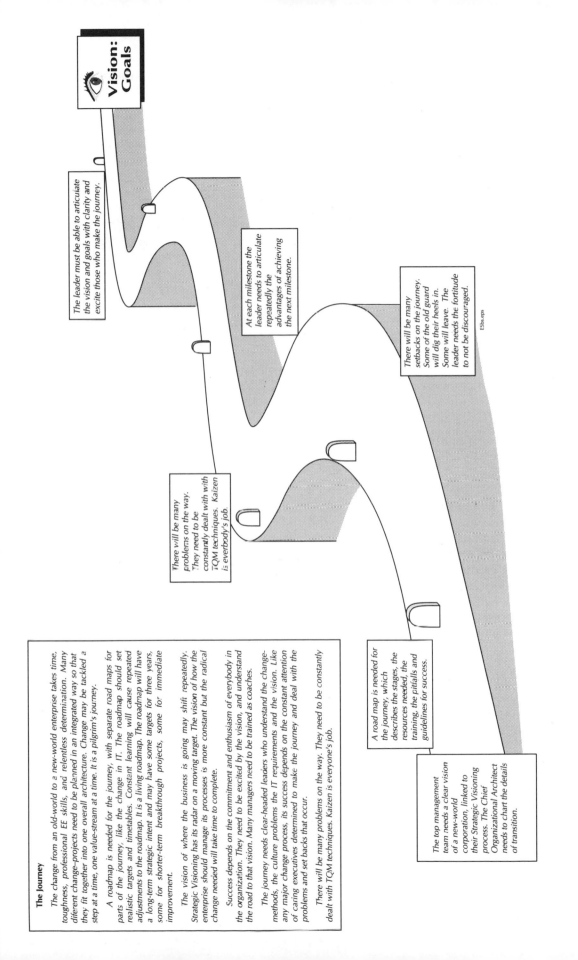

Vision: Goals

The leader must be able to articulate the vision and goals with clarity and excite those who make the journey.

At each milestone the leader needs to articulate repeatedly the advantages of achieving the next milestone.

There will be many setbacks on the journey. Some of the old guard will dig their heels in. Some will leave. The leader needs the fortitude to not be discouraged.

There will be many problems on the way. They need to be constantly dealt with with TQM techniques. Kaizen is everbody's job.

A road map is needed for the journey, which describes the stages, the resources needed, the training, the pitfalls and guidelines for success.

The top management team needs a clear vision of a new-world corporation, linked to their Strategic Visioning process. The Chief Organizational Architect needs to chart the details of transition.

The Journey

The change from an old-world to a new-world enterprise takes time, toughness, professional EE skills, and relentless determination. Many diferent change-projects need to be planned in an integrated way so that they fit together into one overall architecture. Change may be tackled a step at a time, one value-stream at a time. It is a pilgrim's journey.

A roadmap is needed for the journey, with separate road maps for parts of the journey, like the change in IT. The roadmap should set realistic targets and timetables. Constant learning will cause repeated adjustments to the roadmap. It is a living roadmap. The roadmap will have a long-term strategic intent and may have some targets for three years, some for shorter-term breakthrough projects, some for immediate improvement.

The vision of where the business is going may shift repeatedly. Strategic Visioning has its radar on a moving target. The vision of how the enterprise should manage its processes is more constant but the radical change needed will take time to complete.

Success depends on the commitment and enthusiasm of everybody in the organization. They need to be excited by the vision, and understand the road to that vision. Many managers need to be trained as coaches.

The journey needs clear-headed leaders who understand the change-methods, the culture problems the IT requirements and the vision. Like any major change process, its success depends on the constant attention of caring executives determined to make the journey and deal with the problems and set backs that occur.

There will be many problems on the way. They need to be constantly dealt with TQM techniques. Kaizen is everyone's job.

ES0s.eps

Exhibit 28.8   The road map integrating activities of widely differing time horizons

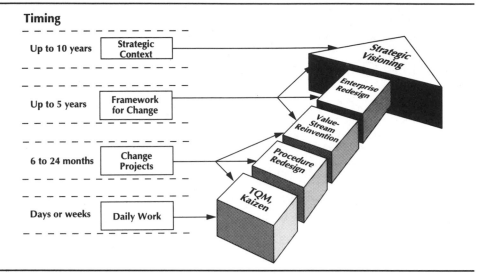

and why, and reiterate the vision over and over again—committed, constantly getting the change process back on track when things go wrong, and constantly encouraging or persuading others in the enterprise. The leaders or chief organizational architect use architecture to show the rest of the organization the way.

The main problem facing organizational architects is complexity. Organizations are systems that interact with their environment and modify themselves continuously. Employees, skills, products, market value, competition—every conceivable organizational attribute changes dynamically. Given this reality, how can one predict what will work a number of years from now? There is a tendency to believe that every situation is unique. At the microlevel that is true; at the macrolevel there is much in one organization that may be repeated with effectiveness to another.

Passionate CEO Leadership

Whether the transition is one reinvented value stream or a corporatewide transition, one prerequisite is crucial: the CEO must be passionately determined to succeed and manage the risks inherent in reengineering.

Top management should understand the entire EE spectrum of change methods, and assess which methods are appropriate.

> The great industrial leaders who have been successful at changing the culture of large organizations have had the tenacity and patience to repeat their vision and consequent demands over and over and over again.

Jack Welch, who spectacularly changed the values and culture of General Electric, used GE's Crotonville educational facility to interact with many thousands of GE managers. He systematically gathered written feedback from the managers. In 1986, five years after he started his campaign, he exploded with frustration while reading the feedback while driving from the Crotonville helipad: "This is unbelievable! I'm getting the same questions I've gotten for five years. Doesn't anyone understand anything? I'm just not getting through to them."

The Crotonville manager, Noel Tichy, asked, "What's the alternative? Don't you just have to keep saying it over and over again?"

"You're right. I've got no alternative."

Two years later Welch commented: "The only way to change people's minds is with consistency. Once you get the ideas, you keep refining and improving them; the more simply your idea is defined, the better it is. You communicate, communicate, then communicate some more. Consistency, simplicity, and repetition is what it's all about."

Noel Tichy later wrote about his years with Jack Welch: "The perseverance to repeat the same message day after day, year after year, with no end in sight, may be Welch's greatest strength."[9]

Similar perseverance can be observed in most of the great corporate change agents of this century. It is said that a great CEO repeats his major message hundreds of times.

Summary

Enterprise redesign is concerned with the following:

- Establishing a clear vision of a new-world enterprise
- Translating the strategic vision into the most appropriate architecture for the enterprise
- Designing the transition to new-world technology, and establishing a road map for the transition
- Determining what areas should be closed, sold, or floated as separate corporations
- Determining whether to establish new business units
- Establishing partner relations with other enterprises
- Establishing a knowledge infrastructure that facilitates corporate learning at all levels

References

1. James Champy, *Managing the Reengineering Organization, Insights*, Vol 6, No. 1 (CSC: Cambridge, Mass., Spring 1994).

2. Charles Handy, *The Age of Unreason* (Harvard Business School Press: Boston, Mass., 1990).
3. D. A. Nadler and M. L. Tushman, *Managing Strategic Organizational Change* (New York: Delta Consulting Group, 1986).
4. Ibid.
5. Ibid.
6. Ibid.
7. Ibid.
8. Comments from SmithKline Beecham Communique, *The Worldwide Manager's Magazine,* Spring, 1993.
9. Noel M. Tichy and Stratford Sherman, *Control Your Destiny or Someone Else Will* (Currency Doubleday: New York 1993).

29

What Replaces the Hierarchy?

The old-world corporation has a well-established hierarchy, and many employees work hard to be promoted within it. The new-world corporation is more horizontal and fluid, but it still needs a structure—the alternative to hierarchy is not anarchy.

What type of structure should replace the traditional hierarchy?

Command and Control

Many corporations in the past have needed a management structure that gathered thousands of pieces of information, summarized them, and reported them to the next-higher management layer. Computer networks changed this routine. For example, on railroads the high-level planners had to know where each locomotive and rail car was, whether it was functioning, where the freight was, and so on. The information coming from many locations had to be integrated. It passed up a hierarchy, decisions were made, and orders were passed down the hierarchy. With computers, however, information from all locations passes over the network into a database. Employees at any location can interrogate the database, generate reports from it, and use powerful computerized tools for decision making. With modern electronics any information is available at any location and can be easily summarized, presented graphically, and fed into decision-support tools. A hierarchical management structure is not needed to process information.

The military exemplified the hierarchical structure. Power resided at the top, and orders were passed down through the chain of command. The troops at the bottom of the hierarchy were drilled to obey orders. The private soldier must not *think;* otherwise he might not do what was required of him. Work is designed at a higher level, and workers are instructed about how to do it. With empowered employees, self-directing teams, and virtuosos, the classical hierarchy breaks down. Managers do not know every detail of the employees' work routines and cannot tell them how to proceed. The higher executives in the hierarchy often set rules or make decisions that impede empowered teams.

The management focus on the 1960s on standardized products and replaceable skills led naturally to a top-down flow of power within enterprises. Everyone, including the workers, believed that the only people who could direct operations were those high in the hierarchy because only they had the full picture. Only they were capable of integrating all the fragmented pieces of work.

In the 1980s work became more complex (partly because of technology in its diverse forms). Products became intricate, with chips in everything. The rate of change greatly increased, necessitating the making of many decisions locally. Automation enabled machines to do simple tasks and left more subtle tasks to people. Decisions based on data and rules (sometimes many rules) were increasingly made by software so did not need layers of planners and middle managers. It became necessary for employees to understand what they were doing and what the customers needed, and to work out how to delight the customer. Employees were empowered to do this. Because of the complexity of the processes, teams that incorporated all the skills necessary carried out the process.

This bottom-up view, motivated by the search for quality and cost effectiveness, led to new models of corporate organization. Management relinquishes much of its integrating power to teams of workers so as to achieve greater effectiveness, speed, quality, and (most importantly) creativity. The workers themselves sense that they, as much as management, are assets of the company. Thus, management's role must inexorably shift away from the detailed design of work fragmented into simple tasks toward an infrastructure that enables empowered workers or teams to do complex work of high quality and to learn continuously how to improve work processes. The faster employees innovate, the more a corporation can stay ahead of its competition, so (as Chapter 31 explains) many characteristics of the workplace should reflect those of the research laboratory.

Self-Reinforcing Cultures

Hierarchical organizations are notorious for preserving themselves. They understand and invest in the qualities that brought success in the past. Their management selection and training emphasizes what used to work. Hierarchies tend to preserve their own culture. Military organizations become more militaristic; bureaucratic organizations become more bureaucratic. The stronger the culture, the more the hierarchy reinforces it. This works well in a stable world, but when paradigms shift it can spell disaster.

IBM was a totally hierarchical company with the most efficient communication channels. If somebody told a joke in the Armonk head office, an hour later IBM managers in Sydney would be telling the same joke. IBM had a powerfully self-reinforcing culture, which believed in "account control" of customers, proprietary architectures, the "glass house," and superb customer service (if the customer obeyed IBM's rules). This culture could not cope effectively with Bill Gates and the iconoclastic hackers who rampaged across the computer industry in the late 1980s. The nerds outfoxed the white-shirted hierarchy over and over again. IBM top management hung on to its culture until it crashed around their ears.

Decades earlier, the Singer Sewing Machine Corporation had crashed from a dominant leading position. A new president remarked that its strictly hierarchical management assumed "All one had to do was what one's predecessors had done before. Everything became ingrained. There were no outside influences acting on the company. It became withdrawn into itself."[1] Empowered teams, dedicated to pleasing the customer, if they were cut loose from the hierarchy, would have detected market changes early and responded to them.

In the past most industries have changed sufficiently slowly that one generation of management does not become technologically obsolete during its tenure. Now technological change is so fast that the cycle of management renewal lags behind the cycle of technological change. The company then has an obsolescent management team. Consciously or subconsciously it tries to reinforce lessons learned years ago, but the game has changed. When paradigms shift, the natural human instinct to stay with what is known and proven is a lethal management trap.

Many industries are now starting to experience the great transition—a furious rate of change. A knowledge society is never static, it constantly changes. Corporations try to learn faster than their competitors. A classical hierarchy does not learn fast. Corporations need to be reorganized so that they learn in every way possible, and put what they learn into operation quickly. Exhibit 29.1 lists problems with hierarchical structures.

Exhibit 29.1   Problems with hierarchies

- Hierarchies tend to build barriers between functional areas so that cross-functional communication is channeled up one hierarchical branch and down another.
- Hierarchies tend to filter or distort information as it is passed upward.
- Hierarchies often prevent fast, fluid, flexible action.
- Most of the important value streams are cross-functional. Hierarchies make cross-functional processes slow, error-prone, inefficient, and difficult to change.
- Hierarchies delay decision making, resulting in lost opportunities.
- Teams close to the customer know what actions to take to delight the customer; higher management does not. Teams doing work know better than anyone else how to improve the work process.
- High-level managers, out of touch with how work is done, often set rules and regulations that cause difficulties.
- Hierarchies tend to create rules and controls that increase complexity.
- Managers pay more attention to political motives, power struggles, and concern with status than to pleasing customers.
- Development of cross-functional human skills is inhibited.
- Hierarchies limit individual accountability ("I was only obeying orders").
- In fast-changing industries those high in the hierarchy become dangerously obsolete.
- Hierarchies tend to multiply themselves (Parkinson's Law) and preserve themselves when not needed.

Parkinson's Law

Hierarchies not only preserve themselves; they multiply themselves. Northcote Parkinson's comic classic on hierarchology explains hierarchical growth with two "axiomatic" statements:[2]

> An official wants to multiply subordinates, not rivals.
> Officials make work for each other.

Parkinson describes an official who feels overworked—and all do sooner or later, because work expands to fill the time available. The official, called A, could ask to share the work with colleague B or could demand the assistance of two subordinates, C and D.

> By having B appointed, on his own level in the hierarchy, he would merely bring in a rival for promotion to his boss's vacancy when his boss (at long last) retires. So A would rather have C and D, junior men, below him. They will add to his consequence and, by dividing the work into two categories, as between C and D, he will have the merit of being the only man who comprehends them both. It is essential to realize at this point that C and D are, as it were, inseparable. To appoint C alone would have been impossible. Why? Because C, if by himself, would divide the work with A and so assume almost the equal status that has been refused in the first instance to B; a status the more emphasized if C is A's only possible successor. Subordinates must thus number two or more, each being thus kept in order by fear of the other's promotion. When C complains in turn of being overworked (as he certainly will), A will, with the concurrence of C, advise the appointment of two assistants to help C. But he can then avert internal friction only by advising the appointment of two more assistants to help D, whose position is much the same. With this recruitment of E, F, G, and H, the promotion of A is now practically certain.[3]

Declining Middle Management

In recent years the number of layers in hierarchical management declined in many enterprises. Each manager managed more people, so the hierarchy become flatter. Corporations cut their middle-management layers.

Layers of Management

	Cut from	To
Detroit Car Companies	15	5
Eastman Kodak	13	4
Intel	10	5

In a management hierarchy the less number of layers, the greater span of control. The span becomes much greater when self-directing teams are employed. Information systems make possible a larger span of control.

Layers of	Span of Control					
Management	5	10	15	20	25	
1	5	10	15	20	25	Number of
2	25	100	225	400	625	employees that
3	125	1,000	3,375	8,000	15,625	can be managed
4	625	10,00	50,625	160,000	390,625	

If the span of control is 5—in other words, if each manager has 5 subordinates—four layers of management can handle a maximum of 625 employees.

If the span of control is 25, four layers of management can handle a maximum of 390,625 employees. The world's largest corporations could be handled, at least in principle, with four layers.

Alternative forms of organization structure are illustrated in Exhibit 29.2.

Becoming Horizontal

Reducing the number of layers in the hierarchy is not, by itself, enough. Many corporations have done that and have not achieved the rises in productivity that are possible. Employees still look upward to bosses rather than outward to customers; their loyalty and commitment is still to the corporate fiefdom rather than to the customer-oriented goals of the enterprise. A more fundamental change occurs when the vertical structure is changed to a horizontal structure, and organized as value-stream teams rather than functional silos. The value-stream teams are entirely focused on the customer of the value stream and on measurements that relate to customer satisfaction and the profitability of delivering customer results.

In the move toward horizontal corporations, the type of structure that usually works best is the value-stream organization. Value-stream teams assume a diversity of forms, depending on the complexity of the specific value stream. A corporation may have a dozen or so types of value stream. The value streams, each with its own management, may report to a top-management team (Exhibit 29.3).

The value-stream organization works well because each value stream has clear goals. It is customer focused; its purpose is to delight its customer (internal or external). It has clear measurements related to its goals, and it can be highly innovative in improving how it achieves its goals. In such an environment it is practical to build high-performance teams that enthusiastically strive to meet tough challenges.

The functionally oriented hierarchy wastes a tremendous amount of energy running its own internal machinery—managing relations among departments,

Exhibit 29.2   Forms of organization structure

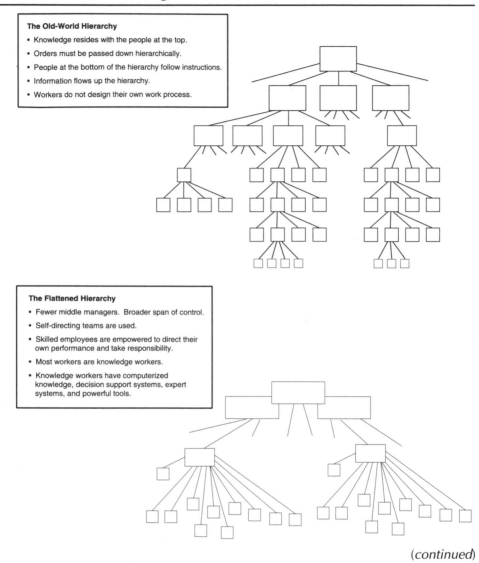

The Old-World Hierarchy
- Knowledge resides with the people at the top.
- Orders must be passed down hierarchically.
- People at the bottom of the hierarchy follow instructions.
- Information flows up the hierarchy.
- Workers do not design their own work process.

The Flattened Hierarchy
- Fewer middle managers. Broader span of control.
- Self-directing teams are used.
- Skilled employees are empowered to direct their own performance and take responsibility.
- Most workers are knowledge workers.
- Knowledge workers have computerized knowledge, decision support systems, expert systems, and powerful tools.

(continued)

controlling problems caused by hand-overs, passing information up and down the hierarchy, controlling noncustomer-related politics, and so on. The value-stream organization eliminates most of those tasks and focuses most of its energies on the value-stream customers.

Even with a value-stream organization, central-support functions—such as financial control, human resources, and building the IT infrastructure—are needed. Some of the support functions should themselves be value streams. Exhibit 29.4 shows support activities as well as operational value streams.

Exhibit 29.2 *continued*

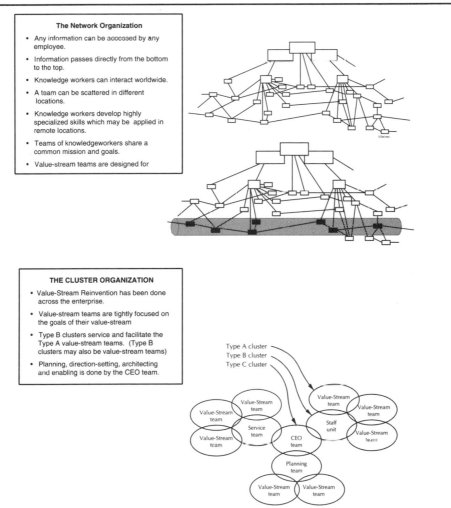

The Network Organization

- Any information can be accessed by any employee.
- Information passes directly from the bottom to the top.
- Knowledge workers can interact worldwide.
- A team can be scattered in different locations.
- Knowledge workers develop highly specialized skills which may be applied in remote locations.
- Teams of knowledgeworkers share a common mission and goals.
- Value-stream teams are designed for

THE CLUSTER ORGANIZATION

- Value-Stream Reinvention has been done across the enterprise.
- Value-stream teams are tightly focused on the goals of their value-stream
- Type B clusters service and facilitate the Type A value-stream teams. (Type B clusters may also be value-stream teams)
- Planning, direction-setting, architecting and enabling is done by the CEO team.

The term *horizontal* organization should not imply that there are no vertical linkages. Some hierarchy survives in nonhierarchical enterprises. Top management must set the direction, establish the strategic vision, and design the enterprise. Financial control is needed of all of the activities. Different parts of the organization need to share a common computer network and services.

Each value stream needs somebody in charge even if it operates with self-managing teams. AT & T's network division, for example, reorganized itself around 13 value streams, each having an "owner" and a "champion." The owner focuses on the day-to-day operations of the value stream, and the champion ensures that the value stream is linked with overall business strategies and goals.[4]

Exhibit 29.3

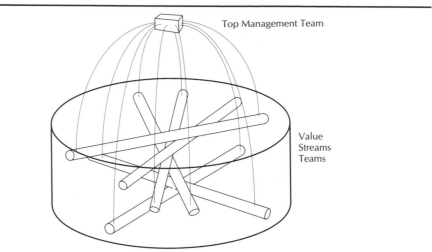

Exhibit 29.4

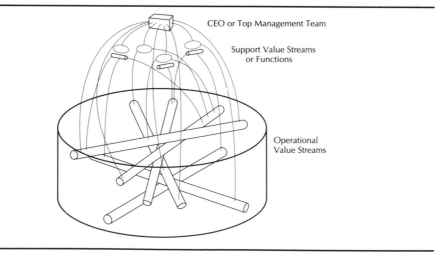

The value-stream organization needs budgets based on value-stream operation rather than on functions and departments. Its bonuses should be based on
value-stream performance and where possible on customer evaluations of value-
stream work. It makes sense, as in many Japanese corporations, to base a high
proportion of employee compensation on results or customer satisfaction.

Residual Hierarchy

Some management literature, advocating corporations that are run by teams or "clusters" of employees, gives the impression that the hierarchy would disappear. In reality, except for very small corporations, a hierarchy is still necessary, though with few levels.

A CEO or top-management team needs to establish the strategic vision and set the course. A middle-management group may need to establish the teams for achieving the vision, set targets, motivate the teams, monitor their results, and take corrective action when necessary. A corporation cannot operate without a clear structure that enables people to work autonomously and creatively toward established goals.

The goals should be clear, large-scale ones such as value-stream results, rather than fragmented work steps such as Frederick Taylor–style management. End-to-end value-stream goals give teams freedom in how they achieve those goals.

New Organization Charts

Various corporations have tried to draw charts to illustrate the new forms of organization. Exhibit 29.5 shows examples. It is difficult to show the new structures on a chart which replaces the traditional hierarchy chart.

Some corporations, Pepsi Co. for example, have turned the traditional pyramid chart upside down. Pepsi Co. put the people who dealt directly with customers at the top; the rest of the organization existed to support them. CEO Craig Weathup called Pepsi-Cola the "right-side up company."[5]

Eastman Chemical Company President Ernest W. Deavenport, Jr., described his organization chart as a "pizza chart"; it looked like a pizza with a lot of pepperoni spread over it. The president was the pepperoni at the center of the pizza. He explained, "We did it in circular form to show that everybody is equal in the organization."[6] Each pepperoni typically represents a cross-functional team, responsible for managing a business, a geographical area, a function, or a core competence.

The bottom picture in Fig. 29.5 shows the organization as a dome structure. Architectural domes provide an efficient and robust way of enclosing large spaces. They are relatively thin compared with the distances they span—unlike pyramids. A dome has a series of ribs radiating down from its center and a series of parallel spars linking the radial ribs. The radial ribs distribute the dome's weight, and the horizontal spars prevent the ribs from spreading apart. The result is a very stable structure. Somewhat similarly, a corporation needs teams linked to the center without layers of middle management and horizontal links to avoid communication's having to be channeled via the top. In the dome structure in

Exhibit 29.5   Attempts to draw new organizational structures

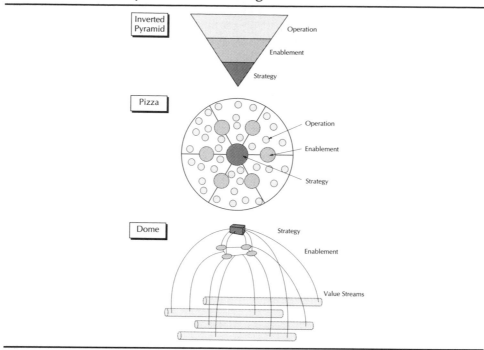

Exhibit 29.3 or 29.4 the operational activities are organized as value streams. Various services are provided to the value-stream teams. This can be a very effective form of enterprise structure.

The Corporation and the Brain

The cybernetic corporation has characteristics similar to the human brain. The brain, like a corporation, has to interact with a complex and ever-changing environment. It has many components with diverse functions that must work together but that must be flexible enough to constantly learn and adapt. Peter Schwartz, a key player in scenario planning that helped Shell to prosper through the OPEC shocks to the oil industry (Chapter 26), comments: "An organization of the scale and complexity of Shell functions very much like a brain. Research in cognitive science might help people who want to make large organizations operate more effectively."[7]

The brain is not organized hierarchically. Like a corporation, it has many parts that have specialized capabilities. Brain researchers who have probed brains electrically have located small modules of brain tissue that govern specific skills. Some deal with physical skills, some with spatial perception, some with logical-mathematical skills, some with music, and so on. These areas are relatively independent, like departments or teams in an enterprise. Cognitive psychologist Howard Gardner discusses these brain mechanisms in his book, *Frames of Mind*. He describes "the existence of several relatively autonomous human intellectual competencies. . . . These are relatively independent of one another, and they can be fashioned and combined in a multiplicity of adaptive ways by individuals and cultures."[8]

Each component of the brain learns to function and improve its functioning as the individual learns. Marvin Minsky sees the brain as a dynamic, very loosely integrated collection of specialized learning agents—similar to what organizations must become.[9] Minsky developed a theory of learning based on how these agents do their simple individual tasks in ever more complex alliances. Many of the functions of the brain require more than one "agent" to work in tight cooperation. The cooperating agents are usually located in separate parts of the brain but coordinate in complex and dynamically changing patterns. Much of the power of the brain seems to stem from just the messy ways its agents cross-connect.[10]

Most people today still think about organizations in spatial metaphors—the "shape" of the boxes and lines on a organizational chart, which managers are "higher" in the "chain of command," how many people are "in" a particular function. Spatial metaphors and language shape how people behave in organizations. For example, their ideas about boxes and lines on organization charts limit how people communicate (for example, "one ought to follow the organizational lines"). The organizational boxes define group "turf" to be protected. Such conversations are based on the old hierarchical organization; workers carried out fragments of work that had to be integrated by a higher level of management. When empowered teams are used, employees become knowledge workers, and computer networks pervade every nook and cranny, we need a new language and new metaphors. The old spatial hierarchical metaphors block real organizational change. The brain has many separate areas, each physically small and having different capabilities, which are not linked hierarchically but with a multiplicity of parallel channels that adapt to changing needs.

Loose and Tight Coupling

An organization needs a mixture of tight and loose coupling. A tightly coupled organization can be engineered and tuned for a specific purpose so that it carries out that purpose as efficiently as possible. A loosely coupled organization is more flexible and adaptable; it can exploit unpredictable changes.

A loosely coupled organization may have many clusters or teams who do the basic work, each of which adjusts and optimizes how it carries out its activities. Each team is itself tightly coupled, with the team members interacting closely with one another. Each team decides how best to change in response to its environment and continuously learns how to meet its goals better. However, there is loose coupling between the teams. Learning is not easily passed from one team to another, and it is difficult to tune the interaction among the teams to optimize the behavior of the organization as a whole. This can be contrasted with the hierarchical command-and-control organization, in which detailed operating instructions are passed down from the center and detailed feedback is sent back to the center.

Tightly coupled organizations can be more integrated. Tight coupling can produce high leverage and economies of scale but may do so at the expense of adapting less well to local needs, inhibiting the spread of team learning, and failing to develop the creativity and energy of employees.

An enterprise may organize with type A teams (who do the basic work), each deciding with creative enthusiasm how best to change in response to its environment, as well as with type B teams (who systematize what is done by type A workers), whose members interact closely in order to maximize systematic learning from the diverse experiences of the type A groups. The type B groups are tightly coupled with the type A groups in order to create infrastructural order within the enterprise. The type C workers (high management concerned with direction setting and strategy) are loosely interconnected so as to maximize their individual creativity; yet, as a group, they are tightly coupled with the enterprise as a whole. (Exhibit 30.2, in the next chapter, describes these types of employees in more detail).

The nature of this set of work-group couplings ought to drive the architecture of the technological infrastructure of the organization. There must be *both* tightly coupled centralized systems and databases, and loosely coupled decentralized systems and databases. Underlying the entire technological structure must be an architecture that allows diversity yet facilitates interconnection across the enterprise's systems and teams.

New corporations can build the new types of human-technological structure as they grow. Older corporations have to make a transition from the old models to the new. It is usually more difficult to transform an old organization than to build a new one.

Summary

The old-world enterprise is hierarchical, with many layers of management. The new-world enterprise has self-managing teams and little need for middle management. The old-world is organized as functional fiefdoms, the new-world as value streams (Exhibit 29.6). The new-world enterprise needs new-world IT, with enterprisewide networks, distributed computing, and nimble, easy-to-change systems rather than difficult-to-change mainframes. The new-world corporation is a cybernetic corporation.

Within this boundaryless framework, data is accessible to all employees. All are challenged to excel, experiment, solve problems, learn continuously, and

Exhibit 29.6

Old World: Hierarchy and Stovepipes

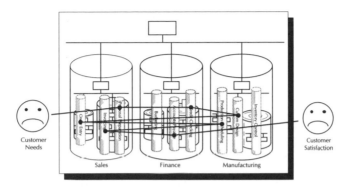

New World: Value Streams

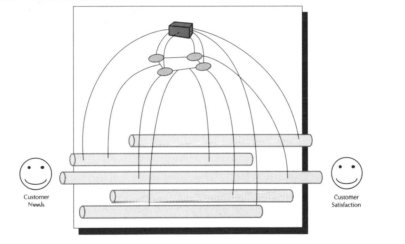

broaden their skills. Virtuosos are encouraged and empowered. The entire enterprise is designed to learn and climb learning curves as fast as possible.

Only part of the contributions are made by full-time employees. Some employees are part-time or hired when needed. Careful thought is given to what work should be out-sourced to external contractors, service organizations, or suppliers. The term *virtual enterprise* is used to mean that people scattered in different corporations, or individuals who provide services, are linked so that they work together as in one enterprise. A virtual enterprise can be tightly knit with computer networks but scattered to the winds geographically and organizationally.

The new-world enterprise has computerized links to customers, suppliers, retailers, distributors, and trading partners. The relationships among enterprises are reinvented to take advantage of computer-to-computer links and just-in-time techniques, and to facilitate the joint climbing of learning curves.

In the new-world corporation almost every aspect of corporate life is different from that in the old-world—compensation, motivation, education, unions, measurements, rewards, appraisal, and overall culture.

References

1. Donald Kircher, President of Singer Sewing Machine Corporation, quoted in *Management Today,* June 1966.
2. C. Northcote Parkinson, *Parkinson's Law* (Ballantine Books: New York, 1957).
3. Ibid.
4. "The Horizontal Corporation," *Business Week,* December 20, 1993.
5. Ibid.
6. Ernest W. Deavenport, Jr., quoted in "The Horizontal Corporation."
7. Peter Schwartz, *The Art of the Long View* (Doubleday Currency: New York, 1991).
8. Howard Gardener, *Frames of Mind: The Theory of Multiple Intelligences* (Basic Books: New York, 1983).
9. Marvin Minsky, *Society of Mind* (Touchstone: New York, 1985).
10. Ibid.

30

The Many Facets of Enterprise Learning

A learning enterprise is one skilled at acquiring, creating, storing, and transferring knowledge, and using it to change the way work is done.

We have emphasized the view of Arie de Geus, Shell's former coordinator of group planning, that the only *sustainable* competitive advantage is the ability to team faster than one's competition.[1] This seems particularly true when we ask how a country with high wages can compete with an aggressively evolving country with low wages.

An enterprise can learn in many different ways. Some publications describe one form of enterprise learning and ignore the others. Top management today should be building an enterprise that learns in every way, not just one, and records the results of its learning. Planners at all levels should plan for multiple types of learning. An enterprise can be *taught to learn* in multiple ways. Those corporations that prosper into the twenty-first century will be learning-efficient organizations. All of today's corporations should seek to accelerate their rate of learning.

The enterprise that knows how to learn better than its competitors has a significant edge. The learning in a large enterprise is continuous, largely unseen, and unfortunately largely underutilized. Sales and service people are always learning—customers are constantly communicating about products and how the enterprise satisfies their needs—but this information may not reach the product designers. Engineers too encounter interesting things in their work that may not be channeled into helping the organization. And management also learns to solve problems but may continue to correct the same problem over and over without reflecting on and addressing its source.

An organization must "learn how to learn." The clusters in an enterprise need tools and skills as leverage for the various types of learning appropriate to their mission. Learning must be *systematic* throughout the enterprise of the future.

Types of Enterprise Learning

An enterprise should learn in multiple ways and record the results of its learning.

Kaizen

A culture of *kaizen,* in which everybody improves everything all the time—TQM (total quality management) and CPI (continuous-process improvement)—should pervade the enterprise, employing techniques such as the following:

- Quantitative analysis of problems
- In-depth analysis of the causes of problems
- Statistical quality control
- Systematic suggestion schemes
- Awards for suggestions and improvements
- *Kaizen* targets for managers, foremen, and supervisors
- Focus on delighting the customer
- Quality circles
- Self-motivated teams
- Top management driving *kaizen* culture

Learning by Reinvention

Value-stream reinvention is a dramatic form of learning. An outdated, clumsy set of processes is replaced with one thought out from scratch. In this learning experience many new ideas are explored. A diversity of work processes link together to form the new value stream, and contributions from many areas help to design the new value stream. The challenge of quantum-leap reinvention puts the learning processes into high gear for a time. When the new value-stream teams go to work, they should be trained to search for constant improvements with the techniques of *kaizen*-style learning.

Learning Teams

Much learning takes place in teams. Teams, either permanent or convened for a short-term purpose, should be deliberately designed for this purpose. They can be at any level—type A (at the workplace), type B (designing the infrastructure), type C (top management), or type D (external). (See Exhibit 30.1.)

Team members learn from each other and stimulate each other. They have different sets of knowledge. They are often people who need one another in order to act so that the sum is greater than the parts. No one individual embodies all the learning of the team as a whole. Members should consciously employ both debate and dialogue.[2] In debate different arguments are presented and defended in an attempt to choose the best. In dialogue explanations and exploration of ideas involve deep listening and suspension of individual views so one can learn from others.

Team Problem Solving

Learning often occurs rapidly when there are urgent and tough problems to be solved. High-performance team members tend to come together when jointly confronted with tough problems. Teams may be deliberately assembled to learn how to deal with tough problems. In some cases this has dramatically changed corporate processes. Value-stream teams have explicit goals that they are determined to achieve. With such clear goals and motivation, the learning process can be actively managed for maximum effectiveness.

Simulation and Prototypes

When a complex process is to be performed, it makes sense to simulate it in order to train the participants. In a new factory with fundamentally new methods, for example, factory workers may be trained with simulated operations before they work on the factory floor. Simulations range from the use of Lego blocks to elaborate computerized models. When preparing to make a reinvented value stream operational, a value-stream "laboratory" should be set up so that team members can learn their new roles and at the same time help to "debug" the processes. Prototypes of the future computer systems can often be created quickly. The laboratory simulations and prototypes can elicit substantial modifications to the processes.

The laboratory should be an ongoing resource for training new recruits and trying out new ideas.

Experimentation

Most people love to experiment, try out new ideas, and discover different ways of doing things. Experimentation should be encouraged at all levels so as to explore ways of improving the work processes. Experimentation is often part of team learning. Techniques for efficient design of experiments should be taught. A means for transferring successful experiments into formal operating procedures is needed.

Some value streams should be operated as a laboratory, with the encouragement of continuous experimentation and research to acquire new learning. In some cases the entire corporation is run as a learning laboratory, as described in the next chapter.

Customer Observation

Customers often find difficulties with a new product or can suggest changes in it. Often the only way to learn what improvements are needed is to observe the customer in action. Milliken uses "first-delivery teams" to accompany the first shipment of all products.[3] The team follows the product through the customer's processes, records any difficulties, observes how the product is used, and develops ideas for improving the product. Some companies employ "usability labs" to videotape users learning to use the product and recording their difficulties and "human-factor" problems. Customer difficulties often surprise the designers of the product, and many iterations of improvement are possible.

Benchmarking

Benchmarking involves systematic study of processes in other corporations to identify which corporations are doing a process in a better way or are achieving better results. Where possible, a process of systematic comparison should measure the results achieved. There is usually a large difference between the best and the average in an industry. Benchmarking should be an ongoing investigation to uncover analyze, adopt, improve, and implement the best practices. ("Benchmarking" is often too narrowly defined.)

Facilitated Workshops

Workshops with diverse participants are conducted under the guidance of a "facilitator" to achieve specified results, such as redesigning a work process, creating specifications for a system, and validating enterprise models. Facilitated workshops can be powerful collective-learning experiences that generate many new ideas, solve communication problems, and engender excitement about new directions.

Workout Sessions

The term *workout session* was used in GE for thousands of facilitated workshops to designate the following:

- A psychological "workout" with management
- Collective "working out" of how to improve processes
- Taking the work out of processes

These exercises in collective learning have resulted in many major changes in how enterprises function.

Quality Circles

An employee can convene a *quality circle* to deal with a problem or something that could be improved. The circle is an appropriate chosen group of people who, collectively, are likely to find a solution. The circle has meetings until they correct the problem. In some organizations any employee can convene a quality circle and can ask for any person he wants to be involved.

Brainstorming

Brainstorming may be a component of workshops, in which for a period everyone is encouraged to voice wild ideas without criticism and then to refine the ideas if possible into something workable. Various scenarios may be used to encourage the voicing of new ideas.

Enterprise Modeling

Models of the enterprise are created in a computer and steadily refined. The models may reflect the work flow, policies, and rules for running the business. They permit the simulation of alternative work flows, rules, and procedures. Management or designers can experiment with the models and use them to learn more about how the enterprise functions. The models are used for business process redesign and for fundamental reengineering. The models represent a growing body of know-how about how the enterprise should function.

Demonstration Projects

Demonstration projects are sometimes established for clean-sheet or discontinuous changes. They range from relatively inexpensive demonstrations such as the introduction of a self-managing team, to massive demonstrations such as a new type of factory. For General Motors the Saturn car plan was a multibillion-dollar demonstration of what it took to build cars in a fundamentally different way—a massively expensive learning experience.

Demonstration projects are usually the first to adopt principles and approaches that the corporation hopes to adopt later on a larger scale. They invoke much learning by doing. Mistakes, backtracking, and evolution of ideas are expected on demonstration projects. Such projects must be designed so that experimentation and learning are substantial and the knowledge acquired is recorded so that it is transferable. There must be explicit strategies for benefiting from the learning experience. A goal should be to progress from empirical design and superficial knowledge to precise guidelines for design and deep understanding of cause-and-effect relationships.

Study of Successes and Failures

Failure can be a great teacher. It is desirable to analyze the reasons for failure in detail and record them in such a way that they can be applied to future projects. Similarly, success stories should be examined and an analysis of the reasons for success disseminated. Too often failures are hushed up rather than milked for the insight and understanding that they can provide. Enough time needs to be available to study and record the experience from successes and failures. Many organizations waste this valuable source of learning.

Scenario Exploration

A useful technique to assist top management visioning is to create a variety of possible future scenarios. Management then works out what it would do if such scenarios become reality. Shell was much better prepared than the other oil companies for the OPEC crisis of the 1970s because it had used this technique and had thoroughly explored what it would do if such a situation occurred.[4] Scenario exploration helps a corporation to avoid being caught by surprise. It learns ahead of time what actions may be needed if its market or external forces change, or if crises occur. It may then make preparatory plans and establish readiness in its management.

When South Africa moved toward constitutional change in the early 1990s, various large South African corporations mapped the possible scenarios for the decade and explored their options under these scenarios.

Counterintuitive Learning

Intuitive human learning takes place where cause and effect are close so that human beings can associate them. However, enterprises conduct activities in which cause and effect are separated in complex ways. Because of this, enterprises engage in systemic behavior that can be counterintuitive. Managers often blame problems on external factors when in reality the system itself is causing the problem. Unless management learns to understand the systemic behavior, it may repeatedly take action that causes problems. Computer systems can be built that help managers understand systemic behavior, and systems can often be reengineered to lessen the problems associated with systemic behavior.

When complex systems behave in counterintuitive ways, it is necessary to lessen the counterintuitive behavior where possible and to educate management's intuition.

Cross-Communication of Learning

When a group in one location learns and hence improves its work processes, the improvements need to be transmitted to groups in other locations that can benefit from them. Putting deliberate procedures into place and managing them achieves this cross-communication of learning.

The cross-communication can employ recorded knowledge—checklists, guidelines, operating procedures, and so on—recorded in a computer in such a way that they can be constantly refined and used by others. Cross-communication needs meetings and conferences to share and discuss experience.

Conferences to Exchange Experience

When people discuss their experiences at conferences, they learn from each other informally. Conferences should bring together groups doing similar work. Groups doing dissimilar work can often gain creative insight from listening to one another's experiences and examining one another's methods. Certain employees should participate in industrywide conferences to learn from the experience of others.

Industry Seminars

Much can be learned at external seminars. Some of the better industry "gurus" have much to communicate. This source of knowledge should be tapped and disseminated through the enterprise. Some experts conduct internal seminars that help an enterprise to learn and change.

Computerized Representation of Procedures

Operating procedures and methodologies should be represented in computers in such a way that they can continually evolve and be improved to reflect continuous learning. Details of problems and how to avoid them should be recorded.

Expert Systems

Expert systems can be built to capture specialized knowledge and make it available to other people. The knowledge in expert systems should be added to continuously as more is learned. Expert systems use rules and facts with logical inferencing techniques to derive conclusions and hence guide their users. Some expert systems contain the knowledge of several people, which enables them to solve problems too difficult for any one person.

The best expert systems have become a valuable resource enabling employees to use expertise culled from others effectively. The best expert systems, like other powerful tools, have the effect of making a person who is already skilled more so. In some cases they have greatly improved the productivity or results of top professionals.

Repository-Based Systems

A growing collection of objects stored in the repository allows systems to be built and changed quickly, capturing the learning of many IT professionals. Repository-based tools permit the building of information systems from templates, models, objects, and designs that already exist. The collection of such knowledge in repositories grows continuously and allows computer-based systems to be built better and faster. The knowledge in the repository is continuously refined and replaced as more is learned.

Kaizen-Capable IT

Computer systems in many enterprises are a straightjacket that prevents rapid change of procedures. Modern tools enable us to build computer applications that can be rapidly and constantly changed and improved. The continuous learning processes of *kaizen* can then apply to computer systems. Ideally, all future information technology should be *kaizen*-capable and that this should pervade the culture of the IT organization.

A Knowledge Infrastructure

Computers can act as accumulators of information or knowledge. Information systems can accumulate much of the learning of an enterprise, making it available at any location or time. The collected information may be in the form of corporate models, designs, or objects stored in a repository; expert systems; database text-retrieval systems; hyperdocuments; spreadsheets; and so on. An infrastructure is needed to accumulate the learning of an enterprise, store it, refine it, and make it available where it is useful.

An enterprise should learn both from external sources, such as industry seminars and authorities, and from its own internal experiences. It should record the insight it obtains from learning so that this insight can be disseminated and put to use.

A learning-efficient corporation constantly seeks new ideas in its products, its processes, and its management. It tries out new ideas and reflects on the outcome, determining how they might be improved. As new insights are gained from this process, it records the knowledge and disseminates it. The enterprise should incorporate the new learning into its day-to-day practices. A learning-efficient corporation does this extensively with a short cycle time.

Four Types of Learning

Learning is acquired by both individuals and clusters of employees, who can be work groups, teams, virtual teams that are geographically scattered but linked by electronics, loose networks of people, task forces, or autonomous business units.

Corporations have four types of clusters or individuals, shown in Exhibit 30.1. The four types learn in different ways, as illustrated in Exhibit 30.2. Enterprise Engineering needs to provide methods, tools, and practical help to grow and support these four learning clusters and agents.

These four types of learning agents are increasingly linked to webs of technology. The fundamental nature of work is changing from a loose relationship between people and machines to a close relationship in which it is becoming increasingly difficult to determine who does the work, people or machines. The new paradigm for work can be thought of as an "empowering human-

Exhibit 30.1 Four types of clusters

Type		*Examples*
A	***Employees who do the basic work***—They make things, repair things, interact with customers, and provide basic services. They interact directly with the environment of the enterprise.	▪ Value-stream teams ▪ Combined sales and service teams ▪ Concurrent product-engineering teams ▪ Task forces ▪ Quality circle groups in TQM
B	***Employees who systematize and monitor***—what is done by type A employees. They do finance and human-resource functions. They create information systems and the infrastructure of the enterprise, and make it work.	▪ Joint IT and user system-development groups ▪ Finance, accountants ▪ Human-resource cluster ▪ System-reengineering team ▪ Training cluster
C	***High-level management and staff***—They are concerned with the overall direction setting of the enterprise. They plot the course of the enterprise and plan its overall architecture.	▪ The CEO team ▪ Corporate-architecture teams ▪ Strategic task forces ▪ Planning groups
D	***People who are separate from the enterprise***—provide an external view and help the enterprise to grow beyond its current paradigms where necessary. They include external consultants, board members, auditors, and customer focus groups.	▪ Boards ▪ Consultants ▪ Auditors ▪ Customer focus groups

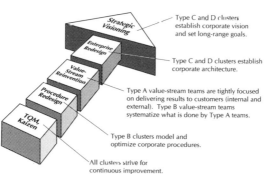

Exhibit 30.2   Learning in the four types of clusters

Type A—Employees who do the basic work

Employees who interact directly with customers, or with the work processes, do most of the dynamic learning within the organization. Type A workers should experiment with work processes continually. They learn how to make the work processes better, how to eliminate problems, how to improve products, and (particularly important) how to please the customer.

Primary Learning Processes

- Direct learning from customers
- Direct learning from work process
- Problem solving
- Experimentation
- Focus on effectiveness and efficiency of work

Type B—Employees who systematize what is done by type A employees

Type B employees learn at a more conceptual level. They record and systematize the learning done by type A employees and produce new leverage for the enterprise's learning: They build systems, create training, create alliances, etcetera. The creation of a powerful enterprisewide knowledge infrastructure should be a primary task of type B employees, who are the primary creators of architecture, shared information, and other integrating and order-bringing features of an enterprise.

Primary Learning Processes

- Learning from A-type experiences
- Focus on infrastructure
- Focus on information needs or IT
- Models of work flow, processes and date
- Design of experiments. Organized learning from A-type experiments
- Focus on effectiveness and efficiency of the overall enterprise

Type C—Top-level employees concerned with the overall direction setting of the enterprise

High-level management and staff learn about the enterprise as a whole, its markets, competition, environment, architecture, overall processes, and strategic vision. Type C employees are mainly oriented toward the future and directing the enterprise toward learning in anticipation of the demands of that future.

Primary Learning Processes

- Focus on current and future environment
- Focus on enterprise architectural issues and problems
- Focus on overall enterprise direction setting
- Focus on overall enterprise learning performance
- Strategic visioning
- Scenario planning
- Technology impact analysis

(continued)

Exhibit 30.2 *continued*

Type D—People separate from the enterprise who provide an external view

People separate from the enterprise can critique its learning and help move it through new stages of growth beyond its current paradigms. This class of persons includes external consultants, board members, auditors, and customer focus groups. It may also include internal "wild ducks" consciously empowered by type C employees to balance their inherent learning barriers.

Primary Learning Processes

- Focus on current and future environment
- Learning from other enterprises
- Organized interchange in consulting companies
- Focus on effectiveness or problems of the overall enterprise
- Scenario planning
- Critique of the strategy

technological partnership" rather than as human productivity enhanced by technology. In other words, we cannot look at a model for human organizations unless we integrate technology into the model. This is rarely done today—there is a profound gap between organizational and technological models in most organizations, and between business managers and IT professionals. The practitioners of TQM, for instance, usually do not discuss software; they focus on improving human processes without regard for IT capabilities that should be integral to these processes.

Different people tend to learn in different ways. Some managers rely on "street smarts"—their learning based on experience and hard knocks. Their view of learning may be shaded toward opportunism and learning on the fly. Others learn analytically by collecting and studying facts, numerically analyzing possible causes of problems, building models of reality. Others stress literary research, the searching for ideas, brainstorming, and innovation. Still others emphasize experimentation and R & D. All these and other models of learning are essential ingredients of the learning enterprise.

Paradox: Empowerment vs. Cohesion

The modern organization faces a paradox. On the one hand, it needs to *empower* and energize individuals, giving them freedom to act, participate in inventing their own work processes, and constantly improve these processes. We should stimulate and harness their creativity, originality, and on-the-job capability to solve problems. On the other hand, we need the leverage that comes from cohesion, discipline, globalization, tight control, economies of scale, and enterprisewide integration. We need farsighted plans. As in society, freedom is made possible by discipline, planning, and infrastructure.

To tackle this paradox, all four types of learning must take place. Type A employees learn to improve their own work processes or meet the needs of customers better. Type B employees learn how to improve the infrastructure and spread the knowledge of type A employees through the enterprise. Type C employees think about needed structural changes and learn to respond to the corporation's changing environment. Type D people apply learning gathered on the outside to help guide the corporation.

Value-Stream Learning

The new or reengineered corporation should be thought of in terms of its value streams. A particularly effective unit for learning is the value-stream team, which (if designed as described in Part II) has clear goals and high motivation. Each team should be continuously learning how to achieve its goals better, and the results of this learning should be communicated to other teams of the same type. Experiments are performed in the search for improvement. Low-cost experiments are done by one team; high-cost experiments may involve several.

A value stream, reinvented from end to end, with new work teams should have electronics which does the following:

- Processes material automatically where possible
- Provides the team with the right information at the right time
- Guides the team doing the work
- Helps enforce accuracy and consistency
- Facilitates constant improvement of the work process
- Facilitates experimentation
- Stores and disseminates knowledge learned about improving the work process

Joint Learning with Trading Partners

A particularly important type of learning that happens rarely in some corporations is *joint* learning with suppliers, customers, agents, or other trading partners.

As a manufacturer strives to improve its manufacturing process, it needs better-quality components from its suppliers and often components that are fundamentally redesigned so that the assembly process can be more automated. The manufacturer and the supplier both learn how to improve their processes. They can help each other, so it makes sense to climb a joint learning curve. This may need very close cooperation.

A corporation should be constantly trying to delight its customers. It may need to find out, in detail, how customers use its products and then to work with the customers to improve the customers' processes, perhaps making major product improvements to achieve this. Joint learning requires a redesign of business relationships.

Maximizing Experiential Learning

Much effective learning comes *from experience*. People reflect on their experience and learn from it. The efficient learner experiments and broadens his experience. *Teams* can sometimes learn better than individuals because the team consists of people with different talents who discuss their collective experience from different points of view. Exhibit 30.3 illustrates experience-based corporate learning.

> Boeing top management established a high-level employee team to study the development processes of the Boeing 707, 727, 737, and 747 aircraft. Boeing had many more difficulties with the 737 and 747 than with the profitable 707 and 727 programs. The study, called Project Homework, established many "lessons learned" and produced hundreds of recommendations for future projects. Several members of the team were transferred to Boeing's 757 and 767 projects. This carefully managed learning from experience resulted in making the 757 and 767 the most successful, error-free aircraft launched in Boeing's history.[5]

An enterprise has certain beliefs that influence behavior. The vision and mission translate into action; new ideas produce action; groups of employees reflect on the outcomes of their action; and reflection leads to certain insights or expanded expertise. If one group learns and improves its procedures, the learning should be documented so that others can benefit from it. The results of the learning ought to be disseminated to other groups in the enterprise. The documentation and dissemination of new insights require work and usually do not happen without a deliberate management effort.

The reflection process is critical to learning. A group needs to examine its

Exhibit 30.3

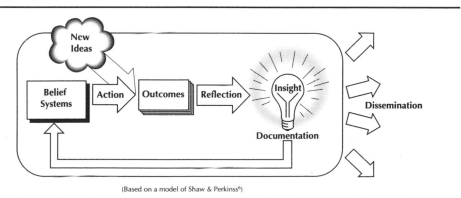

(Based on a model of Shaw & Perkinss[6])

Based on a model of Robert Shaw and Dennis Perkins[6]

experiences, discuss why things happened as they did, and determine how to make improvements. Dissemination of what has been learned helps the reflection process. It brings different perspectives into play in examining the experience. If a group has to disseminate what it has learned, it is forced to think clearly about it and articulate it well. The group gains new information and insight from others, which help it to interpret the experience.

Robert Shaw and Dennis Perkins use a model of enterprise learning like the diagram in Exhibit 30.3. They observe the following:

> Learning is most likely to occur when individuals and groups effectively reflect on and interpret the outcomes of their actions, individuals and groups disseminate new learning throughout an organization, and individuals and groups act on their beliefs and leverage new learning (their own and others) to produce the greatest benefit to their organization.[6]

Barriers to Experiential Learning

Experiential learning is deficient when the components of learning are performed inadequately. Exhibit 30.4 highlights barriers to such learning:

- Insufficient innovation
- Insufficient capacity to act
- Insufficient capacity to reflect

Exhibit 30.4   Barriers to organizational learning

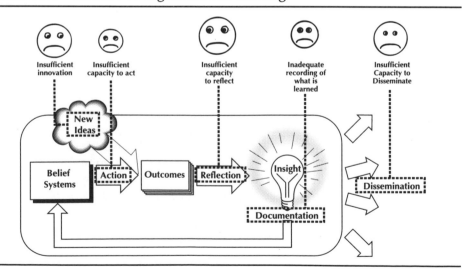

Based on a model of Robert Shaw and Dennis Perkins[6]

- Inadequate recording of what is learned
- Insufficient capacity to disseminate

Insufficient Innovation

A person who learns to be a good photographer constantly experiments—searching for different camera angles, trying new lighting; shooting into the sun to see whether that works; using different lenses, film, portrait settings; experimenting with short depth of focus and very fast shutter speeds. Corporate learning also requires the urge to learn by innovation. Most organizations have many—sometimes subtle—disincentives to experimenting.

Insufficient Capacity to Act

To discover whether innovations work well, one must test them. There are various disincentives to such action, including unwillingness to take risks and fear of failure. Some innovations are bound to fail, but a good but unsuccessful attempt to do something new ought to be applauded, not punished. Many employees are averse to taking risks and uncomfortable with new approaches. Management may be complacent and may ignore problems caused by using traditional methods. Unless management encourages employees to act upon new ideas, learning will be limited.

Sometimes the work pressures are too great to allow for trying out new methods even though they would help. A well-known cartoon shows a machine-gun salesmen approaching a general whose army is fighting only with spears. The general says: "Don't bother me. Can't you see we are in the middle of fighting a war!"

Insufficient Capacity to Reflect

Experiential learning comes from reflecting about the outcome of the approaches tried. Learning is inhibited if there is insufficient reflection. Sometimes the reflection has too narrow a focus. A nineteenth-century artist would have difficulty reflecting about modern art. A manager who controls everything with spreadsheets has difficulty reflecting about things that cannot be put onto one.

Often reflection is limited because employees feel that they must criticize. Even if encouraged to do so, they are aware of certain sacred cows that they dare not challenge. Reflection is frequently biased toward the bible of current practice so may be done better by objective outsiders, who bring different perspectives and do not have to avoid current taboos. Employees can be prisoners of what they understand the best.

Work pressures may seem too great to allow time for reflection. There is frenzied action; everybody keeps busy. Corporate activities may be nonstop, with employees working late into the night, but no learning. Action can be a substitute for thought. Reflection requires a lack of action for certain periods.

Inadequate Recording of What Is Learned

Insights gained should be recorded, or they will be lost. There is often no budget or no time for doing this. Sometimes nobody in the group has the talent or inclination to record the insight. It may be difficult to document; it cannot be done by filling in forms. If the literacy needed to record insight is absent in working groups, an external facilitator may record it. Recording insight may be a type-B task, rather than type-A.

Insufficient Capacity to Disseminate

When one group learns and improves its work process, the learning should be transmitted to other groups in the enterprise. If this dissemination does not occur, much of the potential value of the learning is lost. The dissemination does not occur without deliberate planning.

Sometimes a group does not want to transmit its learning to other groups because it feels competitive with them. Each group may want to be the best and hence may not want to help advance its perceived internal competitor. Often there is a parochial attitude with groups feeling that they can learn nothing from one another. Often each feels that it is "unique." A higher level of management must foster the dissemination.

Groups may not want to discuss their failures. Hoping to increase their own reputation, they may distort the facts for this purpose.

The dissemination process should improve the ability to derive insight from a group's experiences. Effective learners spend time at off-site sessions, comparing notes and going to conferences. Time is spent putting together training programs to disseminate learning. Case studies are written up and presented throughout the enterprise.

Real leverage comes from applying across the enterprise what has been learned. Enterprises need to motivate people to use what others have learned and overcome antipathy toward things "not-invented-here." There should be rewards associated with disseminating know-how, writing up case studies, making presentations. There should be rewards for applying the insights of others. Too often rewards only go to those who create new ideas; they should also go to those who put new ideas to use. Exhibit 30.5 lists the potential causes of barriers to experiential learning.

Exhibit 30.5   Causes of the learning barriers

Barrier to Learning (See Exhibit 30.4)	*Potential Causes*
Insufficient innovation	Taking of risks discouraged
	No time to experiment
	Attitude of "Things have always been done this way."
	Mistakes punished
	Arrogance ("We know what is best.")
	Standard operating procedures regarded as a bible
Insufficient capacity to act	Employees powerless to try new things
	Individuals or teams overcontrolled, "wild ducks" discouraged
	Stress caused by too many priorities
	Unclear objectives
	Inadequate funding
	Poor implementation of new ideas
	Excessive delays
	A blind eye turned to problems
	Complacency
	Discomfort with new approaches
	Incremental improvements permitted but not fundamental redesign
Insufficient capacity to reflect	Time not taken to examine results
	Employees' feeling that they cannot criticize
	Problems denied
	Successes of the past preclude valid reflection on new approaches
	Reflection biased toward the "bible" of current practices
	Incorrect analysis
	Incomplete analyses
	Short-term pressures limiting adequate reflection
	Inadequate set of knowledge brought to focus on the outcomes
	Frenzied action, no reflection
	Excessive performance demands
	Focus only on what can be measured
	Decision makers dependent on spreadsheets ("If it's not in the spreadsheet it doesn't exist.")

(continued)

Exhibit 30.5 *continued*

Barrier to Learning	Potential Causes
Insufficient capacity to reflect (*continued*)	No discussion with people outside the group
	Employees locked into what they understand the best
	Absence of learning forums
	Interpretations blocked if at odds with current philosophy
	Core assumptions unchallenged
	Cause and effect not linked in obvious ways
	Embarrassing conclusions avoided
Inadequate recording of what is learned	No budget for recording insight
	No management directive to record insight
	No talent for recording insight
	No established mechanism
Inadequate capacity to disseminate	No budget for dissemination
	No management directive to disseminate
	No communication between groups
	Parochial attitude
	Competitive attitude
	Uncooperativeness ("We want to be the best. Why should we help competing departments to be the best?")
	Failure of higher management to appreciate the need for, and value of, dissemination of insight
	Reluctance of the group to discuss its failures
	Strong intergroup boundaries
	Internal rivalries and politics
	Distortion of facts to increase group funding
	The myth of uniqueness ("We are different from them.")
	Geographic distances too large

When Learning from Experience Is a Delusion

Learning from experience is clear and understandable. We all do it; it is part of nature. We learn from the consequences of our actions, whether we are learning to ride a bicycle, conduct a meeting, operate a lathe, or manage a team. We can discuss barriers to experiential learning with a diagram such as Exhibit 30.4.

A more dangerous learning disability occurs when learning from experience breaks down, as when we cannot see the consequences of our actions. Many executives make important decisions for which they cannot directly experience the consequences. The results of the decision occur in a distant place or after a long delay.

Experiential learning requires feedback of results to the person learning. The feedback loop may be faulty for the following reasons:

- The delay is too great to allow feedback.
- The consequence is too distant to be visible.
- The cause-and-effect relationship is different from the one expected.
- The decision has unperceived side effects.

Many of the most critical decisions that executives make have consequences years later. Some affect many different areas in the enterprise. Often the most important decisions are those for which there is the least opportunity for trial-and-error learning.

Chapters 20 and 21 examined situations that are counterintuitive, in which learning from experience does not occur. It is vital to recognize such situations and apply corrective action.

Single-Loop and Double-Loop Learning

The learning in a large enterprise goes on continuously, largely unseen and, unfortunately, largely unused. Sales reps are continuously learning—customers are constantly giving feedback about products. Engineers are constantly encountering interesting things in their work that may or may not be put to use in helping the enterprise. Management also learns to solve problems but may continue to correct the immediate problem over and over without addressing its source.

An enterprise needs to learn how to pass on what it learns. It should help individuals to learn well, record what is learned, and disseminate the results of the learning so that the whole enterprise benefits from it.

There are two fundamental types of systematic learning—single-loop and double-loop learning. Single-loop learning is exemplified in the continuous-learning cycle of W. E. Deming, illustrated in Exhibit 30.6. A vision stimulates change and produces results that move an organization toward the desired state. This is experiential learning; it produces effectiveness, quality, "street smarts," and results that move an organization toward the desired vision or end state.

Double-loop learning adds a dimension to the usual learning cycle.[7] It examines the validity of the vision that drives single-loop learning. It observes external reality skeptically (always suspicious that the enterprise's vision may be erroneous), gathers facts, forms new theories, and validates them against the facts. (See Exhibit 30.7.) The result of double-loop learning is sometimes a shift in mental models, which change the fundamental assumptions that drive the organization. Within Enterprise Engineering, strategic visioning and value-stream reinvention employ explicit tools and techniques to stimulate double-loop learning.

Exhibit 30.6

Learning starts with the need to learn—energized by a fresh vision of the future, shared with others—made concrete by performance expectations or benchmarks.

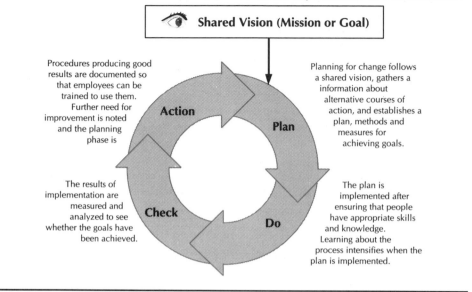

The classical PDCA cycle of W. E. Deming

The Measurement of Learning

It has long been said that if you cannot measure something, you cannot manage it. It is desirable to measure corporate learning, but no measure is comprehensive. Classroom learning can be measured with tests. Competence at certain skills can be measured. Where the objective of learning is to improve a process, various measures of the effectiveness of that process can be made—time to market, percentage of defects, time to respond to customers, productivity cost per unit manufactured, and so on. These measures are sometimes plotted against time on log paper, as shown in Exhibit 30.8.

Curves such as those in Exhibit 30.8 are referred as half-life curves.[8] The performance measure halves (that is, improves) in given time periods and so can be drawn as a straight line on log paper. If the measure (such as time to market or percentage of defects) halves every 12 months, it is said to have a half-life of 12 months. A goal should be to make curves such as those in Exhibit 30.8 as steep as possible, meaning that learning is taking place as fast as possible.

Exhibit 30.7 How can learning be made more effective?

The PDCA cycle (left-hand loop) may be based on a shared vision with an underlying mental model. This vision should be constantly challenged with observation and analysis, and then validated and adjusted (right-hand loop).

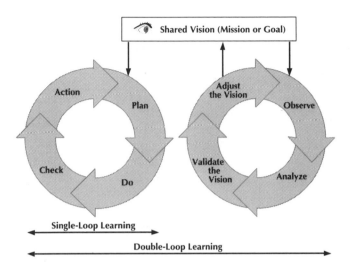

Curves such as those in Exhibit 30.8 measure the results of learning, which takes place in three overlapping stages:

1. *Cognition*—People are exposed to new ideas and begin to think differently.
2. *Behavior*—People start to change their behavior; the new knowledge starts to take effect.
3. *Results*—Performance improves measurably—for example, productivity increases, cycle time declines, defect rates fall, and so on.

Whereas *results* can actually be measured, the first two stages are difficult to measure. *Cognition* can be assessed subjectively, by managers, or in interviews. *Behavior* change can be observed. For example, in the mail-order firm of L. L. Bean, staff members place telephone orders with the firm's own operators to assess service levels.[9] There are various ways to observe employees in action.

Exhibit 30.8 Half-life measures of learning

The measure of performance is plotted on a log scale.

Measure of performance, e.g. time to market or defect rate

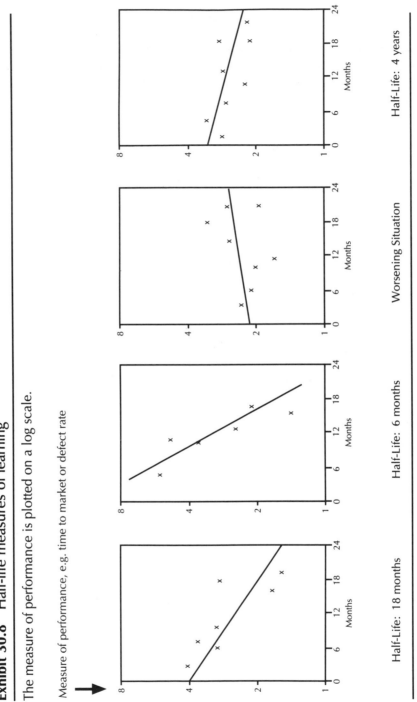

Half-Life: 18 months

Half-Life: 6 months

Worsening Situation

Half-Life: 4 years

Summary

Successful corporations in the future will increasingly be those that learn faster than their competition. Corporations need not only continuous-process improvement but continuous learning—in fact, more than that: *continuous improvement of the ways of learning.*

Managers must understand the many forms of, and barriers to enterprise learning. They must actively manage the learning process and measure it. Learning must improve by design rather than haphazardly. The chief organizational architect must design an enterprise that is skilled at acquiring, creating, storing, and communicating knowledge, and at actively putting it to work.

References

1. Arie de Geus, "Planning as Learning," *Harvard Business Review,* March-April 1988, pp. 70–74.
2. Peter M. Senge, *The Fifth Discipline* (Doubleday Currency: New York, 1990), Chapter 12.
3. David A. Garvin, "Building a Learning Organization," *Harvard Business Review,* July-August, 1993.
4. de Geus, "Planning as Learning."
5. Garvin, "Building a Learning Organization."
6. Robert B. Shaw and Dennis N. T. Perkins, "Teaching Organizations to Learn: The Power of Productive Failures, in David A Nadler et al, *Organizational Architecture* (Jossey-Bass: San Francisco, 1992).
7. Chris Argyris, "Double Loop Learning in Organizations," *Harvard Business Review,* September-October 1977.
8. Garvin (above) gives examples of learning half-life measurements.
9. Ibid.

31

The Corporation as a Learning Laboratory

Many corporations of the future will be run like a laboratory. The purpose of a laboratory is to enable a corporation to have products ahead of its competition. Most laboratories are remote both from the customers and the processes that create products or services. The laboratory research is an isolated function in what ought to be a cross-functional activity. Chapter 13 tells how a newly invented value stream should be operated as a learning laboratory and describes corporations in which an research-and-development attitude pervades the entire corporation. *The entire corporation has become a learning laboratory.*

As was commented earlier, the learning-laboratory corporation is the culmination of the twentieth-century journey from treating employees as mere slaves, who must be made to obey orders, to encouraging every employee to use his intelligence to make new contributions. The century started with Kafkaesque contempt for workers; it ends with the challenge of regarding the entire corporation as a learning laboratory.

The learning-laboratory corporation could not be more different from the hierarchical corporation. Much of what has been learned about running the R & D function applies to the entire enterprise. It encourages and rewards breakthrough thinking whenever this achieves results. A mix of analytical, rational thinking and creative, off-the-beaten-track thinking pervades all of its activities.

A laboratory is an organization dedicated to the creation of new knowledge. It experiments so that it can learn. To add to its pool of knowledge, it should constantly scan the horizon to see what research results are emerging elsewhere. It uses ideas from any source to help achieve its own goals of solving complex problems or improving product designs. It creates, searches for, and integrates knowledge. The goal should be to climb learning curves as fast as possible.

It makes little corporate sense for the laboratory to be an ivory-tower environment, where researchers write papers to impress other researchers but have no contact with the processes that translate research into profits. For development to be as effective as possible, it should be part of a cross-functional activity concerned with changing the products and processes. The experimentation and design that create new ideas should pervade the entire enterprise. How to design effective experiments should be taught throughout the enterprise.

To operate the entire corporation as a learning laboratory requires management practices and values that pervade everything the corporation does.

Chaparral Steel

A spectacular example is Chaparral Steel in Midlothian, Texas. One might think that the steel industry, denigrated as being part of the old "smokestack" world, would be an unlikely place to find a learning-laboratory enterprise. Dorothy Leonard-Barton studied Chaparral Steel and describes the extraordinary benefits that can result from operating a factory as a learning laboratory.[1] She contends that this is the new frontier in manufacturing. In such an enterprise every employee in the factory is challenged to participate in experimentation, the garnering of new ideas, and the improvement of factory processes, tools, parts, and products.

This goes far beyond TQM (total quality management) culture, in which everybody solves problems. A learning-laboratory culture is one in which everybody is helping search for breakthroughs. The goal is to reach far beyond current capability. Breakthroughs often need cross-functional thinking; they are likely to integrate knowledge from across the enterprise.

A learning-laboratory enterprise needs an enterprisewide ecosystem designed to increase the speed of enterprise innovation.

Chaparral Steel was founded in 1975 and from its inception set out to operate as a learning laboratory. Research was done throughout the entire organization instead of in a separate R & D laboratory. Japan and Germany had reputations for being the world's most efficient steel producers. By 1990, however, *Chaparral's productivity was 1.5 worker-hours per rolled ton of steel, whereas the Japanese average was 5.6 and the German average 5.7.*

In addition, Chaparral was recognized for quality. It was the first American company to be awarded the right to use the Japanese Industrial Standard certification on its structural-steel products. It was the only American steel company certified by AIME (American Institute of Mining, Metallurgical, and Petroleum Engineers) for nuclear applications and one of only 2 companies (out of 15) whose steel is certified by the American Builders of Ships.

The difference in productivity between Chaparral and traditional steel companies is so great that one must ask how long old-style steel companies can survive.

If a learning-laboratory corporation makes such a difference in steel, it is likely to make far more difference in corporations whose products or services change rapidly—as with cameras, electronics, training, clothing, entertainment, computers, etcetera. As global competition intensifies, the number of many copy-cat products will increase; the art of innovation will be the key to survival.

Research Cemeteries

Gordon Forward, the appropriately named CEO of Chaparral Steel, describes the large, separate research centers at some companies as being like the Forest Lawn Cemetery: "After you spend some time there, you realize that you are in Forest Lawn. Not because there are no good ideas there, but because the good ideas are dying there all the time."[2]

The legendary Xerox PARC (Palo Alto Research Center) invented the mouse, the dialogue style of the Macintosh computer, local-area networks, Ethernet, object-oriented programming, Smalltalk, client-server systems, and the first conti-nentwide satellite network (XTEN). Any of these could have made a fortune, but Xerox failed to turn any of them into profitable products. IBM's Thomas J. Watson Laboratory at Yorktown has produced an amazing series of breakthroughs (at enormous expense), but they rarely reached customers. Videotape recording was invented and developed in the United States, but today not one videotape ma-chine or camcorder is made here. The United States lost the entire industry first to Japan and then to Japanese subsidiaries in cheap-labor countries. Philips, in Holland, invented optical discs and laser discs for music, data, and video re-cording. As I shop for such products in the United States, I reflect on how much Philips has improved my own quality of life but find the shops full of Japanese, not Philips, products. Over and over again, Western research laboratories have invented things that the Japanese improved and cashed in on.

To help reverse this situation, research and development must not be con-fined to the laboratory; it must pervade the entire corporation. The entire corpora-tion must constantly invent, improve, and record its knowledge, and must imme-diately put its inventions to work. In many corporations there need be no laboratory as such; the whole corporation can be a laboratory. The extent to which the corporation searches for innovations will determine its success only if the innovations are quickly put to use.

Gordon Forward comments, "Every employee is in R & D."

Four Characteristics

A learning-laboratory enterprise needs an ecosystem having the four characteris-tics shown in Exhibit 31.1.[3] These aspects of the enterprise need to be totally integrated into its management practices and underlying values.

A Value-Stream Organization with a *Kaizen* Culture

Although most corporations are far from it today, a value-stream structure (Part II) with a *kaizen* culture (Part III) is likely to become regarded as the bread-and-

Exhibit 31.1   Four characteristics of a learning-laboratory enterprise, which need to be totally integrated

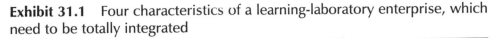
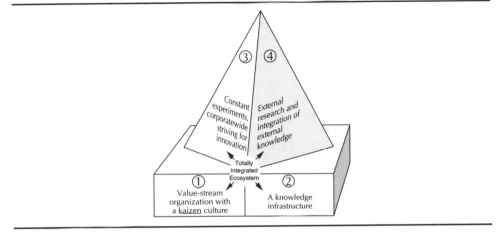

butter necessity for future corporations. On that foundation the other three characteristics of the learning-laboratory enterprise are built.

There must be constant striving to solve problems, make improvements, increase productivity, and generally "raise the bar" of performance. This is best accomplished with value-stream teams focused on delighting their customers and motivated to achieve aggressive goals. The systems and procedures need to be redesigned to support such teams, getting the right information and computer power to the right people at the right time.

A Knowledge Infrastructure

An infrastructure is needed to capture knowledge, improve it, store it, disseminate it, and put it to use. A learning enterprise needs constant education and training. As new knowledge is acquired, anybody may teach it—for example, shop foremen. The knowledge may be built into databases, expert systems, computer-based training, and multimedia computers. Employees with notebook computers may use them for both learning and capturing knowledge.

Knowledge should be freely shared and available to everyone. There should be no "ownership" of ideas and no boundaries that prevent data sharing. The computer network should provide access to databases across the enterprise, with some employees being selected for their skills in coaching and transmitting skills to others.

The knowledge infrastructure, value-stream organization, and *kaizen* culture are the foundation on which the learning-laboratory enterprise is built (Exhibit 31.2).

Exhibit 31.2   Foundations of a learning-laboratory enterprise

(These apply to all modern-style enterprise regardless of parts 3 and 4 of Exhibit 31.1.)

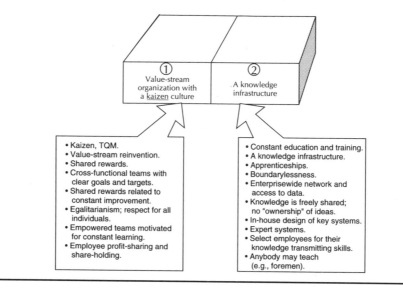

Constant Experimentation—Enterprisewide Striving for Innovation

The learning-laboratory corporation constantly experiments and searches for new ideas. A culture of innovation and experimenting is continuously reaching beyond what is done today. As in an R & D lab, it must be expected that only some new ideas will work out. Failure should not be punished. Risk is always associated with innovation. Management, as in R & D, must strike the right balance between risk and potential reward. To do this, it must be guided by a vision of where the corporation should be going. Innovation should not be random but targeted at certain types of customers, selected goals, core competencies, or strategic value streams of the enterprise.

A corporation that regards itself as a learning laboratory selects employees who are valuable in such an environment. It needs employees who are comfortable challenging the status quo, who look for breakthroughs, and who will participate in teams that make innovation practical.

Some innovation requires rational, analytical skills; some requires creative inspiration. Problems and bottlenecks can be analyzed with disciplined teachable techniques such as the use of fishbone and Pareto diagrams described in Chapter 16. Breakthrough innovation, on the other hand, requires creative minds. Producing totally new ideas is not a rational process. It needs wild, unconventional inspiration.

Most large corporations miss out on uncontrolled unconventional innovation. They encourage and teach analytical thinking, such as that expressed in fishbone diagrams, but do not know how to teach breakthrough, holistic thinking. Many big companies have forgotten how to innovate because, unwittingly or otherwise, they discourage the unconventional thinker who has unusual, even wild, thought processes. The unconventional innovators, if they exist at all, are confined to the research lab.

A learning-laboratory enterprise needs both analytical, rational, fishbone thinkers and wild-duck, imaginative, flash-of-inspiration thinkers. Wild ducks do not fly in teams. Uncontrolled creative people who produce breakthrough ideas are sometimes loners, but sometimes they are excellent members of teams if encouraged to let their wild thoughts flow. The right-brained inventive thinker working alone achieves little. In combination with left-brained analytical thinkers, he can move mountains. As was explained in Chapter 6, team structures that link virtuosos to other workers are invaluable.

In R & D laboratories, several hundred ideas are often generated before one comes to fruition. When the entire corporation becomes a learning laboratory, it should be accepted that many ideas are needed but only the best will be implemented. The corporation having few ideas tends to implement them even if they are not very good. Much effort is often spent on perfecting a new thrust that was a bad idea to begin with. Good R & D executives are skilled at encouraging many ideas and culling the less feasible ones before too much is spent on them.

The culling of ideas must be done by a suitably high level of management. Teams that hatch ideas rarely judge their own ideas objectively. To have an idea terminated does not mean failure. Management should congratulate the person or team that produced it, saying "Now produce some more."

External Research and Integration of External Knowledge

A learning-laboratory corporation should be constantly searching beyond its own walls for ideas and new ways to do things. More valuable ideas are likely to come from outside the corporation than inside it. The search should be systematic and organized.

The term *virtual research organization* is used to refer to a far-flung network of affiliates who provide ideas and information, and who possibly do contract research or out-sourced design. Drug companies and leading-edge high-tech companies in general need their own big-budget R & D laboratories, but most companies can obtain more cost benefit from a virtual research organization than from their own internal laboratories. Employees throughout a learning-laboratory corporation should be scanning the horizon for relevant ideas. It is much less expensive to beg, borrow, or steal new research results than to do the research yourself. In a planned way, employees should be going to conferences and seminars, and visiting other companies. Often there is much to learn from companies not in quite the same business.

The enterprise should *benchmark* the performance of processes in other companies. It should examine in detail competing or noncompeting products from which ideas can be found. The "virtual" research organization may have a collegiate network, organizing visits to universities and monitoring relevant research in universities. Universities are only too eager to talk about their research and to exchange ideas. They are often hoping for research sponsors. The corporation may participate in research done by universities, consulting firms, or other companies, for multiple clients.

An employee who finds ideas or obtains studies from visits or affiliates should be expected to make presentations, create reports, and make videotapes that communicate this information. He should spread the knowledge and educate colleagues. Knowledge from external research is fed into the knowledge infrastructure of the enterprise. The corporation may have a joint arrangement with its customers or suppliers to share results from its network of research sources. Improvement of products, parts, processes, or services often can be accomplished better in conjunction with a supplier or customer than alone.

A virtual R & D organization can tap a much broader range of knowledge sources than an isolated laboratory can. It pays for specific problems to be researched, prototypes to be built and tested, or specific designs to be done externally. This external knowledge and development can enable the enterprise to learn and innovate aggressively.

Exhibit 31.3 summarizes characteristics of internal and external laboratory-

Exhibit 31.3   Aspects of parts 3 and 4 of Exhibit 31.1

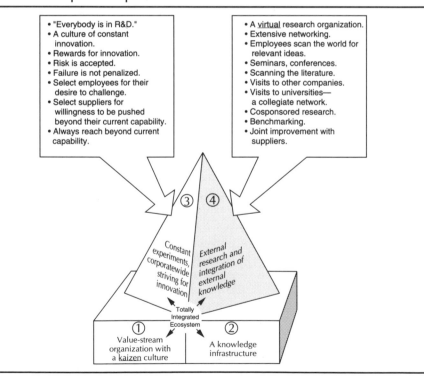

Exhibit 31.4   The four characteristics of the learning-laboratory enterprise that result in a totally integrated ecosystem

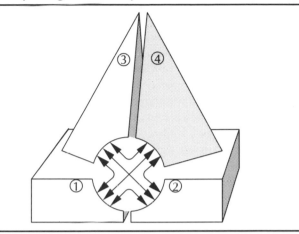

like activities. They work best when built on the foundation illustrated in Exhibit 31.2 and fully integrated (Exhibit 31.4).

Experiments in Steel Making

Chaparral set out to make large structural I-beams for about half the cost of big steel mills. This required a drastic reduction of energy costs and casting steel into a shape closely approximating that of the final product. The more closely the steel could be cast to resemble the final stage, the less expensive rolling would be required. No steel mill had ever cast steel into large I-beams except with a very expensive process.

To achieve this near-net shape, the white-hot steel had to be cast through a copper-alloy mold cooled with high-speed water flow. Vendors thought it impossible to make such a mold. Chaparral wanted to cast the steel horizontally (not vertically as is usual) in almost its final shape so that it could race directly into the rolling mill. Computerized equipment would cut it to the length required for specific customer orders. The steel would pass through the rolling equipment once, stop, reverse, and go through again. This process would demand split-second timing. While the rolling was occurring, the flow of white-hot steel would be diverted. The goal was to divert as little as possible because every second of diversion costs money; the diverted steel would have to be reheated before being rolled.

Endless experimentation went on in Chaparral to increase the efficiency of such processes. The workers joined in the experimentation, constantly remedying problems. Chaparral, unlike most factories, often performed experiments on the production line itself. It wanted the experimental environment to be as similar as possible to the production environment and all production workers to participate in the experiments, learn from them, solve problems, and produce floods of ideas.

In one set of experiments with the near-net-shape casting, the workers had a crazy idea: built prototype splashboards for the molten metal out of plywood. By continuously soaking the plywood with water, they could prevent it from being burnt just long enough to test its function. Many plywood splashboards were built until the shape was perfected. Similarly, the workers experimented with copper molds, as opposed to the more expensive, heat-resistant alloy molds. With the soft copper molds, they could experiment with many variations of shape, although the mold was quickly destroyed by the steel.

As well as experimenting on the actual steel-casting equipment, the employees built a one-sixth scale model that used water to approximate the flow of steel. This model stood alongside the actual steel caster. Employees could compare its operation with that of the actual caster and do many experiments with it quickly, some of which led to improvements in the actual caster. Many such experiments were done by shop-floor employees without authorization from a higher level of management. This gave employees a feeling of "ownership" of the research activities and enabled them to make many innovations in the steel-making process. They had great fun doing it.

Experiments in Software Development

Software development is a field that is evolving very rapidly. Every month there are new tools and methods—code generators, design tools, tools for building the user interface, templates, libraries of Lego-like parts, and so on.

Software-development organizations can be divided into three types.

> *Stagnant Organizations*—The developers continue to write code in the time-honored way, thinking that everything should be written in their favorite language.
>
> *TQM Organizations*—The principles of TQM are used to improve human performance and catch defects as early as possible. ISO 9000 certification may be sought. Major improvements in quality are achieved, but there is little awareness of radical breakthroughs.
>
> *Learning-Laboratory Organizations*—Software is built by small high-performance teams allocated to one project after another. The teams use the most powerful tools with the goal of completing their piece of a project quickly (say, in two to six months). The project work is intense, so a team can spend the less-stressful period between projects looking for better tools, reusable objects, and better methods—and generally consolidating what it has learned. A small control group monitors the teams, ensuring that all teams have their performance measured in consistent ways. The

central group constantly surveys the vendors of tools, templates, objects, and methodologies, examining their new ideas and experimenting with them. Members of this group go to conferences, visit "leading edge" developers, and generally research the field. They introduce new tools and techniques to the development teams. When a team achieves consistently better results than other teams because it has found better tools and techniques, the control group spreads the improved method to other teams. In this way, the whole organization experiments and climbs a learning curve as fast as possible.

General Electric consists of many companies in diverse businesses, all of them striving to improve their information technology applications. A small control group at the GE head office does constant research on development tools and methods. It works with all of the software development groups in the GE corporations to introduce new ideas, tools, and packages, and to ensure that they are relevant. When one team does better than the rest, its methods are studied and, if possible, passed on to the other teams.

Software productivity was measured by the central group in terms of function points per month of developer time. The average IT organization operates at about 5 function points per person a month. GE's best teams achieve 50-to-100 function points per person a month.[4] GE's software reliability metrics shows that its best teams are way ahead of the industry average. In most corporations few projects of a million lines of code are ever completed successfully; GE has completed multiple projects exceeding this size in a relatively short time and has achieved high software reliability. Software maintenance consumes considerable effort in many corporations; one maintenance programmer supports about 500-to-1000 function points. GE pushed this to 7000 function points and aims to drive it higher.

GE succeeded in applying learning-laboratory techniques in a highly disciplined environment.

A Multicorporate Learning Laboratory

A learning-laboratory corporation needs suppliers who can learn also. It should select suppliers who are willing to cooperate in climbing a *joint* learning curve and who are willing to be pushed beyond their current capability. When a corporation invents new tools or equipment, for example, its customers need to change their methodologies. As customers change, they discover new requirements in the tools. Improved tools push the frontier of methodologies; improved methodologies push the frontier of tools. *Joint* learning is needed.

Joint learning demands special relationships and new types of contracts. It is facilitated by teleconferencing, intercorporate computer networks, databases, and new information superhighways. There can be intricate computer-aided joint development between a manufacturer and a supplier or a customer. There can be tightly choreographed interactions in supply chains. The learning-laboratory corporation can be an extended corporation in which partners operate in learning-laboratory mode. The innovation in one corporation may have goals borrowed from the innovation in a customer corporation, or the new ideas of a supplier may initiate learning-laboratory activities in a manufacturer or service company.

A key to Chaparral's goal of casting steel in a shape as close as possible to its final one is a rapidly cooled mold in the form of a tube through which the molten steel passes. The forces on this mold are brutal. It must be made of an alloy that is tough and dissipates heat rapidly. Such a mold has to be specially fabricated. Chaparral identified two mold fabricators who might provide what they needed, one in Italy and one in Germany. The German mold makers were so skeptical of Chaparral's ideas that at first they were unwilling to make molds with such a radical design. They began to overcome their skepticism when they saw how far Chaparral was progressing with their Italian competition.[5]

The hot steel shrinks as it goes through the cooled mold, so the mold is shaped to correspond with the shrinkage. The shape must be just right or the metal will bind. The metal must emerge with a smooth skin, not crinkled by the mold. A mold such as this had never been used before for casting large beams in a shape close to their final one. Much experimentation was needed.

Chaparral employees visited the Italian and German companies frequently, telling them how their experiments were progressing. Sometimes the rate of innovation was so fast that the German mold developers were told not to bother shipping a mold they had built; it already needed redesign. The $37 thousand for the unshipped mold was part of the cost of experimentation.

At Chaparral every employee is in R & D, even machine operators. Nobody understands the practical problems of machinery better than its operators. Operators see everything that goes wrong and try to prevent it. Of the three-person team from Texas that repeatedly visited Germany, trying to perfect the new casting mold, one was an operator.

Eventually the German mold-making expertise combined with constant experiments and improvements in Texas resulted in a new type of mold, which the companies patented. Neither company could have produced it alone. The partnership of factory innovation in both companies gave the result.

Molding the hot steel into its near-net-shape resulted in less rolling of the I-beams. Rolling affects the metallurgical properties of steel, and no one was sure at first whether high-quality beams could be made. Experimentation was needed to learn how to test and adjust the process. Chaparral found a steel-production laboratory in Mexico with equipment sufficiently flexible to do such experiments and simulate future mill design. Chaparral succeeded in producing samples in Mexico with superior metallurgical qualities.

The German and Mexican specialized capabilities acted as a "virtual" research environment for Chaparral.

Risks

There were serious risks in pushing the frontiers of steel making as Chaparral did. The near-net-shape casting might not have worked. Risky experiments such as those at Chaparral would be meticulously avoided in most production environments. However, Chaparral's view was that R & D must take risks. To do so is part of the process of R & D. Without risks no breakthroughs occur. Failures are expected in R & D and are not penalized. Risk has to be accepted and managed.

At Chaparral everyone experiments so everyone may do something that does not work. Individuals are not blamed if their experiment fails; on the contrary, they are commended for trying. If failed experiments were penalized, nobody would experiment.

One mill superintendent championed the installation of an arc saw for curing finished beams. It cost $1.5 million and always had problems. For a year, the employees tried to solve these, but the arc saw never became satisfactory. The superintendent eventually eliminated his own brainchild. He was later promoted to vice-president. Even very expensive failures are regarded as part of the cost of research.

Gordon Forward's view is that *to do nothing* may be a greater risk. If the company does not push the frontiers, its competition will, and the company might lose its market.

Holistic Interplay

A vital characteristic of a learning-laboratory corporation is that it cannot be constructed piecemeal; all the components relate to one another. Just as the parts of our body only make sense in the context of the entire body, so the learning-laboratory corporation needs to be perceived as an organic whole. This whole is in a state of constant flux, continuously and rapidly evolving. The management has to pay constant attention to this integration. The corporation needs holistic systems thinking. A knowledge infrastructure communicates the innovations across the enterprise. There is no "throw-it-over-the-wall-now-it's-his-problem" separation of activities. Computers and networks help choreograph the complex interplay of activities.

Dorothy Leonard-Barton is convinced that Chaparral can only be understood holistically. She concludes that the most important characteristic of a learning-laboratory factory is that it is a totally integrated system. If competitors copy a part of such a system, they achieve little because it is the interrelatedness that makes the system valuable. "When a fragment of the learning laboratory is pulled out to be examined, it comes out trailing roots back to deeply held values and widely observed management practices. It is this interconnectedness that makes such systems difficult to imitate and fragile—but effective."[6] Leaders must be able to see and manage the interconnectedness. They must see not snapshots but how parts of the system interact with one another, constantly changing with time. They must understand not just components but interrelationships. Like appreciating a football game they must understand the holistic interplay of activities, but unlike a football game the activities may be far apart in time and space.

Selecting and Keeping Employees

A learning-laboratory corporation needs to select employees who will be effective in the R & D process. Chaparral's success relates strongly to its selection of employees. Only about one out of ten applicants who are interviewed for jobs at Chaparral are actually hired. The final decision about whether to hire a person belongs to the foreman with direct responsibility.

A learning-laboratory corporation needs employees who can innovate and constantly challenge the way things are done. They must be able to learn and enjoy learning. This does not mean only textbook learning; it means on-the-job learning, learning by doing, learning by talking to people, learning by tinkering and experimenting. Employees must want to contribute. Making contributions must be what makes them happy. Continuous learning depends on selecting employees who are willing to learn. It might be thought that college graduates would be the most capable of learning, but many college graduates want an ivory-tower environment rather than the rough-and-tumble environment of a factory shop floor or the dirt of a fitting shop. The person who learns from books is usually quite different from the person who learns by tinkering. The brilliant hacker who learns at his computer screen is quite different from the manager who learns by asking questions of people. Learning takes many forms and can employ many types of people.

Probably most people could be capable of life-long learning but somewhere along the way lose the ability to learn. Deadly jobs make them afraid to speak up, lacking in confidence, bureaucratic, or suspicious. Just as bad schools can stamp out creativity in children, so most companies stamp it out in employees. If a person stops learning for five years, it is extremely difficult to start learning again. It seems that the learning circuits of the brain can go dead just as a muscle can go dead if not used for several years. In some countries, the civil service hires the best graduates, but by age 35 they are unemployable in an innovative enterprise.

With the exception of a few managers and specialists, Chaparral did not look for employees with experience in the steel industry. It looked for people who could learn new jobs with enthusiasm. It looked for those who were articulate and could communicate well. Spreading the knowledge is as important as creating it. It hired employees who would love the job, be excited about the creativity of Chaparral, and consequently work hard. After hiring, employees went through six weeks of intensive training with daily evaluations, to make sure that they would fit into the unusual corporate culture. Many corporations have a "boot camp" for new employees with a substantial pay increase for those who survive it. Much ongoing training, including external education, is needed in a learning-laboratory corporation.

Trained, indoctrinated employees are valuable, and the corporation should do everything it can to retain them. Innovative people may leave if they see no path for advancement. A flat organization does not have a promotion ladder to climb, so advancement means working on bigger and more interesting projects. Careful attention to each individual is essential to make sure that each person finds his job satisfying.

The pay structure needs to reflect the growth of individuals and reward their learning of greater skills. Chaparral is most unusual among steel companies in that it has salaries, not hourly wages. There are no time clocks. All workers are paid like professionals in a laboratory.

Incentives

Making difficult breakthroughs work is a challenge that has rewards of its own; innovation is exciting. Nevertheless, a learning-laboratory corporation needs to link its demands for innovation to an appropriate reward structure.

At Chaparral Steel, 93 percent of the employees are stockholders. In addition to being allocated shares, 62 percent buy additional shares each month through payroll deductions. Many corporations have profit-sharing schemes for management; in a learning-laboratory enterprise, profit-related bonuses may apply to those at other levels. Sometimes bonuses relate to specific goals, such as completing projects on time, increasing productivity measures, or closing large orders.

Employees should be made proud of their accomplishments. This may be done with reward ceremonies, wall plaques, tie clips, or other forms of recognition. In Texas Instruments at some locations, all employees wear badges for security purposes. The badges have a variety of stars and symbols for accomplishment, almost like displaying medals in the military.

Establishing a Learning-Laboratory Corporation

A conventional corporation does not grow into a learning-laboratory corporation by a process of evolution. Learning-laboratory corporations come into existence only by strong, deliberate, well-thought-out acts of top management.

It seems certain that some learning-laboratory corporations, such as Chaparral, will grow and take their competition by storm. Just as lean-manufacturing plants have caused some mass-production plants to close their doors, so learning-laboratory factories will cause some traditional factories to close. Many start-up corporations will build themselves in a learning-laboratory fashion. As such corporations grow and become better understood, they may wipe out much of their competition. In some industries, the only long-term survivors will be learning-laboratory corporations.

In many corporations, top management works in pristine surroundings designed by expensive architects. At Chaparral the workers' locker room is in the one-story head-office building. Sweaty steel workers interact with high executives. Many ideas originate from meetings in the corridors. There is no executive dining room; everybody lines up and eats in the same cafeteria. All employees can make their views known to top management. To maintain this interchange, Chaparral deliberately held its size to less than a thousand employees. With a thousand people, meetings that unify the entire corporation are possible. (Mahler's Eighth Symphony requires a thousand performers whom the conductor has to unify.) The plant layout is designed to facilitate constant interaction among employees and management.

Top executives who create such corporations need to be consistent in their vision for many years. They must put into place a culture with a strong sense of values that pervades the entire corporation. Management must be seen to be excited by the constant experimentation. It must be apparent that innovation is supported and rewarded. Employees must feel that their job is to make constant improvements, with most of them never even having been discussed in planning meetings. Employees should feel free to discuss ideas openly with managers. Managers should talk to workers anywhere they may be and ask them what they are excited about. The mechanisms must be in place for constant learning, research, and discovery, for the search for knowledge and transfer of knowledge.

There must be continuous management effort in communicating this sense of values and checking the smallest details to ensure that employees' behavior grows to support the learning-laboratory culture. Like creating a spectacular garden, management attention must be constant and thorough, or the weeds take over.

References

1. Dorothy Leonard-Barton, "The Factory as a Learning Laboratory," *Sloan Management Review,* Fall 1992.
2. Interview by A. M. Kantrow (1986), quoted by Leonard-Barton in "The Factory as a Learning Laboratory."
3. These four characteristics are described in Leonard-Barton's excellent paper, above. They have been adjusted here to correlate with the themes of this book.
4. Function points are a measure of the complexity of transaction-processing systems, independent of the tools or programming languages used. Guidelines for calculating function points are kept up to date by IFPUG (the International Function Point Users Group).
5. Figures about GE's software-development productivity are from Don McNamara, GE Head Office, Fairfield, Connecticut. Mr. McNamara was the driving force behind GE's dramatic improvements in application development capability.
6. The Chaparral experience is put under the microscope in Leonard-Barton's paper (reference 1, above).

32

The New Employment Deal

In new-world corporations just about every aspect of employment is different from that in old-world corporations—teams, measurements, management, compensation, education, appraisal, rewards, motivation, unions. Making the transition can cause human chaos if it is done badly. Change agents need skilled HR (human resource) professionals to help them design and implement the human changes. Like IT (information technology) professionals, many HR professionals are not trained in organizational design. They need to work closely with the chief organizational architect and executives who are changing the organizational design.

In the old-world organization many employees lived in hope of promotion. When the hierarchy is largely removed and replaced with a horizontal structure, there is little scope for climbing the corporate ladder.

Perhaps more alarming to employees, the pay scales associated with the corporate ladder are gone. Compensation schemes in a horizontal enterprise are quite different from those in a vertical enterprise.

Employees in traditional corporations often expect pay increases at regular

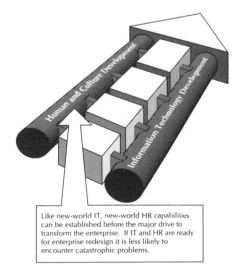

Like new-world IT, new-world HR capabilities can be established before the major drive to transform the enterprise. If IT and HR are ready for enterprise redesign it is less likely to encounter catastrophic problems.

intervals even though the value of their contribution has not increased. In the new-world corporation, employees cannot expect automatically to climb a hierarchy or automatically climb to higher pay levels. Instead pay is related, as far as possible, to the employees' contributions. Employees increase their pay by making themselves more valuable—by increasing their knowledge, capability, or contribution to competitiveness. The Hay Group conducted a survey of trends in payment schemes in the United States and concluded "The age of 'entitlement' to automatic salary increases is over."[1] "Employers and employees alike must understand the new framework for compensation, collaborate on creating good systems of performance measurement, and agree to use pay as a strategic force in moving the organization ahead."[2]

Vanishing Job Security

Old-world corporations looked after their employees and gave them job security. Ironclad job security was appropriate in a static world with routine work. In the new-world, routine work is done by machines, competition is intense, and the employee skills needed are changing fast.

Employees with "tenure," even university professors, tend to retire on the job. A large New York bank guaranteed that anyone with 20 years' experience would never be laid off. An HR executive at the bank commented, "We found that people who came for security would not adopt new ways of doing things."[3] The 1980s ushered in an era, not only of downsizing but of demands for different types of employees. The job mix changed rapidly, and change accelerated in the 1990s.

Many corporations with no-layoff policies tried to reduce their work force by such means as early-retirement programs. Employees were given financial inducements to leave. The problem with this (as stated earlier) is that the good ones tend to take the financial package and leave, while the less able ones, who might have difficulty finding secure employment elsewhere, stay. As corporations such as IBM discovered, early-retirement programs are not only expensive; they filter off the good people.

When a corporation changes a longstanding policy of employment security, employees often feel betrayed and angry. The deal was that they gave employee loyalty in return for job security. After being loyal for many years, they are now told that they can be laid off. Often candidates for layoff are the ones whose skills are not valuable elsewhere. The drones panic.

The New Deal

The new-world corporation says to employees, in effect, "Promotion prospects are low because the old hierarchy has gone. We cannot guarantee regular salary raises. And there is no longer job security; we have to be free to downsize, to lay off people whose skills are no longer wanted, and to trim back when business is bad."

The age of entitlement is over. Employees are no longer entitled to automatic pay increases above the inflation rate, promotion based on seniority, a career path up the hierarchy, and guaranteed job security.

This bad news must be counterbalanced with a new deal that is attractive to employees: "This is an exciting place to work. We will train you to do interesting jobs and coach you to be members of empowered teams. Pay will be related to results, and you can earn high compensation if your contribution is substantial. You will be constantly challenged to find better ways to do this, and we will provide the resources needed for you to pursue that challenge. This is a learning corporation, and we expect you to participate in the learning processes. As you learn more, you will become more valuable."

The new deal says "You own your own employability. You are responsible. If you make yourself valuable, you will be employable, and compensation will relate to your value. We owe you every opportunity to increase your value." The new-world corporation has much better ways to measure value. Instead of sitting in a department doing repetitive tasks, whose value is difficult to ascertain, most employees will be members of value-stream teams that produce measurable results for customers (internal or external). The teams are challenged constantly to improve the results.

When there is pressure for performance and particularly when performance affects everyone's pay, employees tend to be impatient with nonperformers. They expect management to do something about the drones.

Full Explanation

A particularly important aspect of new-world corporations is that management explains to employees what is happening and why. Management is completely open and honest with employees. The reasons for new compensation schemes are fully described. Companies that candidly explain their problems to employees and solicit their views usually find that employees increase their commitment and work harder.

Intel holds quarterly business-update meetings (BUMs) for all employees. Twice a year it holds meetings describing strategic long-range plans to managers, which help managers understand the shifting demand for skills. It is every manager's job to explain to employees how the demand for skills is changing and to encourage desirable training.

Changing Compensation Schemes

The compensation policies of the new-world corporation are fundamentally different from those of the old world. Many corporations, especially in the United

States, have been restructuring their pay systems and have found that this is a particularly perilous change to make. Other corporations have avoided facing this change. They have reinvented work processes to be boundaryless, creative, empowered, and horizontal, but they still follow pay structures designed for the hierarchy of the past.

Old-world pay systems were often based on one devised by Edward Hay half a century ago. This used 20 to 40 job tiers that mirrored the multilevel hierarchy, each with a strict pay range. The system assigned a number of points to each job based on its level in the hierarchy. Employees aspired to promotion within the hierarchy and protected their turf in ways that reengineering seeks to obliterate.

New-world pay schemes have characteristics such as the following:

- Substantial bonus based on individual or team performance
- Substantial bonus based on results that may involve many work groups—for example, introducing a new product on time
- Sharing in corporate profits
- Stock options or stock ownership
- Base pay linked to knowledge, skill, and capability
- No automatic increase in base pay without a corresponding increase in employee value

Changing the pay scheme is a difficult and emotional thing to do. It is desirable to discuss it openly with the employees affected, explaining the reasons why the change is needed and asking them what they think. They know more about pay schemes than most managers suspect and debate the subject extensively. Managers should make sure they know the hard realities: if there is less profit, there is less money to go around; but if you reach the "superbowl," everybody will benefit. Employees' debates about pay should incorporate debates about performance. After a new pay scheme is implemented, its originators should discuss its effects carefully with the employees, finding out what works and what needs adjusting.

Gain Sharing

It makes sense to base bonuses on results. This gives all employees an incentive to improve the results. Collective bonuses for achievements—such as completing projects on time, making a quota, or operating within budget—tend to create peer pressure to achieve the target. Nobody wants to let colleagues down and cause the bonus to be lost.

There is a wide diversity of schemes for bonuses based on results. Such schemes are often referred to as *gain sharing*. Gain sharing is a group-based incentive program in which employees earn bonuses by finding ways to save money, hit targets, or achieve measurable results. Speed may be an important measure for one group, customer satisfaction for another, profits for another. The measurement must be carefully thought out. Employees can make repairs when no repairs are needed if paid for the volume of their repairs. Programmers can fill programs with excessive lines of code if paid a bonus for number of lines of code written.

Payment schemes based on rigid job descriptions can be harmful. They encourage employees to do only what is in their job description. Today, jobs are changing fast, and corporations need employees who are empowered and creative at reinventing work, and who develop new skills and learn how to please value-stream customers. It is often easy to create effective gain-sharing schemes for employees organized as value-stream teams rather than in traditional departments. The value-stream team has a clear customer and measurable goals. Appropriate bonuses can encourage value-stream teams to do the best job possible.

Many employers want to make pay variable so that it reflects the corporation's fortunes. If bonuses are a substantial part of compensation, there is less need to lay off employees when business is bad.

Pay-for-Knowledge Schemes

One of the appalling aspects of old-world corporations was work rules and job restrictions, often imposed by unions. An electrician could not saw wood; a carpenter could not change a light bulb. Workers were forbidden to move from one job to another. A supervisor was forbidden by union rules to fill in for an employee who went to the bathroom. If an employee assigned to a job was not available, the job did not get done, even when this caused other workers to be idle. A worker was not allowed to deal with a problem on his machine; that was the repairman's job. Peter Drucker has written that work rules and job restrictions are the main cause of the productivity gap between the West and Japan.[4]

In the new-world enterprise each worker needs to be as useful as possible. Teams should be able to perform well even when some of their members are missing. Employees should be able to do multiple tasks so that a small team can be self-sufficient and not have to pass work on to other groups. Employees should be able to test the work done to verify that it has zero defects. On an assembly line, workers may be trained to do the jobs upstream and downstream of their own positions to help ensure continuous operation. In general it is desirable to have flexibility in job assignments.

To encourage employees to learn skills that make them more useful, employees should be given pay raises when they improve their skills. A pay-for-knowledge scheme ties base pay to knowledge. Instead of aspiring to climb a hierarchy, the employee then aspires to have more knowledge or skill, knowing that as his value increases, so does his compensation.

Nucor is a high-performing steel company (competitive with Chaparral, discussed in Chapter 31). Nucor divides its production workers into work groups of 25 to 35 people and pays each work group a bonus based on its production above a certain predetermined standard. If the group produces 50 percent more than the standard, members receive a 50-percent bonus; if they produce 100 percent above the standard they receive a 100-percent bonus. Simple!

During the 1980s Nucor's sales grew 850 percent, and its profits grew 1,250 percent. While most of the American steel industry was laying off workers, Nucor laid off no worker in fifteen years. Nucor does many things well, but its work-group compensation contributes greatly to its performance.

Employee Appraisals

Where employees are members of teams, the appraisal of employees should relate to how valuable they are as team members. Often the best people to make this judgment are the *other* members of the team. The appraisal process in some organizations calls for each team member to appraise each other team member. GE's lighting business put into place "360-degree appraisals" in which employees were appraised by their peers as well as by people above and below them in rank.

Appraisals are sensitive because they are a basis for compensation. If a person is appraised *as an individual* rather than *as a team member,* he will tend to take actions that make himself look good. This is the opposite of good team behavior, in which the team member subordinates his own recognition to the goal of making the team succeed. In a high-performance team each member must help the *other* members to excel. Appraisals and compensation must therefore relate to team performance, not individual performance.

One problem with this is that a team member who is not really trying receives the same bonus as team members who are straining to achieve something. The strong team members resent carrying a weak member who shares their bonus. They complain that this is not fair. For this reason mechanisms have been put into place with which team members appraise their colleagues.

When peer appraisals are made, a manager should use them as a basis for counseling each employee in private and agreeing to goals for improvement and further training.

In many law firms and other professional companies, remuneration relates to seniority. The Los Angeles law firm Munger Tolles & Olson has 53 partners, and pay relates to how the partners assess one another's performance. Each January a sheet showing the previous year's profits is distributed. The sheet contains each partner's name, and each partner assigns a number to each other partner based on his evaluation of that person's contribution to the profits. The firm assembles this information in a spreadsheet showing how each partner is rated by his peers and what his total rating is. A compensation committee reviews the numbers, talks privately to each partner, and arrives at a compensation figure. The best-paid partner can make at least five times what the lowest-paid partner can.[5]

This system seems to work well. It encourages partners to be cordial to one another because, if you are hostile to someone, that might affect your pay.

Employee Stock Option Plans

If employees own part of a company they are likely to take a greater interest in its success. They pay attention not only to their own activity but to the corporation as a whole. With ESOPs (Employee Stock Option Plans) employees encourage their colleagues across the corporation to cut costs and increase performance. A study in the United States showed that corporations grew 40 to 46 percent faster after setting up an ESOP; companies grew even faster when they had an ESOP *and* a high level of employee participation in decision making.[6] Employees benefit not only from receiving a bonus in the form of stock options but also from the appreciation of the stock.

If the shares of a company are not public, employees may be contractually required to sell them back to the company at fair market value if they leave the company.

In the new-world corporation, employees should learn as much as they can about the corporation and its competitive strategy. Stock ownership encourages this. Employees become financial partners in the corporation.

Different Classes of Employment Package

Sometimes employee deals are talked about as though they are the same for all employees. In reality it makes sense to define different classes of employees who receive different deals. Exhibit 32.1 shows four classes of employees.

Class 1

Core employees are uniquely valuable. The corporation would be damaged if they left, so every attempt is made to lock them in. This may be done with stock options, vesting schemes, long-term benefits, and generally making them feel an important part of the corporation. Vital in this group are employees who advance the building and perfection of strategic "predator" capabilities as discussed in Chapter 24. Even the core employees change with time as new strategic capabilities become important and earlier ones become outdated. Major education programs are needed for focusing the core executives and professionals on the implication of changing markets and discontinuities in technology.

Class 2

Employees who would be expensive to replace (in Exhibit 32.1) include members of high-performance teams, employees with expensive skills, employees who are particularly good with customers. Class 2 employees need to be rewarded for their skills in ways that encourage them to stay. Class 1 and 2 employees may be made to feel that, while not exactly having "tenure," they have job security and will have good rewards as long as they continue to make themselves valuable.

Exhibit 32.1

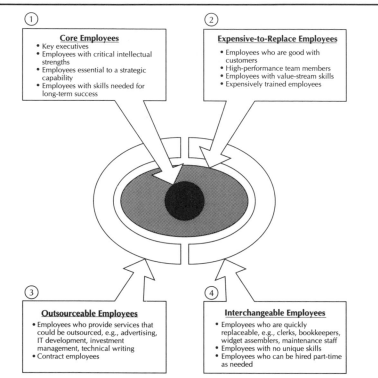

Different classes of employees may receive very different packages of compensation and reward.

Such employees should feel that they will not be laid off casually when recessions or reorganizations occur.

Class 3

Thsee employees do professional tasks that could be out-sourced. A corporation has a choice about whether it creates its own advertisement, writes its own product manuals, programs its own computer applications, manages its own cash reserves, and so on. These are capabilities that outside firms can provide and that corporations can decide whether to out-source. Such employees may be paid for results on a contract basis and should understand that they, in effect, compete with external service providers.

Class 4

Employees are indeed laid off by some corporations when business is bad. Usually they are employees with no unique skills and so are quickly replaceable.

Exhibit 32.2 Federal Express's PRISM system which reinvented the human-resource function

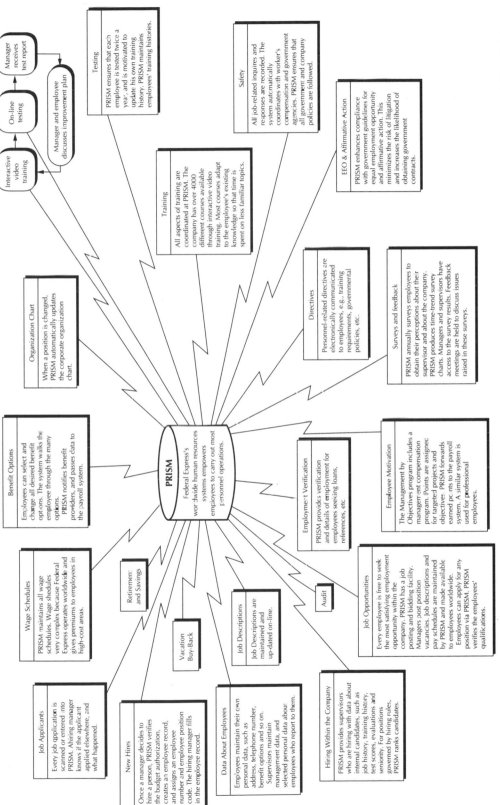

PRISM

Federal Express's worldwide human resources systems empowers employees to carry out most personnel operations.

Manager receives test report

On-line testing

Interactive video training

Manager and employee discusses improvement plan

Testing

PRISM ensures that each employee is tested twice a year, and is motivated to update his own training history. PRISM maintains employees' training histories.

Safety

All job-related inquires and responses are recorded. The system automatically coordinates with worker's compensation and government agencies. PRISM ensures that all government and company policies are followed.

EEO & Affirmative Action

PRISM enhances compliance with government guidelines for equal employment opportunity and affirmative action. This minimizes the risk of litigation and increases the likelihood of obtaining government contracts.

Training

All aspects of training are coordinated at PRISM. The company has over 4000 different courses available through interactive video training. Most courses adapt to the employee's existing knowledge so that time is spent on less familiar topics.

Organization Chart

When a position is changed, PRISM automatically updates the corporate organization chart.

Directives

Personnel-related directives are electronically communicated to employees, e.g., training requirements, governmental policies, etc.

Surveys and feedback

PRISM annually surveys employees to obtain their perceptions about their supervisor and about the company. PRISM produces time-trend survey charts. Managers and supervisors have access to the survey results. Feedback meetings are held to discuss issues raised in these surveys.

Benefit Options

Employees can select and change all desired benefit options. The system walks the employee through the many options. PRISM notifies benefit providers, and passes data to the payroll system.

Employment Verification

PRISM provides verification and details of employment for employees seeking loans, references, etc.

Employee Motivation

The Management by Objectives program includes a management compensation program. Points are assigned for targeted projects and objectives. PRISM forwards earned points to the payroll system. A similar system is used for professional employees.

Wage Schedules

PRISM maintains all wage schedules. Wage schedules very complex because Federal Express operates worldwide and gives premiums to employees in high-cost areas.

Retirement and Savings

Vacation Buy-Back

Job Descriptions

Job Descriptions are maintained and up-dated on-line.

Audit

Job Opportunities

Every employee is free to seek the most satisfying employment opportunity within the company. PRISM has a job posting and bidding facility. Managers post position vacancies. Job descriptions and pay schedules are maintained by PRISM and made available to employees worldwide. Employees can apply for any position via PRISM. PRISM verifies the employees' qualifications.

Job Applicants

Every job application is scanned or entered into PRISM. A hiring manager knows if the applicant applied elsewhere, and what happened.

New Hires

Once a manager decides to hire a person, PRISM verifies the budget authorization, creates an employee record, and assigns an employee number and employee position code. The hiring manager fills in the employee record.

Data About Employees

Employees maintain their own personal data, such as address, telephone number, benefit options and so on. Supervisors maintain management data, and selected personal data about employees who report to them.

Hiring Within the Company

PRISM provides supervisors who are hiring with data about internal candidates, such as job history, training history, test scores, evaluations and seniority. For positions governed by hiring rules, PRISM ranks candidates.

They can be hired part-time as needed. They include laborers, clerks, widget assemblers, and people who can be quickly trained to do simple tasks. These employees are paid for the job, with incentives for good work, but may have no long-term security or long-term benefits.

In the new-world corporation, employees should be able to use their own computers to help manage their own careers. The computer should tell them about all vacancies and opportunities, training courses, benefit options, and so on. Employees should maintain their own electronic résumés.

Federal Express reinvented the corporate-personnel function. Corporate philosophy puts great emphasis on the development of its employees. It stresses its "people-service-profit" view: Focus on developing employees and management; that leads to higher levels of service and hence to higher profits. A corporatewide system called PRISM empowers employees and managers to carry out personnel functions that in most other companies are done by an HR department. PRISM helps to ensure that employees are well trained and motivated, feel that they are treated fairly, and have advancement opportunities open to them.

Exhibit 32.2 shows some of the functions of PRISM. Managers can enter into PRISM details about their employees, and employees enter details about themselves. All employees can examine on their screen their own personnel data and are securely locked out of data about other employees. Employees can see what positions exist or are available, and they can bid for these positions. The system is concerned with developing and motivating employees. It helps to ensure that their skills are constantly upgraded, often with on-line training and testing. The system has an on-line management-by-objectives implementation. It conducts periodic surveys, which show that the system has substantially increased employee commitment and morale.[7]

References

1. Thomas R. Horton, "Compensation in Changing Times," *Management Review*, March 1987.
2. "The End of an Era?" *Compensation Quarterly*, Hay Management Consultants, Fall 1987.
3. Brian O'Reilly, "The New Deal," *Fortune*, June 13, 1994.
4. Peter Drucker, "Workers Hands Bound by Tradition," *The Wall Street Journal*, August 2, 1988.
5. Jaclyn Fierman, "The Perilous New World of Fair Pay," *Fortune*, June 13, 1994.
6. Corey Rosen, "Using ESOPs to Boost Corporate Performance," *Management Review* (March 1988): 30.
7. Prashant C. Palvia, James A. Perkins, and Steven M. Zeltmann, "The PRISM System: A Key to Organizational Effectiveness at Federal Express Corporation," *MIS Quarterly*, Sept 1992.

33

The Changing of Corporate Culture

Corporations that have been successful for a long time usually have a strong *culture*. Great corporate leaders such as Thomas Watson (father and son) of IBM, Harley Proctor of Proctor and Gamble, General Johnson of Johnson and Johnson, and (more recently) Jim Treibig of Tandem and Anita Roddick of The Body Shop have believed that a strong culture brought success. Toyota, Rolls Royce, Sony, 3M—in fact most of the greatest corporations of this century—have had a strong culture reinforced by a strong CEO.

Webster's Dictionary defined culture as "the behaviors and beliefs of a particular group ... the integrated pattern of human behavior." An ex-CEO of McKinsey had a more informal definition: "The way we do things around here."[1] As new members join an organization, they learn its culture and are made to conform to its culture, which is passed on to successive waves of employees just as a society's culture is passed to successive generations.

The term *culture* refers to a total communication pattern within a community. Some of this communication pattern is explicit. It is in memos, organization charts, and classroom material. Much of it is hidden: We are often unaware of what we communicate, or fail to communicate.

As organizations grow, their cultures adapt. Mature organizations have a deeply entrenched culture, like the roots of an old tree. The problem with most mature corporations is that they have the wrong culture for the present era. It was set into place before the age of value streams, empowered teams, *kaizen*, computer networks, and so on.

New corporations focus on survival and tend to pay very close attention to market changes, cash flows, responsiveness to customers, etcetera. Organizations that have a history of successes tend to become complacent and allow policies, procedures, and bureaucracies to replace the flexibility and adaptability that contributed to their success. Old organizations have strong mechanisms for preserving their entrenched cultures.

Enterprise Engineering is concerned with changing corporations in major ways. This requires careful attention to corporate culture. Change agents need to be aware of corporate culture and must understand its strong resistance to change. They must be aware of which techniques can successfully change the culture and which are likely to fail because of the culture's protective barriers. They need to distinguish different components of culture and know which to leave intact. Many attempted changes fail because corporate culture subtly rejects them.

The culture of a community is a system of behavior made up of thousands of details. Nobody writes down most of the rules of behavior; only when they are broken do we know that the rules exist. Cultural anthropologists who have studied cultures in communities are now switching their attention to cultures of enterprises. Ed Hall, a cultural anthropologist comments, "Culture hides much more than it reveals, and strangely enough what it hides, it hides most effectively from its own participants."[2] There is an "out-of-awareness" communication, which can cause serious problems. It is particularly important when we interact in a different culture. An American woman doing business in Japan, for example, has cultural land mines all around her. A computer expert making a presentation to the board of directors may face greater cultural obstacles than the American woman in Japan.

Basic human nature has not changed for centuries. Shakespeare describes with astonishing skill human nature as we observe it today. We have the same power struggles, greed, love, kindness, jealousy, and treachery as in Shakespeare's day, four hundred years ago. It is a fair bet that human nature will be the same in our reengineered enterprises. Culture is a complex veneer that overlays human nature. Culture is something we invent, but substantial skill is required in order to change it. The change agents of Enterprise Engineering must acquire this skill. If they charge ahead without understanding the nature of the enterprise culture and how it can be changed, they will fail.

Many managers are strongly concerned with change but do not focus on the cultural issues of change; as a result, the changes they plan do not occur as intended. Employees become angry and demoralized; they often become emotional wrecks. The recommendations and plans for change are embraced with enthusiasm, but then nothing happens. The management of change is the management of cultural transformation.

The Protective Barrier

A well-established culture is hostile to changes in its inherent patterns. It develops elaborate and powerful mechanisms for protecting itself. Only in this way can it survive. In corporations, people believe that their own survival in the enterprise is based on "what the company stands for" or following "the correct way to do things." So they oppose cultural threats, enveloping them with protective barriers and routines—procrastination, endless discussion and reviews, crises that provide no time for change, blame laid on those who do not change, and so on.

Cultural anthropologists say that "out-of-awareness" communication is the part of the cultural iceberg under the water.

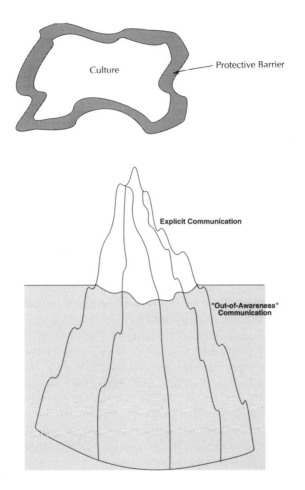

"*We must never assume that we are fully aware of what we communicate to someone else. There exists tremendous distortion in meaning as we try to communicate. The job of achieving understanding and insight in mental processes of others is much more difficult and the situation much more serious than most of us care to admit.*"

—Edward Hall, *The Silent Language*[3]

The enterprise defends itself against novelty, "change for change's sake," and any attempts to change the total communication pattern which is its culture. A corporate body is similar in some ways to a biological body, which protects itself in three ways. It prevents foreign organisms from entering if it can; it attacks those that do enter; it inactivates those organisms that it cannot kill. The corporate body tries to keep out an alien culture. If one enters the corporate body, the alien culture tries to kill it. If it cannot kill it, if finds ways to neutralize it.[4]

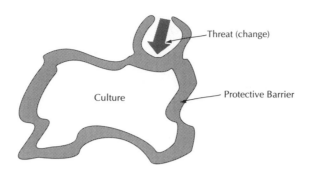

Alien Life Forms

When empowered teams or high-performance work groups are placed into a traditional hierarchical organization, they can be like an alien life form. The bureaucratically minded hierarchy does not accept them. The organization detects their presence and tries to destroy them. There are numerous examples of this.[5] They may survive for a time with a protective sponsor, but eventually they will not survive unless the host organization is changed. There have been many attempts to introduce TQM into organizations at a low level—even when highly successful the success was short-lived. The introduction of SWAT teams into IT organizations to achieve fast development has sometimes been quashed by older-style managers.

Cray Computer CEO John Rollwagen resigned from his position to go to the U.S. Department of Commerce to assist the Clinton administration in transforming government; he resigned after several weeks because he could not change Commerce's culture even in subtle ways.

> The National Education Corporation had long been successful in creating and selling correspondence courses and other training for secretaries and low-level employees. It then took over two companies, Deltak and ASI, which were highly successful at training IT professionals with videotapes and computer-based training to form a subsidiary, ALI, later called NETG. This was a different world from NEC. The culture clash caused political battles and repeated firings of the CEOs of NETG. The revenue of NETG shrank to a fraction of its former value, even though its market was growing, and the financial loss grew until in 1993 the loss was more than a third of the revenue.
>
> NETG formed a subsidiary, a Trojan horse within its walls, to create IT education, targeted at the hot subjects of the day. The subsidiary was small, highly aggressive, fast moving, and felt that it did not need the bureaucracy of the parent company or its dinosaur of a television studio. In 1991 and 1992 it was the only part of NETG that made courses which met customer needs. The new group became an alien culture, a dozen or so people in a large corporation

that had a different way of operating. The antibodies went to work. The book-keepers of the parent company loaded all manner of costs onto the new subsidiary. The managers tried to impose unworkable laws. The European subsidiary did not sell the products of the new group to avoid paying royalties. The finance executives changed the charging rules so that the subsidiary could not win. The subsidiary, NETG's main hope for the future, lasted two years.

An Enterprise Engineering change agent needs to understand the cultural protection mechanisms asking, What can penetrate the protective barrier, and what will be rejected? Once a change is established, what antibodies will try to kill it? How can a change in culture be achieved that will be solid and long-lasting?

When an attempt made to change the culture fails, a second attempt may encounter even more difficulty. The antibodies are alert and active. Just as an inoculation can increase a body's resistance to chicken pox, so can a corporate management team, union, or board alert itself to attacks on its beliefs. It can regard the change agent with self-reinforcing cynicism.

Three Cultural Components

A culture has three components to it described in Exhibit 33.1.

Formal culture provides a rigid set of rules and beliefs. It serves as the glue that ties a community together. Formal culture is highly tenacious, and this tenacity makes life in societies possible. Formal culture is highly resistant to change from the outside. Many enterprises with long-term success have had powerful formal cultures.

Edward Hall comments: "Formal culture does a job closely analogous to instinct. Everybody can depend upon it almost as though it were instinctual."[7]

Informal culture describes patterns of behavior not found in manuals or textbooks, largely copied from other people.

People are often unaware of informal cultural behavior; indeed we *need* to be unaware of how we do certain complex actions. If a centipede thinks rationally about what sequence it should move its legs in, it will get in a tangle. A person learning shorthand or touch-typing is told to "get it in the fingers"; thinking about it slows down the process.

Being unaware of informal culture can create serious problems when different cultures meet. Corporations have unique informally learned behavior patterns. We are unaware of subtle ways in which Japanese business people interpret our gestures or words, and vice versa. Japanese people laugh when they are embarrassed or uncomfortable in a business situation; Westerners may completely misinterpret the laughter. The Japanese may say yes to avoid confrontation when they really think no, and Westerners mistakenly take the yes literally. The Japa-

Exhibit 33.1   Three types of culture blended together in an enterprise[6]

Culture is of three types, learned three ways:
formal, informal, and technical.

Formal Culture

Formal culture acknowledges only a "right" and a "wrong" way to do things. It is taught by admonition. Children are taught, "You can't do that," in a tone of voice indicating that the child is doing the unthinkable. Employees are taught, "This is the way we do things here." No other way is conceivably acceptable. There is no rational explanation for the culture's often emotionally held views. Formal learning has a binary, yes/no, right/wrong character. You either break the rules or you do not. Hundreds of such rules contribute to a formal culture that nobody questions. In many corporations today the formal culture needs to be changed.

Informal Culture

Informal culture is learned by imitation. A child imitates his parents, dancers, pop stars, heroes or villains on television, or other children. An apprentice is shown, "Do it this way." A new employee is told, "Do what other people do; you'll soon learn the ropes." Much informal culture is acquired without any deliberate awareness either by the learner or the person being imitated. Much informal culture is "out-of-awareness" communication such as body language, hidden meaning to words, knee-jerk reactions, subtle political triggers, style, and so on.

Technical Culture

Technical culture is taught and explained rationally. It is based on logical analysis. Its success, unlike formal and informal culture, depends upon how well the analysis and teaching is done. The techniques and methodologies of business form its technical culture. Whereas formal cultural matters are emotionally held, technical culture tries to avoid emotion because emotion tends to impede efficient operation and change. Sometimes advocates of technical culture become upset if the technical foundation is not adhered to. They avoid emotion about the details but become highly emotional if the principles are violated.

Sometimes culture that starts as technical becomes so observed and entrenched that it becomes a formal culture and people say, "Is there any other way?" It takes on the emotional trappings of a formal culture.

---

nese are often trying to be charming and polite, but Westerners think they are being devious.

Sexual behavior is largely learned informally. Only recently have we had technical aids to learning sex, such as books and video tapes. Even with these, sex is learned mainly from informal human interaction. Earlier in the century sex had major formal rules. Intimacy was not permitted outside marriage. To help obey the formal rules, the culture had a support system: women were chaperoned at house parties and wore clothes that covered everything below the neck. In stages throughout this century the technical support system was removed and then reversed. Teen-age girls changed to bikinis, spent evenings alone with men in cars, and watched movies with them showing explicit, outrageous sex. When Cole Porter wrote "Anything Goes," most women were still expected to be chaste before marriage. The formal culture remained after informal and technical aspects of the culture had changed.

In the 1950s a cultural anthropologist stated what seemed to him inevitable: the formal culture of premarital chastity would be gone in a decade.[8] He was hysterically attacked by the press and public. The reaction was typical of someone who predicts the collapse of a formal culture.

Technical culture is rational. In a corporation it relates to the behavior taught in classes and devised by work groups or analysts. Because it is logical, it is the easiest of the three to change. Naive systems analysts often assume that all behavior is logical. They are astonished at opposition to new procedures which to them are an obvious improvement.

A skillful corporate change agent, like a skillful courtroom lawyer, is fully aware of culture and uses cultural factors to help bring about the changes needed.

Edward Hall describes the legendary lawyer Clarence Darrow, who succeeded in having thieves and murderers acquitted. The law, like systems analysis, is technical and unemotional. Juries, like corporations, are steeped in a formal culture that is emotional.

> The success of Clarence Darrow was attributable to his being a past master at invoking formal culture to sway juries.... Darrow dressed in an old sloppy suit. He appealed to the common man—people could identify with him. He was their type, the country bumpkin who outsmarts the city slicker. Now it is obvious that in addition to knowing his law well he also knew his culture. He realized that most people do not understand the law but will stand up for their own formal systems and even weep over them when they see them outraged. This was Darrow's strength. However, he failed when he was called to Honolulu. There he faced a jury made up of members who had different formal systems. The Chinese jurors weren't a bit moved by his culture-rooted strategies.[9]

The corporate change agent should adopt the informal culture and language of those he wants to change and should determine what formal aspects of culture need to change. The agent should *use* those aspects of formal culture that do not change so as to bolster his effectiveness.

Sudden Shifts

Formal culture can undergo sudden quantum-change shifts. Cultural anthropologists record that a common characteristic of culture change in society is that a practice holds on persistently, apparently resisting all efforts to change it, and then suddenly, without notice, collapses.[10] The same is true in corporations. The rapid shift occurs because people cannot tolerate existing in two systems at the same time, the old formal culture and the new technical culture. The new technical culture often requires changes in the formal culture.

Once the change has occurred, the people involved would be extremely opposed to returning to the previous culture. Employees who have been successfully through value-stream reinvention totally resist a return to the previous form of management. Once individuals are *empowered*, it is almost impossible to reverse their condition. For instance, employees at the General Motors Saturn plant work in self-managed teams in which they have responsibility for making decisions on an ongoing basis; they are not interested in transferring to other GM facilities, and unfortunately older facilities are not interested in embracing them and their foreign ways of working.

The Level of Cultural Change

A culture protects itself against change in diverse ways in order to survive. The technical part of culture is relatively easy to change; the formal part is difficult. A change agent should change the technical culture and leave the formal culture intact, if possible, or else make single changes to formal culture cautiously.

Kaizen (or TQM), once it is well established, avoids changing the formal culture most of the time. It changes informal and technical behavior patterns. However, the introduction of *kaizen* in the first place is a change in formal culture. People who would not dare criticize management are told to look for problems, to articulate them, and to make suggestions for solving them. This is a radical change in behavior patterns. Because cultures resist formal change vigorously, the introduction of TQM has failed in many corporations. Once it is well established, it succeeds.

Value-stream reinvention attacks the formal culture. Naive, and in the final analysis inept, change agents of business reengineering often perceive a corporation's formal cultural behavior as obsolete, irrational, unnecessary, a remnant of an era before modern technology. It is fun to attack it. Mike Hammer describes business reengineering as "heavy blasting." He also states that 70 percent of organizations undertaking a business-reengineering effort fail.[11] There are multiple reasons for failure, but resistance to culture change is the least often discussed. Failure is predictable when change agents ignore the profound impact of culture. They must understand culture's pervasive impact on the process of making and sustaining organizational change; otherwise, their methodology is systematically flawed.

The "sacred cows" described in Chapter 12 are part of formal culture. If not removed, they inhibit the necessary changes. The team reinventing the value stream says, Identify the sacred cows and shoot them. However, care and skill are required in the technique for changing formal culture. Analysts with brilliant new designs often blunder into an organization, unaware of cultural issues. Removing the sacred cows requires constant repetitive persuasion by top management.

Management Directives

A management directive ordering change that is insensitive to formal culture usually fails. Management decrees something should happen, but the antibodies go to work. Management's instructions are adjusted in subtle ways that make them conform to what employees assume is right—the rules of the formal culture.

Sometimes a CEO is put in charge of an unprofitable corporation to "turn it around." Some have a reputation as turn-around artists. They move as many losses as possible into a category that can be blamed on their predecessor. They slash expenses, boost sales, and slash development. Usually they do not succeed in building a new culture that will make the corporation stronger in the future.

Marvin Runyon was hired by the Tennessee Valley Authority to reduce its expenses significantly. He succeeded by slashing payrolls of thousands of employees. He left the TVA to become Postmaster General, in which position he repeated the slashing technique; within ninety days of taking over, he had eliminated 50 percent of the executive leadership of the organization. Though costs were reduced significantly, it is believed by many that irreparable damage has been done to both organizations.[12]

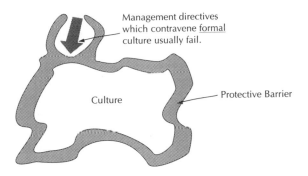

Management directives which contravene <u>formal</u> culture usually fail.

Culture

Protective Barrier

Marketplace Demands

It might be thought that marketplace demands cannot be ignored; but all the evidence is that if responding to them violates the rules of the formal culture, the demands will indeed be ignored. There are many examples of corporations responding to a severe decline in sales by increasing research-and-development expenditures on products of the same type, when the market was asking for products of a different type. IBM, in the years before its great crash in 1993, intensified its development of proprietary mainframes and mainframe-related architectures

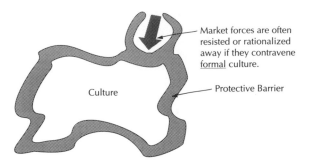

(SNA, SAA, AD/Cycle, etc.), when the marketplace was clearly demanding open systems, downsizing, local-area networks, and client-server systems. IBM's formal culture emphasized mainframes and proprietary systems. Its culture said "main-frame account control" when its customers said, "Choose the best of the breed rather than be controlled."

New Technology

New technology often can penetrate a culture without setting off its cultural inva-sion alarms. It seems to have a numbing effect on the culture like a dentist's needle. This century has seen diverse societies eagerly absorbing new technology such as cars, radio, telephone, television, drugs, and so on, not realizing that this absorption of technology will fundamentally change their culture. Most corpora-tions (at least in the United States) are fascinated by technology. People become excited about new technology (even when the CEO is not). They want the latest personal computer, the latest software. Hospitals buy the latest equipment, and factories buy the latest machines. Employees accept the spread of computer net-works not imagining that they might change the culture.

Technology can be a Trojan horse which, if skillfully used by change agents, can start cultural change.

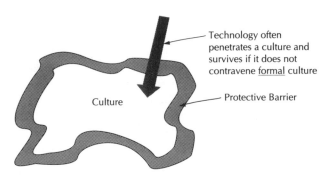

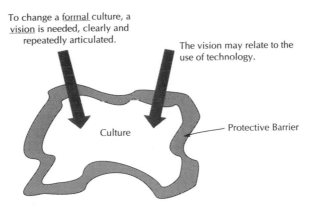

New Vision

To change formal culture, a vision is needed that can excite people. The vision must be clearly articulated and communicated to everybody. The vision may relate to something made possible by the use of technology. The vision may describe the goals of a value stream. It could be Federal Express's "All packages will be delivered by 10:30 A.M. tomorrow," or Ford's "Quality is Job #1," or "Process a coil of strip steel in ten minutes" or "Build *kaizen*-capable software." It could be "Provide the best health care possible," or "Provide the best customer service in the world." The concept of value-stream teams focusing on value-stream customers could be the vision that changes old culture patterns.

Sometimes the creator of a culture-changing vision cannot express it or teach it clearly. He needs a translator. Skillful wording of the vision is critical. Vision communicators should read books on advertising such as *Ogilvy on Advertising*.[13] Many visions that are intended to change corporate culture are very badly expressed. Churchill's brilliant use of the English language in World War II enabled him to energize an entire nation.

The language in enterprises is increasingly the language of specialists. The language of IT professionals is not understood by business people. The language of the research chemist is not understood by the drugstore chemist. The vision must be translated into the language of those whose culture is to be changed.

Threatening words should be avoided. The term *business reengineering* is threatening to people who do not want to be reengineered. Michael Hammer's phraseology, although it may be true is threatening: "Business Reengineering means scrapping what exists and starting over" and "Traditional counts for nothing."[14] It might be preferable to use Michaelangelo's language: "The block of marble contains an image; I have to set it free." People will buy into change efforts if they feel that they are involved in the process, rather than that it is something being done to them.

Trojan Horse

To summarize, change agents should avoid directly confronting an organization with management directives or market thrusts that change formal culture. Instead they should introduce helpful tools (technology) and well-articulated visions. These together may be a Trojan Horse that the culture embraces and later refines on its own terms. Managers have an implicit belief that the enterprise must have a vision (meaningful to *them*) and that the work force must be empowered by technology. That is why they actively pull the Trojan Horse of vision and technology, and the hidden changes these bring with them, into the inner core of the enterprise, beginning culture modification. The same Trojan Horse's contents would set off cultural invasion alarms if introduced with pressure by an outside change agent.

Basic Values

Corporations with a strong culture have certain basic beliefs or values. Values are the bedrock of corporate culture, the essence of a company's view of how it should behave, and they provide guidelines for employees' day-to-day behavior. They are deeply held beliefs that are repeatedly reinforced in corporate rituals, myths, and ceremonies.

Terrence Deal and Allen Kennedy studied corporate culture extensively.[15] Surveying 80 major American companies, they found that 25 had clearly articulated corporate beliefs or values. Of this 25, 18 had qualitative values such as those in the paragraph above rather than financially oriented goals. All of these 18 companies were outstanding performers, whereas among the other 62 companies there was "no correlation of any relevance—some did OK, some poorly, most had their ups and downs." Deal and Kennedy concluded that powerful communication of qualitative values, so that a strong culture is formed around them, has helped to build great corporations.

Where a corporation has a strong set of values, reengineering efforts can usually support and reinforce those values. The values can be restated to help employees accept the changes that are needed. Any violation of the basic values will make change much more difficult. Where a corporation does not have an articulated set of beliefs these should be created with the participation of employees as described in Chapter 27. Corporations that do have basic values often need to rethink them today because of empowerment, high-performance teams, value streams, and extended enterprise connections. Each value stream should itself have an articulated set of values that incorporates the enterprise values but also includes values specific to the value stream.

Occasionally, the traditional deeply held values of a corporation are in serious conflict with its current situation. ATT, after divestiture, still had strong values relating to "universal service" in which everyone who wanted a phone could have one. Suddenly, the telephone business was competitive but ATT's culture did not change quickly in the direction of high-speed response, many choices of instruments and service, and intense marketing. Its preoccupation with total system integrity allowed competitors to move fast in specialized niches of their choice. ATT's top management understood the threats of competition, but the culture of ordinary employees took years to change. Low-key, likable, "Mother Bell" people chatted to customers and wanted to give them plain old telephone service with no frills. They even advised customers to buy the new gadgets elsewhere.

The strength of a culture can become a negative factor if the culture becomes obsolete.

Pounding Home the Vision

The value and overall vision of the corporation need to be stated over and over again. Leaders who have changed corporate cultures, such as the Watsons of IBM or SAS's Jan Carlzon, lost no opportunity to preach their vision. They repeated it tirelessly. When Thomas Watson, Jr., lectured his troops, he was as hypnotic as Billy Graham. Carlzon explained to all SAS employees his vision of turning the organization chart upside down so that workers with the most customer contact were at the top of the chart and everybody else was expected to serve those who served customers. Over and over he discussed his vision with managers. He constantly attended employee parties in aircraft hangers. The visionary leader is often emphatic, fluent, and extreme both in condemnation and congratulation. His effectiveness relates to the clarity of his message, the number of "kilowatts" he radiates, and the number of employees he reaches.

Repeating the message endlessly requires considerable patience. Sometimes ex-schoolteachers have been particularly good at changing formal culture. They have the tolerance to explain over and over again why the new way is right. "There is now one right way to do it. Any other way is unthinkable. Today's way of doing it is different from earlier times. There is no choice. This is the right way."

The repetitive delivery of the message may be accompanied by a slogan campaign, posters on the walls, pads of paper with the message on each sheet, three-ring binders with the message of the cover, and so on. Individuals or teams should be given performance plans which reward them for making the culture change happen. During the change period they may be repeatedly counseled. Individuals who resist the change should have special counseling.

Many corporations have fired resisters. Some have fired large groups of them in an attempt to make a clean sweep. Some corporations have done clean-sweep firing without giving those fired a chance to change. These heavy-handed practices, more prevalent in the United States than most countries, send a highly negative message to the employees. It says, "Do things wrong and you'll be fired," "Keep your head down," "It's them versus us," "There's no safe career path." A different message is needed—a highly positive message about an exciting vision. The vision energizes everybody. The message is "To achieve the vision we all have to pull together."

When major culture changes occur, some individuals do not make the transition. They should be coached carefully, but even so they may choose to leave or ask for a transfer. When Oticon, the Danish hearing-aid company, eliminated paper throughout the entire company, some people left of their own choosing. When IT organizations have moved aggressively from hand programming to an environment with code generators and advanced tools, some professionals have opted out. If coaching is done well, the good people stay.

Sometimes managers think it is *macho* to do a clean sweep. Firing people demonstrates that they are capable of taking strong action. Sometimes they get rid of potential political opponents. However French Revolution–style management almost always lowers long-term corporate profits. Managing the culture transition skillfully without losing good people is the sign of good management.

The Cost of Attempting to Change Culture

Many change efforts fail because insufficient money is spent on achieving the change. Deal and Kennedy, studying corporate cultures, identified ten major projects in which the desired end product was organization and culture change.[16] They determined the cost of the change and commented that "the conclusions were startling." In addition to the fees of consultants and salaries of change agents, an amount was required equivalent to between 5 and 10 percent of the annual budget for the personnel whose behavior was supposed to be changed. To get people to change, management had to capture between 5 and 10 percent of their time for a year. Sometimes the cost is even higher. In creating its highly successful Opel factory in East Germany, General Motors required that employees spend months learning their new jobs in a simulated environment.

Mercury Communications in Britain set out to change its culture and required that all of its 10 thousand employees attend training classes. Xerox had 100 thousand employees when it set out to change itself so that it could compete against the Japanese. Deal and Kennedy estimate that the cost to Xerox was between $150 million and $300 million. To change the U.S. auto industry in the 1980s, Deal and Kennedy feel that around $5 billion to $10 billion should have been spent on culture change. Because it was not spent, Deal and Kennedy predicted correctly in 1982 that "red ink will continue to flow."[17] The total cost of changing IBM's culture after its crash in 1992 was likely to be much more than $1 billion.

Given a rule of thumb that culture change costs 5 to 10 percent of the annual personnel budget for those involved, an executive may decide to attack certain cultural problems and walk away from others, to attack some value streams and not others. In some cases an attempt to make a major cultural change is not economical. Sometimes it is more cost-effective to close down the part of an enterprise that is losing money than to attempt to change its culture. It may be better to start a new green-field operation rather than attempt to convert a moribund one.

Not only does it cost more to change culture than most executives expect; it takes much more time. It can take years to accomplish deep-rooted change in an organization's culture. The stronger the culture the more it will stubbornly remain. People find subtle and often emotional reasons for rejecting the new culture. Culture tends to change faster in times of impending doom. When a crisis puts jobs at risk, people are more willing to learn new ways.

Stage-by-Stage Cultural Change

A widespread culture change may be broken into stages. It is much easier to change the culture of small groups then large ones. Teams, designed with the characteristics in Chapter 6, can be quickly imbued with a strong culture. It is often appropriate to tackle one value stream at a time. When one success has been achieved, the next is easier to carry out. The people who have been through the transition say, "We'd never go back to the previous way." A demonstrable success is needed because managers will find excuses not to change. If the success has reduced costs, or increased profits, substantially, the change is hard to resist. Measurable success makes it easier to neutralize people who are skillful at resisting change.

Sometimes an approach that changes formal culture needs to be introduced to the entire enterprise, like Jan Carlzon's "inverting the organization chart" in SAS. This needs enterprisewide missionary work on the part of top management, with every level of management backing up the "missionaries." A move to TQM culture could be tackled in one area at a time. The problem with area-by-area change is that it takes a long time, when usually the benefits are needed as quickly as possible. Top management must decide whether to take the aggressive but riskier road of tackling the culture of the whole enterprise in one sweep.

A change to formal culture is something that goes from top to bottom in an enterprise. It is important to deal with a vertical slice of the organization. One cannot change from a culture at the bottom of an enterprise without involving top management. Top management cannot successfully decree a change without careful attention to how culture is changed at the bottom. Technical culture changes are more easy to confine to one level.

The largest and most difficult culture changes are those that change the whole nature of the enterprise. The transition to a learning enterprise, from a control-oriented culture to an empowered culture, from a vertical to a horizontal organization—these are transitions in which the new culture grows out of repeated patterns of successful behavior. Management repeatedly promotes experiences of successful learning, measures and rewards learning, and demonstrates what they want the organization to be by learning themselves. Such large-scale transitions do not happen overnight. They are an accelerated version of the growth of a society or the transition of a town from a traditional Vermont village to a ski resort.

Exhibit 33.2   The process of changing culture

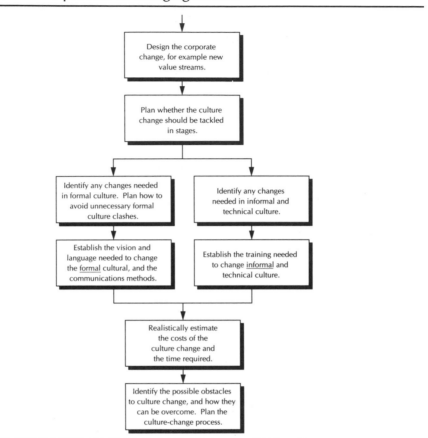

The Cultural Change Process

Exhibit 33.2 suggests steps in a process for changing corporate culture. The details of how culture is changed differ considerably from one situation to another. There are likely to be many variations on the process of Exhibit 33.2. Many analysts and managers who design and implement corporate changes do so without any study of how culture is transformed. This is asking for trouble, and the change process often fails. Even when it succeeds, cost in human wreckage is high. The professional Enterprise Engineer needs to pay careful attention to the steps in Exhibit 33.2.

References

1. Marion Bower, *The Will to Manage* (McGraw-Hill: New York, 1966).
2. Edward T. Hall, *The Silent Language* (Anchor Books: New York, 1981).
3. Ibid.
4. The model of corporate culture's protective barrier and ways to penetrate it is from Dan Silverman in James Martin & Co.
5. P. H. Mirvis and D. N. Berg (eds.), *Failures in Organizational Development and Change: Cases and Essays for Learning* (New York: Wiley, 1977). See R. E. Walton, "The Diffusion of New Work Structures: Explaining Why Success Didn't Take."
6. Ibid.
7. Hall, *The Silent Language*.
8. A. P. Murdock. This story is from Hall, *The Silent Language* (Anchor Books, Doubleday: New York, 1959).
9. Ibid.
10. Ibid.
11. "Missteps, Miscues—Business Reengineering Failures Have Cost Corporations Billions," *InformationWeek*, June 20, 1994.
12. Information from Dan Silverman.
13. David Ogilvy, *Ogilvy on Advertising*.
14. M. Hammer and J. Champy, *Reengineering the Corporation* (Harper Business: New York, 1993).
15. T. E. Deal and A. A. Kennedy, *Corporate Cultures* (Addison Wesley: Reading, Mass., 1982).
16. Ibid.
17. Ibid, page 163.

34

Managing the Risks of Corporate Change

As noted earlier, the United States spent about $32 billion on business reengineering projects in 1994, and a survey of 1,200 corporations indicated that this expenditure will reach more than $50 billion per year by 1997.[1,2] Mike Hammer estimates that 70 percent of business-reengineering efforts fail.[3]

The obstacles that prevent success in reengineering are surprisingly similar from one effort to another. Most consulting organizations that have done multiple reengineering projects have a list of obstacles or risks that they have learned to expect at different phases of a project. The types of obstacles become familiar and infuriatingly predictable. Because of their predictability, the team can be ready for them and can warn CEOs and sponsors to anticipate them.

If a danger is anticipated and thought about in advance by a determined top-management team, it is usually manageable. This chapter describes the types of obstacles that occur so that Enterprise Engineers can forewarn top executives and manage the risks in what is a highly risky process. Enterprise Engineering needs a disciplined approach to avoid failure.

Hammer lists three main reasons why the failures occur:[4]

- People don't know what they are talking about. (The term *business reengineering* is used as a hype word, often having no precise meaning).
- Committed executive leadership is missing. (Reengineering absolutely requires passionate top-down leadership).
- Corporations do not know how to manage corporate change. (They improvise, and reengineering is not something you can make up as you go along).

In this chapter we assume that people *do* know what they are talking about, *do* know how to go about reengineering, and that the CEO *is* committed to the task. Failures still occur. It is necessary to analyze the potential obstacles to success and then remove them.

High-Management Roadblocks

Some of the most dangerous risks relate to the sometimes hidden agenda of upper management. Top executives naturally tend to oppose any scheme that would lessen their own compensation or power.

Executives in charge of functional areas can be like the barons of medieval Europe. European countries were frequently torn by interbaronial rivalries and jealousies even when there were great dangers threatening or great opportunities beckoning from other lands. The barons would not be so naive as to say, "We're all part of the same enterprise, aren't we? Why can't we work together instead of wasting time on these internal wrangles?" The employees in an enterprise understand the strength of the interbaronial rivalries. The barons of Europe, when permitted, would build superbly strong castles. Periodically, kings used to find it necessary to knock down some of the castles. Today is such an age.

The ability to share knowledge widely allows an enterprise to become more fluid. It allows teams to work on the whole life cycle of valuable tasks in an enterprise, reducing functional barriers. Many middle managers want to protect their information, however. The barons of hierarchical management know that "unshared knowledge is power." They have long opposed databases that make "their" data freely available. Now the enterprise needs databases that support cross-functional teams. The functional barons have maintained their power by controlling communications and information flow. This inhibits vital forms of enterprise learning.

Only the CEO can deal with high-management changes. This is one reason the CEO must be *passionate* about reengineering. Enterprise redesign often removes layers of middle management. Cross-functional teams invade the power structures of functional managers. Middle management has to be changed in order to allow the new value streams to be as effective as possible. There must be no inhibitions to value-stream teams constantly learning and implementing what they learn.

Top executives' pay and motivation must be linked to *long-term* corporate performance so that they will make the structural changes necessary for success. They may be compensated with warrants, stock options, or other performance-related incentives. They must participate personally in the long-term success that is the reason for upheaval. The reward systems need to be redesigned from top to bottom.

Enterprise Engineers often develop a clear view of what an enterprise ought to be: a learning enterprise with empowered teams highly focused on delighting the customers of reinvented value streams. The path to this future is blocked by a collection of barriers in today's enterprises. Exhibit 34.1 presents characteristics of what the enterprise ought to be. Exhibit 34.2 shows some formidable barriers blocking the road. Breakthrough results come from overcoming these barriers. The energy to achieve such change comes from seeing the gap that exists between today's level of performance and what could be achieved.

Exhibit 34.1   Characteristics of a reengineered enterprise

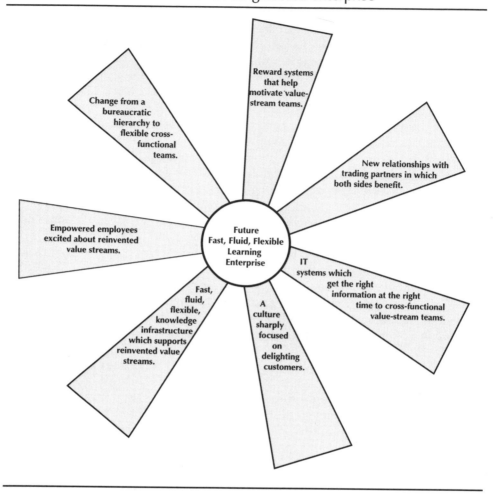

Ishikawa Risk Charts

In Chapter 16 we described the TQM technique of drawing fishbone (Ishikawa) diagrams to break down problems into their possible causes. The formidable risks associated with reengineering should be analyzed in a similar way. Because the risks are somewhat similar from one project to another, a reengineering team can start with a set of such diagrams and adjust them to reflect its own particular circumstances. The special risks of a specific project can be added to the charts. As in TQM, the purpose of the chart is to focus on the causes of problems and pay attention to techniques that can help to minimize the risk. The fishbone diagrams can be linked to Pareto diagrams (as in Chapter 16) for showing estimates

Exhibit 34.2 Barriers to achieving the characteristics in Exhibit 34.1

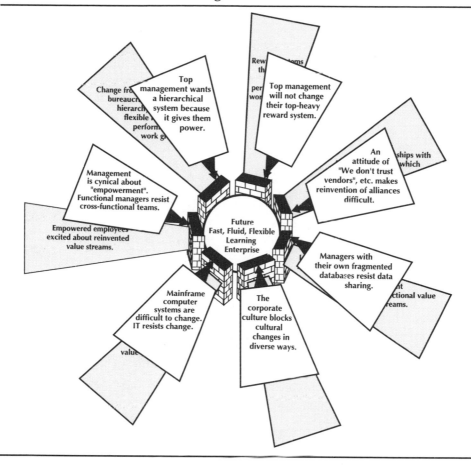

of the relative danger of the risk. (PC software tools exist for editing fishbone diagrams and generating associated Pareto diagrams).

Exhibits 34.3, 34.4, and 34.5 show risk charts for the *planning-and-design* phase of a reengineering project, the *implementation* phase, and the *beginning-operation* phase. Many projects have looked great when the design is done but have never been successfully implemented. Some have been implemented, the software been built, and pilot operations demonstrated, but they have never been transferred into successful operation. Often the major reasons for failure of what appeared excellent in concept are the barriers illustrated in Exhibit 34.2. There are many other problems (shown in Exhibits 34.3, 34.4, and 34.5), but most of these are manageable if management is prepared for them and determined to succeed.

The key to overcoming the obstacles is the determination of the CEO. Without this, reengineering usually fails. The CEO must clearly understand the bene-

Exhibit 34.3

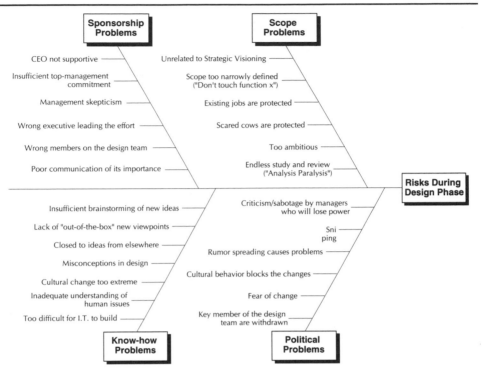

This and the following two exhibits show Ishikawa diagram of the risks encountered in the phases of reengineering. These may be linked to Pareto charts (as in Chapter 16) estimating the relative strengths of the risks. Forewarned, top management can help to manage the risks.

fits, and this ought to be linked to the strategic-visioning process. The reengineering team should discuss the fishbone risk charts and associated Pareto diagrams with the CEO, the chief organizational architect, and the top-management team that is (or should be) driving the reengineering process.

Methodology for Reengineering

Enterprise Engineering employs a family of change methods. These are processes for changing the processes of enterprises. Each change method consists of a set of steps to be accomplished, and each step has various considerations, based on experience, that are intended to make the step successful.

Exhibits 34.3, 34.4, and 34.5 show risk charts for the reengineering process. These can be broken into more detailed charts for each of the steps in the change

Exhibit 34.4 Risks during implementation

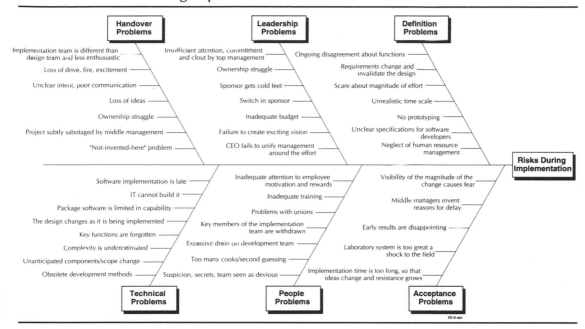

Exhibit 34.5 Risks when starting operation

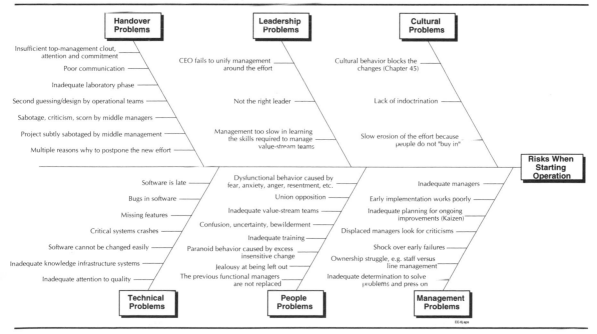

method. At each step various types of risks or obstacles are encountered that tend to repeat themselves from one project to another, so a team that has done many projects can anticipate them. A methodology for reengineering attempts to capture the experience on projects and use it to help ensure the next time. The reengineering team should be trained in such a methodology.

> *Just as civil engineers have methodologies for building skyscrapers, so Enterprise Engineers have methodologies for changing business processes. Both types of methodologies should be represented as PERT charts linked to computerized tools for project management. Both types of methodologies should have fishbone diagrams of the risks and problems likely to be encountered at each step.*

When risk charts are associated with each step in the methodology, they can have finer resolution and greater detail than those in Exhibits 34.3, 34.4, and 34.5.

EE Laboratory

Computer system development without prototyping usually produces bad results. It is only when prototypes are built and thoroughly tested by prospective users that the development organization can be sure it is building the right thing. Prototyping usually reveals all manner of misconceptions and aspects of faulty human factoring. Today, the users of computer systems should employ a "graphical user interface" (GUI) like that of the Macintosh system or Windows program. Tools exist for building such GUI prototypes very rapidly. These tools are used to prototype the user interface at an early stage of a project so that prospective users can see what the system will do. Many changes are made as a result of this.

When a value stream is reinvented, it needs more than software prototypes. It creates new types of jobs in which the tasks and activities are far more interrelated than before. At an early stage in the implementation cycle it is desirable to set up a laboratory environment in which the new work is performed in a simulated fashion. Employees who will form the future teams work to carry out the intended tasks, using the IT prototypes. This EE laboratory environment should be used as early as possible even if the simulation is crude and incomplete, because many new ideas are generated in the laboratory and subsequent brainstorming sessions. As well as triggering ideas, the EE laboratory reveals aspects of the design that do not work well or need thinking out in more detail.

Many projects reach the time when they should become operational only to find that pieces of the new jigsaw puzzle are missing. This is sometimes referred to as "the Swiss-cheese effect"—there are holes in the cheese. The Swiss-cheese effect has wrecked some massively funded redesign efforts. The EE laboratory helps to ensure that holes in the cheese are discovered before they become catastrophic.

In general much polishing and improvement results from the simulated operations of the EE lab. Sometimes surprising changes in direction occur. It may be discovered that higher levels of automation are possible than were imagined during the initial design or, conversely, that some aspects of the work are more subtle than was originally thought and cannot be fully automated. Only by setting up laboratory operations can the reengineering team find the best solutions.

When designing computer applications it is good practice to conduct a *facilitated workshop* with the potential users of the application, often called a JAD workshop (joint application design). The users and IT professionals together work out what the software ought to do, experiment with prototypes, and jointly create a design of the application. Such workshops are very important when reengineering is done, and several workshops may be used as the new process evolves and the new ways of working become steadily clearer. Workshops and brainstorming are used during the planning, design, and laboratory operations.

The laboratory makes it possible to experiment with new processes, make mistakes without incurring wrath, and explore alternatives in a much more realistic way than when doing design on paper.

Pilot Operation

Even after prototyping and laboratory operation, real-world operation is going to bring surprises. It makes sense to test the new way of working in one location, in a controlled way, and adjust it as required before going to full operation. After laboratory operation there should be pilot operation (Exhibit 34.6). The reengineering team then receives its first real-world feedback. It discovers how value-stream customers react to a reinvented value stream and is likely to discover that various changes are necessary in order to implement the value stream smoothly.

Sometimes pilot operation triggers a major crisis. The operation does not go as expected. Employees have difficulty doing what is required of them. The first results are disappointing. It is discovered that much more training is needed, or that the training should take place in a simulated environment. It may be found that the computer systems do not work as intended. They may be difficult to learn. LAN (local-area network) crashes may wreak havoc on the operation. Backup procedures are needed. The value-stream team needs more access to external help than originally envisioned.

It is desirable to find out about such problems and find solutions for them before full operation is attempted. A substantial period may be needed of the new process running concurrently with the old.

When things go wrong during the pilot operation (and they usually do) the reengineering team needs leadership that is determined to overcome the problems. The CEO should have been told to expect teething troubles and must protect the team from the anti-reengineering voices who will be vigorously saying "We told you so." Often the pilot operation is crude, but it reveals that the new way of working is possible and encourages the CEO to drive for the many improvements that are needed.

Exhibit 34.6   Phases of reengineering

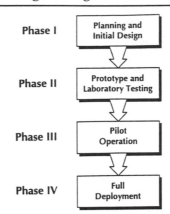

Phase I	Planning and Initial Design
Phase II	Prototype and Laboratory Testing
Phase III	Pilot Operation
Phase IV	Full Deployment

The initial design usually changes substantially in phase 3 (prototyping and laboratory testing). It may change substantially during (phase 3) pilot operation.

Kaizen during Operation

Even when the new way of working is fully deployed, it should be regarded as a start-up phase of something which will improve dramatically. The first video cameras, airplanes, personal computers, and so on, were very primitive. The first version of any invention is crude compared to what the invention will eventually become. This is true of reinvented value streams.

The months or years after a reinvented value stream becomes operational should be a period of intense *kaizen* activity. Everybody should be analyzing problems and brainstorming solutions. There should be an intense drive for rapid improvement.

IT Failures

Many of the most valuable examples of reengineering require major new IT systems. This is especially so when building the "predator" capabilities discussed in Chapter 30 which enable a corporation to push vigorously ahead of its competition. The survey mentioned earlier forecast that of $52 billion spend on business reengineering in the United States in 1997, nearly $40 billion would pay for information systems.[5] Often the most expensive failure during implementation is failure to build the right IT systems. William Stoddard, a partner in charge of reengineering at Anderson Consulting, described a company that brought in Anderson because "one project after another had died in its tracks" when the company spent a great deal of time "building castles in the air without paying attention to information technology."[6] This has happened in many reengineering efforts. Citibank N.A. wasted $50 million in an effort to reengineer the handling of its custody and master-trust product lines. *Information Week* reported "Citibank booted IBM's Integrated Systems Solutions Corp. (ISSC) and a slew of subcontractors off the project . . . the mistake was to try to modify the source code of an off-the-shelf solution. . . . Citibank has taken the systems development efforts back in-house."[7]

The Need for Speed

A reengineering project needs to be done quickly. Some authorities have stated that it typically takes three years. This is far too long. A three-year project has a high probability of failure.

There are two major reasons why *long* reengineering projects fail.

First, there is a major impact on jobs, including jobs of powerful or highly paid people. Once the rumor mill starts, people who do not want their jobs changed try to block the change. People who do not want to lose power or comfort attempt to sabotage the reengineering in subtle ways. One executive who had been involved in multiple projects referred to a period when rumors and bad news about change spread as "the Valley of Death." People are worried about their future. It is desirable to pass through the Valley of Death as quickly as possible.

Second, the business and competition are changing while the reengineering is being done. If the reengineering takes three years, the world will have changed before it is finished.

To speed up implementation, the IT organization has to build or acquire the necessary systems *fast*. It may buy packages; it may out-source the development, or it may build the systems in-house—but speed is essential. The old two-to-three-year development cycle, common with COBOL or C programming, is not acceptable for business reengineering. Fast development needs code generators and power tools, and teams that use them well. The IT development process itself is a prime target for reengineering in many corporations.

Even though laboratory operation is essential, it should not be an excuse for endless experimentation. Rapid prototyping should speed up the design process, and rapid laboratory testing should speed up the polishing and tuning. Many good projects fail because of "analysis paralysis" or a never-ending search for perfection. A motto of reengineering should be the following:

> *A workable solution implemented next month is better than a perfect solution implemented next year.*

No solution is likely to be very good until it has been used in live operation and many improvements made as a result. The sooner it gets into live operation the better so that real-life improvements can begin.

Risks Associated with Hand-overs

A particularly risky time is after one team hands over the work to a different team.

It is generally a bad idea to separate design and implementation. The design team should be responsible for the reengineered process until it is operational. The design team should "contract out" the implementation work such as software development, even though that development may be done in-house. The design team must monitor and control the implementation very closely.

Nevertheless, one sometimes finds one team conceptualizing and designing a reengineered process and the implementation being handed over to a different organization, which must build the IT systems needed or work out the detailed compensation plans, hiring policies, and so on. The original design team was excited about its own "baby," but the implementation group is less enthusiastic as its members confront the details and difficulties of implementing the reengineered process. During implementation, there may be sniping and obstacles raised by people who do not welcome the change in jobs or in the power structure.

Even if one team does the design and implementation of the new procedure, its members are not the people who have to live with it. When it is handed over to operational managers or the new value-stream teams, many difficulties are encountered or new forms of opposition raised. Managers are frightened of the change; workers are uncomfortable with it and long for the old sacred cows.

The design team may be wildly enthusiastic about its plans but may run into open hostility, with everything possible being done to sink the scheme. Many excellent reinventions of value streams are never launched, and many that are launched sink soon afterward.

Continuity of sponsorship needs to be maintained throughout such transitions. If the same sponsor is determined to make it work, there is a far better chance of success. Often, chaos occurs when the sponsor or CEO changes. A new CEO may have different ideas about how to make things work.

Dysfunctional Behavior

A major reason for problems or failure is employees' behaving in harmful ways. They may be coping with negative feelings caused by fear, anxiety, resentment, or regret at the loss of a role they were comfortable with. To deal with such feelings, sensitive human attention is needed. Employee emotions should be anticipated and dealt with in a caring manner, almost like corporate psychotherapy. Dysfunctional behavior may be caused by bewilderment, uncertainty, and lack of understanding. To avoid this problem, relentless attention must be paid to good communications, education, and explanation of reasons.

Fears, resentment, anger, and panic may be understandable (see Chapter 32). There may be sudden layoffs, breaking of the perceived employee compact that traded employee loyalty for job security, loss of opportunities for promotion up a multilevel hierarchy, loss of entitlement to regular pay increases, and restructuring of the pay scheme. As noted in Chapter 32, if the human-resources organization has already addressed these issues and established a new deal for employment, the transitions caused by changes such as value-stream reinvention can be smoother.

The resistance to cultural change, discussed in Chapter 32, is a reason for dysfunctional behavior. An understanding of corporate culture and how to change it is desirable. Particularly valuable is an understanding of when change in formal culture has a high probability of failure. It may be easier to start a new business unit than to change a deeply rooted formal culture. If such a culture must be changed, it needs totally concerted management effort.

Cynical employees have been confronted with threats of change before and may be saying to themselves, "This too shall pass," "Keep your head down, and it will blow over," "If I ignore it, it will go away." Management must demonstrate relentlessly, over and over again: "We are serious. It is going to happen. It needs full commitment from everybody"—in Mike Hammer's expression, "We will take care of the wounded but shoot the stragglers."

Some employees or managers may be active, rather than passive, in their resistance. They believe they can stop the reengineering and set about doing so through either overt or underground means. It may be necessary for management to demonstrate that it will root out the dissidents. The dissidents often say, "The whole thing is crazy. They don't know what they're doing. It's unnecessary. The process works well today, and this will wreck it." Management needs to spell out in detail and with clarity why the change must happen and how the results will be better. Management needs to develop champions and enthusiasts of the change who will spread their enthusiasm. Clear, relentless communication is essential.

Many employees alarmed by the change have fears that it is bad for them. Management needs to address these fears carefully and put together packages that makes the change attractive. "It is exciting. Jobs will be more interesting, more fun. You will be empowered. You will be constantly challenged to use your creativity." Particularly important, management must design a good employment deal for the key players (class 1 and class 2 in Exhibit 32.1) and demonstrate how they participate financially in the improvement. The change agents must design new jobs that are exciting, creative, fun, and financially rewarding when successful.

To make reengineering succeed, sensitive care and attention is needed to the human issues. Good executives have generated a sense of excitement for the entire corporation, surrounding the adventurous journey into the new world.

Pavlov's Dogs

Often the most serious inhibitor to learning in an enterprise is employees' belief that mistakes may be punished, perhaps indirectly. They reason, If you do everything "by the book," you are safe; any deviation from the book is risky and may incur wrath if there are complaints. This widespread stultifying attitude is reinforced by the impression that doing everything "by the book" will eventually result in seniority upgrade or promotion; attracting wrath may eliminate this possibility, so "Don't rock the boat."

Edgar Schein, a professor of management at the Sloane School, compares learned emotional behavior in enterprises to Pavlov's experiments with dogs.[8] A dog can be conditioned with rewards or with punishments, but negative reinforcement is stronger than positive.

If you always ring a bell before you feed a dog, the dog learns to associate the bell with the reward. If the food then stops coming when the bell is rung, the dog unlearns the association fairly quickly. On the other hand, if you put a dog in a green room and give it a painful electric shock when a bell rings, it will quickly learn to avoid green rooms. When the shocks are turned off, it will still avoid green rooms. If the dog *had* to spend much time in the green room full of bells, it would acquire a severe phobia about green rooms. It would be difficult to remove this phobia when the shocks were turned off.

Pavlov's experiments indicate that behavior learned through punishment is more stable than behavior learned through reward. This finding was put to use in some unpleasant organizations in the past. When things change, and we want the dog to go into the green room, we have difficulty making that happen. People who have been conditioned with punishment limit their behavior to what they think is safe. They avoid trial-and-error learning. When the cause of the phobia has gone, they do not lose the phobia.

We can motivate people with sticks and carrots. In times of rapid change, carrots work well but sticks do not. If we establish behavior with sticks, when we need to change that behavior we cannot easily remove the phobia caused by sticks. People continue to use behavior patterns that avoided punishment in the past.

Organizations that have emphasized punishment over reward are extremely difficult to change. Communist enterprises, Kafkaesque bureaucracies, the Chinese Cultural Revolution, military boot camps, or their corporate equivalents leave long-lasting phobias. Executives building learning enterprises have found it easier to start from scratch than to convert organizations in which people were strongly conditioned by punishment.

Many managers have actually enjoyed using punishment. It makes them feel tough. They think that the mark of a strong executive is that he "kicks ass." The most difficult organization to change is one in which conditioning by retribution is combined with upgrades in seniority. Employees avoid any unsafe behavior under such circumstances. They keep their heads down, incur no risks, and wait for promotion. A dreaded form of punishment is delay of a seniority upgrade. Such organizations ought to be regarded as part of the obsolete past, as inappropriate for competitive corporations as Frederick Taylor's stopwatches. They worked in static situations when work consisted of repetitive processing, but today repetitive processing can largely be done by computers. Routine work is for machines; work that requires change is for human beings.

Successful corporations are those that change faster than their competitors, who are always "moving in" to copy what works well. But conditioning by punishment inhibits change. The dog who got electric shocks cowers in areas that are safe.

Fear of Reorganization

Sometimes the "green room" is any form of corporate reorganization. People remember previous reorganizations as traumatic, with all employees worrying about whether they would be fired, the corporation being "downsized," or put through other forms of pain. As soon as a new reorganization is announced, or a new leader takes over, the phobias from previous reorganizations are activated. The employees are being forced into Pavlov's green room again. The change agent cannot produce new behavior in a dog agitated by its previous green-room experience.

We have emphasized that a leader must create a vision of an exciting future. The problem with that approach is the failure to consider that for many people the vision represents a green room. They have established some degree of job comfort, but now the prospect exists of entering the green room again. The exciting vision does not overcome the green-room anxieties. Schein explains, "Our complex human mind is able to defend itself against messages which make it anxious." There are three common defenses:

- Employees do not hear the message.
- Employees deny that the message applies to them.
- Employees rationalize that their leaders do not understand the situation.

Given this collective set of responses, how can the change agent move forward?

A Counter-Anxiety

Schein described anxieties that produce resistance to change as "anxiety 1."[9] Anxiety 1 is associated with unwillingness to learn new behavior because it appears too disruptive, difficult, or potentially traumatic. The difficulty of learning something new is such that for a period you may be made to feel a fool. Worse, you may not succeed in learning it, may not fit in with the changed behavior, or may make serious mistakes. To avoid anxiety 1, employees deny the need for change, project the need for change onto others, or manage to avoid learning by means of various defensive mechanisms.

Anxiety 1 needs to be countered with a different anxiety—anxiety 2, concern that bad things will happen if you do *not* change. It represents fear of the consequences of failing to learn new behavior. These consequences include shame, guilt, lack of respect, demotion, not being part of the success, being bypassed, the closing of one's department, and (at worst) corporate failure—losing one's job.

When anxiety 1 dominates, people find subtle ways to rationalize away the need for change. They will cling to old habits. They will avoid confrontations with uncertainty. Schein states that it is necessary for the change agent to make anxiety 2 substantially larger than anxiety 1. Only then will change happen.

To make employees understand that the corporation needs to change can be difficult. Often they have been made to take pride in both the corporation and the way they work. They believe that incremental improvement is needed but see no reason for traumatic upheaval. A careful education process is needed to make them understand that major change is needed. Benchmarking helps with this. It can be demonstrated that a different corporation is operating a process with much greater productivity, speed, or reliability.

Often employees do not believe it when management says, "We are in trouble." They have to be given detailed figures with a detailed explanation of what the figures mean. Even then they may reason that the cause of the problem has nothing to do with them. "It's not my fault that the sales are low."

The change agent has to relate the need for new behavior to the individuals he wishes to change. They must be made to feel that if they do not do something new, bad consequences will occur. Their jobs may be in jeopardy; they may be moved to a different area; they may lose seniority, title, bonus, or status. The change agent has to "get their attention."

The corporation's change might be thought of as being like a group in a movie reaching a swaying wire bridge across a precipitous gorge. The group looks at the bridge and says, "There's no way we're going across that!" (anxiety 1). The danger of *not* crossing it must be perceived to be greater than the danger of crossing it. A desperate criminal gang is pursuing the fleeing people fast with machine guns (anxiety 2). Those group needs to perceive that the danger is real; the enemy is not in sight, but if those being pursued wait until it is they will be too late.

The leader needs not only to make anxiety 2 seem real and severe enough to warrant risk but also must minimize the dangers inherent in anxiety 1. To minimize anxiety 1, the leader needs to demonstrate a clear path forward with appropriate safeguards. The leader shows the others what to do, equips them with safety ropes, and goes across the bridge first.

Countering one anxiety by emphasizing a worse one must not preclude careful attention to the human reaction. Pavlov set up experiments in which the only alternative to the green room was a red room. If the dog fleeing the green room is given shocks in the red room, and then all shocks were turned off, the dog rushes back and forth between the green room and red room until totally exhausted. It does not learn that the shocks have been turned off. Some corporations allow both anxiety 1 and anxiety 2 to become phobias, and in the general agitation employees do little that is useful; they become paralyzed with concern about either course. Morale goes to pieces. The skilled change agent is a coach who skillfully balances anxiety 2 with a demonstration of how to succeed in the new way ahead. He creates, as far as he can, conditions of psychological comfort with the new behavior. This approach calls for careful training and education, clear guidelines, coaching, praise, and rewards for moving ahead.

If the road ahead is clear, the vision of the future is exciting, and people know that they will be well trained and not punished for mistakes, employees may become exhilarated, and work hard not to let their team down. In Chaparral Steel, described in Chapter 31, radical change is always in the air, but the absentee rate is about a quarter of that reported by the U.S. National Association of Manufacturers.[10]

Psychological comfort in an environment of rapid change needs the following:

- Careful coaching with attention to employees' feelings
- Good education and training
- Opportunities for practice with supportive groups
- Carrots, not sticks
- No punishment
- Encouragement to overcome the shame associated with making errors
- Encouragement of experimentation
- Rewards for innovation
- Membership of a team whose members all help fellow members ("We're all in this together.")
- Clear term goals
- Constant demonstration from management that innovation is important
- A fully supportive environment
- Full explanation from management of the directions of the business and the reasons for the corporation's actions

In general, sensitive human care is needed when major changes are made. A sledge-hammer approach to reengineering can cause vitally needed changes to fail. Only too often managers attempt to bulldoze changes through without addressing the fears and emotions of employees with care and attention.

Different Risk Profiles

The different change methods of Enterprise Engineering have different risk profiles associated with them. Value-stream reinvention is much riskier than procedure redesign. Enterprise redesign may expose the whole enterprise to high risk. The largest benefits often come from the riskiest changes (otherwise those changes should not be incurred). The chief organizational architect needs to understand the alternative change methods, the associated risks, and the techniques for minimizing and managing those risks.

TQM/*Kaizen*

TQM/*kaizen* can be accomplished with little change to the organization structure. However, to succeed a major change in culture and reward systems is needed. Enterprises that have been successful at TQM have gone to extraordinary lengths to enroll the entire management in a new language of empowerment to make these programs work. The programs can thus be viewed as largely cultural change processes rather than as business process redesign.

Procedural Redesign

This process is chosen specifically to avoid pervasive structural and cultural change. The chief organizational architect may judge that the organization is not ready to enroll itself in the upheaval that value-stream reinvention demands, so specific processes are chosen for redesign to achieve performance improvements in a limited region of the enterprise.

Value-Stream Reinvention

Value-stream reinvention involves radical change in both structure and culture. It replaces the existing value stream with something entirely different. It deliberately kills the sacred cows in order to rethink the basic means by which value should be delivered. Because of this revolutionary flavor, the design team usually isolates itself from the organization—its thinking seems too radical for everyone, perhaps even its sponsor. The new value stream must be tried in a laboratory environment and piloted to ease it into the organization. The people involved on the project and the pilots need significant cultural transition support themselves.

Enterprise Redesign

When an enterprise contemplates changing its fundamental reasons for existence, it faces a daunting cultural task. Anyone who has been part of an acquisition or merger knows how long the two cultures persist in conflict with one another. The structural-cultural transition becomes a major project itself. (In fact, the ability to carry out such transitions is a hallmark of companies that compete via these means.) That is why performing major enterprise transition by building a new part of the enterprise at a new site is often more desirable than attempting to change a strongly embedded resistive culture.

Strategic Visioning

The cultural issues in strategic visioning involve the top-management team itself. Members must set aside their defensiveness in order to invent a new strategic context for the organization. This almost always involves engaging in type D learning through the use of outside agents such as consultants. Sometimes it is extremely difficult to change the culture and beliefs of top management. The profound effects produced by the new strategic context may reverberate throughout the enterprise. Strategic visioning is done precisely to produce an energizing context that can transform organizational culture from the top down.

Exhibit 34.7

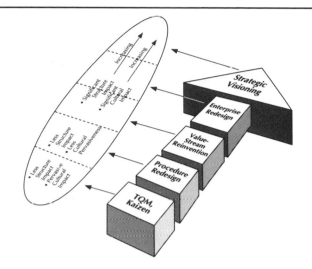

Different risks are associated with the different EE change methods. The chief organizational architect needs to invoke the categories of change that are appropriate to the circumstances.

References

1. Bruce Caldwell, "Missteps, Miscues," *Information Week,* June 20, 1994.
2. Survey by *Systems Reengineering Economics,* newsletter (Computer Economics, Inc.: Carlsbad, Cal., 1994).
3. Mike Hammer's estimate is repeatedly quoted as in Caldwell, "Missteps, Miscues," *Information Week,* June 20, 1994.
4. "Hammer's Belief: Reengineering Requires Passionate Leadership," *Information Week,* June 20, 1994.
5. Survey by *Systems Reengineering Economics,* newsletter (Computer Economics, Inc.: Carlsbad, Cal., 1994).
6. William Stoddard, quoted in *Information Week,* June 20, 1994.
7. "Citi Falls Asleep," *Information Week,* June 20, 1994.
8. Edgar H. Schein, "How Can Organizations Learn Faster? The Challenge of Entering the Green Room," *Sloan Management Review,* Winter 1993.
9. Ibid.
10. Dorothy Leonard-Barton, "The Factory as a Learning Laboratory," *Sloan Management Review,* Fall 1992.

35

Starting Afresh

A friend who can imitate a strong Irish accent likes to tell a story about asking the way to Dublin. The reply is "Now, if I was going to Dublin, I wouldn't start from here!"

If long-term survival requires a boundaryless, value-stream, learning-laboratory corporation (or whatever other characteristics describe the survivor), a critical question is "Can you get there if you start from here? It is difficult and painful to transform a 1970s-style enterprise into a new-world enterprise operating in top gear. It is just about impossible to turn a bureaucracy or an aristocracy into a learning laboratory. Brute force will not do it; the Chinese Cultural Revolution was one of the biggest disasters in human history.

It would be almost impossible to turn a traditional big-steel corporation into a learning-laboratory corporation like Chaparral. But if big steel is in competition with many Chaparrals, big steel will die. It is interesting to note that in staffing Chaparral, its management avoided workers with steel-industry experience. They hired, and continue to hire, farmers and ranchers from the local area with mechanical experience. They look for "a twinkle in the eye, a zest for life, basically conscientious people who can put in a strong day's work and enjoy what they're doing . . . people who have not been exposed to other companies' bad habits."[1]

To say it again, Chaparral, the United States' tenth-largest steel producer, has a productivity more than three times the industry average.

Productivity, Worker-hours per rolled ton of steel:[2]

US average	:	5.3
Japanese average	:	5.6
German average	:	5.7
Chaparral	:	1.5

Can the legendary steel mills of the Ruhr survive unless they turn themselves into Chaparrals?

Many other corporations that are harbingers of the twenty-first century are new corporations, not born-again old corporations.

Often the best strategy for the existing traditional corporation is to start up green-field subsidiaries. Design them from the beginning to follow the principles summarized in this book. Design them to be learning laboratories and make sure they are not contaminated by the old-style executives, bean-counters, unions, clergy, lawyers, bureaucrats, personnel managers, or guardians of past methodology.

The MIT International Motor Vehicle Program showed that there are almost no examples of mass-production car factories, or European craft-style car factories, having converted successfully to lean manufacturing. The lean factories with high productivity and high quality were new start-from-scratch operations. Pygmalion stories are for the theater. In General Motors the NUMMI plant, the Saturn plant, and the East German Opel plant are the most interesting steps toward the future car factory, and all were green-field factories, fundamentally rethinking what a GM factory ought to be like.

One reason why German and Japanese corporations became so successful in the decades after World War II was that their factories had been bombed until the rubble bounced. They had to rethink and begin again.

Green-Field Value Streams

Value-stream reinvention, in its most extreme form, means *scrapping* existing business structure and processes and starting again. Change agents determine what the results of the value stream ought to be in the future and work backwards as if unconstrained by present processes or management. They say, "If this were a start-up company, how would we operate the end-to-end process?"

Scrapping and starting over is shock treatment in many enterprises. Not surprisingly, it meets with much resistance. The reengineering czar needs to be the CEO, COO, or a person with top-level clout. Mike Hammer comments, "A lot of people have to be clouted."[3] Failures occur when a sledge-hammer approach is taken to changing corporate culture. Done right, starting over with new value-stream teams can generate a new level of energy and excitement. Creating excitement about a new way of working can be much more successful than endlessly patching the old way of working.

There can be problems operating a fundamentally reinvented value stream in an otherwise-traditional enterprise. It creates a group who play by different rules; have a different type of compensation, appraisal, and rewards; and have a different relationship with management. Unless carefully managed it can be an alien body within a strong culture, which causes the cultural antibodies to go to work as described in Chapter 33. For this reason some CEOs have planned an *enterprisewide* transition and all employees are made to feel part of that transition. All employees are given a vision that excites them and are made to feel part of a long-range journey toward that vision.

This enterprise-wide transition has occurred in corporations of ten thousand people (such as Britain's Mercury) but is extremely difficult to achieve in very large, hierarchical, or bureaucratic enterprises. The large enterprise may choose to transform one location at a time, or to establish one or more new green-field locations. It is often advisable to establish new business units with new-style architecture.

It can be difficult to transform one value stream fundamentally. The difficulties are compounded if many value streams are tackled at once. An attempt to switch the whole of Russia from communism to capitalism doomed it to chaos.

The most risk-free approach may therefore be to grow new subsidiaries in which learning occurs at a rapid rate. The learning is documented, and as the subsidiaries succeed they are multiplied rapidly. If new growth occurs vigorously, the deadwood can be removed as in pruning an apple tree. To do this humanely, the deadwood employees are retrained, indoctrinated, and made part of the new organization, where their success with new-style work will be appraised along with everyone else's.

George Gilder describing how revolutionary change occurred in the microelectronics industry comments, "No matter how persuasive the advocates of change, it is very rare that an entrenched establishment will reform its ways. Establishments die or retire themselves, or fall in revolutions; they only rarely transform themselves."[4] He describes how some microelectronics companies did succeed in learning and transforming themselves. Today, equally fast changes are needed in many companies because of the pressures of globalism, new technology, intensified competition, automation, rapid product change, and custom demand for quality and service. Companies that do not change fast enough get into trouble, as IBM did.

Green-Field Business Units

Many corporations are now beginning to build small business units. Hitachi Ltd. has 600 companies (27 publicly traded). Johnson & Johnson has 106. Some large corporations in the future may have thousands of small business units. The autonomous business units may obtain services such as financing, advertising, and global distribution from their large parent. The new business units, however, should be built with value-stream teams and new-world principles. This may become the primary form of transition to the new world.

To make sure that it has its own new-world culture, a small business unit has to be autonomous and separate from its parent company. It must be free to hire its own people and build its own culture, although it may be guided at arm's length by the chief organizational architect of the parent company. It is necessary to decide what services of the parent it can use without inhibiting the building of its new culture. The knowledge infrastructure of the parent may be important for spreading what is learned.

The four categories of Enterprise Engineering change methods may be interpreted as in Exhibit 35.1, with the fourth category being "Start afresh rather then attempt to change an existing organization." Sometimes the existing organization has so much baggage and overhead, and is so resistant to change, that it is easier to start afresh. Bulldoze the old factory and build a new one with new principles.

Exhibit 35.1 The fourth option: starting green-field operations

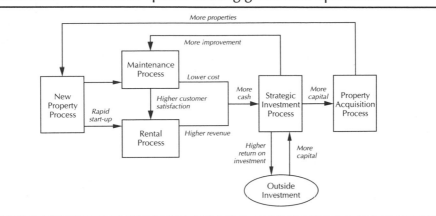

New, or transformed, corporations must be so structured that change happens constantly and easily. This can happen if the corporation is built with value-stream teams that learn constantly. A well-designed infrastructure is a crucial component of any enduring organization in a time of accelerating change. Today, most enterprises are not structured in a form that allows much rapid change. They often rely on computer systems that have been built to produce next year changes needed next month. Many enterprises fail to harness the energy and ingenuity of their employees as they should. Employees have untapped reservoirs of creativity. Most employees could contribute much more than they have the opportunity to do.

The difficulty is transforming from the old architecture with its power structure to the new architectures, which facilitate constant learning. Once the new architecture is in place, change can happen continuously. But it is virtually impossible to change a big-steel mill into a Chaparral.

Reinventing Government?

An alarming scenario is that the transition from old-world to new-world will happen vigorously in competitive corporations, but not in government. Government could be old-world in a society where everything else is new-world.

In 1993 U.S. Vice-President Al Gore started a vigorous initiative for "reinventing government" with the intent of avoiding that scenario. In some pockets of government, changes occurred, but most bodies seemed to subscribe to this view: "Keep your head down. This problem will go away after the next election." Seven months after Al Gore's report on the subject first went to President Clinton, the Vice-President began visits to key federal agencies to celebrate reengineering successes.[5] The "successes" were minor changes within a traditional old-world structure. There was no value-stream reinvention as described in Part II.

Peter Drucker, in his book *Post-Capitalist Society*, lists reasons why the techniques of business reengineering are unlikely to work in government. Because of this he states that any activity of government that could be out-sourced to competitive corporations should be.[6] It is the forces of competition that drive the reinvention of corporations; these forces say "Reinvent or die." Most (but not all) of the activities now being done in government could be done by competitive enterprise.

Between 1939 and 1954 Britain lost most of its colonies. It changed from having the largest empire in history to having a few colonies, which were mostly vacation islands such as Bermuda and Malta. During the same period the Colonial Office, the central administration for the Empire, grew from 420 to 1,661 people. It became larger than at the height of the British Empire.[7]

At the Ochoco National Forest in Oregon five district rangers oversee a million acres of timber. However they spend most of their time with paper, not trees. There are 53 separate budgets, 577 management codes, and 1,769 accounting lines.[8] The Agriculture Department operates many extension offices to give free advice to farmers. In Georgia's Douglas County it serves only 17 farmers but costs $85 thousand to operate. Almost all of those farmers do not use its free advice.

It is estimated that an average of 23 signatures are needed when the U.S. Federal Government buys goods or services. There are ten pages of specifications for ashtrays (called "ash receivers, tobacco, desk type"). The General Services Administration approval process for ordering a computer takes as long as three years; computers become outdated in one year.

When an organization grows for a long time without the forces of competition weeds can choke the garden. The most effective solution is to plough the garden and start afresh.

Global Rebuilding

Enterprise Engineering has massive social and national implications. The planet is shrinking. Nations once designated "Third-World countries" are industrializing rapidly. Countries with reengineered enterprises will pull ahead of those stuck with traditional enterprises. Parts of the world that have vigorous new growth, such as Southeast Asia, will build new-style corporations capable of competing better than nonreengineered Western corporations.

The United States has an entrepreneurial tradition. Its venture-capital structure, bankruptcy laws, and absence of layoff inhibitions encourage fast growth of new corporations that recreate the rules. The United States may reinvent itself faster than Europe.

Europe has double the unemployment rate of that in the United States, but most of its large enterprises could (and probably should) be run with far fewer of people. Probably the reason why the United States has lower unemployment is that it creates new corporations faster. New corporations provide new employment, whereas old corporations are cutting back their staff. New business start-ups nearly tripled in the United States from about 270 thousand in 1978 to some 750 thousand in 1988, creating 15 million new jobs.

Japan's *kaizen* culture impels Japanese corporations to improve continuously until they achieve excellence. Traits such as discipline, conformity, and uniformity help greatly with TQM. But Japan generally avoids traumatic human upheaval. Value-stream reinvention involves traumatic change, but (in the Western view) to scrap and rebuild is often better than continuous improvement in an era when business's paradigms are shifting fast.

The American dream is to have a "piece of the action." America's fast growth of new corporations, driven by entrepreneurs who reinvent everything, lends power to the United States economy. Japan discourages nonconformists; America thrives on them. Diversity, nonconformity, autonomy, inventiveness, originality, and entrepreneurism are strengths that the West must tap in order to compete with Japan.

The danger in the West is its large number of old, self-satisfied enterprises with overpaid executives protecting their power structure. While China, India, and the Pacific Rim are vigorously building new corporations according to the new principles, the Western country-club set is complacently unaware of the revolution. The West has allowed its schools to go to pieces at a time when reading, communication skills, and basic mathematics are particularly badly needed. Many skilled employees in countries such as Indonesia and the Philippines earn one-tenth of what people in similar positions do in Europe and America. This differential obviously cannot last. The country-club set of the West seems like the aristocracy of the 1920s—destined to be swept away.

The challenge for the West now is, Can it build new corporations fast enough using the principles described in this book?

References

1. Chaparral's Administrative Vice-President Dennis Beach, quoted in Dorothy Leonard-Barton: "The Factory as a Learning Laboratory," *Sloan Management Review,* Fall 1992.
2. Figures quoted in Leonard-Barton article above.
3. J. Champy and M. Hammer, *Reengineering the Corporation,* Harper Business: New York, 1993.
4. George Gilder, *Microcosm* (Touchstone, Simon and Schuster: Englewood Cliffs, N.J., 1988).
5. National Performance Review, *Reinventing Government Update,* Office of the Vice President, Washington, May 1994.
6. Peter Drucker, *Post-Capitalist Society* (Harper Business: New York, 1993).
7. C. Northcote Parkinson, *Parkinson's Law* (Ballantine Books, New York, 1957).
8. "Godzilla Zaps the System," *Time,* September 19, 1993.

Glossary

The basic concepts and terms of Enterprise Engineering are listed here along with the chapter in which an introductory explanation or definition of them appears.

Anticipatory vs. reactive change	28
Arrow (spectrum) of EE approaches	5
Attacker's advantage	25
Automation of HR function	32
Barriers to experimental learning	30
Benchmarking	11
Beyond-the-call-of-duty awards (BCD)	10
Boundarylessness	2
Business rules in software	31
Bypass of middleman	13
Capability predator	24
Cause-and-effect diagram	16
Chief organizational architect (COA)	4
Companywide quality control	15
Continuous-discontinuity management	25
Continuous-process improvement	5
Continuous vs. discontinuous change	18
Core competency	23
Corporate transparency	4
Corporate vision	27
Counterintuitive behavior	20
Culture: formal, informal and technical	33
Customer-delight factors	10
Cybercorp	1
Dangerous feedback	21
Deming Prize	15
Design of experiments (DOE)	16
Discontinuities	25
Discontinuity management	25
Discontinuous change	5
Discontinuous vs. continuous change	18
Double-loop learning	30
Dysfunctional behavior	34
EE laboratory	35
Elapsed-time–work-time ratio	8
Employee types (A, B, G, and D)	36
Empowerment	2
Enterprise Engineer (professional)	5
Enterprise Engineering	Preface
Enterprise redesign	5
Fishbone (Ishikawa) diagram	16
Five *Why*s	15
Five *Why*s for the CEO	22
Formal culture	33
Half-life measures of learning	30
High-performance team	6
HR	32
Informal culture	33
Investment life cycle (for technology)	25

Ishikawa (fishbone) diagram	16	Quality-function deployment	10
Ishikawa risk charts	34	Real team	6
ISO 9000	15	Risk charts (Ishikawa)	34
IT (information technology)	7	Roadmap for corporate change	28
Kaizen	14	S-curve	25
Kaizen awards ceremony	15	Sacred cows	12
Kaizen-capable computing	13	Scenarios	26
Knowledge infrastructure	30	Shamrock organization	19
Laboratory for EE	34	Simultaneous engineering	8
Laboratory for value-stream		Single-loop learning	30
testing	10	Six-sigma quality	16
Laboratory in business	2	Statistical quality control	16
Lean manufacturing	13	Stovepipe systems	8
Learning-laboratory		Strategic capability	23
corporation	31	Strategic competency	23
Learning-laboratory value		Strategic-learning laboratory	24
stream	9	Strategic value stream	24
Legos	16	Strategic visioning	22
Life-cycle curve (of technology)	15	Support of value stream	8
Long-span activity webs	19	System dynamics	20
Malcolm Baldrige Award	15	Systemic behavior	20
Maslow's Hierarchy of Human		Taylorism	2
Needs	2	Team (versus working group)	6
Mental models	16	Technical culture	33
Multicorporate organism	4	Technology S-curves	25
Multicorporate TQM	18	360-degree appraisals	32
Negative feedback	21	Total quality control (TQC)	15
New deal for employment	32	Total quality management	
New world architecture	28	(TQM)	15
Official future	26	Triage	13
Organizational-interaction chart	12	Valley of Death	34
Out-of-awareness		Value chain	7
communication	33	Value stream	7
Pareto diagram	16	Value stream, primary and	
Pay-for-knowledge schemes	32	strategic	8
PDCA cycle	14	Value stream as a learning	
Pilot operation (of reengineered		laboratory	9
activity)	34	Value-stream laboratory	13
Positive feedback	21	Value-stream learning	7
Postcapitalist society	1	Value-stream reinvention	7
Primary value stream	8	Value-stream team	11
Procedure redesign	5	Value-stream vision	27
Prototype operation	34	Virtual enterprise	29
Pseudoteams	6	Virtuosos	6
Quality circle	15	Zero defections	10
Quality control	15	Zero defects	14

Index

Accountability
  individual and collective, 87
  team, 89–90
Ackoff, Russell, 38, 294
Activities web, enterprise, 267–69
Administrative process redesign,
  36–37
Architecture
  of an enterprise, 56
  goals of new-world enterprise,
    374–76
  value-stream, 136–38
Artificial intelligence, 43–44
Automation
  firm changes required with,
    33–36
  of new value stream, 114
  use by advanced corporations,
    42–43

Barnacles, 181–83
Bateson, Gregory, 6
Behavior
  dysfunctional, 482–83
  systemic, 267
Belasco, James, 359–60
Benchmarking, 171–73
Blanchard, Ken, 153, 156
Bonuses, 448
Boundarylessness, 26
Bowles, Sheldon, 156
Branson, Richard, 21
Breakthrough thinking, 82–83
Business reengineering
  implications of, 114
  obstacles to success, 472
  probability of success in govern-
    ment, 494
  resistance to culture change,
    462
  risk charts for, 475–78
  time frame for implementation,
    481
  as value-stream reinvention, 66,
    112
  See also Enterprise Engineering

Capabilities
  development of core, 78–79
  end-to-end, 305
  strategic capablity as value
    stream, 297–98, 305–6
  as value streams, 305
Carlzon, Jan, 467, 469
Champy, James, 169, 366, 376–77
Change
  anticipatory, 383
  with automation, 33–36
  corporate culture, 469–70
  discontinuous change in rede-
    sign, 62–63, 71–72
  Enterprise Engineering methods
    of, 60–61, 476–88, 493–94
  leadership required for, 388–91
  levels to achieve goals, 377–80
  management of, 456
  reactive strategic, 383–84
  resistance to, 456–57, 462
  visions required for, 465
change
  kaizen culture of constant, 212–15
Chief executive officer (CEO)
  as architect of enterprise, 56–57
  commitment to value-stream re-
    invention, 114
  leadership in change, 388–91
  role in business reengineering,
    475–76
  value-stream reinvention driven
    by, 321–22
Clusters. See Employee clusters
Compensation
  new-world corporations, 446–47
  pay-for-knowledge scheme,
    449–50
  policies of new-world corpora-
    tion, 447–48
Competitive advantage
  in knowledge and learning, 4–5
  of learning, 5
  sustainable, 407
Computer-aided design (CAD),
  187

Computer-aided software engineering (CASE), 187
Computing
  intercorporate, 47–48
  kaizen-capable, 212–15
  See also Neurocomputers
Concurrent engineering, 188–89
Continuous process improvement
  (CPI), 201
Control procedures, 176–77
Core competency, 305–6
  link to value streams, 316–17
  masters enabling technology or
    skill, 306–8, 311
  uses for, 324
  See also Capabilities
Corporate culture
  beliefs or values, 466
  with change, 455–56
  hostility to change, 456–57
  management of, 467–68
  stage-by-stage change, 469–70
Corporations, new-world
  continuum of, 388
  employment in, 445–47, 450–54
  goal of architecture of, 374–76
  information technology in, 374–
    76, 480–81
  pay-for-knowledge schemes,
    449–50
  principles of transition to, 380
  teams in, 449
  transition to, 376–79
  with value-stream architecture,
    136–38
CPI. See Continuous-process improvement (CPI)
Culture
  defined, 455
  formal, informal, and technical,
    459–70
  See also Corporate culture
Customer needs
  assessing, 142
  case worker to meet, 131–32
  differences, 154–56

Customer needs (*cont.*)
  focus on, 157–61
  quality function deployment to
      analyze, 162–63
Customers
  identifying value-stream, 158–60
  redesign of value stream for,
      128–29
  as target of value-stream team,
      168
Customer service, zero-defection
      standard, 164
Cybercorp (cybernetic corporation)
  defined, 5–6, 8
  electronic reaction times in,
      48–49
Cybernetics, 5
Cyberspace, 6

Deal, Terence, 466, 468
Decision making
  mental models, 344–45
  new tools for, 50–51
  scenario planning in, 349–50
de Geus, Arie, 5
Deming, W. Edwards, 207–8, 218–
      19, 425–26
Deming Prize, 228–29
Distribution systems
  problems of manufacturing,
      193–95
  simulations of, 270–74
Drucker, Peter, 4, 449, 494

Electronics
  growth in capability, 43
  systems to bypass intermediar-
      ies, 190–91
Electronic technology
  for information access, 144–45
  intelligent documents, 147
  speech storage using, 146–47
Employee clusters
  learning in different types of,
      414–17
  properties of, 84
  team as, 85
  virtuosos as part of, 99
Employees
  appraisals in new-world corpora-
      tion, 450
  dysfunctional behavior, 482–87
  encouragement to provide good
      service, 156
  in new-world corporations,
      445–50
  in redesigned enterprise, 375–76
  stock-option plans for, 451
Employment
  different classes in new-world
      corporation, 451–54

in new-world corporations,
      445–46
  reinvention, 24–25
Empowerment, 14, 84, 462
Enterprise, old-world, 393–95
Enterprise Engineering
  basic diagram of, 61
  change methods, 60–61, 476–89,
      493–94
  concern with corporate culture,
      455–56
  defined, 58
  identification of core capability,
      78
  implications of, 494–95
  transition to new-world enter-
      prise, 376–79
  See also Business reengineering
Enterprise Engineers
  breakthrough thinking mode of,
      82–83
  capabilities required for, 80–82
  role of, 59
Enterprise Redesign, 391
Enterprises
  architecture of, 56
  with autonomous functional
      areas, 124–25
  move to horizontal organization
      in, 397–401
  reengineering entire, 380–82
  survival characteristics, 20–22
  synchronization of elements in
      redesign, 114–16
  ways to learn, 407–14
  See also Business reengineering;
      Corporations, new-world;
      Virtual enterprise
Entrepreneurs
  loners as, 97
  value-stream teams as, 167
Evans, P., 305
Executive information systems,
      value-stream, 192

Feedback loops
  positive and negative, 72–73,
      282–85
  quick-and slow-response, 286–
      87
Fishbone diagrams
  cause-and-effect, 234
  in problem analysis, 195–96,
      474–75
Ford, Henry, 23
Forrester, Jay, 269
Foster, Richard N., 327, 330, 332

Gain sharing, 448–49
Gardner, Howard, 403
Gilder, George, 492

Goals
  of new-world enterprise architec-
      ture, 374–76
  setting goals in value-stream re-
      invention, 140–41
  team performance goals, 90–92
  of value-stream reinvention, 195
  value-stream teams, 165–68
Gore, Al, 494

Hall, Edward, 456, 457, 459, 461
Hamel, Gary, 305
Hammer, Michael, 66, 70, 169, 366,
      462, 472, 491
Harari, Oren, 242, 249
Harper, Mike, 27
Harvey-Jones, John, 71, 308–9
Hay, Edward, 448
Hay Group, 446
Hierarchies
  empowered teams in, 458–59
  of old-world enterprises, 393–97
  residual, 401, 445
  of traditional enterprises, 111–12
Horizontal organization
  effect of, 445–47
  enterprise move to, 397–401,
      445–47
Human intelligence, 44
Humanity (in firm redesign), 28
Human needs hierarchy, 15–16, 29
Human resource professionals, 445

Image processing, 145–46
Imai, Kenichi, 256
Imai, Masaaki, 202, 204, 207, 209,
      256
Information
  electronic access, 144–45
  patterns detected by neurocom-
      puters, 50–51
  See also Executive information
      systems
Information technology (IT)
  in new-world enterprise, 374–76,
      480–81
  requirements for organization,
      114
  uses in system redesign, 276–9
Innovation, 300–302, 421
Insight, executive, 78
Integration of work, 169–71
Interactions, multiple, 286–87
Ishikawa diagrams. *See* Fishbone
      diagrams
ISO 9000 standards, 227–28, 229,
      231
IT. *See* Information technology (IT)

Juran, J. M., 218–19
Just-in-time (JIT) inventory sys-
      tems, 193

Kaizen concept
    after value-stream reinvention,
        480
    applications of, 205–6
    applied to new value stream,
        211
    comparison with TQM, 251–58
    as continuous improvement,
        201–2
    difference from procedure rede-
        sign, 262–66
    effect of culture, 462
    enterprise learning, 203
    in learning enterprise, 408
    as method of enterprise change,
        60–62, 193
    strategy, 22
    total quality management imple-
        mentation of, 212
    See also ISO 9000 standards; Total
        quality management (TQM)
Katzenbach, Jon, 88, 89, 91, 94
Kennedy, Allen, 466, 468
Knowledge
    accumulation in an enterprise,
        150–52
    pay-for-knowledge schemes in
        new-world corporation,
        449–50
    power of unshared, 5
    value of, 4–5

Leadership
    constancy of, 388–91
    in statement of corporate values
        and vision, 467
    for TQM strategy, 243
Lean manufacturing concept
    applications of, 192–93
    Japanese car industry, 35–36
Learning
    barriers to learning from experi-
        ence, 420–24
    competitive advantage of, 5
    corporate, 287–88
    delusional aspects of learning
        from experience, 424–25
    different types of employee,
        414–18
    enterprise vision as, 22
    from experience, 419–20
    kaizen as form of enterprise, 203
    measurement of, 426–29
    single- and double-loop, 425–26
    with trading partners, 418
    value-stream, 418
Learning enterprise, 29, 407
Learning laboratory
    corporation as, 430–44
    value stream as, 319–21
Leverage, 279–80, 417

Life-cycle curve
    of investment in new technology,
        329–38
    of technology, 325–29
Loners in corporations, 96

Malcolm Baldrige Award
    examination for, 228–29, 231
    winners' improvements, 242–43
Management
    of change, 456
    of continuity-discontinuity,
        340–42
    of cultural transition, 467–68
    directives, 463
    in new-world corporation, 447
    of redesign risks, 487–89
    team self-management, 85–86
    of value-stream teams, 377
    See also Total quality manage-
        ment (TQM)
Maslow, Abraham, 15, 29
Mills, D. Quinn, 84
Minsky, Marvin, 403
Mitroff, Ian, 367

Nadler, David, 383
Networks, corporate
    intercorporate networks, 47–49
    for transparency, 44–45
Neurocomputers, 50–51
Nishimura, Ko, 18

O'Brien, Bill, 359
OCC (our contribution counts)
    circles, 219–20
Ogilvy, David, 97
Ohmae, Kenichi, 3, 294, 302
Out-sourcing, 321

Pareto diagrams, 236–38, 474–75
P-criteria (process-oriented), 204–5
PDCA cycle, 207–9
Perot, Ross, 128
Politics, corporate, 186
Porter, Michael, 106
Potter, David, 367
Power
    in redesigned enterprise, 375–77
    unshared knowledge as, 5
Prahalad, C. K., 305
Procedure redesign
    difference from value-stream re-
        invention and *kaizen*, 261–66
    examples, 275–77
    information technology in,
        276–79
Process reengineering
    actions to limit harmful interac-
        tions, 288–90
    for speed, 142–44

Prototypes
    in Enterprise Engineering labora-
        tory, 478–79
    value-stream, 195
Pseudoteams, 91

Quality circles, 219–20
Quality control, 234, 238–40
Quality function deployment
    (QFD), 162
Quality improvements
    campaigns for, 244
    reward system for, 244
    staff to implement, 246–47
Quality standards
    ISO 9000, 227–28
    Japanese, 27–28
    See also Total quality manage-
        ment (TQM)

Raving-fan recipe, 156–57
R-criteria (results-oriented), 204–5
Redesign, enterprise
    circumstances for, 33–36
    circumstances for and methods
        of, 73–75
    procedure as discontinuous
        change, 71–72
    themes in, 27–29
Reich, Robert B., 8
Reimann, Curt, 211
Research & development activities,
    148–50
Reward systems, 244
Risks
    charts for business reengineer-
        ing, 475–78
    in enterprise redesign, 487–88
Rollwagen, John, 458
Runyon, Marvin, 463
Rupport, Bruce, 116

SABRE (American Airlines soft-
    ware), 49–50
Sacred cows
    dealing with, 176–81
    identifying, 174–76
    as part of formal culture, 462–63
    See also Superstitions
Sakuma, Akimitsu, 256
Scenario planning
    official future derived from,
        343
Shell Oil, 345–48
Scenarios
    process of using, 356
    test of effectivenes, 355–56
Schein, Edgar, 16; 484, 485
Schwartz, Peter, 343, 349, 402
Self-actualization concept, 16–17
Self-management (team), 85–86

Self-reliance (value-stream teams), 185
Senge, Peter, 269–70, 274–75, 368
Shaw, George Bernard, 97
Shulman, L. E., 305
Simultaneous engineering
 defined, 130
 parallel tasks as, 188–89
Skills
 in new-world corporation, 445–46, 449–50
 team, 89
Smith, Adam, 17
Smith, Douglas, 88, 89, 91, 94
Software, corporate, 49–50
Speed, 142–44
Spreadsheets
 intelligent, 50
 rule-based processing, 50
Stalk, George, 305, 313, 322
Statistical charts, 233
Stock option plans, 451
Stoddard, William, 480
Strategic planning, 294
Strategic visioning
 defined, 293
 difference from strategic planning, 294
 enterprise redesign in context of, 382–83
 example of, 295
 as ongoing process, 385–88
Suggestion scheme, *kaizen*-oriented, 220–21
Superstitions, 176
System dynamics, 269–70
Systems
 changing structure of, 275–76
 defined, 267
 value systems, 118–20

Taylor, Frederick Winslow, 17
Teams
 characteristics of true, 88–90
 distinct from working groups, 87–88
 as employee clusters, 85
 enterprise learning in, 408–9
 factors in working together, 91–92
 high-performance, 92–95
 importance of, 86
 individuals within, 87–88
 in new-world corporation, 449
 in old-style hierarchy, 458–59
 for redesign of value stream, 128–29
 self-management of, 85–86
 value stream problem-solving, 195, 197

work with virtuosos, 99
 See also Pseudoteams; Value-stream teams
Technology
 effect on culture of new, 464
 in firm redesign, 28
 identification and acquisition of new, 339–40
 investment in, 329–38
 life-cycle curve of, 325–27
 protection of investment, 338–39
Telecommunications technology
 advances in, 43–44
 as tool for corporate consolidation, 46
Total quality management (TQM)
 application of, 19, 38
 applied to reinvented value streams, 250–51
 companies making progress with, 247–48
 comparison with *kaizen,* 251–58
 defined, 216
 delight customer goal, 217
 ingredients and roles of, 226
 integration, 242–43
 multicorporate, 258
 origins, 218
 reasons of failure and success, 241–42, 245, 247–48
 techniques of, 62, 64–65
 with value-stream reinvention, 211
 when to apply, 70
Transparency, corporate, 44–45
Triage, 189–90
Tushman, Michael, 383

Uncertainty (in firm redesign), 27
U. S. General Accounting Office (GAO), 242–43, 247–48
Usilaner, Brian, 242

Value chain, 106
Values
 of corporate culture, 466–67
 statement of corporate, 467
Value-stream customer, 127–28
Value-stream laboratory, 197, 319–21
Value stream reinvention
 requirements, 71–72
Value-stream reinvention
 application of TQM to, 250–51
 basic idea of, 108–13, 491–92
 business reengineering as, 6, 112
 concept, 63–70
 difference from procedure design, 261–66
 effect on culture, 462

enterprise learning by, 408
 minimizing interaction, 183–84
 problem-solving goals of, 195
 prototypes, 478
 teams as products of, 95–96
 testing and refinement, 195
 in work simplification, 76–77
Value streams
 activities of, 108
 avoidance of reinvention, 133–34
 corporations composed of, 95–96, 106–7, 121–24
 cross multiple enterprise functions, 125–27
 customers of, 158–60
 defined, 104–5
 identification of, 118
 one-person, 131–32
 prototyping, 195
 redesign priorities, 132–33
 relation to core capability, 78–79
 strategic, 134–38, 311–2
 strategic capabilities as, 297–98
 symptoms of unhealthy, 132–33
 See also Value systems
Value-stream teams, 95–96
 innovation-seeking, 311
 organization and goals of, 165–68
 role of managers with, 377
Value systems, primary and support, 118–20
Virtual enterprise, 403
Virtuosos, 98–99
Vision
 to change formal culture, 465
 constancy of, 388–90
 effective, 359–60
 enterprise need for, 20–22
 sources of and suport for, 360–63
 statement of corporate, 467
 translation into action, 363–64
 value-stream, 364–65
 See also Strategic visioning
Vision statements, 365–69

Waste, 221–23
Watson, Thomas J., Jr., 358, 467
Webs of activities, feedback loops, 72–73
Weiner, Norbert, 5
Welch, Jack, 26
Work
 changes with redesign of firm, 27–28
 reasons for simplification of, 76–77
 reinvention to please customer, 110–11

Work flow
  "breakthrough" improvements,
    67–69
  faults in Exhibit 7.4, 18–9
  See also Value stream

Working groups, 87–88

Young, John, 143

Zero-defect standard
  in customer service, 164
  efforts to achieve, 209–11